ICONS OF THE
AMERICAN WEST

Recent Titles in
Greenwood Icons

Icons of Horror and the Supernatural: An Encyclopedia of Our Worst Nightmares
Edited by S.T. Joshi

Icons of Business: An Encyclopedia of Mavericks, Movers, and Shakers
Edited by Kateri Drexler

Icons of Hip Hop: An Encyclopedia of the Movement, Music, and Culture
Edited by Mickey Hess

Icons of Evolution: An Encyclopedia of People, Evidence, and Controversies
Edited by Brian Regal

Icons of Rock: An Encyclopedia of the Legends Who Changed Music Forever
Edited by Scott Schinder and Andy Schwartz

Icons of R&B and Soul: An Encyclopedia of the Artists Who Revolutionized Rhythm
Bob Gulla

African American Icons of Sport: Triumph, Courage, and Excellence
Matthew C. Whitaker

ICONS OF THE AMERICAN WEST

From Cowgirls to Silicon Valley

VOLUME 1

Edited by Gordon Morris Bakken

Greenwood Icons

GREENWOOD PRESS
Westport, Connecticut · London

Library of Congress Cataloging-in-Publication Data

Icons of the American West : from cowgirls to Silicon Valley / edited by Gordon Morris Bakken.
       p. cm. — (Greenwood icons)
  Includes bibliographical references and index.
   ISBN 978-0-313-34148-9 (set : alk. paper) — ISBN 978-0-313-34149-6 (v. 1 : alk. paper) — ISBN 978-0-313-34150-2 (v. 2 : alk. paper)
   1. West (U.S.)—History 2. West (U.S.)—Biography. 3. West (U.S.)—In popular culture. 4. Frontier and pioneer life—West (U.S.) 5. Popular culture—West (U.S.) I. Bakken, Gordon Morris.
F591.I36 2008
978—dc22   2008006650

British Library Cataloguing in Publication Data is available.

Library of Congress Catalog Card Number: 2008006650
ISBN-13: 978-0-313-34148-9 (set)
       978-0-313-34149-6 (vol. 1)
       978-0-313-34150-2 (vol. 2)

First published in 2008

Greenwood Press, 88 Post Road West, Westport, CT 06881
An imprint of Greenwood Publishing Group, Inc.
www.greenwood.com

Printed in the United States of America

The paper used in this book complies with the Permanent Paper Standard issued by the National Information Standards Organization (Z39.48–1984).

10 9 8 7 6 5 4 3 2 1

To
Allan G. Bogue
of
Madison, Wisconsin

Contents

List of Photos

Series Foreword

Worshipped and cursed. Loved and loathed. Obsessed about the world over. What does it take to become an icon? Regardless of subject, culture, or era, the requisite qualifications are the same: (1) challenge the status quo, (2) influence millions, and (3) impact history.

Using these criteria, Greenwood Press introduces a new reference format and approach to popular culture. Spanning a wide range of subjects, volumes in the Greenwood Icons series provide students and general readers a port of entry into the most fascinating and influential topics of the day. Every title offers an in-depth look at 27 iconic figures, each of which captures the essence of a broad subject. These icons typically embody a group of values, elicit strong reactions, reflect the essence of a particular time and place, and link different traditions and periods. Among those featured are artists and activists, superheroes and spies, inventors and athletes, the legends and mythmakers of entire generations. Yet icons can also come from unexpected places: the heroine who transcends the pages of a novel or the revolutionary idea that shatters our previously held beliefs. Whether people, places, or things, such icons serve as a bridge between the past and the present, the canonical and the contemporary. By focusing on icons central to popular culture, this series encourages students to appreciate cultural diversity and critically analyze issues of enduring significance.

Most important, these books are as entertaining as they are provocative. Is Disneyland a more influential icon of the American West than Las Vegas? How do ghosts and ghouls reflect our collective psyche? Is Barry Bonds an inspiring or deplorable icon of baseball?

Designed to foster debate, the series serves as a unique resource that is ideal for paper writing or report purposes. Insightful, in-depth entries provide far more information than conventional reference articles but are less intimidating and more accessible than a book-length biography. The most revered and reviled icons of American and world history are brought to life with related sidebars, timelines, fact boxes, and quotations. Authoritative entries are accompanied by bibliographies, making these titles an ideal starting point for further research. Spanning a wide range of popular topics including business, literature, civil rights, politics, music, and more, books in the series provide fresh insights for the student and popular reader into the power and influence of icons, a topic of as vital interest today as in any previous era.

Preface

Icons of the American West exist in the American mind focused on the Old West and a New West. The Old West, sometimes called the Wild West, was a place where white Americans clashed with American Indians in the great battles of the Indians Wars; men and women made fortunes and as often failed in enterprise, men fought gun battles in mining towns and cattle towns, and the gun was the law of the land. The Old West was the stomping ground of mountain men, great Indian chiefs, crack shots, and pioneers rushing to California for gold. The Old West also was the place where the environment was pure and where the conservation and preservationist movements started. It was an eden to be exploited for enterprise, but it contained holy places in nature that had to be preserved for all generations.

The New West is a place of incredible imagination. It is the built environment of Disneyland and Las Vegas. It is a place where all of the world could exist in a valley. It gives the nation dynamic women who become iconic politicians and peace advocates. Presidents with clearly Western packaging forged in Hollywood dominate the American political imagination. Computers and software spring from the minds of Westerners who build empires. Environment still tops the list of priorities for Westerners and its national parks are symbols for the nation. New environmentalists emerge and women take their place at the head of the movement. Indian chiefs now wield economic clout backed by Indian casinos. Western women now sit in the state house and in the Congress. The New West is an exciting place because it is home to people of vision, whose imaginations have changed the image of the West.

The First Peoples of the West were American Indians. War chiefs, particularly of the late nineteenth century, were iconic because of their deeds and Hollywood's images—Sitting Bull and Crazy Horse are practically household names. They defeated George Armstrong Custer at the Little Bighorn in 1876, and popular literature and art depicted Custer's Last Stand as heroic for over a century. On closer inspection, Custer lost because of a failure of reconnaissance, communications, and command. Geronimo and Chief Joseph of the Nez Perce waged strategic retreats and tactical surprises in their wars with American forces. Sacagawea was an exceptional woman who enabled Lewis and Clark to conduct a successful expedition over the Louisiana Purchase. These American Indians earned a place in American memory for their exploits in the nineteenth century in the Old West.

In the New West of the twentieth and twenty-first centuries, American Indians are part of the gaming industry. They participate in state and national politics. They manage businesses and tribal enterprises. Their casinos are the icons of the present. Their management of revenues enhances state budgets, builds tribal infrastructure, and advances tribal culture.

In the Old West, American Indians had extensive tribal trade networks that became the paths others would mark. Explorers like Lewis and Clark found tribal traders to be shrewd bargainers. Later intruders in the West sought fur-bearing animals. The mountain men traded with the First Peoples, fought them, and marked their lands on maps and in memory. The paths they marked out became the highways for the Mormon pioneers. Brigham Young led the Latter-Day Saints to Utah and established a kingdom initially free from the religious bigotry and violence they had experienced in the Midwest. The discovery of gold in California resulted in a mass migration of Americans to California. The migration was so dramatic that "seeing the elephant" became an iconic phrase forever linked to the Gold Rush to California.

The West was a place of extreme violence or as Ned Blackhawk put it, "violence over the land." Intertribal violence characterized Western life for many tribes. The efforts of the American government to press tribes into confined spaces furthered violence. George Armstrong Custer's military defeat at the Little Bighorn in 1876 left a cultural marker for the American mind. There, iconic personalities Custer and Crazy Horse met in deadly battle using the iconic weapons of the West, the Winchester rifle and the Colt Single Action revolver. Western violence was more than deadly combat. Gunfighters, gun violence, and crime marked many a Western town. Outlaws and lawmen became popular figures of pulp fact and fiction.

Helping the American people to imagine this West, Buffalo Bill Cody brought the "Wild West Show" to the nation and the world. Cody featured cowboys and cowgirls, American Indians, and displays of marksmanship. Annie Oakley was the markswoman most remembered from these shows. She demonstrated that a woman could outshoot most men. In broader terms, Annie Oakley reminded Americans that women were very much a part of the West albeit little noticed in pulp fiction. Annie Oakley also believed that every woman should know how to shoot. She personally taught 15,000 women the skills necessary to use firearms. Yet she was committed to ladylike behavior in public. She embraced a version of pioneer life that was genteel, making her public appearances model a female pioneer experience that was as simple as her shooting seemed to the audience. It was not the reality of pioneer life facing the elements and the soil.

In reality, women were pioneers in the American West contributing to every facet of life. Many women were authors of local and national fame. Fannie Baker Darden became known as the "Poet Laureate" of Columbus, Texas. Eliza Wood Burhans Farnham published her *Woman and Her Era* in 1864, Mollie Evelyn Moore Davis's came out in 1867. Sara Winnemucca's *Life Among the Paiutes* and Mary Hallock Foote's *The Led-Horse Claim* found print in 1883. Sophie Alice Callahan's *Wynema* came out eight years later. Mary Hunter Austin's *Land of Little Rain* started to fascinate readers in 1903. Alice Eastwood's *A Handbook of the Trees of California* came out two years later. In 1906 Elsie Clews Parsons's *The Family* and Bertha Muzzy Sinclair's *Chip of the Flying U* were published. Willa Cather's *O Pioneers!* won critical acclaim in 1913. Hildegarde Flanner's *Younger Girl and Other Poems* and Ruth Murray Underhill's *White Moth* hit the bookstores in 1920. Nine years later Ruth Leah Bunzel's *The Pueblo Potter* was published joined three years afterward by Ella Cara Deloria's *Dakota Texts*. In 1934 Gladys Amanda Reichard's *Spider Woman* was released to the public followed in 1935 by Mari Sandoz's *Old Jules*, a tale of life on the Nebraska frontier. Nina Otero Warren's *Old Spain in our Southwest* (1936) told of Hispanic roots in Western soils. Similarly, Cleofas Martinez Jamamillo told cultural tales in *Cuentos del hogar/ Spanish Fairy Tales* (1939) and Elsie Clews Parsons analyzed American Indian religious practices in *Pueblo Indian Religion* (1939). Two years later Agnes Morley Cleaveland's *No Life for a Lady* arrived at bookstore shelves. Betty Freidan shook up gender relations with *The Feminine Mystique* (1963) identifying the problem with no name. Numerous other women were successful authors such as Octavia Butler, *Crossover* (1971), Leslie Marmon Silko, *Laguna Woman Poems* (1974), Maxine Hong Kingston, *The Warrior Woman* (1974), Phyllis Schlafly, *The Power of the Positive Woman* (1977), Margaret Coel, *Chief Left Hand: Southern Arapaho* (1981), Gloria Anzaldua, *Borderlands/ La fontera: The New Mestiza* (1984), Linda M. Hasselstrom, *Going Over East* (1987), Amy Tan, *The Joy Luck Club* (1988), Janet Campbell Hale, *Bloodline* (1993), Wilma Mankiller, *Mankiller: A Chief and Her People* (1993), and Delphine Red Shirt, *Turtle Lung Woman's Granddaughter* (2002).

Women joined the professions and made substantial contributions in the West. Harriet Bunce Wright was a teacher and co-founder of the Wheellock Academy, Choctaw Nation, Indian Territory. Mary Avery Loughridge was a teacher at the Koweta Manual Labor Boarding School, Cherokee Nation, Indian Territory. Mother Magdalen Hayden was the first superior of the Sisters of Loretto in New Mexico Territory. Elizabeth Fulton Hester was a founder-teacher at the Muskogee Day Nursery in Indian Territory in 1856 commencing seventy years of service to American Indians in Oklahoma. Mary Bridget Hayden was named Mother Superior at the Osage Mission School, Indian Territory in 1859. Abigail Scott Duniway won election to President of the Oregon Equal Suffrage Association in 1873. In 1877 Elizabeth Culver became the first female school superintendent in Hamilton County, Kansas. Mary E. Foy won appointment as the first Los Angeles City Librarian in 1880. In 1878 Clara

Shortridge Foltz was the first woman admitted to the California Bar. Mary Elizabeth Lease was admitted to the Kansas Bar in 1885 and Ella L. Knowles passed the Montana Bar examination with distinction in 1889. In 1914 Gloria Bullock graduated from the University of Southern California Law School starting a distinguished career in the bar and on the bench. These professional pioneers showed America that women could achieve at high levels in the professions.

Women also distinguished themselves in politics. Jeannette Rankin of Montana was the first woman elected to the United States House of Representatives in 1916. The people of Montana returned her to the House in 1940 and she became the only person to vote against declarations of war in World War I and World War II. Rankin devoted her life to the cause of world peace. Minnie Grinstead became the first woman elected to the Kansas legislature in 1918. Oklahoma voters sent Alice Mary Robertson to the House in 1921 and Texas voters put Miriam Amanda Wallace "Ma" Ferguson in the governor's seat in 1924. The next year Emma Grigsby Meharg was appointed the first female Secretary of State in Texas and Edith Eunice Therrel Wilmans was appointed to the Texas Supreme Court. In 1926 Texas voters sent Margie Elizabeth Neal to the state senate, the same year that Laura Scudder introduced "Mayflower Chips" to California inaugurating a dynamic food business. Arizona voters sent Isabella Selmes Greenway to the House of Representatives in 1929 and four years later Kathryn O'Loughlin of Kansas joined her. California voters sent Helen Gahagan Douglas to the House in 1945. She later became Richard Nixon's U.S. Senate opponent and "the pink lady." Many other women won election to Congress, and in 2007 Nancy Pelosi achieved the distinction of being the first woman elected Speaker of the House of Representatives.

The West inspired artists who represented both its scenic beauty and its colorful people. Frederick Remington and scores of other artists gave America their impression in images that remain iconic. The scenic beauty also inspired people like John Muir and Harriet Monroe to campaign to preserve natural monuments to nature's designs. Yosemite Valley and the Hetch Hetchy were two ends of their campaign. In the New West Yellowstone National Park and Grand Canyon National Park continue to draw thousands of tourists to view these natural wonders. Environmentalists like Jeanne Marie Souvigney and environmental advocacy groups like the Sierra Club and the Greater Yellowstone Coalition continue to fight to maintain a nature for future generations of Americans. Suzanne Lewis became the first female superintendent of Yellowstone in winter 2002. Lewis is now one of many women serving in the Park Service providing visitors with a view of the wonders of nature and protecting our cherished national parks.

The New West is the site of built scenic wonders that draw millions to them. Las Vegas, Nevada, emerged in the mid-twentieth century as a neon metropolis of entertainment. Its nightlife centered in the casino continues to lure millions to this desert icon. Strong Western competition for these entertainment dollars centers in the growing number of Indian casinos. Disneyland in Anaheim, California, was another part of the built environment that lured tours to the West.

The New West also produced innovators of national repute. Politicians like Ronald Reagan, Ann Richards, Diane Feinstein, Barbara Boxer, and Barbara Jordan captured the American imagination. Aviation pioneers like Glenn Martin made the West famous for aircraft. Bill Gates, Steve Jobs, Steve Wozniak, and Sandra Kurtzig brought computers and electronic innovation to national prominence.

The outlaws and iconic lawmen of the Old West retained their national reputations preserved in film, fiction, and history. In the New West, modern policing was the territory of innovators such as Eugene Biscailuz, the Los Angeles County sheriff to the stars. Biscailuz put deputies into the air and modern policing techniques on the national stage. Biscailuz was sheriff from 1932 until 1958, and "he transformed the department into a professional law enforcement agency." He pioneered the practice of putting good prisoners to work on honor farms and ranches in an effort to rehabilitate them. Cecilia Rasmussen penned this October 21, 2007, description in the *Los Angeles Times*, "Long arm of this lawman bridged a city's history: Eugene Biscailuz was descended from settlers; his long, colorful career as sheriff was marked by modernization." He did more than create "the volunteer Aero Squadron, now an official county search and rescue team." Biscailuz recruited Hoot Gibson and Howard Hughes as pilots for the Aero Squadron. He was a "descendant of Jose Maria Claudio Lopez, a Spanish soldier at the San Gabriel Mission," and French Basque sheepherders. "During Prohibition, Biscailuz was one of an influential band of revelers who called themselves the Uplifters Club." Members included Will Rogers, Walt Disney, Spencer Tracy, Clark Gable, Harold Lloyd, and Daryl F. Zanuck. Biscailuz was, as Cecilia Rasmussen so ably described, an icon of the American West. He "was virtually a 'human bridge' between the old Pueblo de Los Angeles and the huge metropolis of today, and his identification with the city ranked with its orange groves, motion pictures and passion for progress." His Western-style hat and boots placed him in the West he left so important a mark on in Los Angeles.

The New West is also the place where recreation and environment combine to create ideal places to live. Bozeman, Montana, is one such place where people can find the world in the Gallatin Valley. Despite the Montana winter people find all that is desirable for quality life in a cultural setting with recreational opportunities within easy reach.

The Old West set the stage for the New West we find in fact and fiction. This work is divided into two volumes with the first dedicated to exploring the icons of the Old West and the second identifying the icons of the New West of the twentieth and twenty-first centuries. Read volume 1 with care as you will find it prelude to volume 2's New West. It is the last best place for many Americans.

Timeline

1784	John Jacob Astor arrives in New York. He would make a fortune in the fur trade.
1785	William Ashley born.
1787	Sacagawea born.
1801	Brigham Young born.
1804	Jim Bridger born.
1805–1806	Lewis and Clark explore the West with the help of Sacagawea.
1806	John Colter, Joseph Dickson, and Forest Hancock travel up the Missouri River to the Yellowstone River on the first fur-trapping expedition.
1807	Manuel Lisa commands a fur-trapping expedition up the Missouri to the mouth of the Bighorn River.
1808	John Jacob Astor founds the American Fur Company.
1809	St. Louis Missouri Fur Company formed.
1823	Mexico grants Stephen Austin the right to settle in Texas with three hundred families.
1824	Jedediah Strong Smith discovers South Pass.
1826	William Ashley sells the Rocky Mountain Fur Company.
1829	Fannie Baker Darden, "The Poet Laureate of Columbus, Texas" born; Geronimo born.
1832	Harriet Bunce Wright is teacher/co-founder of Wheelock Academy, Choctaw Nation, Indian Territory.
1833	Lydia Maria Child publishes *An Appeal for that Class of Americans Called Africans*.
1836	Sarah Josepha Hale becomes editor of *Godey's Lady's Book*; Eliza Hart Spalding and Narcissa Whitman become the first two white women to cross the Rocky Mountains on their way to Oregon; Emily Morgan [Emily D. West] becomes "The

Yellow Rose of Texas" for her exploits in the Texas war with Mexico.

1838   John Muir born.

1839   Mary Avery Loughridge becomes a teacher at the Koweta Manual Labor Boarding School, Cherokee Nation, Indian Territory.

1840   Crazy Horse born in the season of Stole-One-Hundred Horses; Chief Joseph of the Nez Perce born.

1841   Nancy Kelsey departs Missouri for California with the Bartleson/Bidwell Company.

1844   John C. Fremont's expedition visits Las Vegas.

1846   Susan Shelby Magoffin sets off down the Santa Fe Trail.

1847   Tamsen Donner dies in Donner Pass, the victim of a man who would not ask for directions; Mary Bridget Hayden arrives at Osage Mission Government School; William F. "Buffalo Bill" Cody born; Brigham Young leads the first group of pioneers from Winter Quarters to the Salt Lake Valley.

1848   Women's Rights Convention held at Seneca Falls, New York; James Marshall discovers gold at Sutter's Mill in California; Gold Rush to California begins.

1849   Elizabeth Blackwell receives a medical degree from Geneva College; Gold Rush to California begins.

1850   The Deseret Dramatic Association founded in Salt Lake City.

1852   Vicar Apostolic Jean-Baptiste Lamy accompanies the first Sisters of Loretto to New Mexico with Mother Magdalen Hayden as their first superior.

1853   Sisters of Loretto open the Academy of Our Lady of Light in Santa Fe.

1855   Sara Robinson arrives in Lawrence, Kansas. Brigham Young dispatches thirty Mormons to Las Vegas to build a fort.

1856   Elizabeth Fulton Hester, teacher/founder of Muskogee Day Nursery, begins seventy years of service to American Indian people in Oklahoma.

1859   Mary Bridget Hayden named Mother Superior at Osage Mission School; Clear Creek, Colorado, and "Comstock Lode" in Nevada strikes continue migration to mining regions.

1864   Eliza Wood Burhans Farnham's *Woman and Her Era* published; John Muir left the University of Wisconsin; On June 30, 1864, President Abraham Lincoln signed a bill granting Yosemite Valley and the Mariposa Grove of Giant Sequoias to the state of California as an inalienable public trust. This was the first time in history that a federal government had set aside scenic lands simply to protect them and to allow for their enjoyment by all people; town of Bozeman, Montana, founded.

1865	The first all-women's college founded at Vassar.
1867	Kansas legislature refuses to extend voting rights to women; Mollie Evelyn Moore Davis's *Minding the Gap* published; Young Women's Christian Association (YWCA) founded.
1868	Laura de Force Gordon delivers her first speech for women's suffrage in California.
1869	Wyoming Territory passes a female suffrage statute; Eagle Woman takes over the Grand River Agency trading post; National Woman Suffrage Association founded; American Woman Suffrage Association founded; Transcontinental Railroad completed; Zions Cooperative Mercantile Institution opens in Salt Lake City.
1870	Utah Territory passes a female suffrage law.
1871	Lawrence, Kansas, Friends in Council founded; Lizzy Johnson buys land and cattle and registers her CY brand.
1872	Yellowstone designated the first national park in the United States; Victoria Woodhull runs for President of the United States; William F. "Buffalo Bill" Cody awarded the Congressional Medal of Honor.
1873	Abigail Scott Duniway named president of the Oregon Equal Suffrage Association; [Women's] *Home Companion* founded; Winchester introduces Model 1873 to the American public.
1874	Women's Christian Temperance Union established; Occidental Mission Home for Girls opened by the Presbyterian Church to Minister to Asian females in San Francisco; Women's Christian Temperance Union (WYCU) emerges as a national organization from its Midwestern roots; Sharps Buffalo Rifle becomes a favorite of Western hunters; Joseph F. Glidden patents barbed wire.
1876	Oakland Ebell Society founded; Annie Oakley outshoots Frank Butler in a demonstration of world-class marksmanship; George Armstrong Custer loses the Battle of the Little Bighorn; Chiricahua Reservation closes and Geronimo's raids from the Warm Springs Agency, New Mexico, begin; William F. "Buffalo Bill" Cody kills a Cheyenne warrior, perhaps Yellow Hair, at Warbonnet Creek, Nebraska.
1877	Salt Lake City Lady's Literary Society founded; Elizabeth Culver elected first female school superintendent in Hamilton County, Kansas; Chief Joseph and 800 non-treaty Nez Perce trek 1500 miles through Idaho, Montana, and Wyoming Territories; Brigham Young dies.
1878	Clara Shortridge Foltz is the first woman admitted to the California bar; Buffalo Calf Road led Cheyenne in battle against the United States Army.

1879	Frances Willard named president of the WYCU; Teddy Blue Abbott sets out on his "mixed outfit" trail ride.
1880	Mary E. Foy appointed the first Los Angeles City Librarian.
1881	First suffrage bill introduced in Arizona Territorial Legislature.
1882	Association of Collegiate Alumnae founded; Buffalo Bill Cody introduces the "Old Glory Blowout" in North Platte, Nebraska.
1883	Washington Territory extends voting rights and jury service to women, but the statutes are declared unconstitutional by the Territorial Supreme Court; Caroline M. Severance founds the Los Angeles Women's Club; Sarah Winnemucca's *Life Among the Paiutes* published; Mary Hallock Foote's *The Led-Horse Claim* published; *Ladies Home Journal* founded; Eugene Warren Biscailuz born; William F. "Buffalo Bill" Cody's Wild West Show opens in Omaha, Nebraska.
1885	Mary Elizabeth "Hell Raising" Lease admitted to the Kansas bar; *Good Housekeeping* founded; severe winter destroys range cattle industry.
1886	Rebecca Lee Dorsey opens a medical practice in Los Angeles; Geronimo surrenders to General Nelson A. Miles.
1887	Congress disfranchises women in Utah Territory with the Edmunds-Tucker Act; Congress passes the Dawes Act or General Allotment Act further depriving American Indians of land.
1889	Ella L. Knowles passes the Montana bar examination with distinction; Jane Addams and Ellen Gates Starr establish Hull House in Chicago.
1890	Wyoming is admitted as a state with women suffrage, the first in the nation; General Federation of Women's Clubs founded.
1891	Sophie Alice Callahan's *Wynema* published; Friday Morning Club of Los Angeles founded; Katherine Drexel founded the Sisters of the Blessed Sacrament for Colored and Indian People.
1892	Sierra Club founded in San Francisco.
1893	Colorado amends its constitution to grant women the vote.
1896	Utah enters the union with woman suffrage; Idaho adopts a woman suffrage amendment to the state constitution; woman suffrage lost at the polls in California.
1898	Freda Ehmann starts the Ehmann Olive Company in Oroville, California; W.S. James's *A Cowboy's Life in Texas* published.
1900	Carrie Nation starts her prohibition campaign at the Cary Hotel in Wichita, Kansas; Donaldina MacKenzie Cameron becomes superintendent of the Mission Home of the Women's Occidental Board of Foreign Missions in San Francisco; William E. Colby named secretary of the Sierra Club.

1901	William E. Colby leads the first Sierra Club High Trip into Yosemite.
1902	St. Frances Xavier Cabrini visits Denver.
1903	Women first compete at rodeo at Cheyenne Frontier Days; Mary Hunter Austin's *The Land of Little Rain* published; Women's Trade Union League founded.
1904	Annette Abbott Adams is the first woman to graduate from the University of California Law School (Boalt Hall).
1905	Alice Eastwood's *A Handbook of the Trees of California* published.
1906	Elsie Clews Parsons's *The Family* published; Bertha Muzzy Sinclair's *Chip of the Flying U* published.
1908	Woman's Club of Huntington Beach, California, founded.
1910	Frances Marion signs a contract with Bosworth Studios; Alice Stebbins Wells becomes the first policewoman of the Los Angeles Police Department; Thomas Byron Story builds the Story Mansion in Bozeman, Montana.
1911	California extends the franchise to women; Triangle Shirtwaist fire in New York kills 146 workers, mostly women.
1912	Kansas and Arizona extend the franchise to women; Zane Grey's *Riders of the Purple Sage* published.
1913	Montana and Nevada extend the franchise to women; Willa Cather's *O Pioneers!* published; Raker Act authorizes the flooding of the Hetch Hetchy Valley.
1914	Gloria Bullock graduates from the University of Southern California Law School.
1915	Alice Stebbins Wells organizes the International Association of Policewomen; Woman's Peace Party founded; Joseph Nisbet LeConte elected president of the Sierra Club.
1916	Annie Webb Blanton becomes the first female president of the Texas State Teachers Association; Jeannette Rankin of Montana elected to the United States House of Representatives.
1917	North Dakota and Nebraska extend presidential suffrage to women.
1918	Minnie Grinstead becomes the first woman elected to the Kansas legislature.
1919	Grand Canyon becomes a national park.
1920	Nineteenth Amendment ratified giving women the right to vote; Nellie Trent Bush elected to the Arizona legislature; Hildegarde Flanner's *Younger Girl and Other Poems* published; Ruth Murray Underhill's *White Moth* published.
1921	National Woman's Party starts a state-by-state campaign for an Equal Rights Bill; Sheppard-Towner Act passes in Congress to provide maternal and infant health education; Alice Mary

Robertson (R, OK) elected to the United States House of
Representatives.

1923   Aimee Semple McPherson opens the Angelus Temple in Los
        Angeles; Mae Ella Nolan (R, CA) elected to the United States
        House of Representatives; Congress holds hearings on an Equal
        Rights Amendment; Winchester ends production of Model
        1873 after 700,000 sold.

1924   Miriam Amanda Wallace "Ma" Ferguson elected governor of
        Texas.

1925   Emma Grigsby Meharg appointed first female secretary of State
        in Texas; Edith Eunice Therrel Wilmans appointed to the Texas
        Supreme Court; Florence Prag Kahn (R, CA) elected to the
        United States House of Representatives.

1926   Margie Elizabeth Neal becomes the first woman elected to the
        Texas Senate; Laura Scudder introduces "Mayflower Chips" to
        California; Anne Martin is a delegate to the 5th Biennial
        International Congress of the Women's International League for
        Peace and Freedom.

1928   Boulder Canyon Project Act signed into law.

1929   Florence "Pancho" Barnes wins the First Women's Air Race in
        Glendale, California; Ruth Leah Bunzel's *The Pueblo Potter*
        published; Isabella Selmes Greenway (D, AZ) elected to the
        United States House of Representatives.

1930   Jessie Daniel Ames helps found the Association of Southern
        Women for the Prevention of Lynching.

1931   Ruth Winifred Brown elected president of the Oklahoma
        Library Association; Gloria Bullock is the first woman ap-
        pointed to the California Superior Court bench.

1932   Helen S. Richt graduates from the veterinary medicine program
        at Kansas State University; Ella Cara Deloria's *Dakota Texts*
        published; Amelia Earhart makes her solo flight over the Atlantic.

1933   Kathryn O'Loughlin (McCarthy) (D, KS) elected to the United
        States House of Representatives; Francis P. Farquhar elected
        president of the Sierra Club.

1934   Gladys Amanda Reichard's *Spider Woman* published; Ansel
        Adams joins the Sierra Club board of directors.

1935   Sarah Tilghman Hughes becomes first woman to serve as a
        Texas District Judge; Mari Sandoz's *Old Jules* published.

1936   Katherine Cheung obtains her commercial pilot's license; Nina
        Otero Warren's *Old Spain in Our Southwest* published; Mary
        McLeod Bethune named Negro Affairs Director of the National
        Youth Administration.

1937   Nan Wood Honeyman (D, OR) elected to the United States
        House of Representatives.

1938	Lorna Lockwood elected to the Arizona legislature.
1939	Cleofas Martinez Jaramillo's *Cuentos del hogar/Spanish Fairy Tales* published; Elsie Clews Parsons's *Pueblo Indian Religion* published.
1940	Jeannette Rankin of Montana wins a seat in the United States House of Representatives a second time.
1941	Agnes Morley Cleaveland's *No Life for a Lady* published.
1942	Charolette Winter King wins a seat on the South Pasadena City Council; Maria Tallchief becomes America Prima Ballerina with Ballet Russe de Monte Carlo.
1944	Mildred Jeffrey and Lillian Hatcher lead the United Auto Workers Women's Bureau.
1945	Helen Gahagan Douglas (D, CA) elected to the United States House of Representatives.
1946	Guy McAfee opens the Golden Nugget casino on the Las Vegas "strip"; Ben "Bugsy" Siegel's Flamingo casino holds its grand opening.
1947	Rose Hum Lee completes her doctorate at the University of Chicago; Georgia Lee Lusk (D, NM) elected to the United States House of Representatives; Sandra Kurtzig born.
1948	Marie Callender starts selling her pies commercially to Long Beach, California, eateries.
1949	Georgia Neese Clark Gray named United States Treasurer; Reva Boone (D, UT) elected to United States House of Representatives.
1950	Steven Wozniak born.
1953	Ivy Baker Priest appointed United States Treasurer; *Kinsey Report* issued; Gracie Pfost (D, ID) elected to the United States House of Representatives.
1955	Adlai Stevenson exhorts Smith College graduates to become republican mothers; Del Martin and Phyllis Lyon founded the Daughters of Belitis in San Francisco; Rosa Parks refuses to sit in the "colored" section of a Montgomery, Alabama, bus; Edith Green (D, OR) elected to the United States House of Representatives; Bill Gates born.
1958	Donna Joy McGladrey starts teaching in Alaska.
1959	Ruth Handler creates Barbie; Catherine Dean May (R, WA) elected to the United States House of Representatives.
1960	Alice Ramsey named "Woman Motorist of the Century"; Julia Butler Hansen (D, WA) elected to the United States House of Representatives.
1963	Betty Friedan's *The Feminine Mystique* published; Presidential Commission on the Status of Women, chaired by Eleanor Roosevelt, issues its report and only Marguerite Rewalt supports an Equal Rights Amendment; Equal Pay Act becomes law.

1964	Civil Rights Act of 1964 becomes law.
1966	Barbara Jordan elected to the Texas Senate; National Organization of Women founded; Ivy Baker Priest elected treasurer of California; Lera Thomas (D, TX) elected to the United States House of Representatives.
1967	Ronald Reagan elected California governor.
1968	Shirley Ann Mount Hufstedler appointed to the Ninth Circuit Court of Appeals; Kuniko Terasawa receives the Order of the Sacred Treasure, Zuiosho-5th Class.
1969	Hattie Burnstad is named Washakie County, Wyoming, teacher of the year.
1971	Octavia Butler's *Crossover* published; Ann Willis Richards manages the successful campaign of Sara Ragle Weddinton for the Texas House of Representatives.
1972	Barbara Jordan elected to the United States House of Representatives; Sarah Ragle Weddinton is the first woman elected to the Texas House of Representatives; Title IX of the Higher Education Act becomes law increasing access to higher education for women, particularly athletics; Congresswoman Shirley Chisholm runs for president of the United States; the journal *Women's Studies* founded; the journal *Feminist Studies* founded; Equal Rights Amendment to the United States Constitution approved by Congress; Patricia Schroeder (D, CO) elected to the United States House of Representatives.
1973	Sarah Ragle Weddinton successfully argues *Roe v. Wade*; Billie Jean King defeats Bobby Riggs in a tennis match; Yvonne Brathwaite Burke (D, CA) and Barbara Jordan (D, TX) elected to the United States House of Representatives.
1974	Leslie Marmon Silko's *Laguna Woman Poems* published; Mary Ann Graf is the first female graduate of the University of California, Davis enology program; March Fong Eu elected California's first female secretary of state; Sandra and Ari Kurtzig found ASK Computer Systems Company.
1976	Steven Wozniak and Steve Jobs demonstrate Apple 1 computer in the Jobs family garage; Ann Willis Richards elected Travis County Commissioner and serves Texas until 1982.
1975	The journal *Signs* founded; Congress mandates that United States military academies admit women; Shirley Pettis (R, CA), Martha Keys (D, KS), and Virginia Smith (R, NV) elected to the United States House of Representatives; Bill Gates founds Microsoft Corporation.
1976	Maxine Hong Kingston's *The Warrior Woman* published.
1977	Rose Elizabeth Bird becomes the first female Chief Justice of the California Supreme Court; United Nations International

Women's Year declared; Phillis Schlafly's *The Power of the Positive Woman* published.

1978   Sally K. Ride joins NASA.

1979   Mildred Imach Cleghorn named chair of Fort Sill Apache tribe; Dorothy Wright Nelson appointed to the Ninth Circuit Court of Appeals; Ruth Murray Underhill's *Papago Woman* published.

1980   Kathleen M. Conley is the first woman to graduate from the United States Air Force Academy; Ronald Reagan elected president of the United States.

1981   Margaret Coel's *Chief Left Hand: Southern Arapaho* published; Linda Hogan's *Daughters, I Love You* published; Molly Ivins takes a job with the *Dallas Times Herald*; Bobbi Fiedler (R, CA) elected to the United States House of Representatives; Court of Appeals decides *Florida v. Butterworth*.

1982   A sufficient number of states fail to ratify the Equal Rights Amendment; Ann Willis Richards elected Texas state treasurer.

1983   Barbara Boxer (D, CA), Sala Burton (D, CA), and Barbara Vucanocick (R, NV) elected to the United States House of Representatives; Sally K. Ride is first female in space on the shuttle *Challenger*; Greater Yellowstone Coalition founded.

1984   Gloria Anzaldua's *Borderlands/La fontera: The New Mestiza* published; Cynthia Holcomb Hall appointed to the Ninth Circuit Court of Appeals.

1985   Jan Meyers (R, KS) elected to the United States House of Representatives.

1987   Linda M. Hasselstrom's *Going Over East* published; National Museum of Women in the Arts opens in Washington, DC; Wilma Mankiller becomes Principal Chief of the Cherokee Nation; Nancy Pelosi (D, CA) is elected to the United States House of Representatives; United States Supreme Court decides *Cabazon Band of Mission Indians v. California* ushering in Indian gaming.

1988   Amy Tan's *The Joy Luck Club* published; Dr. Mae C. Jemison becomes first African American woman in space; Congress passes the Family Support Act to collect from "deadbeat dads."

1989   Joyce Kennard appointed to the California Supreme Court; Patricia Schroeder's *Champion of the Great American Family* published; Jolene Unsoeld (D, WA) elected to the United States House of Representatives.

1990   Ann Willis Richards elected governor of Texas; Maxine Waters elected to the United States House of Representatives.

1991	Congresswoman Patricia Schroeder's rider to a Department of Defense bill leads to the assignment of women to combat aircraft.
1992	Dianne Feinstein (D, CA) elected to the United States Senate; Ann Willis Richards chaired the Democratic National Committee.
1993	Barbara Boxer (D, CA) elected to the United States Senate; Mary Crow Dog's *Ohitika Woman* published; Janet Campbell Hale's *Bloodlines* published; Karan English (D, AZ), Anna Eshoo (D, CA), Jane Harman (D, CA), Lucille Roybal-Allard (D, CA), Lynne Schenk (D, CA), Lynn Woolsey (D, CA), Elizabeth Furse (D, OR), Eddie Bernice Johnson (D, TX), Karen Sheperd (D, UT), Maria Cantwell (D, WA), and Jennifer Dunn (D, WA) elected to the United States House of Representatives; Wilma Mankiller's *Mankiller: A Chief and Her People* published.
1994	Kathryn M. Werdegar appointed to the California Supreme Court.
1995	Eileen M. Collins of San Antonio, Texas, becomes first woman to fly the space shuttle; Zoe Lofgren (D, CA), Andrea Seastrand (R, CA), Juanita Millender-McDonald (D, CA), Helen Chenoweth (R, ID), Darlene Hooley (D, OR), Sheila Jackson-Lee (C, TX), Enid Green (Waldholtz) (R, UT), Linda Smith (R, WA), and Barbara Cubin (R, WY) elected to the United States House of Representatives.
1996	Janice Rogers Brown appointed to California Supreme Court.
1997	Ellen Tauscher (D, CA), Loretta Sanchez (D, CA), Lois Capps (D, CA), Diana DeBette (D, CO), and Kay Granger (R, TX) elected to the United States House of Representatives; Maria Tallchief receives Kennedy Center Honor.
1998	Patricia Schroeder's *24 Years of House Work . . . and the Place is Still a Mess* published; Lois Capps (D, CA), Mary Bono (R, CA), Barbara Lee (D, CA), and Heather Wilson (R, NM) elected to the United States House of Representatives; California voters approve Proposition 5, the Tribal Government Gaming and Economic Self-Sufficiency Act of 1998.
1999	Dawnine Dyer named "Mentor of the Year" by winemakers; Team USA wins Women's World Cup of soccer; Eileen M. Collins becomes the first woman space shuttle commander; Shelley Berkley (D, NV) and Grace Napolitano (D, CA) elected to the United States House of Representatives.
2000	United States Senator Kay Bailey Hutchison (R, TX) named Border Texan of the Year.
2001	Rosario Marin named United States Treasurer; Susan Davis (D, CA), Hilda Solis (D, CA), and Diane Watson (D, CA) elected to the United States House of Representatives.

2002	Delphine Red Shirt's *Turtle Lung Woman's Granddaughter* published.
2003	Representative Nancy Pelosi (D, CA) named House Democratic Whip.
2007	Representative Nancy Pelosi named Speaker of the House of Representatives, the first woman ever to serve as Speaker.

Legendary horse bandit Joaquin Murieta. Courtesy of The Bancroft Library, University of California, Berkeley.

Banditry in California, 1850–1875

Paul R. Spitzzeri

Banditry, both by individuals and by groups, flourished in frontier California from the 1850s through the mid-1870s. Especially prominent during the Gold Rush period, bandits committed robberies, murders, and other criminal acts throughout the state with the more prominent of them becoming icons in the state. Chief among these were Joaquin Murieta and Tiburcio Vasquez, who remain figures of fascination for some who claim them to be "social bandits" or heroes. As social bandits, Murieta and Vasquez, it is claimed, were fighting against the American conquest of California and American and European mistreatment of native Spanish-speaking Californians (or *Californios*) and Mexicans. Others dispute the social bandit label and contend that the mythical and legendary status of Murieta, Vasquez, and others assigned to them in recent decades obscures the idea that they were instead common criminals. Murieta and Vasquez have even become part of popular culture with their stories, real or imagined, represented in films, art, theater, and literature.

Although Murieta and Vasquez have received the lion's share of the attention from California's era of banditry, there were many others who were well known in their time, including Americans and Europeans. Among these were Jack Powers, John "Red" Irving, and Tom Bell. Although they did not have the status of social bandit attached to them, these men were, to lesser degrees, icons in California as well. In a number of cases, bandit gangs included members from different ethnic groups.

Contributing to the rise of banditry were major changes in California after the American conquest in 1846–1847. The discovery of gold; the flood of gold-seekers and immigrants who followed; mistrust, hatred, and misunderstanding among the many ethnic and racial groups who lived in Gold Rush–era California; the difficulties in providing a stable government; and the lack of professionalization in the criminal justice system were among many factors that enabled bandits to operate in California. As the criminal justice system developed and professionalized, banditry began to wane, so that by the late 1870s it was not nearly as significant a threat as before.

Still, the iconic status of some bandits, particularly Murieta and Vasquez, continued to resonate with many. Purported histories, novels, movies, plays, songs, works of art, and other elements of popular culture continued to perpetuate the perception of bandits as romantic and often sympathetic figures. In many ways, this followed traditions about bandits from other portions of the world, especially Europe.

The foment of the civil rights movement of the 1960s, however, gave a fresh impetus for reclaiming the iconic status of the California bandit. The Chicano movement, especially, tended to embrace the rebelliousness of figures such as Che Guevara, Hernando Villa, Murieta, and Vasquez. This was not limited to political activism or popular culture, however, but also extended to some academics, who first sought to establish a link to the theory of the social bandit as exemplified in the work of British historian Eric Hobsbawm. Although the Chicano movement peaked in the early 1970s, the idea of Murieta and

Vasquez as social bandits persists even as some historians have taken pains to counter the concept in recent interpretations.

HISTORICAL BACKGROUND

Perhaps because of its small and relatively homogeneous Spanish and Mexican-era population, California experienced little documented banditry before the American conquest and the onset of the Gold Rush. A primary contributing cause to the change in the California environment that fostered the rise of banditry was the Mexican-American War. The campaign generated much controversy in the United States when war was declared in 1846, led to great political and social upheaval within the Mexican territory of Alta California during the campaigns of 1846 and 1847, and left a lingering atmosphere of conflict and tension between the native Californians, often called *Californios*, and the American conquerors. It has often been stated that the conquest and persistent difficulties between Americans and Europeans and Californios and Mexicans led many of the latter to turn to banditry in response. What is little recognized is that some of the most notorious bandits in California in the following decade were soldiers mustered out of volunteer service with American forces. One example is John "Jack" Powers, son of Irish immigrants, who joined the New York Volunteers regiment commanded by Captain Jonathan D. Stevenson.

A second factor in banditry's ascension was the timely coincidence of James Marshall's stunning discovery of gold at Coloma in January 1848, and the ratification just days later by the Mexican Congress of the Treaty of Guadalupe Hidalgo, which formally ended the war. This led to an even more transformative effect on California: the immigration of a couple hundred thousand gold seekers, settlers, and others within a few short years. As with any immigrant population, embedded within the new arrivals were those who would find banditry an alluring avocation, particularly as the promise of golden riches proved to be elusive to almost everyone who dug for the precious mineral. As the new arrivals streamed in from Mexico, Chile, China, the eastern United States, and Europe, people who had never lived among such an assemblage of different races and ethnicities found themselves at odds with others who spoke strange languages, dressed in different clothing, observed unfamiliar social practices, and had varying views about the right to settle in the newly obtained American territory. Consequently, intense racial and ethnic prejudice and violence was present in the gold fields and other portions of California almost immediately. It has been claimed that these conditions fostered the rise of banditry. There was, however, an economic impetus with the Gold Rush that fed the motivations of bandits, whether they found no luck in the gold fields or quickly realized that there was money to be earned in robbery among the merchants and suppliers of all types who thrived on trade in the gold-producing region; in the major cities and towns, such as San Francisco, Sacramento, Stockton, and Los Angeles; and on the vast cattle ranches of central and southern California. Typically, the more urban bandits were loosely organized, such as was the case with the Hounds and Sydney Ducks in San Francisco, while rural bandit gangs would associate under a leader but were otherwise not generally organized in any specific way.

A third element to the rise of banditry in California was the near absence of effective political and judicial authority, especially in the years between the conquest in 1846–1847 and the admission of California into the union in September 1850. Although almost immediately there were calls for California to be admitted as a state, Congress could not efficiently address California's status in the years following the conquest. The Missouri Compromise had governed the admission of alternating free and slave states since 1820, but California's unusual status as geographically north and south greatly complicated matters. In 1847 and 1848, the matter did not seem as pressing as it became after the hordes of gold seekers began to pour into California in 1849. The government of California had been left to the military with governors appointed and then deciding to largely leave the political and legal systems of Mexico in place. These systems, however, had functioned fairly effectively for decades with a small, fundamentally homogeneous population. After 1848, California teemed with new residents from around the world, deeply suspicious of each other but relatively unfettered by the restraints of government and law. By mid-1849, influential citizens, many of them arrivals within the previous year or two and faced with a seemingly intractable deadlock in Congress, decided to take matters into their own hands and write their own constitution and create their own government, goals which were accomplished at the end of 1849 and into the early months of 1850. Forced to act, Congress finally enacted the Compromise of 1850, which concerned a whole range of issues involving conquered Mexican territory after the war, including the status of slavery. California was admitted to the union on 9 September 1850 as a free state. Yet, the previous spring, civilian governmental and judicial systems had been put into place through elections and begun their operations.

A related issue was that, even with American-style systems of government and jurisprudence enacted, the early 1850s was an era in which, because of low taxation and a lack of widespread monetary and material support for the administration of justice, the effectiveness of crime prevention was limited. This was an era in which peace officers, who were elected and lacked any training, were few and underpaid, lawyers often were admitted to the bar without any formal education or training, and judges were not nearly the respected authority figures they later became. Most jails were flimsily built wooden, brick, or adobe structures allowing generally easy escapes for some prisoners, and state prisons, such as at San Quentin and later Folsom were built with cost rather than efficiency in mind and were heavily overcrowded soon after construction. Without a well-funded, professional criminal justice system, California was particularly ill equipped to deal with the presence of banditry in a rapidly growing, gold-producing state. This condition was hardly limited to California, as the United States as a whole lacked a sense of professionalization in the administration of criminal justice, though there was a gradual movement toward it from the 1850s onward. In addition, there was a heavy reliance on extralegal resolutions to criminal behavior, leading to a strong movement for popular justice, such as popular tribunals mimicking the legal courts, and lynching. This was also a national phenomenon in 1850s America, where popular justice was in its heyday. As a result, especially in the 1850s, California was rife with examples of popular tribunals, in which citizens held trials with judges, prosecutors, defense attorneys, witnesses, and the like in some imitation of the established courts, and vigilantism, in which citizens tended to dispense with any formalities except, perhaps, for a public meeting and storm a jail, seize a suspected criminal, and execute them, usually by hanging or firing squad. It is notable that, in those cases where vigilantes explained their actions, they almost always justified their actions by stating that they were acting to uphold, rather than circumvent, the law. The common complaint, moreover, was that the law was ineffective and weak, which was often an accurate statement because of the lack of support given to the administration of justice.

The heyday of the bandit coincides with the salad days of the Gold Rush. Consequently, as gold production dropped government became more established and effective. As the administration of criminal justice became more financially and socially supported and professionalized, reported instances of banditry declined, even if the romance associated with it lived on. The capture and execution of Vasquez in 1874–1875 has generally been considered to be the end of the era of banditry that started during the Gold Rush years.

THE GENESIS OF BANDITRY IN CALIFORNIA, 1848–1855

On 4 December 1848, the first documented incident of banditry doubled as a horrific massacre at the Mission San Miguel. Two Irish-born former military men, Peter Raymond, formerly with Frémont's California Battalion, and Peter Quinn, a sailor with the Navy, were implicated in a murder at Sutter's Mill, the very birthplace of the Gold Rush. Raymond, who escaped after being captured in this homicide, fled with Quinn to Mission Soledad where they joined forces with three other men, including another ex-soldier from Stevenson's New York Volunteers (the same regiment that brought famed bandit Jack Powers to California). The five men, with an Indian guide, then descended south to San Miguel where they were welcomed into the home of William Reed and his wife Maria Antonia Vallejo. The six visitors stayed one night and headed south the following morning, but Reed's boast about his cache of gold from his months in the gold fields led them to double back and try to relieve Reed of his bounty. Not content with mere robbery, the six men enacted one of the worst massacres anywhere in America at the time. Ten people including the family and employees were murdered. But by chance famed mountain man James Beckwourth happened to stop at the site and discovered the horrible tragedy. Racing to Monterey, Beckwourth found a young Army lieutenant, William Tecumseh Sherman, later a Civil War hero as a Union Army general, and related what he had found. Military governor William Mason was notified and sent Lieutenant Edward O.C. Ord south to investigate. Either brazenly or foolishly, the murderers ventured south and entered Santa Barbara in broad daylight. By then, news of the San Miguel massacre had spread and a posse of fifteen men, twelve of them Californio, from Santa Barbara descended on the six desperadoes. In a battle on a beach south of the mission town, one posse member and three of the bandits were killed. The remaining three men from the gang were seized then taken to town for a popular tribunal. The day after Christmas, with a jury of twelve and Lieutenant Ord representing military authority, the three prisoners were adjudged guilty and sentenced to death by firing squad. The execution occurred on 28 December and ended the first documented incident of banditry in American-era California.

In the meantime, a cadre of soldiers mustered out from Stevenson's regiment of New York Volunteers created a loosely confederated gang called the Hounds. Although not, perhaps, bandits in the sense of those who rode through California committing crimes, the criminal activities of the Hounds in San Francisco certainly merits referring to them as close in kinship to bandits. Through much of 1849, the ruffians, many of whom had associations with New York street gangs, even called their headquarters "Tammany Hall." After a particularly vicious attack on Chilean residents, Americans and Europeans who had generally tolerated their presence cracked down and broke up the gang. One of the alleged Hounds was former New York Volunteer Jack Powers.

There was any number of especially violent depredations carried out by bandits throughout the Gold Rush years and afterward. Some of the names of these desperadoes are unknown to history, such as the gang of nine Mexicans and one American who committed two brutal robberies, including several murders, in Amador County in August 1855 that led to a bloody two weeks unprecedented anywhere else in an otherwise unusually violent California. As horrendous as these attacks were, the responses, fueled by anger, hysteria, and paranoia, were about equally so—Latino men were strung up somewhat indiscriminately or by the machinations of an American looking to usurp a Latino's mining claim. Eventually, some of the accused bandits were tracked down to the area near Columbia in Tuolumne County where more gun battles and hangings of suspects occurred. By the time the bloodletting was finished, some twenty-three persons had been killed, either victims of the bandits, members of the gang, or innocents accused of involvement.

FIRST AMONG ICONS: JOAQUIN MURIETA (Ca. 1830–1853)

Murieta is as shadowy a figure as any in California history. Much of the elusiveness in finding tangible examples of his existence is due simply to the transitory and anonymous nature of life in rural California in the early 1850s and the fact that bandits operated on the fringes of society, while a significant part is due to his several biographers. The earliest and most influential of the Murieta chroniclers was Yellow Bird, also known as John Rollin Ridge, a half-Cherokee native of Georgia who was, as a child, part of the Indian Removal to Oklahoma. In his *The Life and Adventures of Joaquin Murieta* (1854), Yellow Bird immediately lays out the template for Murieta's future iconic status by identifying him as "the Rinaldo Rinaldini of California." Rinaldini was a bandit on the French island of Corsica in the 1770s identified by some as driven to rebel against both French domination of the former Italian-held island as well as against the modern conventions he loathed. Rinaldini was, in fact, just one of many famous bandits throughout the centuries in Europe, including Stenka Razin in Russia, Marco Sciarra in Naples, Perot Rocaguinarda in Spain, Johann Buckler in Germany, Louis Dominique Cartouche in France, and Robin Hood and Dick Turpin in England. There was also a more contemporary development of a romance around bandits in Mexico, which coalesced from the period of the war of independence from Spain onward. Yellow Bird's immediate attempts to determine Murieta's pedigree among iconic, romantic, and legendary bandits suggests more of a literary rather than historical motivation for the book.

The descendants of Yellow Bird's heroic Murieta included a variety of unknown and undistinguished writers, but also numbered two of the nineteenth century's most influential historians, Hubert Howe Bancroft and Theodore Hittell, whose massive histories of California remain important sources of information. Both liberally used Yellow Bird's biography, though Hittell did note that unreliability was the order of the day when it came to documenting Murieta's life. Bancroft was more romantic chronicler than historian in his discussion of Murieta, offering little specific information as to Murieta's activities. Eventually, the iconic force of Murieta was rendered onto the dramatic stage and motion pictures to become some part of popular culture, which further blurred the line between history and myth. All followed the Yellow Bird template in identifying revenge for racist actions (stolen land, ravished mistress/wife), with the latest of the films, an unsold television pilot from 1969 starring Ricardo Montalban, boasting the tag line "The Man Who Didn't Give a Damn."

Documentation about Murieta is very difficult to find. There are some references to him in many California newspapers, but the tendency of the press to reprint "accounts" from unnamed sources, the reliability of which are impossible to determine, makes for a problematic association of fact with someone as inherently mysterious as Murieta. For example, one press account from 1853 stated that Murieta was from Jalisco state in Mexico, identifying the particular town, and that he was thirty-five years of age. Other sources identify Murieta as a native of Sonora, which seems plausible considering that most of the early arrivals in the Gold Rush were highly experienced in gold mines, but the attribution is not definitive. Other statements from newspapers claim Murieta was well educated and spoke English fluently. Another newspaper reference from spring 1853, albeit derived "from several sources" and purporting to be in Murieta's own words, notes that the bandit had declared himself the victim of American prejudice and robbery in the mines. This account is the only contemporary newspaper that relates injustices committed against Murieta that might have provided the impetus for his career in banditry. There is, however, a likely antecedent in Yellow Bird's work, claiming that in 1850 Murieta swore revenge against Americans after his half-brother was lynched and Murieta whipped in an accusation and punishment by Americans for horse thievery. This came from a serialized story by "Dame Shirley" (Amelia Clappe), whose version of a Mexican who was whipped and sought revenge against his American oppressors is almost exactly mimicked by Yellow Bird. Elements of the story later included an assertion that Murieta's Sonora-born sweetheart (or wife) Rosita (or Rosalia) was raped and Murieta tied to a post and whipped by Americans. Notably, though Yellow Bird has Murieta frequently reinforcing his hatred for Americans often with dialogue. There are a number of examples, though vague, where the bandit is described as robbing Chinese, German, and French victims, though these crimes were, perhaps, purely for financial gain as opposed to the reaction against racism imputed to Murieta by the author. At one point in the narrative, a party of travelers robbed by Murieta happened to be rather neatly divided into a group of four Frenchmen, six Germans, and three Americans.

Yellow Bird, having identified the impetus for Murieta's criminal career, claimed that Joaquin methodically tracked down members of the mob that whipped him and killed his brother and exacted his revenge. The author also identified some of Murieta's confederates, including the "monster" Manuel Garcia, or "Three-Fingered Jack"; the youthful Reyes Feliz, whose sister was purported to be Murieta's lover; a man known only as Claudio; Joaquin Valenzuela; and Pedro Gonzalez; and claimed that there were more than fifty men—an incredible number—in the Murieta gang.

It appears that Murieta's first exploit was committed in fall 1851, if a later confession by an accused criminal said to be Joaquin's brother-in-law is accepted. This robbery, committed east of Los Angeles, involved twenty-nine horses. This was followed in November 1852 by the crime that led to the aforementioned confession. General Joshua Bean, commander of a volunteer force that brutally ended a conflict with southern California Indians the previous year, was established at the mission town of San Gabriel, near Los Angeles, as proprietor of a store and saloon. Living with him was his brother, Roy, later the notorious "judge" of Langtry, Texas. Joshua Bean was shot and killed as he was returning to his home after attending a maromo [dance]. In the aftermath, six men were arrested, all said to be members of the gang led by Salomon Pico, relative of ex-governor Pio Pico. In the investigation that ensued, it was reported that Murieta was in San Gabriel that evening with a woman named Ana Benitez, though it was not clear if he had any involvement in the events surrounding Bean's death. Benitez, however, claimed that one accused man, Cipriano Sandoval, confessed his involvement in the incident to her and Murieta. Another accused man was Reyes Feliz, the same person mentioned in Yellow Bird's story, who claimed he heard two men identify Murieta as the assassin. Another witness, identified as part of Pico's gang, testified before the tribunal that another man was with Benitez and that she had said Joaquin was in the San Joaquin to sell stolen horses. Evidently, based on Benitez's testimony, Sandoval along with four other men, including Reyes Feliz (who admitted to being associated with Murieta), was tried by a popular tribunal, adjudged guilty, and lynched. Interestingly, Yellow Bird's narrative had Feliz left behind somewhere north of Los Angeles mortally wounded from a bear mauling and begging Murieta to leave him to die, faithfully attended by his wife. Later in the manuscript, however, Feliz reappears in Los Angeles, recovered from his wounds, attended by his prototypically devoted wife Carmelita, and accused of complicity in Bean's death, for which he was hung. In Yellow Bird's story, Feliz approached death beatifically and leaped to his death from the platform before the trap was opened. Moreover, Carmelita, who wandered through the mountains wailing in grief and torment, was found dead, stretched upon a rock as if in sleep.

Notably, as suspects were being rounded up in the Bean incident, some one hundred horses were stolen from the San Gabriel area. According to a Los Angeles judge, one of the thieves was said to be Murieta. It is notable that, in Yellow Bird's life of Murieta there is ample dialogue provided between the bandit and his henchman Claudio about the need to kill Bean for his harassment of Claudio, who had been, in this account, thwarted in his attempts to commit robberies in the area. Moreover, Yellow Bird introduces Harry Love into the story at this point as a deputy sheriff of Los Angeles. The murder of Bean is deemed to have occurred away from the village of San Gabriel with Bean wrestled from his horse by Murieta and Three-Fingered Jack, killed and left on the spot. Yellow Bird even embellished his account by claiming that Three-Fingered Jack robbed and killed two Chinese camped near San Gabriel, a highly unlikely event because there were almost no Chinese known to have been living in the Los Angeles area at the time. This one example illustrates the issue of Yellow Bird's account being a romantic legend rather than anything connected to history, even given the lack of documentation available about the bandit.

As Yellow Bird moved closer in the narrative to the fateful year of 1853, the violence and desperation in his story increases, although, as throughout his story, the worst excesses are not those of Murieta, who retains thereby his heroic posture, but the brutish and monstrous Three-Fingered Jack whose capacity for grotesque killing is graphically detailed by Yellow Bird.

In addition, there was a frenzy in the gold fields during spring and early summer 1853 that led to reports of virtually any robbery or murder in the area to be the work of Murieta. It was also supposed that Murieta had committed depredations in other parts of the state, including Los Angeles, where the local newspaper in fall 1852 reported him to be present at the mission town of San Gabriel during the murder of General Joshua Bean.

Eventually, the hysteria about Murieta led Governor John Bigler to issue a $1000 reward for "Joaquin Carrillo." As attributed Joaquin crimes mounted, a new proclamation raised the bounty to $5000, but confusingly indicated that there were five Joaquins covered under the provisions, including Valenzuela, Botiller, Carrillo, Ocomorenia, and "Muriati." On 17 May 1853, a posse known as the California Rangers was appointed by legislative fiat and organized under Captain Harry Love, a figure of some shadowy repute in his own right. While the establishment of the reward and organization of the posse is about the most reliable information of all about Murieta, even as it named five different men as targets, the posse itself only contained one man who had any claim of knowing Murieta by sight. Consequently, when the posse in July killed a man purported to be Murieta and, among others, one of his notorious henchmen known as Three-Fingered Jack Garcia, it was decided to preserve by pickling the hand of Jack and the head of the man alleged to be Joaquin. These gruesome relics were toured throughout the state to try to establish proof of the identity of Murieta and Garcia. One problem was that the appearance of the five Joaquins in the governor's proclamation noted that Murieta had black hair and eyes, while that of the man killed by the Rangers had lighter color in both. There was considerable suspicion voiced among the press about the authenticity of the head in the jar, but Love received a $1000 reward and a $5000 appropriation by the legislature for his work. To this day, stories persist that Murieta eluded capture and went to Mexico to live out a full life. Meanwhile the pickled head in the jar is assumed to have been destroyed in the great San Francisco earthquake and fire of 1906, only adding more to the legend of Murieta, of whom so little is factually and historically known.

HEIR TO JOAQUIN: TIBURCIO VASQUEZ (1835–1875)

Compared to Murieta, Tiburcio Vasquez is a well-documented figure, much of this being attributable to the length of his career, the fact that he was captured alive and processed through the machinations of law, and that interviews of him were conducted after his capture and published. Still, Vasquez is no less a romantic figure if not as much a myth and legend, and he may, in some ways, be the first criminal celebrity in California who experienced some of his fame while still alive. Yet he appears to have attracted little attention until over twenty years after he first identified his entry in banditry. His crimes were largely out of the public eye and seemingly minor until the Tres Piños robbery in 1873, which led to the death of three men and for which Vasquez was convicted of murder and hung at San Jose in 1875. After his capture near Los Angeles in spring 1874, Vasquez was the subject of a play in that city within weeks, interviews with him were published in local newspapers, photographs of him sold to raise funds for his court defense, and hordes of visitors, including the curious and well-wishers, visited him both at Los Angeles and San Jose, where his trial was held.

Vasquez stated in interviews that he was a native of Monterey, the Spanish and Mexican-era capital of Alta California, born 11 August 1835. By 1874, his parents were dead, but there were three brothers and two sisters. In Monterey County in the 1850 census, there is a Tiburcio Vasquez who appears as a fifteen-year-old boy in a household that does not have a parent. This does not square with Vasquez's own recollection that he sought his mother's blessing to embark on a criminal career about two years after this, so the attribution is uncertain. Historian Hubert Howe Bancroft believed that two men, also named Tiburcio Vasquez, were the father and grandfather of the bandit. The elder was born in 1777 at Yerba Buena (San Francisco) and the second was born in 1793 and the dates seem close together for them to be father and son, but possible. Bancroft notes the second Tiburcio was alive as late as 1855 and lists ten children born between 1825 and 1840, but none named Tiburcio. A biographer of the bandit, Eugene Sawyer, gives names of four of Vasquez's siblings, only one of which matches the names from Bancroft's list. In short, Vasquez's pedigree is not known, but more of his background is available than for Murieta.

According to a Los Angeles interview in 1874, Vasquez commenced his career as a robber in 1852, based, he claimed, on an incident at a dance where he and other Californios were subjected to racial abuse. From that incident, Vasquez remarked nearly a quarter century later, he chose banditry as his vehicle to fight for social rights for himself and his fellow countrymen. The bandit went on to say that he received his mother's blessing for his wish to become a robber and stated that the first victim of his "defense" was the theft and money and clothes from peddlers in his home county of Monterey.

It is, however, five years later that Vasquez first enters the official public record for a crime committed against another Californio. After stealing a mule and nine horses with an accomplice named Librado Corona from Juan Francisco of Los Angeles County (this hearkens back to the question about Vasquez's status as a social bandit when his victim was of the same general ethnicity), the bandit was tried and convicted on a grand larceny charge in Los Angeles. He was sentenced to five years at San Quentin, but after less than two years in prison Vasquez joined a prison break in June 1859. He fled to Amador County in the gold country but was caught and returned to prison within two months. Vasquez remained at San Quentin, appearing there in the 1860 census, was the subject of a pardon petition that was rejected, and completed his sentence in 1863. In an interview with San Francisco journalist George Beers, Vasquez stated that he returned to his mother seeking gainful employment as a ranch laborer, but that suspicion of him led him to return to crime. By his own description, Vasquez's robberies involved stagecoaches and other conveyances and houses. Specific information about his activities from 1863 to 1873 is sketchy and his crimes attracted little attention. In 1866, he was arrested and convicted on charges of cattle thievery in Sonoma County and returned to San Quentin for his second stint, serving his term until release in June 1870. Notably, when Vasquez associated himself with compatriots such as Cleovaro Chavez, who continued his criminal career after Vasquez's execution, and Abdon Leiva, who figured prominently in Vasquez's downfall, he also took up with a French native named August de Bert.

After 1870, Vasquez attempted more daring robberies, such as a $30,000 robbery from cattle baron Henry Miller and a holdup of a Southern Pacific Railroad payroll train between Gilroy and San Jose, before the Tres Piños incident. Yet these and his final attempt at robbery, of a sheep rancher near Los Angeles in spring 1874, were all failures and an examination of Vasquez's career does not show a list of prominent robberies. Instead, the rumor of Vasquez's exploits fed by his own shows of bravado in his jailhouse interviews appear to have been fodder for future interpretations of his stature and nature as a bandit rather than the record of his banditry.

The affair in the San Benito County hamlet of Tres Piños, south of Hollister, in August 1873 was the result of a botched robbery of a store, leading to the deaths of three men. Interestingly, Vasquez, whose capture was in no small measure due to Leiva (whose wife had an affair of some duration with Vasquez), claimed that it was Leiva and another man who committed the killings before Vasquez and Chavez arrived on the scene. Regardless, what was left of the gang rode south toward Los Angeles where another robbery was planned to get them money to go to Mexico. For a time in September, a posse led by Santa Clara County sheriff John H. Adams and Los Angeles County sheriff William R. Rowland chased after Vasquez and his gang, during which time Abdon Leiva turned himself in to authorities. Vasquez, however, was able to elude capture in the rough San Gabriel Mountains north of Los Angeles.

Thwarted evidently in his plans to go to Mexico, Vasquez stated later that he went back north to Tulare and Fresno counties and then eastward to Inyo County to commit further depredations. By then, Governor Newton Booth had issued two proclamations providing for rewards for the capture of Vasquez. The first, after the Tres Piños murders, was for $1000. The second, issued in January 1874, was for $2000 dead and $3000 alive. In the meantime, Sheriff Adams negotiated a $5000 appropriation from the state legislature to form a new posse and commence the chase of Vasquez. Meanwhile, Vasquez had returned to the San Gabriel Mountains occasionally, according to one source, staying at a home west of Los Angeles at the base of the Santa Monica Mountains.

In mid-April, Vasquez and his gang attempted their last robbery together, selecting Alessandro Repetto, a sheep rancher in the hills of today's city of Monterey Park, a few miles east of Los Angeles. Believing that Repetto had a large sum of cash from the sale of wool, Vasquez confronted the rancher in his home only to find that there was no such sum. Instead, Vasquez sent a son or nephew of Repetto to Los Angeles to withdraw funds the rancher had at the bank of Temple and Workman. One version of the story has it that when the young man entered the bank and was visibly nervous, bank president F.P.F. Temple called in Sheriff Rowland and the whereabouts of Vasquez was discovered. The boy was entreated by the sheriff to return to the ranch, with Rowland to follow in close pursuit, but not to reveal the sheriff's presence. The story further observed that Temple, moved by the young man's concern for the fate of Repetto, allowed him to leave and warn Vasquez before Rowland gave permission, thus allowing the bandit to flee.

Whatever the particulars, Rowland arrived at the Repetto ranch not long after Vasquez's departure so that in giving chase Rowland found himself within sight of the bandit and his gang. During the chase, Vasquez even stopped to quickly relieve a group of men of valuables after they finished work laying pipes for the Indiana Colony, a new settlement soon renamed Pasadena. For several days, Vasquez and Rowland were engaged in a wild cat-and-mouse chase through the San Gabriel Mountains, prompting rumors of Vasquez's appearance in several Los Angeles area sites in a microcosm of what was reported with Murieta throughout California in spring 1853. In this encounter, as with the previous September, Vasquez made another escape after a dangerous journey down a very steep canyon.

An interesting component to Vasquez and the chase by Rowland that is not part of the Murieta story is the degree to which the former may have been given aid by his fellow Californios, a point discussed by some of the Los Angeles newspapers.

In late March, meanwhile, the legislature appropriated another $15,000 to bring Vasquez to justice and Alameda County sheriff Harry Morse, who had been part of the Adams posse the previous summer, formed a posse to find Vasquez and headed down to Los Angeles to confer with Sheriff Rowland. A second proclamation by Governor Booth raised the reward for Vasquez to $6000 if returned dead and $8000 if alive. When Morse met Rowland, the latter assured the former that he would capture Vasquez if the bandit remained in Los Angeles County and Morse returned north.

Finally, on 14 May 1874, a farmer named D.K. Smith rode into Los Angeles from his place on the plain west of Los Angeles and reported that Vasquez was at a nearby house situated near today's famed Hollywood. To avoid arousing Vasquez's suspicion, Rowland conspicuously remained in Los Angeles while sending an undersheriff and several men to capture the bandit. Using a little subterfuge in concealing themselves in the bed of a wagon that happened to be driving by, the posse members surrounded the house, interrupted Vasquez at a meal, and captured him as he tried to run by bringing him down with a few gunshots.

Vasquez's tenure in the Los Angeles jail immediately brought immense interest in the notorious bandido, who found himself in an unprecedented position of criminal celebrity. From newspaper accounts and histories, it appears that most visitors were there out of curiosity, although there were reports of women, including, to the disgust of a Los Angeles merchant, white women, bringing Vasquez flowers. A Los Angeles newspaper publisher, Benjamin Truman of the *Los Angeles Daily Star*, who secured the first interview with the bandit, quickly offered a little paperbound book titled *Life, Adventures and Capture of the Great California Bandit, Tiburcio Vasquez*. A Los Angeles photographer printed five hundred copies of a portrait taken of the bandit, with part of the proceeds apparently designated for the subject after his capture, and other sittings were held in San Francisco to provide funds for Vasquez's court defense. The nature of Vasquez's celebrity even extended to the world of commercial advertising, as, for example, a Los Angeles dry goods and clothing merchant placed an ad in a paper that stated the bandit recommended the store and its fine and complete stock of items. Finally, the enterprising proprietor of the Merced Theater rushed a farce called "The Capture of Tiburcio Vasquez" into production, which was positively reviewed in one paper for its clever use of burlesque and close enough resemblance to the facts of the capture. Also of note was a card taken out by Vasquez in a newspaper that claimed that he was approaching death and counted himself an unfortunate and sinful person, but innocent of the crimes of which he was accused, if not indicted. Accordingly, to prepare for a fair and impartial court proceeding, Vasquez issued the card as an appeal for a defense fund.

Tiburcio's Tale

"My career grew out of the circumstances by which I was surrounded. As I grew up to manhood, I was in the habit of attending balls and parties given by the native Californians, into which the Americans, then beginning to become numerous, would force themselves and shove the native-born men aside, monopolizing the dance and the women. This was about 1852. A spirit of hatred and revenge took possession of me. I had numerous fights in defense of what I believed to be my rights and those of my countrymen . . . I went to my mother and told her I intended to commence a different life. I asked for and obtained her blessing, and at once commenced the career of a robber. My first exploit consisted in robbing some peddlers of money and clothes in Monterey County."

From a May 1874 Los Angeles jailhouse interview with *Los Angeles Star* publisher Benjamin C. Truman, reproduced in Truman's *Occidental Sketches*, 1881.

The next day, however, on 23 May, Vasquez was taken from jail and sent by railroad to San Pedro Harbor south of Los Angeles, where he was sent aboard a steamer for San Francisco and his extradition to the Sheriff of Monterey County, which then included Tres Piños in its jurisdiction, although the new county of San Benito was soon created with Tres Piños within its boundaries. In mid-June, several indictments were handed down by the Monterey County grand jury. After a July hearing, the proceedings were moved to San Jose, presumably to establish a less prejudiced setting, and the trial postponed until January 1875. After four days of prosecution witnesses the people rested. The only witness testimony for the defense was that of Sheriff Adams and Vasquez himself, who tried to assign blame primarily to Leiva as responsible for the murders.

On 7 January, after three and a half hours of deliberations, the jury returned its verdict of guilty, with ten jurors calling for the death penalty and two recommending life imprisonment. At the time, unanimity was not required for a capital case. After a dramatic lecture by Judge David Belden, the sentence of hanging was set for 19 March. There was a quick appeal to the state Supreme Court with Vasquez's counsel claiming that Belden's jury instructions went too far afield from his mandated instructions on applicable law. The opinion offered by Justice Augustus Rhodes succinctly dismissed the claims by Vasquez's attorneys, ruled that Judge Belden's instructions were well within the law, and upheld the conviction.

At nearly the eleventh hour, three days before the scheduled execution, Governor Romualdo Pacheco, the only Latino governor in California state history who had recently ascended to the office from lieutenant governor when Newton Booth was elected to the U. S. Senate, received telegrams from prominent citizens in San Jose and Los Angeles, including District Judge Ygnacio Sepulveda, asking for a commutation of the sentence to life imprisonment out of concern for potential violence in the wake of Vasquez's hanging.

Consequently, the execution was carried out on 19 March with two sisters, a brother, and several nieces present. As Vasquez approached the gallows, his attorney produced a letter addressed to the bandit's associates in crime. In the missive, Vasquez denied murdering anyone, but seemed to take some responsibility for the commission of those crimes under his leadership. Moreover, he warned against actions of revenge for his death and called upon his colleagues to learn from his example. Another letter addressed generally to parents advised them to look at his example in raising their progeny and then turned to religion as Vasquez accepted his fate. It was reported that although he had maintained an imperturbable calm thus far, Vasquez wept at the conclusion of this second letter before recovering his wits to sign the documents. With a glass of claret and a cigar consumed, Vasquez rapidly ascended the gallows stair and was calm until, by some accounts, the black cap covering his head was lowered and the bandit showing an alarmed look uttered *"Pronto!"* or "Be quick!" Then, the platform door was opened and in a wink of an eye,

Vasquez was left hanging, his neck broken. After twenty-five minutes, the body was cut down and turned over to family members who buried him at Santa Clara Cemetery, where he still rests. For some in Los Angeles, the capture and death of Vasquez signaled the end of a violent era in that part of California and, for the most part, banditry was in decline.

THE TEFLON BANDIT: JACK POWERS (1827–1860)

If there was an American corollary to Murieta, Jack Powers perhaps best qualifies. As with Murieta, Powers has been described as handsome, dashing, and charismatic. Documentation concerning his involvement in banditry, however, is somewhat elusive and seems to be more by association with other known bandits and his penchant for making enemies than on hard evidence. Well known as a gambler and horseman, whose one hundred and fifty mile race in under seven hours in 1858 was statewide news, Powers was almost constantly in suspicion of criminal activities from his arrival in California in 1847 until he fled the state under accusation of wrongdoing in 1858. His reputation as a bandit and criminal remained long after he was murdered on his Arizona ranch in 1860.

The son of Irish immigrants and born in New York City, Powers makes his appearance in public records in summer 1846 when he signed on with the First Regiment of New York Volunteers, commanded by Jonathan D. Stevenson. He gave his name as John A. Powers and his age as nineteen and was following an older brother and brother-in-law in the regiment. A hint of Powers's future nonconformity seems to be a notation on his army record as a deserter, after he snuck ashore before his ship left Governor's Island where the regiment was trained and didn't return for roll call. After over five months at sea, Powers arrived in San Francisco in early March 1847, by which time hostilities in the brief campaign in California had ceased. The New York Volunteers were sent to various portions of California for garrison duty in the newly occupied territory, with Stevenson given command of southern California from his headquarters at Los Angeles. Powers was transferred to a different company and sent to Santa Barbara, which would be his main area of residence for his ten years in California. In short order, Powers's company became notorious for its lack of discipline, love of gambling and drink, and bad relations with the Californios of Santa Barbara, prompting military governor Richard Mason and his aide William Tecumseh Sherman to travel to Santa Barbara and attempt to instill some order and discipline.

In spring 1848 news of the discovery of gold reached Santa Barbara, followed within a couple of months by word that a peace treaty with Mexico was signed, meaning that American forces in California would be mustered out soon. This happened in September, prompting most soldiers to head for the gold fields at a time when, other than Sonoran, Chilean, and Peruvian miners, few others from the outside world had yet made it to California to prospect. It appears that Powers spent the last couple of months along the Stanislaus River digging and made enough money (or took enough work) to convince him to take his bounty and head for San Francisco. The latter was a far different place than the dusty, nearly uninhabited hamlet Powers had first seen less than two years before. By the end of February 1849, the first of the 49ers arrived by steamship and San Francisco began its rapid, rollicking ascent into a full-fledged Gold Rush city.

Many of the New York Volunteers had set up a headquarters and clubhouse in the form of a tent, naturally bearing the sign "Tammany Hall" on it, close to the Mexican-era plaza at Commercial and Kearney Streets. Though they called themselves "The Society of Regulators" they were more commonly known by the notorious moniker of "The Hounds," a group that, in the rapidly urbanizing setting of Gold Rush San Francisco, could be equated with a very large group of bandits. The mayor of San Francisco in 1849 was former New York Volunteers chaplain Reverend Thomas Leavenworth, and the sheriff was regimental sergeant John Pulis. Powers arrived in San Francisco and naturally became associated with his former Army comrades-in-arms. Pulis frequently used the Hounds in his capacity as sheriff to enforce writs and orders. More often, the Hounds preyed on Chilean miners and others who were the target of demands for protection and general unruly raids. In July 1849 a raid on the Chilean settlement turned particularly violent as about a hundred Hounds destroyed tents, seized property, and killed and wounded several persons. Although previous acts of violence and lawlessness by the Hounds had been tolerated, this affair led Sam Brannan and other prominent citizens to muster a vigilante force to disperse the Hounds. Seventeen men, including Powers, accused of being involved in the attack on the Chileans were seized and held aboard a ship in the harbor, a common tactic for jailing persons since no jails then existed in San Francisco. A public tribunal was held, and though there were nine convictions, several men including Powers were acquitted.

Realizing that the city by the bay was not a welcome place for the time being, Powers returned to the gold fields in the Mokelumne region and mined for several months, evidently returning with a healthy amount of cash. He then returned to San Francisco where he remained until spring 1851, when he decided to make his way back to Santa Barbara. Soon after his arrival in the mission town, Powers decided to settle on a ranch north of town that was claimed by Richard S. Den, an early American resident of the area. Eventually, Powers was forced off the ranch, although Den later lost his own claim to the property. At one point, violence broke out over the dispute leading to the death of one of Den's ranchmen. Powers's biographer includes a quote attributed to him about his efforts to reform being thwarted by those trying to prevent him from doing so and that, if he were left alone he would live a good life, but if not, he would become bad and desperate. Notably, Powers is quoted as saying that if his claim to the ranch were invalidated he would no longer seek to reform. In many ways, this resembles the rationale given by Tiburcio Vasquez in his claims that his attempts to settle down were denied by those out to get him, thereby forcing him back to a life of crime.

His denied land claim, his fondness with drinking, horse racing, and gambling, as well as his associations with questionable Californios and former soldier friends continued to cast suspicion on Powers regarding the many robberies that were committed along the El Camino Real (King's Highway), the main north-south road through the Central Coast. One of the supposed locations of Powers's misdeeds was the stretch of the El Camino Real near present-day Los Alamos between Santa Barbara and Santa Maria. Rumors abounded that after bandit Salomon Pico left California for Baja, California, Powers took up with the members of the disbanded gang and that among Powers's most prominent criminal associates were Pio Linares, Rafael Herrada, and Joaquin Valenzuela (Ocomorenia), the latter being one of the five Joaquins who were the subject of Governor Bigler's reward in the hunt for Murieta. Powers's prowess as a horseman lent credence in many minds that he was able to commit crimes in wide-ranging locations because the speed he could reach on his horses could provide him an alibi for being far from the scene of the incident. In later years writers such as Stephen Powers (no relation), who was a federal Indian ethnologist, and Charles Nordhoff, whose books on California were widely read, both treated Powers as a known brigand and bandit. Both claimed that prominent ranchers (in Nordhoff's case Edward F. Beale of the El Tejon Rancho, north of Los Angeles) related that Powers and his gangs entered their properties. Yet both sources claimed that Powers behaved toward them in a courteous and chivalrous manner, not unlike how Murieta was often described.

There were at least two incidents where Powers was charged with a crime. In summer 1853, Powers was indicted by the Santa Barbara Grand Jury for alleged involvement in the killing of a man by Powers's longtime friend Patrick Dunne, another former New York Volunteer. After a trial in Santa Barbara resulted in a deadlock, the charges stood although the case was transferred to Los Angeles in a change of venue. There, Powers and Dunne were tried in District Court, but with the indictment the only evidence presented against them, the two were acquitted and released. Three years later, after Edward McGowan, a police court judge said to be implicated in the famous 1856 murder of San Francisco newspaper publisher James King of William that led to the creation of that city's second vigilance committee, frantically left the city by the bay, Powers was present to assist McGowan when the fugitive arrived at Santa Barbara. McGowan, although calling Powers his "guardian angel" also described him as a "bandit and destroying angel." Though McGowan eventually returned to face trial in the King of William assassination and was acquitted, Powers was arrested and charged with harboring a fugitive. This trial was also moved to Los Angeles from Santa Barbara, but in July 1856, Powers was discharged on grounds of insufficient evidence and allowed to return to his home.

Powers's involvement in the McGowan affair incurred the considerable wrath of James King of William's brother Thomas, who took over the management of the *San Francisco Bulletin* after his brother's death. Whatever support Powers received in the *Herald* was countered aggressively in the *Bulletin*, which almost never failed to mention Powers's name without calling him the "notorious Jack Powers."

In January 1857, after a group of bandits known as the Flores-Daniel gang killed Los Angeles County sheriff James Barton and some of his deputies near San Juan Capistrano, Powers was accused of burglary and was the subject of a warrant issued by the county judge in Los Angeles, though rumor had it that he was linked with the Barton murders. Powers went to San Francisco, perhaps to escape, but was found there and arrested. Eventually, a judge there ordered Powers to return to Los Angeles to face a hearing, but without much evidence produced to link Powers to a crime, he was discharged.

Later in the year, further problems from the association Powers had with some less-than-reputable people arose. In November, two Basques looking to buy cattle vanished near Mission San Miguel, although after a few weeks the body of one of them was found. Suspicion fell on a vaquero named Robles who had been with the two men and was known to be a friend of Powers. It was said Powers visited Robles in jail and counseled him. When Robles was acquitted in a court in San Luis Obispo, talk of forming a vigilante group became rampant. Later, after Powers's famed horse race in May 1858, two of his associates, Pio Linares and Rafael Herrada, delivered some horses to San Luis Obispo that Powers bought in San Francisco. Soon afterward, the two men were part of a group that committed a robbery and four murders, which set loose an organized vigilante committee in San Luis Obispo. A manhunt occurred that included a raid at Linares's home and from which he barely escaped. Three men thought to be his accomplices were tracked down and lynched, although there is significant doubt as to their involvement in the attacks. One of these men, in an elicited confession, implicated Powers as central to the murder of the Basque men the previous fall. Finally, at Los Osos Rancho near the coast, Linares was discovered and confronted by the vigilantes. He was killed and two other men were captured, tried by the committee, and hung, although Herrada escaped. Robles, acquitted in the murder of the two Basque men, was found in Los Angeles by a posse led by then–state senator and future governor Romualdo Pacheco, returned to San Luis Obispo, and hung. Before his death, Robles also implicated in a signed confession extracted by the vigilantes the role of Powers in the death of the Basques.

An arrest warrant with a $500 reward approved by Governor John Weller was made out at the end of May for Powers, who was still in San Francisco, as part of the manhunt, and members of the San Luis Obispo vigilance committee traveled there to make the arrest. Evidently Powers was tipped off by his old friend Patrick Dunne and vanished from the city. Rumors in newspapers during June had him in his archetypal lightning-fast horse ride through

California, so that he was said to be in the Mariposa gold country, in San Bernardino sixty miles east of Los Angeles, and in the San Fernando Valley and Santa Ana in Los Angeles County. Instead, Powers took a steamer bound for the Gulf of California and Sonora in northern Mexico and settled in Hermosillo. According to the *Los Angeles Star* newspaper, Powers was quoted as saying that he would return to San Francisco in two years.

Two years later, however, Powers was dead, though not by law enforcement or a citizens' vigilance committee. Instead, hearing about opportunities to run cattle to a mining area near the Mimbres River in southeastern Arizona, Powers gathered animals and made his way up from Hermosillo only to learn that the mining speculation had failed. Settling in with several hundred cattle at a ranch near Tubac a few miles north of the Mexican border, Powers was killed in late October 1860, perhaps by some Mexicans in his employ. He was buried in nearby Calabasas, which is today a ghost town. Yet Powers's fame continued on years after his lifetime, though he was more kindly recalled as described by his enemy Thomas King of the *San Francisco Bulletin* as a "sporting man."

THE UNITED NATIONS OF BANDITRY: THE TOM BELL GANG

Thomas J. Hodges, whose alias was Tom Bell, was a native of Tennessee who was educated and had some medical training. After serving as a medical orderly with a volunteer regiment from his home state in the Mexican American War, Hodges arrived in California in 1850. Within a year or so, he was convicted of grand larceny in Sacramento County and sentenced to five years in prison, which was then a converted ship at Angel Island in San Francisco Bay. After feigning illness and transferring to the decrepit county jail in San Francisco, Hodges escaped, though he was soon recaptured. Soon after, San Quentin, California's first true prison, was completed and Hodges installed there.

In May 1855, Hodges was part of a group escape from wood-chopping detail and formed a multiracial gang that committed crimes in the gold country from Marysville on the north to the Kings River area in the south. Eventually there were associated with the man who now called himself Tom Bell bandits (including a black man) from several American states, Mexico, Chile, England, Canada, Australia, Sweden, and Germany. Primarily the Bell gang worked in the northern mines, especially around Marysville, Auburn, and the Nevada City area. Express stages and pack trains were particularly lucrative targets, because they usually carried several thousands of dollars. Bell's robberies were carefully planned and choreographed, but after an attempt at robbing an express stagecoach with passengers led to resistance from the driver and the killing of a passenger, the group lost many of its men to a posse, abandoned the northern mines area, and moved south near Firebaugh's Ferry in Fresno County.

A few minor crimes were committed, one of which led to the arrest of some of Bell's most trusted and long-term associates. A new posse, discovering Bell's whereabouts, descended on his ranch in early October 1856 and rounded up almost everyone else associated with the bandit except the leader, who escaped for a few more days. When he returned to his ranch, however, a group of settlers led by a prominent Stockton man, George G. Belt, were alerted to his presence and surprised Bell in conversation with someone. Belt told the bandit to prepare for execution on the spot. Giving Bell time to write letters to a woman who had housed him in California and to his mother in Tennessee, Belt then arranged for a noose and, moving quickly because of impending darkness, lynched Bell from a strong sycamore tree. Members of Bell's gang, meanwhile, continued to be hunted and most of them were killed or imprisoned. One, Jim Webster, was caught and jailed by Henry Plummer, the marshal of Nevada City. Here was a case, however, where the line between bandit and lawman became very blurred. It is likely that Plummer deliberately arranged Webster's escape so that he could claim a reward for his recapture. Whether this was the case isn't known with certainty, but Plummer's future actions showed him to be capable of criminal behavior with the best of them. In 1857 he killed the husband of a woman he was having an affair with. After being convicted of murder and sentenced to San Quentin, Plummer, as Bell had done, faked an illness and received a pardon from the governor. Not long after returning to Nevada City, Plummer killed a man in a drunken gun battle in a brothel and fled the state. It has been said that Plummer turned to crime full time after fleeing toward Oregon and then turning to Washington Territory, where he stopped for a time in Lewiston. In the new mining town of Bannack, Montana, Plummer ran for sheriff, lost the election, and chased off the incumbent with threats of violence. But he was also said to be the leader of a gang of men, called the Innocents, including Bell's former henchmen Cyrus Skinner and Cherokee Bob Talbott, that went on a spree of highway robberies. The famous Montana Vigilantes that was spawned that year brought an end to the thirty-one-year-old sheriff, who was lynched in January 1864. Still, the ruthlessness of the vigilantes, the questionable nature of forced confessions of condemned men who claimed Plummer as the head of the "road agents" gang, and the fact that little direct evidence exists to either implicate or exonerate him leaves the matter of Plummer's criminal career in some doubt.

Rattlesnake Dick Barter, a British Canadian, took some of Bell's men and formed his own gang after Bell's demise. For three years Barter and his men committed a number of brash robberies of stagecoaches and Wells Fargo offices. In battles with his nemesis, Auburn constable John Boggs, Barter escaped arrest and confinement in jail several times. When Barter was finally killed in summer 1859, it was by a Placer County undersheriff in a fight in which Barter wounded a man he thought was Boggs. Having escaped from the battle mortally wounded, Barter had time to sketch a last note that was found in his hand when his body was discovered. The note read, in part, "If J. Boggs is dead, I am satisfied."

DOUBLE BANDITRY: THE JOHN "RED" IRVING GANG

An unusual example of banditry that had more than one manifestation in a single event is what has been called the "Lugo Case" in Los Angeles during 1851. It can be viewed as a matter of "double banditry" because what led to the incident was a series of raids committed by Indians in the desert areas north of Cajon Pass, some sixty miles east of Los Angeles. Indian incursions into the greater Los Angeles area were frequent and the prize targets were horses. Although not generally referred to as such, there is no reason not to view these raids as acts of banditry.

In the first days of 1851, horse thefts by Ute Indians led by the famous Chief Walkara at the Rancho San Bernardino led to attempts by the family to find and punish the perpetrators. On one such mission Jose Maria Lugo, the owner of the San Bernardino, organized a posse of some twenty men, including ranch vaqueros, Cahuilla Indians who were also employed by the Lugos to guard against such raids, and Lugo's sons Chico and Menito. While ascending Cajon Pass to track down the Indians, the posse came upon Patrick McSwiggin and a Creek Indian named Sam, teamsters in the Amargosa mine owned by Los Angeles investors, in the high desert area above the pass and questioned them as to any sighting of Indians. Evidently the reply was that the Utes were armed with only bows and arrows, and the Lugos continued on only to be confronted by Indians amply armed with guns. In the ensuing gun battle, a member of the Lugo party was killed and the Indians escaped.

When the posse broke up as they returned to San Bernardino, a segment, including the Lugo brothers and three other men, came upon McSwiggin and Sam, whom they believed had deliberately misled them about the Utes and their armaments. According to one of the posse members, Ysidro Higuera, who testified in a trial held for the Lugos, Chico decided to confront the two men and drew his gun. Sam was killed in the first exchange and when McSwiggin sought cover behind his wagon, he was seized, taken out in the open on the road, and shot. Within a few days a detachment of soldiers marching through the pass found the bodies. During a coroner's inquest, the jury could only conclude that the two men met their ends from someone in the Lugo posse. When Justice of the Peace Jonathan R. Scott held hearings to investigate the matter, he ordered Sheriff G. Thompson Burrill to arrest the Lugo brothers. It was during these hearings that Higuera told his story. Representing the state in the hearing was Los Angeles County Attorney (and future District Judge) Benjamin I. Hayes.

Entering into the drama was the fact that Scott and Hayes were just recently legal counsel for Los Angeles jailor George Robinson in a case in which Robinson and Jose Maria Lugo were charged with assault over an incident that occurred at Rancho San Bernardino. It was alleged that Robinson, who with his wife were guests of Jose Maria Lugo at San Bernardino as they were immigrating to Los Angeles in September 1850, hit his wife during an argument. Lugo intervened and a fight broke out between him and Robinson. The two men were charged in District Court on assault and battery charges and fined $2.50. Shortly thereafter, Robinson was hired as jailor. The enmity between Jose Maria Lugo and Robinson continued in civil court as the latter sued the former claiming false imprisonment at the San Bernardino ranch home, as well as assault and battery. In June 1852, after two mistrials, the case was continued.

The allegation later surfaced that under Robinson's influence with the motive of revenge against the Lugos Higuera concocted his story about the McSwiggin and Sam murders to implicate Chico and Menito. It was also noted that Higuera was arrested on separate charges of murder and a charge of grand larceny, intimating that he issued his accusations against the Lugos to assist his cause in court. Higuera, in fact, had been found guilty of grand larceny in District Court in summer 1850 and fined $10. Subsequent to his confession, he faced trial before the Sessions Court in the second larceny case, though there is no known disposition. Another Lugo posse member who Higuera identified as complicit in the deaths was Mariano Elisalde, also charged with the Lugo brothers in the murders.

The accusations against Robinson, Scott, and Hayes were made by Joseph Lancaster Brent, a Los Angeles attorney hired by Jose Maria Lugo, allegedly for $20,000 (an enormous sum), to defend the Lugo brothers. Brent, whose manuscript on the affair was written in 1900 and published twenty-six years later, claimed center stage in the events that followed his hiring.

In the meantime, months passed, and in April 1851 some twenty-five men, led by John "Red" Irving—said to have been a Texas Ranger during the Mexican-American War—descended Cajon Pass into Rancho San Bernardino. There seemed little doubt that the Irving gang was one committed to banditry, although any specific information about their doings is not known. Once Irving learned about the arrest of the Lugos, however, he offered to storm the jail, free the Lugo boys, and take them to Mexico, where the gang was evidently heading to commit robberies and/or join an expedition organized by the Mexican government to fight Indians in Sonora. The price for this service, according to Brent, was $10,000, although a newspaper account stated the amount was a staggering $50,000. Moreover, the attorney wrote, when Jose Maria Lugo refused Irving's offer and instructed Brent to try and get his sons out on bail, Irving sent a lieutenant named George Evans accompanied by a contingent of the gang with a threat that the boys would be killed if the money was not forthcoming.

Brent's narrative continued with the story that as the Lugos brought some friends into Los Angeles as bondsmen, Evans and his men surrounded the simple adobe jail where Chico and Menito were held. Brent claimed that he told the Lugos that a force of Californios was needed to oppose the bandits and that it was not safe to try to convey the boys to court. Next day, a cadre of Californios was stationed opposite Evans and company and a violent standoff loomed. Suddenly, seemingly out of nowhere, a squadron of fifty soldiers marching north from San Diego arrived in town and were requested to assist in keeping order by Sheriff Burrill while the Lugo boys were escorted to court for the bond hearing. During this drama, as narrated by Brent, Irving arrived in town and was infuriated to find that his plan was not working out. Although Brent claimed that Irving confronted him at dinner and told him he had challenged Fitzgerald and his squadron to battle the next day, Irving ordered his men to leave town and head east, where they stole cattle and horses from prominent local rancheros William Workman, Ricardo Vejar, Ignacio Palomares, and Isaac Williams. Irving then divided his gang again, sending some on the road to the Colorado River and toward Mexico, while he, Evans, and ten others went to seek revenge on the Lugo family at Rancho San Bernardino.

In the meantime, Irving's theft of cattle raised an alarm and a posse was formed to track him down. Simultaneously, a messenger was dispatched to warn the Lugos of Irving's movements, so that when the bandit leader arrived at San Bernardino, he found the ranch house virtually abandoned except for a vaquero who was ordered by the Lugos to call in Chief Juan Antonio of the Cahuilla band of Indians for help. Irving fired on the Indians and rode off with his men, the Cahuillas trailing close behind. With no knowledge of the area, Irving fell into a trap set by Chief Juan Antonio and his men who chased them into San Timoteo Canyon near today's city of Redlands. Irving and his men soon found themselves hemmed into a box canyon with the Indians taking up positions to prevent their escape. Though the bandits attempted to fight back, they were quickly cut down, except for Evans, who played dead and managed to escape.

The following day, the Los Angeles posse, consisting of Americans, Europeans, and Californios, arrived at the scene of the slaughter. It was reported by Brent that many of the former were enraged at the carnage when the charge against Irving was only cattle theft, but the Lugo attorney is the only source for this assertion. The coroner's jury, however, consisting of four Latinos and two whites, came back with a judgment that the killings were justified. The local Indian agent concurred, to a degree, stating that Chief Juan Antonio and his men were acting on the behalf of the Lugos, although he opined that Indians generally should not be permitted to punish whites for their crimes.

In the meantime, the Lugo brothers were subjected to, for the era, a very lengthy journey through the Los Angeles County court system. Indictments brought by County Attorney Hayes through the court of his former law partner, Justice Scott, were found faulty after they were sent to the District Court, which had jurisdiction in murder cases. Scott resigned his office in August after the Lugo brothers' case had been continued in the District Court, and

Hayes gave way to a new County Attorney in the fall. The problems of faulty indictments and new indictments and bench warrants that were challenged by Brent were accompanied by the attempted murder of Hayes in the fall. Rumors spread that the assassin was famed bandit Salomon Pico and in December 1851 the Lugos were held without bail during an examination to determine whether they were involved. This was after they had been indicted in August but advised by Brent to hide because he feared that they would be lynched. Although they were not indicted in the attempted killing of Hayes and, finally, in October 1852 the case was dropped due to a lack of evidence, one source has indicated that Chico and Menito Lugo later joined Pico's gang.

One notable artifact from the Lugo case was a report in the *Los Angeles Star* newspaper from October 1851 in which a deputy sheriff provided the paper with a list of homicides committed in the previous fifteen months. Organized by townships, the list gave the number of forty-four homicides, including at San Bernardino, seventeen persons "including Irving's party, killed by the Indians." This list has been used by historians as proof of Los Angeles's exceptionally high rate of murder per capita, far surpassing that of any city in American history. It is a matter of debate, however, as to whether the fate of the Irving "party" or gang was a matter of homicide in the same sense as other reported homicides rather than an outright battle. Even if the Irving gang numbers were removed from the list, reducing the total number by over one-quarter, and accepting that the remaining thirty-three reported homicides actually were homicides, the list would still indicate a very high rate of homicide per capita.

BANDITRY AND POPULAR JUSTICE:
THE SHERIFF BARTON KILLINGS

As banditry waxed and waned, so did popular justice, in which citizens circumvented, though almost always claimed to support, the law and established courts, which were chronically under-funded and short-staffed. Bandits, whether as individuals or in groups, were perennial targets of vigilantes, whose concern for protection of private property and maintaining peace for the public good were not unwarranted. One of the more iconic examples of the response of popular justice against banditry happened in Los Angeles County in 1857.

In early January, a group of bandits commonly known as the Flores-Daniel gang for its leaders Juan Flores and Francisco "Pancho" Daniel engaged in robberies throughout the southern part of Los Angeles County, including the mission town of San Juan Capistrano (now in Orange County). At San Juan, the stores of four men were robbed and one of them, George Pflugardt, was killed. When news of Pflugardt's murder reached Los Angeles, Sheriff James Barton formed a small posse of five men and headed out for the fifty-mile ride to catch the perpetrators. Barton had been sheriff from 1852 to 1855 and had been through more than his share of rough justice in frontier Los Angeles. In September 1856, however, Barton was elected for one more term and took office in December, just weeks before the Flores-Daniel gang conducted its raid on San Juan Capistrano.

In present-day Irvine, Barton met with what was assumed to be the Flores-Daniel gang, but not in a position that favored him. Trapped in an area in which they were completely surrounded, the posse tried to fight the numerically superior gang. The sheriff and three of his men were killed with the other two posse members barely escaping with their lives. The survivors headed for Los Angeles and the suburban town of El Monte, known for its disproportionate number of vigilantes, to raise an alarm.

What resulted was a massive manhunt that was certainly the largest in nineteenth-century Los Angeles County and probably one of the biggest in California. In particular, the death of the popular, if somewhat reckless, sheriff rocked the community and the response, driven by anger and fear, led to reprisals that led to the deaths of nearly two dozen suspects, many of whom likely had little or nothing to do with the Flores-Daniel gang.

The formation of several posses was largely done on the basis of ethnicity, including groups from the German, French, and Californio portions of society, in addition to a group of Americans from the relatively new suburban town of El Monte led by a future sheriff James Thompson; the mustering of an existing militia under former Santa Barbara County Sheriff William W. Twist; and a new company led by a physician, Dr. John S. Griffin, who assumed general leadership over the entire effort to track down the Daniel-Flores gang.

For some reason, the first acts of retribution were not near the scene of the murders of Barton and his posse members but in the mission town of San Gabriel where four Hispanic men, reported to be members of the Daniel-Flores gang, were captured and executed by citizens from El Monte. One of the lynched men, Miguel Soto, was shot and, perhaps in imitation of the alleged Joaquin Murieta killing, his head was decapitated and taken to Los Angeles. While Soto had been examined in 1856 before a Justice of the Peace for robbery and the attempted murder of militia leader Twist, there was significant controversy over whether Soto and the three others killed at San Gabriel had anything to do with the Barton murders or were lynched because they were thought to be involved in crime generally. The decapitation of Soto further added to the inflamed feelings generated by the incident, which was reflected in the combative reporting between the Spanish-language *El Clamor Publico* and the English-language *Los Angeles Star*.

In the meantime, the company of Mounted Californians led by Andres Pico, which included up to eighty Californios and Indians, were joined by the El Monte posse of some forty men and cornered the accused banditti in Trabuco Canyon. Five men, including Juan Flores, were captured and three temporarily escaped, though these latter were caught a short time later. When poor security allowed for all of the prisoners the ability to escape, only two of them were recaptured right away and Pico decided to hang the two, Juan Silvas and Francisco Ardillero. Juan Flores, who rode across the county some eighty or more miles, was captured at the Rancho Simi near the border with Ventura County and placed under arrest in Los Angeles. Two other of the gang escaped through Simi Pass. At least fifty persons were arrested and six men were lynched in the initial manhunt. There were, however, other reports of lynching, included three men killed at Los Nietos, southeast of Los Angeles, and, at Santa Barbara, the executions of two other men, one of whom issued a confession to his involvement in the Flores-Daniel gang.

Flores, however, though lodged in jail was soon the subject of a large public meeting about his fate. Said to be without any dissent, the vote generated by the meeting called for the hanging of the bandit chieftain, which was conducted on Fort Moore Hill overlooking the city on 14 February.

Later in the year, Luciano Tapia, arrested on accusation of being in the Flores-Daniel gang, went on trial at the District Court for the murder of George Pflugardt. He was duly convicted and sentenced to death. He and an American named Thomas King were executed one after the other in February 1858.

This left Pancho Daniel, the other leader of the bandit gang. He was arrested in San Jose early in 1858, extradited to Los Angeles, and indicted. His trial began in March, but Daniel secured a continuation of the case to the July term. When the case resumed in the summer, however, problems in jury selection in which the defense challenged on the basis of alleged bias in juror selection by Los Angeles County Sheriff James Thompson, a member of the El Monte posse that sought the gang after the Barton murders, led to another continuation to November. The trial resumed on 22 November but further defense challenges to the jury selection process were followed by a motion for a change of venue. This had been refused by Judge Benjamin Hayes before, but the problem of seating a jury likely led him to agree and the case was transferred to Santa Barbara County, also part of Hayes's district. The citizens of Los Angeles, however, were not disposed to let Daniel leave the county and, on 30 November 1858, seized the prisoner as he was being removed from his cell for the transfer and lynched him. In the register of action for the District Court, the County Clerk pointedly noted that Daniel was "accidentally hung, through the carelessness of some American citizens."

Popular justice continued for another fifteen years in Los Angeles, but reached its brutal pinnacle with the aftermath of the Barton murders. Although there is no doubt that some of its victims were guilty of the crimes they were accused of committing, there is considerably less certainty about the execution of many of the others, including the four men in San Gabriel. A community greatly excited by the San Juan robberies and murder, followed by the killing of Barton and his posse members, could not control their anger, fear, and desire for revenge and excesses seemed to be the order of the day.

CONCLUSION

The subject of banditry has received surprisingly little attention among academic historians, quite likely because of the lack of documented information about the individuals and, in many cases, the specifics of their activities. It is also probable that the nature of banditry as steeped deeply in legend and myth makes an academic analysis difficult. These conditions, however, have not deterred amateur and popular historians from taking up the topic of banditry, and there is no shortage of books and articles on such figures as Murieta and Vasquez, while American and European bandits are frequently discussed in general works about nineteenth-century lawlessness.

The issue is whether the myths and legends can be sufficiently separated from reliable evidence, even if the iconic presence of the former in the stories of Murieta and Vasquez almost always trumps the latter.

FURTHER READING

Boessenecker, John. *Gold Dust & Gunsmoke: Tales of Gold Rush Outlaws, Gunfighters, Lawmen, and Vigilantes* (New York: John Wiley & Sons, 1999).

Brent, Joseph Lancaster. *Life in California*, unpublished manuscript from 1900, Huntington Library.

Farquhar, Francis Peloubet. *Joaquin Murieta: The Brigand Chief of California* (Reprint ed., Fresno: Valley Publishers, 1969).

Greenwood, Robert, comp. *The California Outlaw, Tiburcio Vasquez* (Reprint ed., New York: Arno Press, 1974).

Hanks, Richard A. "Vicissitudes of Justice: Massacre at San Timoteo Canyon," *Southern California Quarterly*, 82(3): 2000; 233–256.

Nadeau, Remi. *The Real Joaquin Murieta: Robin Hood Hero or Gold Rush Gangster* (Corona del Mar, CA: Trans-Anglo Books, 1974).

Robinson, W.W. *People Versus Lugo* (Los Angeles: Dawson's Book Shop, 1962).

Ross, Dudley T. *Devil on Horseback: A Biography of the "Notorious" Jack Powers* (Fresno, CA: Valley Publishers, 1975).

Sawyer, Eugene T. *The Life and Career of Tiburcio Vasquez, The California Stage Robber* (Oakland, CA: Biobooks, 1944).

Secrest, William B. *California Desperadoes: Stories of Early California Outlaws in Their Own Words* (Clovis, CA: Word Dancer Press, 2000).

Spitzzeri, Paul R. "The Retirement of Judge Lynch: Justice in 1870s Los Angeles," unpublished master's thesis, California State University, Fullerton, 1999.

Thornton, Bruce. *Searching for Joaquin: Myth, Murieta and History in California* (San Francisco: Encounter Books, 2003).

Truman, Major Ben C. *Occidental Sketches* (San Francisco: San Francisco News Company Publishers, 1881).

Yellow Bird (John Rollin Ridge). *The Life and Adventures of Joaquin Murieta, The Celebrated California Bandit* (Reprint ed., Norman: University of Oklahoma Press, 1955).

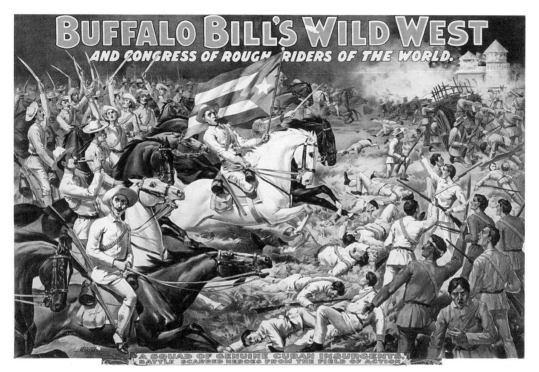

Circus poster showing battle between Buffalo Bill's congress of rough riders and Cuban insurgents, ca. 1898. Courtesy of Library of Congress.

Buffalo Bill Cody

Jennifer Mizzell

William Cody—soldier, showman, entrepreneur, and founder of the Wild West Show—helped shape the popular concept of the American West. By blending historical events such as the Battle of Little Bighorn with mythical portrayals of the West inspired by dime novels and melodramas, Cody entertained late nineteenth- and early twentieth-century audiences with what many people believed an authentic representation of the Wild West. Turn of the century audiences, uncertain about the future and nostalgic for the past, looked to the Wild West Show as both a vehicle for escapism and as an adventure back in time. What many audiences failed to realize, however, was that Buffalo Bill's Wild West Show was, in fact, very modern, both in its concept and in its relationship with American mass media and culture. Buffalo Bill inspired a new form of celebrity, understood the powerful link between American culture and media, and offered Americans new memories of their own histories.

EARLY LIFE

William Frederick "Buffalo Bill" Cody was born near Leclaire, Iowa, on 26 February 1847. In 1854, while the country was in the midst of growing pro- and anti-slavery tensions, the Cody family moved to the Kansas territory and settled within the Salt Creek Valley. Cody's father Isaac was a Free Soil Democrat. Yet the Salt Creek Squatters Association, an organization that worked to maintain order and settle claim disputes in the territory, was controlled primarily by pro-slavery men. The tension between Isaac Cody and his pro-slavery neighbors escalated into violence and in September 1854, Isaac Cody was stabbed during a claim dispute with pro-slavery man, Charles Dunn. Isaac Cody survived the attack, but remained the target of pro-slavery violence.

According to William Cody's own memoir, as a boy, Cody saved his father from a trap set by his enemies. After learning of the danger that awaited his father, who was away from home, the young Cody decided to meet Isaac before he returned to Grasshopper Falls and warn him of the impending threat. Sick with the flu, he got out of bed and onto a horse. He traveled over nine miles, fleeing a gang of men who recognized him as the son of an abolitionist. Eventually, Cody stopped at the home of a family friend, who, noticing the vomit-covered horse, put Cody to bed. Later, the friend related that he had communicated with Cody's father and that Isaac Cody's return date had been postponed. Yet Cody insisted on carrying the message to his father. In 1879, Cody retold the story of his ride to rescue his father in *The Life of Buffalo Bill*. Cody's 1879 account, however, excludes the help he received from the family friend and ignores the fact that Cody's father was not in any real danger.

AUTOBIOGRAPHICAL ACCOUNTS

Cody's autobiographical accounts tend to omit many details of his early life, primarily those that threatened to diminish the character of Buffalo Bill, the American Hero. Cody's account of his efforts to save his father from ambush by pro-slavery men, for example, excludes many details later added by Cody's sister, Julia.

After Isaac's death in 1857, Mary and Julia Cody, Cody's mother and sister, continued to work on the Cody farm, renting out rooms in the family house to help raise money. Cody sought employment as a teamster. Guerilla warfare continued to escalate in Kansas and Missouri, however, and by 1862 Cody joined "The Red Legs," a paramilitary group and the self-proclaimed protectors of Kansas. Yet many of the Red Leg expeditions involved instances of robbery, including theft of property belonging to pro-Union settlers. Frequently away from home, Cody returned to the family farm in 1863 to care for his sick mother. Following the death of Mary Cody, Cody grew despondent and turned to drinking. After recovering from his binge, Cody alleged that he unknowingly awoke as a soldier in the Seventh Kansas Volunteer Cavalry.

During the Civil War, Cody claimed to have witnessed heavy combat and to have been employed as both a scout and as a spy. During this time, according to Cody, he renewed his friendship with James Butler "Wild Bill" Hickok, who was also serving as a spy. According to official military records, however, Cody served as both a hospital orderly and a messenger for the Freedmen's Bureau in St. Louis.

After the Civil War, Cody returned home and resumed employment as a stage driver. In 1866 he married Louisa Maude Frederici, the daughter of an Austro-Italian immigrant. After the war, Cody hoped to start a new family and to reverse the financial ruin his family had suffered at the death of Cody's father. Cody returned with his new bride to his mother's home in Leavenworth, Kansas. Mary Cody died during the war in 1863 and the house was under new ownership. Cody rented the house and transformed it into a hotel called the Golden Rule House. Cody hoped the hotel would prove a lucrative investment, capitalizing on the rising numbers of travelers moving through the area. The business venture failed due, in part, to Cody's own poor money management skills.

As Cody's hotel venture fell short of success, his marriage, too, suffered. At first, the Codys shared a home with Cody's sister Eliza and her husband. After Cody's sister and brother-in-law moved out, Cody's younger sister Helen moved in, depriving Louisa, as she saw it, of her own home. In addition, Cody's financial problems aggravated the tension between Cody and his now pregnant wife. Louisa, the daughter of merchants, had anticipated a fairly settled and comfortable life. Disappointed by her husband's failures, unable to get along with her sister-in-law, and frustrated by the want of her own house, Louisa Cody was left to give birth to her first daughter, Arta, alone. After Golden Rule House failed, Cody left his wife and sister and started out for Salina, Kansas.

According to Cody, his first year away from Louisa was spent "railroading, trading, and hunting." With a mind to make money, Cody was open to a variety of employments including the resumption of various odd jobs and failed business ventures. It was at this time, however, that Cody first acquired the moniker "Buffalo Bill." Although the name "Buffalo" was not uncommon on the Plains, the name assigned to Cody was inspired by one of his many business schemes; that is, as a supplier of buffalo meats. Even before his fame as an entertainer, the nickname "Buffalo Bill" already made Cody a celebrity on the frontier.

After a series of unsuccessful business endeavors, Cody teamed up with William Rose in 1867 to found a town near Fort Hays. The partnership between Cody and Rose began when the men were contracted to grade track for the United Pacific Eastern Division. The new town was founded along the railroad track and given the name "Rome." Cody and Rose designed the town, cleared the land, graded roads, and offered free lots to potential settlers. Eventually the town consisted of thirty houses, saloons, and stores; including one owned by Cody. Cody immediately sent word to Louisa, boasting that he had settled and was now worth $250,000. Soon Cody's wife and new baby joined him in the Kansas frontier. Unfortunately Rome's success was short-lived. After a failed attempt to negotiate Rome as the next town site for the railroad, Cody witnessed the town's dissolution as men tore down their homes and buildings and moved to Hays City, the site of the new railroad stop. Cody and Louisa followed the Rome settlers to Hays City and attempted to set up business in a new hotel. Within several months, Louisa left her husband and moved back to St. Louis.

After Louisa's departure, Cody took up buffalo hunting, an occupation that garnered little respect. In June 1868, Cody invited Louisa to meet him in Leavenworth. Louisa agreed and arrived with the baby. The meeting was brief and after an argument, the couple agreed, according to Cody, that they were not suited for each other. Louisa returned again to St. Louis. Back in Hays, Cody, a successful buffalo hunter, took up scouting for the military as well. Civilians were frequently hired by the army to serve as scouts, teamsters, and guides. In the spring of 1868, Cody was promoted to detective to help catch deserters and thieves. During his service as a low-ranking army detective, Cody rode alongside his old friend Deputy Marshal Bill Hickok.

After a brief career sleuthing for the military, Cody returned to west Kansas and took up work as a scout and hunter for the U.S. Tenth Cavalry. By 1869, Cody had become popular with the local press. Despite the myths surrounding Cody's military exploits during the Indian Wars, though, Cody never actually served as a soldier. The lifestyle of a scout was distinctly different than that of the common soldier. Scouts not only functioned outside the military chain of command, they also lived relatively private lives and garnered greater pay than the average soldier. In addition, Cody supplemented both his income and his celebrity by giving and selling Indian ornaments and captured horses to followers. Scouting was a way for Cody to repair his wounded finances and to differentiate himself from the common soldier, but even as a scout Cody was not exempt from battle; during the 1860s, Cody was involved in at least nine conflicts.

In 1868, Cody volunteered to courier a message from General Philip Sheridan to troops in Fort Dodge, ninety-five miles from Fort Hays. Sheridan received notice that two local Indian tribes were in the process of relocating from the area around Fort Larned. Sheridan feared that the Indians were moving in preparation for an attack on neighboring settlements. Cody covered 350 miles in sixty hours without respite, carrying messages both to Fort Dodge and to Fort Larned. Sheridan, impressed with Cody's ride, proclaimed that Cody's was service indispensable in the campaign against the Indians and appointed Cody as chief of scouts for the Fifth Cavalry.

In late 1868, Cody and the Fifth Cavalry encountered a band of Cheyenne Dog Men north of Fort Hays. Cody and the cavalry followed the Dog Men through a moving battle into Nebraska. Eventually the Indians dispersed, however, and Cody and the cavalry returned to camp. That same winter, Cody and the troops joined Sheridan in his offensive against Indian warriors. Cody scouted for General Eugene Carr and at the end of the campaign in 1869 Carr kept Cody on as his scout. In May 1869, Cody battled bands of Sioux and Cheyenne warriors. Carr commended Cody's courage and skill as a scout and petitioned for a bonus of one hundred dollars for Cody as a token of his admiration and approval.

Within the same month, Cody along with 400 men, including 150 Pawnee scouts, set out to track a band of Dog Men who had kidnapped two women and an infant in northern Kansas. During the expedition, Cody was involved in numerous skirmishes with Sioux and Cheyenne warriors. In one instance, Cody and a crew of scouts chased a Sioux riding party sent to stampede the army mule herd. The chase continued into the night and resulted in the killing of two Sioux raiders. When Cody and the scouts returned to camp, however, Carr was infuriated. Instead of complaining to Cody, though, Carr voiced his frustration to another scout, warning that separating soldiers from the main army was a common Sioux tactic. On 11 July, Carr embarked on a mission to overtake the retreating Cheyenne, fleeing from recent skirmishes. Within three days, Carr's troops clashed with the Cheyenne, crushing the Dog Men and rescuing the only surviving captive, Maria Weichell. Cody's career with the Fifth Cavalry continued through the fall and after 1869, the military kept Cody on as chief herder for Fort McPherson's livestock.

Within the same year, Cody invited Louisa, their daughter Arta, and two of his sisters to stay with him in Kansas. Hostilities between Indian tribes and the military had declined and Cody was now in a position, at least financially, to care for his family. Cody's invitation was accepted and the family settled at Fort McPherson. Cody oversaw the construction of a small house and Louisa, hoping to help supplement the family income, opened a dressmaking business. A year after reuniting with her husband, Louisa gave birth to a boy, Kit Carson Cody. The Cody family, having finally achieved middle-class status, settled into their new lifestyle.

During the 1870s, Cody scouted both for military expeditions and wealthy hunting parties. In 1872 Cody was awarded the Congressional Medal of Honor after leading a detachment of the Third Cavalry into a skirmish with Sioux raiders outside a Sioux Indian camp. Eyewitness accounts commended Cody's bravery and quick thinking, defending his party. Cody's reputation had so preceded him, one onlooker commented, that there was no need to describe Cody's brave feats; rather, all the public needed to know was that Cody had behaved as he usually did. Years after his death, however, the military revoked Cody's medal, claiming that Cody had been a civilian scout rather than a soldier when he earned the award.

On 7 July 1876 Cody and the Fifth Cavalry received word of the defeat of General George A. Custer and the Seventh Cavalry at Little Bighorn. The Fifth Cavalry, determined to prevent additional losses at the hands of the Cheyenne and the Sioux, traveled 150 miles, intercepting a band of Cheyenne at Warbonnet Creek. The Cheyenne engaged the Fifth Cavalry in battle. During the skirmish, Cody dressed in full stage regalia, allegedly shot and scalped Cheyenne chief Yellow Hair. The confrontation between Cody and Yellow Hair was apparently an accident. Many of the details of the encounter have been muddied by unreliable accounts, including the version depicted by Cody in his Wild West Show. Despite the controversy over exactly how the fight between Yellow Hair and Cody unraveled, however, it seems certain that Cody killed the Cheyenne warrior. After the encounter, Cody sent word to Louisa describing the event in eccentric detail and announcing that he planned to send Yellow Hair's arms and scalp to a shopkeeper for display in the front window.

Cody's early penchant for showmanship and his skill as a guide and a buffalo hunter meshed well with his "Western" persona. During the 1870s, for example, Cody's careers as an entertainer and as a scout frequently overlapped. By 1868, railroads advertised buffalo hunts in hopes of both attracting passengers and devising an effective solution for the problem of buffalo herds crowding the railroad tracks. Passengers aboard trains were encouraged to hunt buffalo and trains often stopped to give their travelers a clear shot at the buffalo from the tracks. Tourists were drawn to the buffalo hunts in hopes of experiencing the West; that is, the popularized West that they had seen and heard about in paintings, novels, magazines, and newspapers. Tourists who dreamed of living the Western life flocked to the buffalo hunts in hopes of making a mark, albeit small, upon history. Yet buffalo hunting via train little compared to the experience and excitement of a mounted buffalo hunt.

Cody's familiarity with mounted buffalo hunting preceded his days as an army scout. In fact, Cody had taken railroad agent and Rome nemesis William Webb on a buffalo hunt in 1867. According to Webb, Cody was the best scout he had ever seen and hunting on horseback was the only true way to hunt.

Horseback buffalo hunting represented much more than the fulfillment of fantasies or the expansion of the tourist industry, though. Guided hunts helped cultivate an exclusive social environment, a sort of clique comprised of hunters not defined by urban social mores such as class or tradition. For a guide, satisfying the position of both leader and a hired hand was often an ambiguous task. Cody's strategy for navigating the precarious social terrain was to play practical jokes. For instance, Cody's most remarkable "joke" was the staged Indian attack. In 1871, Cody organized a mock attack, instructing his Pawnee guides to ambush himself and his companion "Mr. McCarthy." The joke backfired when McCarthy fled his false attackers. When Cody finally overtook his client, troops had already been dispatched in pursuit of McCarthy's phony assailants.

Cody's guiding persona, therefore, infused aspects of both the Western hunt and Wild West showmanship. In 1871, Cody guided a hunting party for Philip Sheridan comprised of various prominent Americans including lawyers and financiers. Cody conscientiously prepared for the hunt, appearing in a fringed buckskin suit, a crimson shirt, and sombrero, holding a rifle atop a white horse. Cody maintained his performance throughout the hunt, relating tales of Indians and hunting around the campfire at night and showing off his hunting skills by killing a buffalo on horseback.

In 1872, Cody led another famed hunting party for Russian Grand Duke Alexis. According to one newspaper's account, Cody met the grand duke astride a horse and clothed in a buckskin suit. Cody traveled with the grand duke's party for the fifty-mile hunt terminating at Camp Willow Creek. Cody's importance in the grand duke's party was limited, however, by the presence of George A. Custer. For the remainder of the hunt, Cody occupied a more peripheral position, edged out by Custer's celebrity. Cody did not linger long in Custer's shadow, however, and after the hunt with the grand duke came to a close, he accepted an invitation to visit New York. By February 1872, Cody was on his way to New York City.

CELEBRITY AND THE WILD WEST SHOW

In New York, Cody was immediately drawn to the theater. Ironically, Cody's arrival in New York coincided with the opening of the play "Buffalo Bill" by playwright Fred G. Maeder. The play opened at the Bowery Theater and starred actor J.B. Studley as Buffalo Bill. Studley, realizing that Cody was in attendance, notified the crowd that the real Buffalo Bill was in the audience. Cody was eventually called to the stage to make a short speech. Cody, later recalling what it was like to stand before an audience for the first time, said he made a desperate attempt to speak, but he could no longer recall his exact words. After the short speech, Cody bowed and dashed from the stage.

In fall 1872, Cody along with several scouts was invited by writer Ned Buntline to Chicago. Buntline persuaded Cody to play the role of the real Buffalo Bill on stage. After the scouts arrived, however, it became clear that Buntline did not have a script. After the play's backer reneged, Buntline personally rented a theater for a week and led the scouts to a hotel where, within four hours, he produced a script. Cody and the scouts worried that they would not be able to memorize their lines in less than six months. Yet, under the critical eye of Buntline, they memorized their scripts in time and in four days, opened the play titled "Scouts on the Plains," before a mixed audience comprised of Philip Sheridan and the Chicago aristocracy.

Reviews of the play were dismal. Critics noted the stiffness of the actors, the violence, and the confusing, whirlwind plot. Still, the play continued to tour, traveling throughout the Midwest and Northeast. Eventually the group began to fracture and two members split to start their own theater company. Cody continued on, however, under the name of his new theater company, Buffalo Bill Combination. The Buffalo Bill Combination toured for another ten years, Cody playing the lead role of Buffalo Bill. Cody's early stage career was extremely successful; not only did he gain popularity, but by 1880 Cody's annual profits peaked at $50,000.

In 1872, Cody visited St. Louis to star in "Scouts of the Prairie." He reunited with Louisa again, who, along with their three children—daughter Orra Maude was born in 1872—traveled with Cody and the show. In 1873, the Cody family moved to West Chester, Pennsylvania. Louisa, however, continued to travel with Cody and the show and in 1874, the family visited and eventually settled in Rochester, New York. Despite the reunion between Louisa and Cody, family life was anything but tranquil. In 1876, Cody's five-year-old son died of scarlet fever and two years later Louisa moved with Cody's two daughters to North Platte, Nebraska.

Cody continued to work on the stage until the birth of his Wild West Show in 1883. Cody's fame had been on the rise since the early 1870s when he first appeared before a New York audience in "King of the Border Men." Newspapers profited from Cody's celebrity, embellishing the adventures of Buffalo Bill, including an account of the hunt with Grand Duke Alexis. In many ways, Cody seemed to transfer his "Western show," that is, his performance as a scout—telling stories and staging Indian attacks—to the East. Much of Cody's early theater work consisted of impromptu acting and filling in the gaps between forgotten lines with storytelling and campfire narrative. Cody, thus, successfully entertained Eastern audiences with Western tales, and after his apprenticeship with Buntline, Cody turned to managing his own theater troupe. Cody's stage plays seemed to blur the line between the theater and the frontier. In 1877, for example, troupe members abandoned Cody's theater company after being seriously injured during a scene. The actor who had been scripted to play the scalped Indian Yellow Hair claimed that he had been pressured and deserted by Cody and the troupe. The distraught actor reacted to Cody's alleged abuses by starting his own theater company, but without Cody, the actor's new troupe failed to draw as great an audience as that of the "authentic" Buffalo Bill.

Cody's theater work, therefore, embodied a new form of entertainment, one that blended authentic history and events with Cody's trademark storytelling and the stage. The *New York Times* mused over Cody's new approach to theater, calling it "Drama of the Future" in which contemporary history is portrayed by the actual actors involved. Approximately ten years after Cody's first appearance on stage, he participated, along with a contingent of Pawnee actors, in the initial dress rehearsal for the Wild West Show in Colville, Nebraska. According to contemporaries, after a mule-drawn Deadwood stagecoach rolled into the arena, Cody invited the town council and mayor to take a ride in the coach around the show grounds. The coach circled three times before the Pawnee actors charged after it. Buffalo Bill and a rescue party followed, sending the mules into a frenzy. The entire scene whirled past the crowd, the mayor waving from the window of the coach to be let out, but the mules would not stop until they were entirely exhausted. Once they came to a stop, the mayor leaped from the coach and charged toward Buffalo Bill. Fortunately for Cody, another actor distracted the mayor before he unleashed his anger on the show's star.

One of the most attractive characteristics of Cody's show was its sense of authenticity. What the Wild West Show offered, however, was a mixture of fact and fantasy. Many portraits of Cody were taken before painted backdrops depicting western terrain. Although clearly fabricated, the backdrops were regarded by audience members as authentic representations of the West, drawing out the rugged and therefore "Western" attitude of the person in the photograph. Thus the presence of Indians helped emphasize the authenticity of Cody's Wild West Show. In fact, Cody's initial plans were to make Indians the main feature of the show.

As Cody's show grew in size, he acquired a partner, William "Doc" Carver. The Wild West Show, in its maturity, opened with a parade featuring Indians, cowboys, elk, and buffalo. Following the parade, the show began, comprised of three series of acts: races, historical reenactments, and exhibitions of skill and talent, which included acts such as rope demonstrations and bronco riding. Unlike the contemporary circus, the Wild West Show mixed historical memorabilia, Western props, and authentic historical characters, such as Indians and a Deadwood coach, with showmanship and entertainment. The Wild West Show was at its most popular in cities and urban centers, where Cody—on horseback and armed with a gun—amazed audiences, many of whom had never learned to ride. The show also symbolized the fleeting nature of the frontier and triggered the nostalgia for the frontier past. The Wild West Show, therefore, blended aspects of the past and the present, a modern circus depicting historical events as entertainment for the new urban centers.

The Wild West Show, not surprisingly, had its share of strong personalities. Doc Carver, for instance, was an excellent marksman but only a substandard performer. His shooting was inconsistent and in one instance, after failing to hit a series of targets, Carver lost his temper, broke his rifle on his horse's head, and attacked an assistant. In addition, Cody and his crew had a penchant for drinking, which resulted in poor performances and missed shows. The failings of his show seem to reflect Cody's shortcomings as a manager.

While Cody struggled to balance his performance career with his managerial career, his personal life continued to unravel. Beginning with a lawsuit against his cousin who had allegedly sold family property that belonged to Cody's grandfather, the decline of Cody's personal life continued with the deterioration of his marriage. Louisa, according to Cody, had grown jealous of his stage career and particularly of the show's actresses, whom Louisa claimed to have seen Cody kissing. After Louisa returned to North Platte in 1878, Cody continued to support his wife, sending her $3500 to resettle. Four years after Louisa returned to Nebraska, Cody began work on a new ranch also in North Platte, named "Scout's Rest." Cody increased his land holding by four acres and populated it with cattle, horses, new trees, a large Victorian home, and a barn with the words "SCOUT'S REST" painted across the top.

Despite Cody's move to North Platte, Louisa refused to share a home with her husband and declined invitations to live in the house at Scout's Rest. In 1883, Louisa gave birth to a daughter, Irma, but the relationship between the Codys remained fairly precarious. Cody mortgaged his properties to support his show and his new ranch, and was infuriated when Louisa refused to sign the mortgage papers for her home in North Platte. In addition, Louisa had taken the money given to her by Cody and invested it into other properties under her own name. In September 1883, Cody wrote to his sister announcing that he planned to divorce Louisa, whom he accused of attempting to ruin him financially. Cody eventually dropped the divorce suit, however, when his daughter Orra died a month later.

While Cody struggled to keep his marriage intact, the Wild West Show was in danger of falling apart. Cody's finances suffered thanks to his inability to settle differences with his new partner. In addition to financial qualms, Cody also wrestled with negative publicity after the *Chicago Tribune* reported that audience members who attended the show in October 1883 questioned the "respectability" of its multiethnic cast, comprised of Indians and Mexicans. In 1883, Cody and Carver parted ways and two years later Cody won a lawsuit over the use of the name "Wild West." As a result, Cody hired a new theater manager, Nathan Salsbury, whose experience in entertainment ranged from variety shows to musical theater. The combination of Salsbury's managing experience and Cody's familiarity with the melodrama helped reshape the narrative of the Wild West Show. Despite the show's entertainment value, it still lacked a single, clear direction, in particular the inclusion of a single conclusive ending.

Ethnicity in the Cast

The cast of Buffalo Bill's Wild West Show included Indians, white "American" cowboys, and "vaqueros" of Mexican descent. Actors were often dressed in costumes that emphasized their different ethnicities. Yet actors also frequently blurred racial lines to appear in various roles during the season.

The first change Salsbury demanded of the Wild West crew was sobriety. Cody agreed with Salsbury and together they worked to enforce abstinence and order. Salsbury then went to work reorganizing Cody's show and providing it with the sense of direction it clearly lacked. By 1885, Salsbury had added an orchestra that included musicians dressed in Western costume, which began each show with "The Star Spangled Banner." The Wild West Show also adopted a new closing scene known as "The Attack on Settler's Cabin." The scene featured Cody rescuing a white family or white woman and children from an Indian attack. In this way, the Wild West Show appealed to a conservative middle-class audience who considered the home a place of salvation and virtue.

In 1884, the Wild West Show opened in New York and embarked on an Eastern tour, traveling down the Mississippi by steamboat. While en route, the steamboat collided with another boat, resulting in a loss of equipment, including the show's animals. The actors and the crew survived, however, and were able to salvage the Deadwood stagecoach. Despite the boat accident, Cody and the Wild West Show continued to New Orleans and opened on time. Within two weeks, Cody replaced the show's lost property and purchased new livestock, as well as a buffalo. In September, Cody and the Wild West Show received an endorsement from Mark Twain. According to Twain, the show transported him to wilderness of the Great Plains and the Rocky Mountains. Twain called the show "genuine" and urged Cody to send his show abroad. It is generally agreed that many of the attractions sent from America to Europe were unbelievable, said Twain. If Cody were willing to send the Wild West Show to Europe, he could prove that American entertainment was, in truth, rather authentic. Within two years, Cody accepted Twain's suggestion and traveled with the show across the Atlantic to England.

In spite of setbacks in New Orleans, the Wild West Show, with the combined efforts of Salsbury and Cody, continued to grow. In 1885, Anne Oakley joined the show. Oakley, who harbored an aversion to lowbrow entertainment, was attracted to the Wild West Show for its "wholesomeness." For Oakley, the show's frontier hero embodied heroism, not the overt sexuality common in burlesque shows or circus features. In contrast, the Wild West

Show's now famous "Attack on Settler's Cabin" exemplified the importance of protecting the family and preserving domesticity.

Oakley was hired to replace shooter Adam Bogardus, who quit the show during its run in New Orleans. Salsbury offered Oakley a three-day trial with the show in Nashville. At the end of the trial, Oakley was hired and Salsbury and Cody immediately went to work promoting their new star, ordering $7000 worth of advertisements. The fact that the Wild West Show chose to advertise Oakley as an individual star reveals the degree to which Cody and Salsbury recognized Oakley's value. Oakley's appeal, as a young woman heading up a shooting act, satisfied the show's unusual relationship with both the exploitation of violence and the preservation of the family.

Oakley's act tested the boundaries of the traditional female role and included stunts such as aiming a gun at her husband and shooting the end of a cigarette from her husband's mouth. The combination of Oakley's femininity and shooting skill was a winning match for the Wild West Show. Cody and Salsbury did not hesitate to hire other female actresses, including "the California Girl," Lillian Smith. Oakley's embodiment of female virtue, however, outshined Smith's shooting skill. Smith eventually left the show in pursuit of a love interest. It was clear that tension existed between Oakley and the other female actresses. In 1887, the tension became so great that Oakley left the Wild West Show and embarked on an independent European tour. It was not until 1889 that Oakley returned. Oakley remained with the show until 1901.

The acquisition of Oakley was a precursor to the reinvigoration of Cody's efforts to acquire both famous and more "wild" Indians for the show. In 1885, with the help of General William T. Sherman, Cody obtained permission from the Indian Office to take Sioux chief Sitting Bull on tour. Sitting Bull, however, was unsure about joining the show until, according to Salsbury, he saw a postcard of Oakley. Sitting Bull had seen Oakley perform in 1884, had nicknamed her "Little Sure Shot," and, according to Oakley, had adopted her as his daughter. Sitting Bull joined the Wild West Show for the 1885–1886 season. Under contract with the Wild West Show, Sitting Bull earned fifty dollars a week, with two weeks in advance and a $125 bonus. Cody also agreed to allow Sitting Bull to bring an additional five men at twenty-five dollars a month and three women at fifteen dollars a month, along with his interpreter, William Halsey, at sixty dollars a month. Sitting Bull also retained all rights to his photographs and autograph, which he sold as show souvenirs. Sitting Bull's routine consisted of riding a horse around the arena during the show's opening parade.

In 1885, Cody and Salsbury organized a banquet in Boston to which they invited twelve journalists. The banquet was designed to provide the journalists with a "Western experience," complete with a roasting ox, primitive silverware, tin plates, and neither tables nor chairs. Sitting Bull attended the banquet, and after the meal, answered the reporters' questions. The banquet was successful and the journalists printed glowing reviews of Cody, Sitting

Bull, and the Wild West experience. The 1885 tour was profitable for both Cody and Sitting Bull, yet Indian Agent James McLaughlin feared that the chief's growing popularity and profit from the show increased his influence on the reservation. After 1886, Sitting Bull was barred from the show and returned to his home at Standing Rock.

The Wild West Show closed for the season in September. Instead of disbanding the cast and storing the equipment, however, Cody and Salsbury moved the show indoors to Madison Square Garden. Cody and Salsbury, realizing that most New Yorkers had seen the show during its regular run, hired art director Steele Mackaye to revamp the show's narrative. Mackaye rearranged the traditional acts into a new theme tracing the history of American expansion from the colonies to the West, called *The Drama of Civilization*. British artist Matt Morgan was also hired to paint realistic backdrops for the indoor show. Morgan's vitae included a collection of Civil War paintings on display in St. Louis. Morgan's work with the Wild West Show was unique in that the paintings measured at approximately 40 feet high and 150 feet in length. Mackaye also required that the paintings be curved into a panorama.

Buffalo Bill's show at Madison Square Garden was a success. One of the show's central acts, added in 1887, was titled "Custer's Last Rally." The reenactment of Custer's fall appealed to audiences' fascination with the waning frontier and received a valuable endorsement from Custer's widow, Elizabeth Bacon Custer. With the addition of the reenactment of Custer's death, Cody's show at Madison Square Garden blended Morgan's artistry with the myth and history of Little Bighorn. Cody's donning of a red wig and portrayal of Custer effected audiences in a way that inspired respect and reverence. In addition, the illusion of the panoramas made audiences feel as if they were witnessing a historical event in realtime. The show at Madison Square Garden closed in February. The Wild West Show, however, was still on the ascent. Before the show closed, Salsbury and Cody made an agreement with the American Exhibition in London and on 31 March 1887, the Wild West Show boarded the ship *State of Nebraska* for Great Britain.

EUROPEAN TOUR

Buffalo Bill, along with 209 passengers, 200 horses, 18 buffalo, and a collection of mules, donkeys, steers, and deer crossed the sea for London. The trip was difficult for the Wild West crew, with frequent seasickness and the deaths of buffalo and elk. Eventually the Wild West Show arrived at Gravesend and immediately began rehearsing at the showground near the American Exhibition in West London. Not only had Cody and Salsbury ensured that the show received substantial advance press, the American Exhibition itself coincided with Queen Victoria's Golden Jubilee, celebrating Victoria's fiftieth year on the throne. Prime Minister William Gladstone and the Prince of Wales both attended advanced showings and a substantial crowd of hunting enthusiasts, including the Duke of Beaufort and the Prince of Wales, flocked to the show.

Cody's reputation as a scout and as a hunter was advantageous for the showman in England as well as in the United States. Cody's connections with English hunting enthusiasts prompted an introduction to the Prince of Wales. The prince agreed to attend the show's rehearsal on 5 May, and Cody and Salsbury rushed to assemble a makeshift royal box. Before the show, the prince was asked to signal the opening. Following the prince's signal, the Indians let out a yell and swept around the arena on horseback. The prince leaped from his seat and leaned over the edge of the box, enthralled. After the show, the Prince of Wales asked to tour Cody's stables, was shown Cody's old horse, Charlie, and offered cigarettes to the Indian Red Shirt. The prince was also introduced to Annie Oakley, who, failing to acknowledge royal etiquette, promptly shook hands with the prince and Princess Beatrice. The prince, however, seemed not to take offense, and he later recommended to Victoria that she request her own private showing.

Hunting, popular with the British upper class, was associated with courage, masculinity, and individualism. Cody's own persona and the character of the Wild West Show appealed to British hunting enthusiasts who shared similar ideals and interests.

On 11 May, Victoria arrived at the exhibition flanked by a sizeable entourage. The show opened with the presentation of the American flag, as the orator explained, as a token of peace and friendship to the world. The queen, along with the royal party, rose and bowed before the flag. Cody later proclaimed that the queen's presence at the Wild West Show marked the first time since the Declaration of Independence that an English monarch had saluted the American flag. In addition to a private showing, Victoria also requested a private meeting with Annie Oakley, Lillian Smith, and the "chief" of the show Indians, Red Shirt. Victoria's visit to the Wild West Show triggered a flow of royal audience members, eager both to see Buffalo Bill's show as well as to please the queen by accepting her endorsement.

On 20 June, the Prince of Wales along with the king of Denmark, the king of Saxony, the king and queen of the Belgians, and the king of Greece attended the show. During the Deadwood stagecoach scene, the stage circled the arena with four kings and the Prince of Wales as its passengers. After the show, Cody shared a joke with the future king of England. The prince teased Buffalo Bill that the showman had probably never held four kings like those in the coach. Cody retorted that although he had experience with holding four kings, the four royal dignitaries and the Prince of Wales made a unique royal flush. The joke, which was popular throughout the country, as well as the queen's endorsement of Cody's show, helped inspire the Wild West Show's enormous success in England in 1887. Moreover, the Wild West Show appealed to many British citizens who had long been inundated with romanticized tales of Buffalo

Bill and the American frontier. When Cody finally arrived in England, the British public flocked to the show to see the "authentic" Buffalo Bill.

Two months after the show arrived in England, Cody took a coach ride through Oatlands Park with famed British actors Henry Irving, John Lawrence Toole, and writer and future author of *Dracula* Bram Stoker. Cody's relationship with Irving opened a way for Cody into English society. The thin, pale Irving, too, benefited from his friendship with Cody by using his association with Buffalo Bill to bolster his masculinity. In this way, Irving hoped to acquire more masculine and authoritative stage roles. In 1887, Cody took the show's cowboys and Indians to see Irving on stage. The cast of the Wild West Show attended the play in costume at the Lyceum in London. Red Shirt, "chief" of the Indians, and Buck Taylor, "King of the Cowboys," were seated in the royal box, and Irving, realizing the advantages of having Buffalo Bill and members of the Wild West Show in the audience, invited the cowboys and Indians onstage after the show.

As the friendship between Cody and Irving grew, the society columns traced Cody's movements in and out of the English upper class. Irving was invited to attend a pre-showing of the Wild West Show before it opened to the public and was granted a private box seat at the show arena. Irving, in turn, hosted dinner parties in Cody's honor and often accompanied Cody to socially significant dinners at trendy London clubs.

Bram Stoker, as well, maintained a relationship with Buffalo Bill. Yet in comparison to the bond between Cody and Irving, the link between Stoker and Cody was much more formal and muted. Stoker received an autographed photo of Cody in 1887, as well as a complimentary season ticket to the Wild West Show for its next London season in 1892. Stoker also received gifts from Cody and Salsbury, including Indian arrowheads.

Advertisements for the Wild West Show in the United States publicized the show's success in Europe. An 1895 show poster with the title "World's Wondrous Voyages" featured a map of the North Atlantic world with a red line tracing the show's movement through Europe. The poster applauded the show's popularity on two continents and its travels across 63,000 miles. The poster also featured images of European cities such as Glasgow, London, and Hamburg. Other posters and billboards featured images of "Distinguished Visitors to the Wild West," members of the royalty, and images of Cody saluting European "Presidents, Pope and Potentates, Statesmen and Warriors" with his hat.

In addition to England, the Wild West Show traveled to the European continent where it made its Italian debut in Rome. The show, however, did not appear in the Coliseum, but appeared instead before an audience of 65,000 at the amphitheater of Verona. Members of the show also paid a visit to the Vatican, where they met Pope Leo XIII. The Wild West Show company, comprised of both cowboys and Indians, mixed with the enormous crowds present for the celebration of the anniversary of the Pope's coronation. American newspapers called the meeting between the Pope and the Indians a gathering between the Christian pontiff and the heathens. Newspapers also noted the effect that Rome had on the otherwise rowdy company, inspiring the cowboys to bow and one Indian, Rocky Bear, to kneel at the cross and receive a blessing from the Pope. Before arriving in Rome, Cody wrote to a friend, describing the Wild West Show's time in Europe as the trip of his life. Cody also bragged about his triumph over P.T. Barnum, whom he accused of following the Wild West Show overseas. Cody's boast reveals both the intense level of competition between entertainers and Cody's own impression of himself, that is, of an able and blessed manager and showman.

In May 1888, the Wild West Show closed in England and returned to Staten Island. After arriving in New York, the show ran for two months in Erastina. Salsbury, in the meantime, was already planning a second European tour. In 1889, the Wild West Show traveled to Paris and opened in the shadow of the Eiffel Tower at the Exposition Universelle. After the show closed in Paris in November, the troupe continued to tour the continent, stopping in Lyon and Marseilles, and on New Year's Day performed in Barcelona, Spain. Due to an influenza epidemic and low audience turnout, the show in Spain was cut short and relocated to Naples, Italy, for three weeks. Afterward, the Wild West Show continued to travel, playing to audiences in Rome, Florence, Bologna, Milan, Venice, Germany, Austria, Munich, Dresden, Leipzig, Magdeburg, Hanover, Braunschweig, Berlin, Hamburg, Bremen, Cologne, Dusseldorf, Frankfurt, and Stuttgart before the tour ended in winter 1890.

While Cody was abroad his personal life did not improve. From 1885 through 1886, Cody and Louisa occupied separate homes in North Platte, Louisa staying at the house in town while Cody resided at the famed Scout's Rest Ranch. Cody's daughter Arta attempted to reunite her parents by pleading with her father to forgive her mother and to return home. In 1885, Cody met artist and widow Mollie Moses during a show in Illinois. Cody introduced himself to Moses as a bachelor, explaining that although he had yet to obtain a divorce, he and his wife were effectively separated. Cody and Moses maintained a brief, yet close correspondence, often exchanging gifts. In 1886, Cody invited Moses to meet him at St. James Hotel in St. Louis, but the relationship did not progress far and before the end of the year the correspondence had ceased.

Throughout 1886, Cody's married life remained hostile and tense. He continued to feud with Louisa and through most of late 1886 and early 1887, Cody stayed away from his home in North Platte, leaving directly from Madison Square Garden for England. While he was abroad, Cody corresponded with his sister and brother, but not with his wife. Cody perhaps attempted to hide the condition of his personal life from public view by taking daughter Arta with him to London. Arta also traveled to the Continent and enjoyed a two-week tour of Italy with her father. While Arta was away on the Continent, however, Cody was often in the company of American actress Katherine Clemons. Cody complimented Clemons's physical beauty and the two maintained a relationship for over five years. Clemons posed for pictures with members of the Wild West Show in London and traveled with the troupe throughout Europe. In 1891, Cody loaned Clemons Wild West actors and supplies, including members of the management staff, Indians, and trained horses, for the melodrama the *White Lily*. Although the play received average reviews, Cody funded its tour throughout the English provinces. The play never opened in London.

As Cody's married life continued to decline, so did his finances. Despite Cody's abundant income, he was never truly wealthy. Cody's inability to hold onto money, in fact, was the root of many arguments between Cody and Louisa. Much of Cody's funds were invested in properties such as Scout's Rest. Whatever other monies Cody accrued were spent on personal items like the four-in-hand coach he drove through the streets of North Platte. Cody also gave money to friends and employees, as well as to relatives and siblings, including money to fund Louisa's house in town, as well as financial support for his sister Julia and her husband.

The nature of the Wild West Show, as well, made its profit unpredictable. Not only were ticket sales necessarily volatile, but care for the show, the purchasing of new animals, the cost of feed, providing transportation and lodging for members of the cast and crew, and supplying salaries all took a toll on Cody's final profit. Cody was also compelled to compete with contemporary shows and circuses, which required additional publicity funding for increased numbers of elaborate posters and billboards.

On the outside, the Cody family of North Platte appeared content. Cody and Louisa both attended and hosted dinner parties and socials in Buffalo Bill's honor. Cody was also well connected among the lawyers, doctors, and merchants of North Platte. Yet Cody's time in North Platte was always stressful. In 1889, Cody confided to his sister Julia that he could no longer tolerate the tension between himself and his wife. When Cody asked for his sister's advice, Julia insisted that if he remained patient, the tension would subside. Both Cody's sister and her husband persuaded Cody not to separate from Louisa. He remained with his family for the remainder of the year. In 1890, Cody left for Europe.

In the 1890s, perhaps to compound Cody's troubles even more, the Wild West Show was criticized for its treatment of Indians. By the 1880s, reservations were established to enforce conformity, promote "Americanization," and to limit Indian mobility. The Wild West Show, therefore, offered many Indians a way to both earn money and to travel away from the reservation. Engaged with the Wild West Show, Indians such as the Lakota could not only travel to the East Coast, but also to Europe. Moreover, Cody granted the Indians who joined the Wild West Show considerable freedom. While on tour or with the show camp, many Indians participated in walking tours or outings that lasted for several days at a time. Freedom of religious expression, as well, was afforded the Indians in the Wild West camp. Although the Indians had learned to disguise their rituals in public, camp visitors noted the presence of "Indian steam baths," or sweat lodges where Lakotas offered prayers. The Indians' participation in the Wild West Show allowed many Lakotas to preserve aspects of the culture that were banned at reservations. Dancing on reservations, for example, was forbidden in 1883. Yet these dances continued at the Wild West camp and were featured in the show.

The Wild West Show also offered a way for many Indians to supplement their incomes. On Sioux reservations, most Indians depended on rations from the United States government. In the 1880s, government rations were reduced in an effort to force Indians to become more self-supporting. Instead of inspiring Indians such as the Lakota to become more independent, however, the decrease in rations resulted in widespread famine. The Wild West Show, therefore, offered Lakota the opportunity to escape the poverty of the reservations and to rescue their families from destitution. In the Wild West Show, the average wage for Indians was $25 per month and for those designated as translators or chiefs, from $75 to $125 a month. This salary stands in stark contrast to the $8 per month earned serving as a policeman on the reservation. Indian women, as well, were paid $10 and could earn upward of $35–$40 depending on the status of their husbands or the numbers of children they brought into the show.

While the show was on tour, Cody also protected the Indians' properties back home. In 1891, Cody asked that an agent at Pine Ridge reservation look into complaints made by show Indians that other Indians had appropriated their land. Cody also settled disputes between individual Indians and white farmers. When Calls to Name, a Lakota woman whose property had been stolen by a white man named Davidson, received word from her family concerning Davidson's claim to her horse and colt, she asked Cody to intercede for her. Not only did Cody contact the agent, he also wrote to General Nelson Miles requesting that the general help protect Calls the Name's rights and property.

Reformers and assimilationists, however, did not regard the Wild West Show as a positive or beneficial outlet for Indians. Many reformers feared that Cody's show was demoralizing and dangerous. Reservation agents claimed that Cody was corrupting the Indians' innocent minds, stealing them from the reservations, where they were pure, and returning them full of vice and knowledge of gambling, venereal disease, and alcohol.

Although Cody successfully fended off many of these complaints, in 1890 the show ran into hard times. That year in particular witnessed an increase in the number of Indian injuries and deaths. When the show returned to New York, five Indians resigned before the tour's end to return to their homes. The show paid for the Indians' journey and they were driven by the show's stage driver, Fred Matthews. On the way to the reservation, Kills Plenty fell ill. The trip was postponed as Kills Plenty had to be hospitalized. The fallen Indian died soon after.

Many onlookers looked to the Wild West Show as a bastion of Indian cruelty. The assistant superintendent of immigration in New York, General James

O'Beirne, claimed that he had spoken to the show Indians while they were waiting at the Port of New York. According to O'Beirne, the Indians confided that they had decided to return because they had been treated badly and received bad food in the Wild West Show. The retired general forwarded his report to the press, suddenly placing the Wild West Show at the center of controversy. Newspapers ran headlines charging Cody and the show with mistreatment of Indians. Cartoons accompanied the articles depicting Uncle Sam protecting resentful Indians fleeing Europe and the Wild West Show.

Due to accusations of Indian cruelty, the government launched an investigation into the show's treatment of Indians. In fall 1890, several Indians including No Neck, Rocky Bear, and Black Heart were called on to testify before an inquiry in the Office of Indian Affairs. The Indians, however, denied the accusations made against the show and noted the differences between life at Pine Ridge and with Cody. The inquiry concluded in Cody's favor, and it appeared that the charges were due in part to hostility within the show's Indian community itself. The Indians whom O'Beirne met at the Port of New York also made accusations against other Indians, including Rocky Bear, who served as chief, and Bronco Bill. Rivalries among show Indians, in fact, were fairly common.

Other Indians attacked the show, in part, due to the competition on reservations. Red Cloud, for example, prevented the hiring of many Oglalas in 1887, forcing Cody to hire an additional fifteen men before the show left for Europe. In 1889, Red Cloud continued to assert his influence among the show's Indians by demanding that each Indian pay him twenty-five cents a month for their places in the show. In 1901, the Oglala Tribal Council requested that the government disallow the exhibition of Indians, claiming to borrow the language of white critics, that the Indians returning from the show brought home disease and poor habits. Other Indians like graduate of Carlisle Indian School Chauncey Yellow Robe feared that the Wild West Show betrayed Indians into becoming drunkards.

THE CHICAGO WORLD'S FAIR

In 1891, after Wounded Knee, Cody and Salsburg, unsure if they would be permitted to hire Indians again, looked elsewhere for actors to take on the Indian role. By spring, Cody and Salsbury recruited twelve Cossacks, six Argentine gauchos, and two detachments of regular European cavalry, English and German. The newly outfitted Wild West Show began its tour in Germany, where it received praise from Kaiser Wilhelm II. In 1892, the show returned to London and performed another show at Windsor Castle for Queen Victoria. At home in the United States, the show enjoyed an increase in publicity thanks to growing interest over the show's new format. In 1893, the Wild West Show appeared at the Columbian Exposition.

The primary attraction at the World's Columbian Exposition was the White City, a series of neoclassical buildings that depicted the victories and accomplishments of America. The Wild West Show, however, was located immediately outside the fair, designated by fair organizers as the space for attractions too similar to circuses and unfit for inclusion in the White City. Cody had great success, despite his show's peripheral location. With its new additions in mind, the show boasted a new name: "Buffalo Bill's Wild West and Congress of Rough Riders of the World." The Chicago press described Cody as a gentle giant, enormous in person, but friendly and polite in manner. Not only was Cody a genial showman, but he was also a protector of domestic harmony and, particularly emphasized during the Chicago season, a friend of all children. When Cody learned that Exposition organizers were struggling to coordinate a free picnic for the impoverished children of Chicago, he offered to fund the event, as well as a parade and a day at the Wild West Show for children from Chicago's various charitable institutions. Cody's willingness to pay for the children to attend the Exposition was a successful publicity scheme and increased Cody's popularity with the press. It helped draw a sizeable number of spectators to the show. Audience members allegedly stopped at first sight of the Wild West Show, assuming that it was the fair, and left without moving on to the White City. Overall, during 1893, it is estimated that Cody and Salsbury sold over three million tickets.

In addition to European soldiers, the new Wild West Show also featured African American soldiers. In 1895, Cody and Salsbury developed a new show inspired by African American history, perhaps hoping to attract an African American audience. The show, titled *Black America*, opened in 1895 and claimed to portray African Americans in an authentic light. *Black America* traced the legacy of African Americans through slavery, to soldier and to citizen, yet depicted slavery as a necessary component of African American progress from "savage" to citizen. Despite Cody's high hopes, *Black America* failed and closed within weeks of its opening.

By 1894, Buffalo Bill's Wild West Show camp housed a total of 680 people. The show's camp became its primary attraction, drawing audiences into its complex settlement comprised of numerous people, cowboys, buffalo, and Indians. The Wild West camp consisted of a series of tents, organized into rows along paved streets. Along the streets were gardens and flowerbeds. Cody's tent, which was the size of a small farmhouse, was outfitted with a telephone, curtains, desks, easy chairs, and a refrigerator. Conversely, Indian tipis consisted of a dirt floor and a fire, which one spectator described as at once both a chimney and a house.

By the time the Wild West Show had traveled to Brooklyn, New York, in 1890, the borough had adopted electric lighting. When the show arrived, Cody and Salsbury invited nearly 200 members of the New York Electrical Society to tour the Wild West camp's electrical works. New floodlights had been installed by the Edison Electrical Illuminating Company to light the show. Cody hoped the new electrical works would help boost profits. During the show's stint at Coney Island in 1883, one of the features was advertised as Grand Polytechnic and Electric Illuminations.

In the mid-1890s, Cody decided to expand his real estate experience from building ranches to founding towns. Along with real estate partner George Beck, Cody announced that he would establish a new settlement in Bighorn Basin, Wyoming. The site for the town of Cody was fairly remote, resting behind the Wind River Mountains. The neighboring settlement, Red Lodge, was a two-day ride north into Montana. Arta Cody's husband Horton Beal joined Beck and Cody in founding the town. Cody, however, provided the greatest financial support for his town-founding venture, funding the growth of the Bighorn Basin with profits from the Wild West Show. The town of Cody sat on 28,000 acres at the forks of the Shoshone River. In 1897, Cody and Salsbury teamed up to develop an additional 60,000 acres north of the Shoshone River, opposite the Cody town site. Cody and Salsbury planned to build a series of farms and towns alongside a new canal, which Cody planned to develop once the town of Cody was established.

Buffalo Bill's Wild West Show served as a chief source of advertising for the new settlement. Advertisements for Cody, Wyoming, were printed inside show programs. One pitch claimed Cody town was where Buffalo Bill returned in the off-season to relax. Another pitch noted Cody's clean air and open spaces, unlike the crowded urban centers. Cody also had its own newspaper, the *Shoshone News* to circulate the town's advertisements. In addition, in 1899, editor J.H. Peake was hired to run a new paper, the *Cody Enterprise*. Newspaper advertisements for Cody, Wyoming, featured a caricature of Buffalo Bill inviting visitors to enjoy the land and water within the exquisite mountain valley. Cody continued to expand the town, founding a livery stable, and initiating projects on various coal and gold mines, as well as oil fields. In 1902, Cody opened the Irma Hotel, named after his youngest daughter. The hotel reportedly cost $80,000 to build and furnish. The town continued to grow and in 1902, stood alongside the Burlington & Missouri River Railroad.

In addition to investing in the new town, in 1902 Cody invested in a gold mine at the Campo Bonito mine works in Arizona. Drawn to the mine by Colonel D.B. Dyer, member of New York's Union League Club, Cody became an instant investor. In 1903, a gold strike was reported and gold continued to appear in steady although small waves. Cody worked hard to attract investors to the mine. He offered guided trips to the mines, advertising the experience to potential investors as an authentic taste of Western mining. Despite Cody's efforts to woo investors with his showmanship, the mine remained a financial failure. All in all, Cody personally invested approximately $200,000.

Despite the efforts of Cody and Beck to promote their new town, settlers were slow in coming. Although there was a popular interest in Cody, evidenced by the many letters from prospective settlers inquiring about the weather, quality of the land, and job availability, settlers remained hesitant about settling in the town of Cody. While Cody was grappling with the success of his town venture, he was also struggling with a series of personal setbacks. In 1903, Salsbury, who was on substantially poor terms with his longtime partner, died. By the start of the twentieth century, the relationship between Cody and Salsbury had grown tense. In 1901, realizing that he was dying, Salsbury composed a history of his career with Buffalo Bill. Salsbury's account of his time spent with the Wild West Show was caustic. Although Salsbury did not intend to publish the piece, he claimed that if he had, the title would be "Sixteen Years in Hell with Buffalo Bill."

Cody was also facing another domestic trial, which culminated in a divorce suit against his wife. Louisa Cody refused to grant her husband a divorce and the testimony from the battling spouses spiraled into a public scandal. Cody accused Louisa of threatening to poison him and of refusing to admit his friends into their home in North Platte. In addition to these charges, Cody claimed that Louisa refused to sign mortgages, which significantly hindered his ability to carry on his business, and that his wife had accused him of murdering their daughter Arta, who had died a year earlier. Cody's character suffered much during the trial, from accusations of his poisoning Arta to accounts of severe and perpetual drunkenness. Cody's efforts to secure a divorce from his wife failed and to escape the ridicule of the public eye, Cody left the United States for a two-year tour in Europe.

In 1904 and 1905, Cody and the Wild West Show traveled to Scotland and to France. In 1906, the show opened at Marseilles and in 1907 the show finally returned to the United States. Most newspapers, to Cody's relief, ignored Cody's divorce scandal and emphasized the legacy of Buffalo Bill. Still, it was clear Cody's home life had taken a toll on his public persona. The Wild West Show, for example, no longer made references to families or promoted Scout's Ranch. Advertisements for the show no longer featured aspects of Cody's personal life. The show's famous domestic thriller "Attack on Settler's Cabin" also vanished.

As Cody's show was in transition and as he grew more distant from Louisa and his family, Cody's town-founding efforts also suffered. Cody, Wyoming, with completion of the Cody Canal, was fairly self-sufficient. Cody, therefore, turned his attention to a new prospect; the town of Ralston. Ralston was situated east of Cody and across the Shoshone River. Cody hoped that Ralston would yield a sizable profit and waited impatiently for the Reclamation Service to build a canal. The canal was delayed, however, and despite efforts by Cody to speed the process, government officials withdrew their support from Ralston and settled on a new location between Ralston and neighboring Garland. Cody petitioned Wyoming's governor, Wyoming's congressional delegation, and President Theodore Roosevelt to stop construction on the new town, fearing that it would hinder Ralston's success and largely diminish its value. Despite Cody's effort, however, plans to found the new town, Powell, progressed.

LATER YEARS

After the death of James Bailey in 1906, whom Salsbury had hired to help manage the show while it was on tour, one-third interest in the Wild West Show was sold to Gordon "Pawnee Bill" Lillie. Lillie admired Cody and looked forward to working with him, while Cody, tired of managing the show without a partner, hoped to alleviate his troubles with additional help. When Lillie joined the show, however, Cody was weighted down by financial woes. Cody owed Bailey's heirs $12,000. Lillie, however, negotiated a deal with Bailey's heirs, purchased their portion of the show, and paid off Cody's debt. Lillie then permitted Cody to buy back half of the show, allowing Cody to remain part owner. With the two Bills at the helm, the show became known as "Buffalo Bill's Wild West and Pawnee Bill's Great Far East." The show retained many of the Wild West Show's characteristics, except for the addition of "A Dream of the East," which featured animals such as elephants and camels, as well as belly dancers and Arab warriors. The blending of the frontier with the Orient was an enormous success and during a two-week run at Madison Square Garden in 1908, the show sold out.

In 1910, Cody took advantage of the new show's popularity and announced his upcoming retirement. Instead of retiring immediately, however, Cody would embark on a three-year tour. At each tour stop, Cody would announce his performance as the last in that location, therefore drawing, he hoped, an even greater audience. Show programs featured the headline: "Buffalo Bill Bids You Goodbye" and another leaflet included information on Cody's various business ventures, including the town Cody, Wyoming. In 1910, the show grossed approximately $400,000 and in 1912 earned an additional $125,000. Despite earning a substantial profit, Cody's financial troubles continued. The money Cody lost on the Arizona mines grew into an enormous debt. An investigation in 1912 revealed that a worker had been tampering with the mine to make the ore appear richer. Louis Getchell, who had drawn Cody and D.B. Dyer to the mines, was required to forfeit his job. Cody, however, was reluctant to press charges, fearing that the publicity would attract negative attention.

Also in 1910, Cody was persuaded by his daughter Irma to return to North Platte. Cody's return to North Platte triggered reports that he and Louisa had reconciled. In spite of accounts from Louisa's friends and family, who claimed that Louisa had expressed the desire to reunite with Cody, Cody's efforts to meet with his wife were thwarted. By the next year, however, Cody and Louisa, with the urging of their children, had reconciled.

In 1913, Cody, in need of more money after the Wild West Show's slow season, turned to Henry Tamman, owner of the *Denver Post* and the Sells-Floto Circus, for a $20,000 loan. The agreement between Cody and Tamman included both the loan and Cody's assent to enter a partnership with Tamman's circus, therefore abandoning Lillie the following season. Cody denied that he had entered an agreement with Tamman, but Lillie, already alienated, left the Wild West Show and returned to his ranch. Days before Cody's deadline to repay Tamman's loan, the show arrived in Denver. Tamman immediately filed suit against the show. While in Denver, the show and all of its cash and property were seized. Lillie, who had enough money to pay Cody's debt, refused to help the partner who had betrayed him. Friends of Cody purchased his horse, Isham, and sent it to Cody's ranch as a gift. Yet news traveled fast that Buffalo Bill and the Wild West Show were bankrupt.

Cody, now under contract to Tamman, traveled the country with Tamman's Sells-Floto Circus. Cody's salary was $100 a day, along with a portion of the show's ticket proceeds. While involved with Tamman, Cody also experimented in film. With the support of Tamman and Tamman's partner Frederick G. Bonfils, Cody founded "The Col. W.F. Cody Historical Pictures Company." In September 1913, Cody began filming his movie, "The Last Indian War." The film, however, was a flop. Cody toured with the Sells-Floto Circus for two years until Tamman informed Cody that his debt had been repaid. Tamman soon changed his mind, however, and claimed that Cody still owed $20,000. Cody and Tamman finally agreed that if Cody remained with Tamman's circus through the 1915 season, Tamman would stop siphoning payments from his salary. At the end of the year, Cody was unemployed.

Cody continued in show business and founded a new show at a ranch in Oklahoma: "Buffalo Bill Pageant of Military Preparedness and 101 Ranch Wild West." Cody toured with his nephew William Cody Bradford and the show, a modest success, closed in November 1916. Following the show, Cody, feeling unwell, traveled to Denver in search of medical help. At Glenwood Springs, Cody hoped that mineral baths would help restore his health, but after four days, his status remained the same. On 10 January 1917, William Cody died. Cody's posthumous wishes included his burial in a hill overlooking the town of Cody, but Tamman, who offered to pay for the funeral, would permit Cody's burial only in Denver. In June 1917, Cody was buried in a hole in Lookout Mountain, overlooking Denver and the Great Plains.

FURTHER READING

Cody, William F. *The Life of Hon. William F. Cody/Buffalo Bill: An Autobiography* (Lincoln: University of Nebraska Press, 1978).

Fredriksson, Kristine. *American Rodeo: from Buffalo Bill to Big Business* (College Station: Texas A&M University Press, 1985).

Kasson, Joy S. *Buffalo Bill's Wild West: Celebrity, Memory, and Popular History* (New York: Hill and Wang, 2000).

McMurtry, Larry. *The Colonel and Little Missie: Buffalo Bill, Annie Oakley, and the Beginnings of Stardom in America* (New York: Simon & Schuster, 2005).

Warren, Louis S. *Buffalo Bill's America: William Cody and The Wild West Show* (New York: Vintage Books, 2006).

Chief Joseph, wearing warbonnet and several necklaces, ca. 1903. Courtesy of Library of Congress.

Chief Joseph

Vanessa Gunther

One of the most recognizable native leaders of the American West is a man who has taken on almost mythological dimensions—Chief Joseph of the Chopunnish or Nez Perce. A contemporary of Geronimo, Joseph, in the American mind then and now, seemed to be Geronimo's polar opposite. Where the Apache were considered warlike, the Nez Perce are largely remembered as a peaceful tribe. However, as is the case with most myths, reality and fact are often at odds; such would be the case of Hinmahtooyahlatkekht, or Thunder Rising in the Mountains, and the Nez Perce Indians. Archeological evidence suggests that the Nez Perce have lived in the region east of the Columbia Plateau in Washington and west of the Bitterroot Mountains in Idaho for more than 6000 years. However, the storied history of the Nez Perce in the American mind did not begin until 1806, the year Lewis and Clark stumbled into their camp. After spending time with these strange men, who they initially considered might be descended from dogs because of their smell and facial hair, the Nez Perce pledged their undying friendship to them and by extension to America as well. A few decades later, the Nez Perce startled the nation when they asked for missionaries to come to their land and explain the "book of heaven" that seemed to be so important to the white man. By the late 1830s and into the 1840s missionaries descended on the people of the plateau with the intent to Christianize and civilize the Indians. The willingness of some of the Nez Perce to ally with the Americans and to adopt Christian ways would lead to a schism within the tribe, and the creation of one of the iconic images of the West: Chief Joseph of the Nez Perce, the "Red Napoleon."

Joseph was born to be a leader among his people, but not the type of leader many supposed him to be. He was the son of Tuekakas, or Old Joseph, a Cayuse Indian who had married into the Wallowa band of the Nez Perce tribe and over time rose to a leadership position within the band. When the Reverend Henry Spalding and Marcus Whitman established Protestant missions in the land of the Nez Perce and the Cayuse in 1836, Tuekakas was among the earliest supporters of the new religion they brought with them. Within a few years, Tuekakas had been baptized and renamed Joseph. His passion for the religion of the white man had earned him a privileged position with Spalding, one that would be further rewarded when on 12 April 1840 his wife, Khapkhoponomi, gave birth to a boy who was also quickly baptized and named Ephraim, who would later be called Young Joseph. Little information survives about the childhood of Young Joseph. He was the eldest of two sons born to Tuekakas and Khapkhoponomi (in 1843, Ollokot, or "Frog" was born). As the son of the Wallowa Nez Perce chief, Young Joseph would be groomed to become a leader of his people. However, here the story of Joseph begins to diverge from the myth. The leaders of the Nez Perce, despite hereditary leadership roles, retain their positions only through the consent of the people. Additionally, a Nez Perce tribal chief was not the war chief. The tribal chief was responsible for the safety and well-being of the tribe; although all Nez Perce boys were taught to ride and use a bow and arrow, Young Joseph was not to be a war chief. That responsibility fell to his younger brother Ollokot.

Young Joseph began his life near the Spalding mission in the Wallowa Valley, where, because of his father's devotion to Christianity, he was afforded privileges unavailable to other Nez Perce children. He was allowed to play with the white children and began the rudiments of an education at the mission school, where he learned to write his name. However, internal divisions among the increasing numbers of white settlers who came to the lands of the Nez Perce caused many of the Nez Perce, including his father, to question their commitment to the white man's religion and ways. Their suspicion was compounded in summer 1842, when Dr. Elijah White arrived in the Wallowa Valley as the first U.S. official in the Pacific Northwest. White had been appointed as the subagent for Indian relations in the Oregon country. Shortly after his arrival, he established a series of rules that would govern the Indians' behavior. Although the Indians would be required to obey the rules without question, it appeared the white man would not. Additionally, White attempted to appoint a leader over all the Nez Perce, a man who had been educated by missionaries at the Red River school named Ellis. The appointment of Ellis as the chief of all the Nez Perce flew in the face of tradition, and he was often treated with open contempt by his own people. When Spalding wholeheartedly supported the dictates of Elijah White he also sanctioned this reversal of the traditional leadership roles of the Nez Perce. Conflict over tribal rule would not be the only issue that would impair the relationship between the Nez Perce and the whites. As additional settlers filtered into the area squabbles broke out among the missionaries over land and even the proper interpretation of the religion they brought with them. To the Nez Perce, it no longer seemed the white man's religion or his ways had much to offer the tribe. Subsequently, Old Joseph moved his people back to their traditional lands and his band returned to their ancestral ways. However, Christianity had taken hold in the Nez Perce tribe, and although many traditionalists returned to their old ways, another faction remained behind and wholly adopted Christianity and the ways of white civilization.

Though the abrupt change in Young Joseph's upbringing would ensure that he would be raised within the traditional values of his people, simple withdrawal from the presence of the missionaries and the white settlers could not isolate him from their influence. In 1847, the Cayuse, disgruntled by the influx of a seemingly never-ending train of immigrants and the outbreak of disease that left many of their numbers dead, massacred the residents of the Whitman mission. The attack threatened to plunge the Columbia Plateau into war. As the largest of the tribes in the area, the Nez Perce were key to determining whether the war would spread or be limited to the Cayuse tribe. With Tuekakas as the appointed spokesman for the Nez Perce, a peace was brokered and a general Indian war against the settlers was avoided. At seven years, Young Joseph, would not likely have been privileged to accompany his father to the council but would have been aware of his father's wish to remain at peace with the white community.

As Young Joseph grew he, like all Nez Perce boys, maintained a respectful distance from his father. He was schooled in horsemanship and hunting, most likely by his uncles or other male members of the tribe. However, Joseph would not be a warrior. His responsibilities were to protect his people with words and deeds, not actions. To learn these skills he would observe his father and the other head men during councils. Among the young boys who were his contemporaries, he was designated as their leader. To reinforce his distinctiveness among them, he refrained from their games and dressed differently. By the time he had reached adolescence he went on a spirit journey to identify the spirit that would guide him throughout his life. It was this guide, or *wayakin*, that Joseph would need to rely on while fulfilling his responsibilities to his people. Despite the gravity with which Young Joseph was charged to execute his responsibilities, the time for his leadership was years in the future.

Tuekakas and the other Nez Perce leaders may well have wished to have been left alone, but conditions in the Pacific Northwest were changing dramatically throughout the decade of the 1850s. With each passing year the buffer zone that existed between them and white settlement shrank. The Oregon Donation Land Act of 1850 allowed all male residents over the age of eighteen to claim 320 acres of land from the public domain. As if this were not enough to draw settlers into the region, in 1851 gold was discovered in the Rogue and Umpqua Rivers of Oregon, and later throughout what would become Washington State. Each subsequent discovery brought more settlers into the region and conflict over land use often erupted into war. By the time the Washington Territory had been established in 1853, Indian agents had begun to filter through the area making treaties with a number of tribes that dispossessed the Indians of their lands in return for promises that invariably were never honored. Although isolated from these occurrences in the Wallowa Valley, Young Joseph could not escape their influence in his life. To preserve their lands and way of life, fifty-seven Nez Perce leaders, including Joseph's father, agreed to a treaty in 1855 that traded a portion of their traditional land for the promise of perpetual peace with the whites. As the heir apparent to his tribe, Young Joseph was there to witness his father's participation in this council and saw his father concede to the wishes of the whites to preserve peace for their people.

The peace that the Nez Perce brokered in 1855 would be short-lived. By 1860 gold had been discovered on Nez Perce land and the predictable influx of thousands of rapacious miners flooded into an area that had previously seen limited white settlement. This intrusion resulted in depredations on both sides. By 1862, the United States government could no longer afford to ignore a conflict that threatened to ignite the Pacific into an all-out war while it was busy fighting the Civil War in the East. A new treaty was needed, one that would accommodate the new settlers at the expense of the Nez Perce. The Nez Perce met in council to discuss the wishes of the government. Tuekakas, as the representative of the Wallowa people, brought Young Joseph with him as an observer. In what would become known as the Thief Treaty, the U.S. government proposed that the Nez Perce land holdings be reduced to about one-tenth of their original size. To secure the Nez Perce concessions, the government alternately offered promises of schools and teachers mixed with threats and coercion. Despite his conciliatory past, Tuekakas refused to sign the treaty, as did the majority of the non-Christian Nez Perce. However, the treaty was signed by Lawyer (Hallalhotsoot), a Christianized Nez Perce. The treaty preserved the lands of the Christianized Nez Perce by creating the Lapwai Reservation, while sacrificing the lands of the non-Christian Indians. The treaty also divided the Nez Perce into two factions, the Christianized treaty Indians, who numbered about two-thirds of the total tribe, and the non-treaty Indians. When the non-treaty Indians returned to their home in the Wallowa Valley, Young Joseph was aware of his father's sense of betrayal at the hands of the settlers and the government.

Although the political situation was changing around them, the 1860s were years in which Young Joseph would grow to manhood and take a wife. Around the time the bands of the Nez Perce met in 1863 to discuss the Thief Treaty, Joseph took his first wife. In 1865, his wife Toma Alwawonmi, or "Springtime," gave birth to a daughter, Hophoponmi, or "Noise of Running Feet." With their band relatively isolated from the settlers who increasingly claimed the area, it would have seemed that the white world was far away from the Indian world that the Wallowa Nez Perce enjoyed. They lived according to the rhythms of the land, with hunting parties moving occasionally into the Great Plains to hunt buffalo. During his lifetime Joseph only accompanied one of these parties into the Plains. By 1869, Tuekakas's health was failing, and Joseph increasingly assumed the responsibilities of leadership within the tribe.

The Thief Treaty would have little initial impact on the Wallowa band for most of the 1860s; however, when the Civil War ended and the transcontinental railroad project was completed, surveyors began to appear in the region. It was apparent to Tuekakas what would come next, but he also knew that his ability to lead his people much further was fading. Taking a cue from the surveyors, who piled stones to denote areas they had surveyed, he began piling stones and poles at the edges of the land claimed by the Wallowa to identify that this was their land. He also instructed Young Joseph not to agree to sell the lands of their ancestors and to refuse to accept any gift from a white man so he would never be accused of having sold the land. Young Joseph promised his father that he would not sell the land and that he would protect the people as he had been raised to do. In August 1871, having done all that he could to preserve the land for his tribe, Tuekakas died leaving Joseph, at age thirty-one, as the leader of the Wallowa Nez Perce.

Tuekakas's death would serve as a dividing point for the Wallowa Nez Perce. Though they had been party to the 1855 treaty and were aware of the 1863 treaty, the Indians in the Wallowa Valley were still largely untouched by white settlement until the year after Tuekakas's death. As winter 1871–1872 approached, the band left the high country of the Wallowa Mountains for their winter retreat in the Imnaha Valley along the Snake River. When the band returned to their summer camps in the Wallowa Valley in 1872, whites had already built cabins along the waterways and were pasturing their herds in the fields. When confronted by Joseph and the Wallowa, the settlers pointed to the 1863 treaty that had been signed by Lawyer. Despite the attempted intercession by an Indian agent named John Monteith, the Indians and the white settlers came to an impasse. Eventually, the Nez Perce agreed that the settlers could stay, so long as no more came. By early 1873, news of the Modoc War in northern California had made settlers and the government wary of non-treaty Indians and a permanent solution to the dispute was sought. Agent John Monteith and Superintendent of Indian Affairs T.B. Odeneal recommended that the lower part of the Wallowa Valley be set aside for whites for stock-raising and the upper valley be reserved for the Nez Perce. On 16 June 1873, President Ulysses Grant approved the designation and ordered part of the Wallowa Valley to become part of the Nez Perce reservation. However, although the Indians, the settlers, and the agents agreed that the Nez Perce should have the upper valley, the executive order signed by Grant reversed the land grant and the settlers were granted the upper valley.

In 1873, Joseph had been advised of the executive order dividing the land. Despite assurances that the settlers would leave the valley when they had been paid for their improvements, conflicts between settlers and the Nez Perce grew. Through the summer a war of words was waged in the Western press denouncing the decision of the government to allot the lands to the Indians. By 1874, despite an executive order establishing a reservation in the Wallowa Valley, Commissioner of Indian Affairs Edwin P. Smith wrote that "nothing more would be done toward establishing a reservation" in the valley. The government ceased its efforts to oust the settlers from the valley, but did not inform Joseph of the change in plans. Relations between the settlers and the Nez Perce became increasingly more hostile; little was needed to ignite the region into a war. The first of the sparks occurred on 1 September 1874 with the appointment of Oliver Otis Howard as commander of the Department of the Columbia. Howard was a highly moralistic man who had distinguished himself during the Civil War; however, his tactics in dealing with the Indians who resided within his command would prove to be lackluster and unrealistic. The second spark occurred on 10 June 1875, when Grant rescinded the executive order that had established the Wallowa Valley as part of the Nez Perce reservation. The non-treaty Indians met in council to discuss the change in status, but agreed not to go to war against the whites. By summer 1875, the government gave approval for a wagon road to be constructed through the valley. Joseph protested, but nothing was done to halt the construction.

The final spark that ignited the Nez Perce war occurred on 23 June 1876, when a rancher, A.B. Findley, and two escorts, Wells and Oren McNall, confronted a hunting party and accused the Indians of stealing his livestock. Though several accounts of the event remain, none corroborates the other. The end result, however, was the murder of a Nez Perce brave named Wilhautyah, or "Blowing Wind." At Joseph's insistence the men were brought to trial by the middle of September, but acquitted of the murder by an all-white jury when the Indians who had witnessed the murder were not called to testify. Conditions in the valley were now at a boiling point. The military and the settlers were keenly aware of the recent massacre of the Seventh Cavalry at the hands of the Sioux chief Sitting Bull only three months before. Fear and panic gripped the region and was exacerbated by Joseph's insistence that the settlers leave the valley or face attack by the Nez Perce. To prevent further conflict, and in response to mounting pressure from the settlers who refused to abandon the Wallowa, Howard determined to remove the non-treaty Nez Perce to the Lapwai Reservation. This was despite growing evidence that the Indians had a greater legal claim to the valley than the government and that the 1863 treaty with the Christianized Indians had not extinguished their rights to the land. When Joseph and the non-treaty Indians refused to leave, Howard called for a council in May 1877. There he announced to the Indians that they had thirty days to present themselves to the Lapwai Reservation or face the wrath of the U.S. Army.

Despite repeated attempts at conciliation, Joseph and the non-treaty Nez Perce were now presented with a task that would have been almost impossible to perform. However, try they did. Pushed by Joseph, the non-treaty bands did begin their journey to the Lapwai Reservation in June 1877, but some of the young warriors, stung by the fact that the Nez Perce had seemingly lost their rights as men, broke away from the group and massacred several settlers in the area. Their actions resulted in what Joseph and his father had long tried to forestall—a war. Believing the authorities would offer no quarter to the Indians now, the bands voted in council to abandon their traditional homes in favor of a new home with the Crow or the Sioux who had escaped to Canada following the slaughter of the Seventh Cavalry. It was from this point on that a popular myth was created.

Through the summer and into the fall of 1877 more than 800 non-treaty Nez Perce traveled over 1500 miles through Idaho, Montana, and Wyoming territories. Along their journey they successfully eluded five U.S. Army detachments. When Nez Perce were forced into a military encounter, they proved to be exemplary warriors, easily besting the soldiers who had been sent against them. The trail cut by the tribe was marked by the blood of settlers who stood in the way of the sojourners. Each instance of Indian military prowess and each failure on the part of the U.S. Army were monitored by the American public through the correspondence of Thomas Sutherland, a young reporter who accompanied Howard on the trail to capture the Nez Perce. As news of the drama played out in the press, pressure mounted on the government to succeed. At the same time, Sutherland's reporting created an American myth—Joseph as the Chief of the Nez Perce. In the press, he alone was responsible for the depre-dations and the defeat of the U.S. Army. Joseph became the "Red Napoleon," a man whose stature was likened to that of Sitting Bull and who generated fear in the hearts of those his band encountered. However, none of this was true.

The Nez Perce Indians elected their leaders on their march to freedom, and although Joseph was a camp chief, responsible for the well-being of the people while in camp and the maintenance of the horses, he was not the main leader of the refugees, nor did he lead any military engagements. Joseph repeatedly counseled instead for peace and surrender to the American authorities over their continued flight and war. Along the trail Joseph only infrequently fought against the soldiers that dogged their path. He was widely criticized by his own people for abandoning his wife and newborn infant during one raid; at another he was unable to fight because he had no weapon and instead hud-dled on a river bank cradling his infant daughter in his arms while the war-riors fought off the advancing army. In another instance, he took settlers into his own camp to protect them from members of the band who wanted to kill them. Although Joseph did engage the army when pressed, he was not the military leader, or even the primary leader of his people. As a young man, Joseph had been raised to lead his people in peace, to protect them and see to their needs. Though he knew how to wield a rifle, he was not a warrior, a distinction that made no sense to the American mind and subsequently resulted in the creation of the myth that has endured for almost a century and a half. The primary leader of the non-treaty Nez Perce was Looking Glass, or a half-breed Indian named Poker Joe, both of whom would be killed in the final days of the odyssey.

When the end came for the Nez Perce they were camped in a canyon thirty miles from the border of Canada, in an area known as the Bear Paw. Looking Glass had refused to post guards, believing the Nez Perce had outdistanced the army and were safe. The people were preparing food and supplies to take with them into Canada, where they intended to ally with Sitting Bull and the Sioux. While engaged in their labors they were surrounded by a detachment led by Colonel Nelson A. Miles and pinned down. An impasse of almost a week followed, during which time General Howard and his forces joined with Miles. The Nez Perce met in council to discuss a course of action and Joseph announced he would cease fighting. Though many of the other chiefs chided him for trusting the soldiers, Joseph was adamant—no longer could he watch while his people were slowly killed around him. His own daughter, Hopho-ponmi, had escaped with some of the horses when the siege began, and he was uncertain of her fate. Perhaps a cessation of hostilities would allow him the opportunity to search for her. The U.S. military was all too willing to end the chase and the embarrassment they had endured over the past several months. An agreement was reached that would allow the members of the tribe to cease fighting and present themselves to the military authorities. Joseph's negotia-tion was intended not to surrender the Nez Perce to a superior foe, but to end the fighting between two equal and opposing forces. In addition, those who did not wish to present themselves to the military could follow another chief, White Bird, who opted to continue to push on into Canada. By the time Miles recognized that the Nez Perce had only partially surrendered to him, White Bird and the other Nez Perce were safely in Canada.

Joseph is famously credited with stating, "I will fight no more forever" at his surrender to Miles and Howard on 5 October 1877. This again has become part of the myth of both Joseph and the Nez Perce. Though Joseph did utter something close to these words, it was to his own people during the council meeting to discuss the imminent end of their flight. When the final count of the Indians was made, 87 men, 184 women, and 147 children had given themselves over to the control of the U.S. military. Two of the women who accompanied him were the widows of Looking Glass, who Joseph would take as his own wives. Under the terms of their surrender, they were to be returned to the Wallowa Valley the next year, where they would resume the lives they had left behind. There would be no punishment for the flight, or for the depredations that had occurred during the ordeal.

Although these terms had been agreed to by Nelson Miles, they were not agreed to by the U.S. government. The military, under the command of William Tecumseh Sherman, had been clearly outmaneuvered and outfought by a group of "savages." The demand for land in the Wallowa Valley had not lessened because of the events during summer 1877, and concerns about hostile Indians, especially those who might ally with Chief Sitting Bull to attack U.S. interests in the West, had not been abated. The U.S. Army moved Joseph and his people several times in the ensuing weeks, first to Fort Keogh in Montana, then to Fort Lincoln in the Dakota Territory, and then to Fort Leavenworth in Kansas, where they were housed until July 1878 when the Department of the Army transferred the Nez Perce to the Quapaw Agency in Indian Territory, modern-day Oklahoma. There they would be given over to the jurisdiction of the Department of the Interior. During each of these transfers the property of the Nez Perce was gradually reduced to nothing until they arrived at the Quapaw Agency destitute. The hot and humid weather of both Kansas and Oklahoma combined with a lack of food had rendered the Nez Perce almost incapable of caring for themselves. Joseph, his wife, and his infant daughter, who had been born during their flight, fell ill. During the flight and the stress of the journey from Bear Paw to Indian Territory, many of the Nez Perce died, leaving the young orphaned and the elderly too ill to care for themselves. At one point Joseph and his wife adopted an orphaned boy when his mother died. Despite the best efforts of Joseph and his wife, the boy would soon die as well.

At each stop along the way, Joseph continued to look after the welfare of his people. To any of the many thousands of curious white people who came to see him during his incarceration at Fort Leavenworth he related the promise that had been made to return his people to the Wallowa Valley and asked for their assistance. None came. Instead conditions for the Nez Perce would only worsen. At the Quapaw Agency, they were given over to Hiram Jones, a man singly known for his corruption and greed. To combat the man who literally held the life of the Nez Perce in his hands, Joseph enlisted the aid of a former enemy and settler in the Wallowa Valley, Arthur Chapman. Chapman had been hired as an interpreter for the Nez Perce, and as he traveled with them over the course of several months he evolved into their champion. Encouraged by Joseph, Chapman spearheaded a letter-writing campaign that condemned the conditions on the Quapaw Agency and demanded the Nez Perce be returned home. To keep the plight of the Nez Perce at the forefront of the minds of the government and the American people, the Nez Perce raised funds themselves to send Chapman to Washington, DC, to address Congress on their behalf.

While Chapman was politicking for the Nez Perce, the divisions that had resulted in the flight were to come back again. Three Christianized Indians from the Lapwai Reservation were dispatched to the Quapaw Agency in an attempt to further divide the people and to encourage the non-treaty Indians to adopt Christianity and the way of white civilization. For those who were compliant there was the possibility that they would be allowed to return to their home in the north. Recognizing that the survival of the Nez Perce was at stake, Joseph petitioned to be able to go to Washington, DC, himself to plead the case of his people. In January 1879, permission was finally granted and Joseph, Chapman, and Yellow Bull, a sub-chief, made their way to the nation's capital. Along the way Joseph proved himself to be adept at using the newspapers to his advantage, and by the time he arrived in Washington, a much different portrait of the Nez Perce and the reason for their flight had emerged, one that garnered considerable sympathy for the Nez Perce. Joseph would meet with President Rutherford B. Hayes and members of his cabinet to relate the story of his flight and again to insist that the promises the government had made to his people be honored.

Although Joseph and his supporters kept the plight of the Nez Perce in the press, the government did little. Hiram Jones was relieved of his duties as agent for the Quapaw Agency and a more sympathetic agent was installed. By the middle of 1879, the 418 souls who had followed Joseph out of the canyon in the Bear Paw had been reduced to 370. By the following year the divisions between the Christianized Nez Perce and Joseph's Nez Perce had become even more acute. To survive in the harsh weather conditions of Oklahoma, the tribe was forced to adopt agriculture and stock rearing. In addition, funds for the Indians were limited and could not meet their needs. This forced many to seek work in the white world. As this happened, a gradual shift in the leadership of the tribe occurred. One of the Christianized Nez Perce, Reuben, emerged as the leader, and Joseph was relegated to a secondary position among his people. For the Nez Perce their increasing devotion to Christianity was seen as a mark of civilization, and the Presbyterian Church that supported the agent who served them in Indian Territory took up the cause to return them to their home in Idaho. Return to the cool valleys of Idaho could not come soon enough; since their surrender and captivity in Indian Territory, the Nez Perce were unable to maintain their population. Their children died shortly after birth or in the womb. Within a few years almost 100 graves would appear—a constant, sad reminder of what they had lost. The elderly succumbed to diseases that they were unfamiliar with, and the real possibility that the tribe might become extinct loomed greater with each passing year.

As the months stretched into years several forces came together to finally get the Nez Perce back to their homes. The relentless use of the media by Joseph at every opportunity was often overshadowed by the same efforts on the part of the Christianized Nez Perce to return their brethren to their northern home. The Presbyterian congregations across America, noting the wide conversion of the Nez Perce in the Indian Country and their sharply declining numbers, also took up pen to petition the government for their release. Finally, Nelson Miles, the man to whom they had surrendered in 1877, took up their cause. Only he spoke with greater authority than he had in 1877; by 1880 Miles had been promoted to General and in 1881 was made the Commander of the Columbia.

The combined efforts slowly began to bear fruit. In June 1883, thirty-three people were allowed to relocate to the Lapwai Reservation and to take up residence with the Christianized Nez Perce. Joseph was not among them. The government had hoped this small gesture would be enough to put the issue of the Nez Perce behind them, but it only served to strengthen the cause. By July 1884, Congress approved the transfer of the remaining Nez Perce to their homes in the north. However, since hostility still remained in the Wallowa Valley among the whites, it was decided to send the Christianized Indians to the Lapwai Reservation, and the remaining non-Christian Indians to the Colville Reservation in Washington. The following spring 268 Nez Perce made their separate journeys back to the north. One hundred and fifty would voluntarily go with Joseph to exile in Washington and live on the Colville Reservation.

The Colville Reservation offered little hospitality for Joseph or the Nez Perce. The land was already home to several tribes, most of whom had been displaced by white settlement. Additionally, the reputation Joseph had been saddled with as a renegade Indian caused the settlers in the area to complain about his presence.

By the time the Nez Perce had returned to their homeland, the attitude about the Indians had changed. By 1887, the Dawes Allotment Act would attempt to divide the reservations into individual allotments to foster individuality among the Indians and to open up new land for settlement. Though Joseph was given an allotment on the Lapwai Reservation, he never claimed it. Instead, for the remainder of his life he continued to push the government to compensate the Nez Perce for the loss of their property and the return of the Wallowa Valley. His struggle was aided by Nelson Miles, who would eventually be promoted to Commander of the Army, and Wild Bill Cody, who met Joseph during one of his many trips to the East Coast to push the government into action. Nothing would come of their efforts. Joseph was allowed to return to the Wallowa Valley only once after his return from the Indian Territory. The year was 1901, and he had been given hope that the government might consider granting a small reservation to his people. However, white settlement in the area and protest against the return of the Nez Perce was too great.

Unable to return to the land of his ancestors and beaten by a life of hard living, Joseph's health began to deteriorate. On 21 September 1904 he directed his wife to retrieve his headdress as he was preparing to die. When she returned, he had already passed on. Joseph was buried in the Colville Reservation. In his sixty-four years he had achieved a measure of celebrity in the white world as the Red Napoleon, architect of one of the most embarrassing failures on the part of the U.S. Army. Once his true nature was revealed, his name became synonymous with the "noble savage." However, throughout his life, although he was not able to honor his promise to his father to keep the land of their ancestors, he remained steadfast in his devotion to his people. For this devotion he would pay a tremendous price: All of the nine children Joseph fathered during his life would precede him in death, as would the unknown number of orphans he brought into his home. Hophoponmi, the daughter who escaped to Canada during that fateful week at Bear Paw, was returned to the Lapwai Reservation in 1878 and married George Moses in 1879. She would never see her father again. Joseph would marry four times during his lifetime; two of his wives, those he took after the death of Looking Glass, would survive him and live out their final days on the Colville Reservation. The iconic image of the man who had bested the U.S. Army had been exchanged for one of the Indian, exhausted by unrelenting advance of civilization, who had surrendered.

FURTHER READING

Beal, Merrill D. *"I Will Fight No More Forever"; Chief Joseph and the Nez Perce War* (Seattle: University of Washington Press, 1963).

Deloria, Philip Joseph. *Indians in Unexpected Places* (Lawrence: University Press of Kansas, 2004).

Johnson, Virginia Weisel. *The Unregimented General: A Biography of Nelson A. Miles* (Boston: Houghton Mifflin, 1962).

Wooster, Robert. *Nelson A. Miles and the Twilight of the Frontier Army* (Lincoln: University of Nebraska Press, 1993).

Cowgirls at rodeo, AZO Photograph postcard of Rene Harley, Fox Hastings, Rose Smith, Ruth Roach, Mabel Strickland, Prairie Rose, Dorothy Morell, 1921. Photograph by Ralph R. Doubleday. Courtesy of the Museum of the American West, Autry National Research Center. 89.145.6.Western History Collections, Norman, Oklahoma.

Cowboys and Cowgirls

Taran Schindler

In 1893, Buffalo Bill's Wild West Show opened its tenth season just outside the grounds of the World's Columbian Exposition in Chicago. Advertised since its original performance as an authentic portrayal of Western life, the Wild West Show featured a mix of Western-style scenes. Amid the fair's record-breaking crowds, there to celebrate the cultural arts, technology, and the 400 years since Columbus's arrival, William F. "Buffalo Bill" Cody brought to a larger audience than ever the figure of the American cowboy. Fleshed out in colorful clothing and characterized by unique skills and stunning heroism, his presence was integral to Cody's expression of the West. The cowgirl was there, too. Her athleticism and bravery demonstrated by her roping, riding, and skills of derring-do. The Wild West performance immortalized cowboys and cowgirls as American champions. Once low-wage, hard-working cattle herders and ranch hands, their ascent to such a fabled position is a curious one. It begins during the heyday of American cattle ranching and is driven into the twentieth century by a web of popular and sophisticated forms of cultural expression.

To many people, settling on a single interpretation of these late nineteenth century characters is almost impossible. The cowboy easily and equally calls to mind campfires and harmonica tunes, stampedes and whirling lassos, heroic deeds and mysterious identities, and fast-drawing gunslinging justice. The cowgirl, too, evokes several different characterizations. At once, she's the plucky Wild West show performer or, in the same arena, she's an independent, professional athlete challenging the expectations of Victorian domesticity. Sometimes, too, she is a tough but beautiful vigilante riding astride her horse righting wrongs across the fictionalized West, or she's a tomboy who knows her animals and can handle her gear as well as any man.

Clearly, these multiple images are conflations of history and story. In examining that history and looking to the sources of the story, the unique trajectory from ranch workers to symbols of American identity can be followed. It begins, of course, with cows and the culturally mixed origins of American cattle culture. It is extended through the efficient creation and dissemination of the mass-marketed dime novel and the equally efficient production of Buffalo Bill's Wild West as well as later similar Western reenactment exhibitions. Concurrently, elite late nineteenth century Eastern American circles recognized the popularity of the cowboy and, in more sophisticated expressions, deepened his character and furthered his ideological role as authentic denizen and unbeatable guardian of Western space.

Although the cowgirl character was not perpetuated in the same way, her historic participation in Western reenactment shows and in the parallel development of Western rodeo competition asserted her real presence on the range as well as providing the vehicle for her image of independence and competence into the twentieth and twenty-first centuries.

HISTORICAL OVERVIEW

The cowboy rode into American consciousness in the decades after the Civil War. Although Westerners were certainly aware of cattle drives and herdsmen, it was through military movement, East-West migration, journalism, and even early train travel and tourism that word was carried East of the rough, uniquely clad horsemen who pushed longhorn stock through the American West. At this time, thousands of cattle grazed the open ranges of the Southwest. In seasonal shifts, the animals were rounded up and moved through the Oklahoma Territory to railroad access in Kansas and Missouri or into the fertile ranges in Colorado, Wyoming, and Montana. By the second half of the 1880s, however, when overcrowded herds, fencing issues, and railroad expansion forced an end to open-range ranching, what seemed to be the cowboy's short tenure also seemed to be coming to a close.

The cowboy's sudden appearance and stunted career gives an impression that American cattle culture covers only a less than thirty-year period. It is true that the post–Civil War drives marked the high point of the presence of both cowboys and cattle on the range. Importantly, however, the cowboy's (and later the cowgirl's) distinctive look, his specialized skills, his tools and trappings, and the animals he kept came from a long history of cattle culture in North America. These same attributes leave a strong legacy on the modern ranch and rodeo culture as well as in the popular modern literary and cinematic genre of the Western. J. Frank Dobie, the prominent and popular early twentieth century Western historian, observed that "the cowboy became the best-known occupational type that America has given the world. He exists still and will long exist, though much changed from the original. His fame derives from the past."

Early History

The American cowboy's past begins in the mid-sixteenth century when the Spanish first brought horses and cattle into North America. In 1494, on his second journey, Christopher Columbus introduced a herd of cattle to the island of Hispaniola. The animals thrived in the warm climate on lush grassland. In less than ten years, small agricultural and stockbreeding ranches were established throughout the West Indies. In 1519, in search of gold and infamous for his brutal conquest of the Aztec population, Hernán Cortéz brought eleven stallions and five mares to the mainland of New Spain. These small, tough Spanish-bred Andalusians are ancestors to horses used in American cattle ranching today.

Close to the same time that Cortéz was making his presence known, the first cattle were brought to the mainland by soon-to-be lieutenant governor of New Spain, Gregorio de Villalobos. His herd was followed by the import of countless head of cattle. Of the several different breeds that had been relocated to New Spain, one proved most able to acclimate in the hills and grassy regions of the area south of what is now the state of Mexico. This light-bodied, narrow-muzzled variety had long legs and wide spreading curved horns. Not particularly well designed for work, this descendent of the Andalusian fighting bull and ancestor to the Texas Longhorn was more in demand for its hide, tallow, and meat.

New Spain

New Spain was an area of the North and South American continent that was ruled by Spain from 1535 to 1821. It extended from what are now the Cayman Islands to nearly all of the Southwestern United States, and even parts of British Columbia and Alaska. In 1821, Spain's land holdings decreased with the independence of Mexico and in 1898 when Cuba, Puerto Rico, and Guam were ceded to the United States after the Spanish-American War.

The early sixteenth century in New Spain was marked by the abundance of cattle on the open ranges. As the longhorns multiplied rapidly, Spanish ranchers needed a system to protect their herds from theft, predators, and natural injury. This task was perceived by both wealthy cattlemen and religious missionaries as menial labor meant for unskilled workers. It fell on the non-Spanish population: a motley crew of converted Indians, Africans, and Caribbeans. Known in Spanish as *vaqueros*, this socially outcast and very poor labor force learned to ride horses and control livestock with ropes and prods. They were the original cowboys.

Nineteenth-Century History

The next centuries of northern migration, shifts in Mexican and American national borders, and economic opportunity drew the vaquero and his profession into the United States by way of California and Texas. Eighteenth-century California was Spanish land. Cattle from Mexico were driven northwest originally to supply the missions and forts with small herds for food and supplies. Vaqueros had come to California with the young herds but as the cattle population grew and ranching became the primary industry in the region, extra handlers were in demand. Despite a law that forbade Indians the right to horses, the mission padres, very much in control of the economy, bent the rule and trained Indian converts with the skills of the vaquero. When Mexico gained independence in 1821, mission lands were required to be returned to the public. To protect their vast assets, the padres at the twenty-one missions liquidated their herds into hides, tallow, and jerky. Although a percentage of vaqueros left the mission herds for work on privately owned large ranches or *haciendas*, the responsibilities of many Californian vaqueros changed from growing and protecting beef to skinning, fat production, and beef brining. From 1830 to 1842 total mission herd count dropped from close to 535,000 to 28,220 cattle.

Cattle Rendering

Tallow or rendered cow fat was traditionally used for cooking and in the making of candles and soap. Richard Henry Dana's classic novel *Two Years before the Mast*, published in 1840, offers an image of the hide and tallow trade. His adventure story is based on his experiences at sea from Boston, around Cape Horn, and up the California coast. Not only does Dana paint a picture of the danger and beauty of mid-nineteenth-century sailing life, but he also includes timely descriptions of vaquero culture and his participation in the cattle rendering trade.

At the same time the California cattle industry was in decline, wild cattle were thriving across grasslands in Texas and land was readily available. During the years as a Republic, Texas's borders extended into what are now New Mexico, Oklahoma, Kansas, Colorado, and Wyoming, covering over two million acres. When Texas became a state liberal land policies still held, for a time, from earlier days. Original homestead agreements from 1836 offered white families living in Texas 7600 acres and immigrant families arriving between 1836 and 1837 were offered 1280 acres. Even though state congressional policies in 1854 reduced homestead plots to 160 acres, the ethic to acquire land quickly was in place. With state-supported land subsidy, a wealth of wild cattle, and a wide-open range, Texas in the 1850s had become a state of ranching landholders. An 1860 census reported that Texas was home to one-eighth of all American cattle. Over the decades, Mexican vaqueros had been hired to handle these great herds and, as the beef industry flourished, it was their skills that were passed to a new American crew.

Cowboy Ancestry

Most of the new Southwestern cowboys were white. They were Texans or migrants from Southeastern states. In a moment of evident cultural exchange, these European American cowboys acquired skills rooted in Spanish, West Indian, and Mexican experience. The Texas cowboy may have been continuing African American, Irish, and English colonial traditions as well. The origins of the word "cowboy" point in several directions. Cattle raising had long played a part in the agrarian culture of the American colonial South. African and métis—or mixed-heritage—slaves and indentured workers herded cattle as far north and as far to the east as the Appalachian foothills in northeastern Mississippi. On foot, not horseback, and with dogs for assistance, these herders were known as "cow-boys." Following the Louisiana Purchase in 1803, the Eastern cow-boys crossed the Mississippi River. Once this far west, Southern ranching and vaquero traditions most likely had an influence on each other.

The term "cowboy" also appears in second-century Irish history where it was defined as it is today, as a horseman or a cattle herd. Over 500 years later, Irish cowboys who ran afoul of British law were offered to serve their sentences in jail or in America as indentured farmhands. At this time, cattle raisers in the American colonies used the terms "cow-keeper" and "drover" to separate themselves from the reputation of the Irish cowboy troublemakers.

During the American Revolution, the term "cow-boy" remained an unpopular term for those seeking American independence. Calling themselves "cowboys," a contingent of Royalist Tories stole American colonists' cattle to feed British troops. A half century later, during the Texas Revolution, Texan soldiers known as "cow-boys" raided cattle from Mexican ranches along the Rio Grande. After the war, former soldiers remained in the southern region to round up wild cattle for sale in central Texas and Louisiana. An 1874 publication promoting the cattle trade noted that the average cowhand was called a "cow-boy." It wasn't until the turn of the century that the use of the hyphen was discontinued.

As a whole, cowboys were displaced farmers, former soldiers, and, in general, young men in search of work outside of urban areas. At the time cowboys were beginning to drive the Texas longhorn north, the occupation's history of mixed ancestry was still apparent. Mexicans were an ongoing presence on Western ranches. For Texan ranchers, Mexican cowboys promised expert skills and they worked for lower wages than their Anglo partners. Indian cowboys also had a hand in the mix. References to Pawnee herders have been documented, and late in the nineteenth century, the northern Dakota and Montana tribes adopted a ranching culture. Typically, however, mid-century Indian ranch hands were from the five resettled Eastern tribes with previous herding experience. Chickasaw, Cherokee, Choctaw, Creek, and Seminole managed cattle on Oklahoma lands.

Following the Civil War, African American former slaves migrated west in large numbers. Carrying with them ranching experience from the Southeastern back country, many became cowboys on the open Western range. African American cowboys are a well-known part of ranching culture but because cattle, not cowboys, were counted, statistics are difficult to glean. Memoirs from the time period do note an African American presence. Cowboy Teddy Blue Abbott recalled a "mixed outfit" on an 1879 trail ride and Charlie Siringo, in his 1885 autobiographical account *A Texas Cowboy, or Fifteen Years on the Hurricane Deck of a Spanish Pony*, recalls interactions with black cattlemen. On a trail ride of 2500 head of cattle and twenty-five cowboys, he and "negro Gabe" controlled a herd through a rising river and at a different time, he was told to wait for "Ike Word, an old negro . . . who was the best roper in the crowd."

Round Up and Trail Drives

During the post–Civil War years of Southern Reconstruction and Western expansion the cattle culture grew in Texas, especially in the southern region below the San Antonio River. At the same time, the demand for beef was growing in the rapidly industrializing Northeast. To transport beef-on-the-hoof to Eastern markets, and later, to farther Western urban centers, cowboys led thousands of head of cattle up from Texas on long trail drives to northern railroad access points. The trail drives coupled with the seasonal round up of cattle were the cowboy's two most definitive tasks.

To the mid-nineteenth century Western rancher and cowboy, the open range meant the vast open public lands that rolled out as far as a hungry cow could graze. It also meant the more proximal lands closer to each separate home-stead or ranch. Cowboys regularly monitored their home territory, sending wandering cattle to more central areas. However, open range cattle could roam as far as 150 miles. In order to maintain the individually owned herds, each spring and fall cowboys spent a month out on the range, gathering and separating or "cutting" cattle, branding new calves, and driving herds closer to their home range for security or for preparation for the trail. In 1920, cow-boy Hiram G. Craig, quoted in David Dary's informative and detailed text *Cowboy Culture*, remembered a round up from 1881: "The men, so sent out, all going in different directions, formed a veritable spider's web, with the round up grounds in the center. As soon as the boys would 'whoop-em up,' the cattle were on the run, and would make for the grounds."

The trail drives secured their place in the cattle industry in 1867 when Joseph McCoy, an Illinois stockman, arranged with local government to build stockyards on the Kansas-Pacific railroad in Abilene, Kansas. The location was specifically chosen to protect in-state cattle from the potentially devastating Texas Tick Fever—a condition that arched the back, dropped the head, clouded the eyes, and eventually killed or permanently weakened non-Texan cattle. Kansas law required cattle imports to remain west of the sixth princi-pal meridian, close to present day Mahaska. Farther Western stockyards grew in the Dodge City area, especially for herds heading to Denver and further north.

After a round up of market-bound animals, cowboys spent months on the trail. The most well-ridden cattle routes were the Chisholm Trail, the Western Trail, and the Goodnight-Loving Trail. The Chisholm Trail was partly blazed by Cherokee-Scottish trader, guide, and cattle driver Jesse Chisholm. Before the war, Chisholm led a gold-mining expedition up the Arkansas River, through eastern Oklahoma into Kansas, near Wichita. Later he pushed that trail south to the Red River. The full trail eventually extended north from San Antonio,

Texas, through Wichita to the Abilene railroad. Within the first year of the Texas-Kansas drives, 75,000 cattle were steered north. At its highest point, three years later in 1871, the Chisholm Trail fed over 700,000 cattle into Abilene. After 1872, however, the trails were forced west. Abilene residents felt that the cattle industry upset the local economy and that year, too, the animal quarantine boundary became more restrictive.

While the Chisholm Trail was still used to move cattle as far as Wichita, the Western Trail took cattle from San Antonio to Dodge City in western Kansas. Later, Charles Goodnight and Oliver Loving together and separately mapped a course from west Texas to Denver, Colorado, and further north to Cheyenne, Wyoming. Goodnight was a ranching pioneer in the Texas panhandle region. He began ranching in 1876 with his wife, Mary Ann "Molly" Dyer Goodnight. Seven years later, Goodnight and British partner John G. Adair and his wife Cordelia Adair had 700,000 acres. Their JA ranch was the largest ranch at that time in Texas.

The Goodnight Ranch

In 1883 the Goodnight-Adair JA Ranch was the largest privately owned ranch with 700,000 acres. Two years later, the investment firm Taylor, Babcock, and Company received over three million acres of Texas land as payment for the three million dollar subsidy the firm fronted for a new state capital building. At its peak in 1887, the ranch, known as the corporate XIT ranch, employed 150 cowboys, maintained 1000 horses and a cattle herd of close to 150,000. The brand XIT is either a Roman numeral reference to the ten Texas counties represented in the ranch's land holdings or it may more simply imply that it was the largest ranch in the state.

The Goodnight-Loving Trail, and other cattle routes as well, inspired commercial activity at their origins and at their northern rail destinations. In Denver and in Cheyenne, as in Abilene, Wichita, and Dodge City, stockyards brought business that, in turn, invited banks and merchants. At trailhead towns, cowhands could spend their wages on new clothes and the tools of the trade.

Clothing, Equipment, Specialized Skills

Cowboys needed durable, utilitarian clothes. Without the space to carry extra items and always working outside in all weather, the cowboy made sure to be efficiently dressed. However, cowboy W.S. James remarked in his 1898 memoir *A Cowboy's Life in Texas, 27 Years a Maverick* that the "cowboy . . . had his flights of fancy as clearly defined as the most fashionable French belle." Most essential for the practical or the fanciful cowhand was a hat to protect from the sun and rain. Typically made from wool, the width of the brim and the depth of the crown have been key factors in cowboy style. Boots with a high-wedged heel were popular in the earlier years when cowherds stood in their short-stirrups. Later, in the late 1870s, when longer stirrups allowed the rider to sit comfortably straight in the saddle and ride for longer periods, a lower heeled, square-toed boot was worn.

The cowboy's work required freedom of movement. Wool pants, homespun and later store-bought, were tucked into the top of the boot. In this fashion, a wide pant leg never caught in the stirrup or on thorny plants. A belt instead of over-the-shoulder suspenders fixed pants at the waist. To free the arms, a leather vest worn over a collarless wool shirt replaced the sleeved jacket. Rounding out the distinctive outfit was a cotton bandanna, loosely tied at the neck to provide ready access to a dust mask. A cotton rain slicker and tarp, heavily oiled with linseed oil for waterproofing, were often on hand.

Dressed and ready for the range, the cowherd gathered up the necessary gear. Reflecting the connection between vaquero traditions and American herding, much of the cowboy's equipment and techniques have Spanish or Spanish-derivative names. Eighteenth-century vaqueros and their American protégés used a leather rope called a *reata* to catch a cow over the head and around the neck. To a California vaquero this rope was a *lazo*. La reata became the Anglicized lariat and the lazo is a lasso. Today the two are interchangeably used to refer to the cowherd's rope. After the animal had been roped, the lariat or lasso was quickly looped around the horn of the saddle before the cow had run the length of the rope. The cowboy had "dallied" or "dolly welted" the lariat. In Spanish, he had *da la vuelta* or "given a turn" to the rope. When the cowboy was on the trail or working a round up, he would change his tired horse for a rested one at the *remuda* or *remuda de caballeros* or "relay of horses." Once in the saddle, leather chaps, or *chaperreras*, would protect the rider's legs from chaparral, cactus, and other prickly brush prevalent across the Southwest.

Cow herding demanded top riding skills. Cowherds would ride horses provided by large ranching operations while others had their own mounts. In the mid-1870s, the Plains saddle or Western saddle was the most widely used. It featured a low saddle horn, two cinches, leather side fenders, and narrow stirrups. Well-set in the saddle, a cowboy would ride into the herd, turn the horse toward a cow to be separated, and then, without upsetting the herd, urge that single animal forward. Once cut from the herd, the animal often met with another of the cowboy's specialized skills.

For private ranchers to identify their herd, each animal was marked with the ranch's particular symbol or brand. Branding cattle was a harsh process. Calves and unbranded adults known as mavericks were cut from the herd and held down while hot irons seared the ranch's brand onto their side. Often, at the same time, calves were dehorned, had their tails cut, and, in the case of young bulls, were castrated.

Mavericks

Mavericks earned their name from the unbranded cattle of Texas rancher, Samuel A. Maverick. In the mid-1840s, Maverick had settled in Matagorda County where he acquired his original herd as a payment for a debt. Not particularly interested in raising cattle at the time, he neglected his animals and let them roam unbranded. Other ranchers and neighbors knew unmarked cows as "Maverick's." When he sold his herd, to the benefit of the new owners, any unbranded animals found in the area were considered "Maverick's" and claimed as part of the sale. Used in American vernacular speech today, a maverick is an independent and original thinker.

In contrast to the acrid smell and rough work of branding, herding work often required a much more tender skill. On the trail, cattle were nervous. Crowded, in unfamiliar territory, and often tired and thirsty, the animals were quick to react to sudden movements, changes in weather, and disturbing sounds. In panic, cattle "mill" in a circular formation. The motion can become fervent and can break into full stampede. One way to control the animals was to sing to them. The cowboy's songs were sung loudly over the bellowing animals. The songs, typically sung without musical instruments, were simple but the lyrics reflected life on the range as well as future hopes and dreams.

Cowboy Songs

Andy Adams documented in his *Log of a Cowboy*, published in 1903, that the cowboy's songs sounded "like a hybrid between the weirdness of an Indian cry and the croon of a darky mammy. It expresses the open, the prairie, the immutable desert." American film stars Gene Autry and Roy Rogers popularized the image of the clean-cut, singing cowboy. Folklorists, musicologists, and historians have more authentically preserved cowboy songs and poetry. Through the 1930s, John A. Lomax Jr. cataloged countless songs and poems from various Western cattle herding traditions and, in present-day, the Western Folklife Center in Elko, Nevada, keeps manuscript and audio archives. The art form is still thriving in cattle communities across the United States. Each year poets, both young and seasoned, male and female, share their poetic interpretations of the modern Western range at the National Cowboy Poetry Gathering also in Elko, Nevada.

What keeps the herd from running,
Stampeding far and wide?
The cowboy's long, low whistle,
And singing by their side.
  —*anonymous, cowboy song*

Women's History on the Range

The cowboy's way of life was a fusion of diverse cultural traditions and hard outdoor work, American expansion, and economic opportunities. Written between the lines of history is an assumption that the cowherd's craft—the riding, roping, and cattle know-how along with the specialized clothing and riding gear—was exclusively a male thing. Lost in the shadow of a myth of masculinity have been the cattle women of the West. Within the last twenty-five years scholars have found a rich legacy of working women behind the image of the Wild West performing cowgirl. It is true that most of the people who worked the round ups and the trails were men and as Renée M. Laegreid addresses in her 2006 text *Riding Pretty*, ranch work was a masculine sphere. However, when Molly Dyer Goodnight and Cordelia Adair rode into the ranching West, they were not the first and would not be the last women in the area who actively participated in business management as well as in the daily tasks of mid- to late-nineteenth century ranching.

Over the course of the cattle boom, women drove supply wagons, rounded up horses, stood in for absent husbands, and managed their own herds. Some even rode the trail. Willie Matthews, at age nineteen in 1888, masqueraded as a boy and worked, with noticeable skill, as a cowboy in New Mexico and Colorado for four months. At this time, while the term "cowboy" implied the occupation of a cowherd, the term "cowgirl" was not yet a part of ranching culture. Instead, the women who did similar or the same work as men were ranchers, ranch women, or in some cases, cowboys as well.

Ranching in the West provided a unique environment for the Victorian woman. In an age when women were expected to live by standards set by the domestic virtues of "True Womanhood," Western women were learning the physical and business aspects of ranching in their own homes. Often located on an isolated homestead in a remote region, family-run ranches needed all members to complete the daily responsibilities. Out of this necessity, Western women were able to drop some of the restrictive ideologies of passive femininity and submission. Instead, they learned to ride at a young age, participated in the chores of the ranch, and if so inclined, worked outdoors with livestock. Typically, work was designated according to ability not gender. Alice Greenough, an early twentieth-century cowherd and rodeo cowgirl, remembers in *Cowgirls*, Teresa Jordan's 1979 collection of biographies, her father encouraging her to work for a neighbor who was looking seasonal laborers. "She'll work just like a man," her father assured. Her work out-of-doors was not unusual for a woman in her situation nor did it suggest she was unfeminine for pursuing it. Greenough was in a place in which she learned both the ways of the home and the ranch.

Cattle culture had been offering such opportunities for women for close to a century. In the late eighteenth century several women in southern Texas owned and managed large ranching operations. Into the next century, as ranching grew, Mexican women became more involved with handling animals, riding longer distances, and, noticeably more politically active and independent as well. Mexican legend holds one woman in particular, Dona Maria del Carmen Calvillo, in high esteem. In addition to her independent management of her ranch in Floresville, Texas, she made peace with neighboring Indians and provided shelter for Santa Ana's army in the battle for Texan independence.

The Homestead Act of 1862 drew men and women to the West. Between 1862 and 1934 thousands of individual women participated in this surge. Unlike domestic employment available to women in more populated areas, homesteading provided a liberating environment. Some of the women who made land claims were married and used homesteading to supplement their families' assets. However, many were single or widowed, finding in Western land cultivation and ranching real physical freedom and economic opportunity.

The Homestead Act

The Homestead Act of 1862 was designed to encourage agricultural development in the American West. The United States federal government authorized a plan that granted 160 acres of Western land to an adult over the age of twenty-one. The act stipulated that the land was to be lived on for five years. Within that timeframe, the land was to be cultivated and a home, no smaller than twelve by fourteen feet, was to be built. After the designated period, if the homesteader had met the criteria, he or she could apply for ownership and the title to the land.

Ranching opened doors for women, who out of necessity or personal interest chose to raise or work with livestock. Still, their participation in the field, as nineteenth-century women, was not without challenges. Victorian decorum dictated not only her social behavior but also her participation in physical activity and her manner of dress. In the early years of American ranching the sidesaddle

The Sidesaddle: A Spanish Tradition

The sidesaddle came to the American West from two separate but related traditions. In eighth-century Moorish Spain women traveled in a basket-like attachment at the side of a horse. Hundreds of years later, in the late fifteenth and early sixteenth centuries, the Spanish with their horses headed for North America in search of gold. By this point the basket had evolved into the sidesaddle and was seen as a symbol or aristocracy. At the same time, Spanish princess Catherine of Aragon married into the British royal family carrying her riding traditions with her. The sidesaddle made its way into North America through both English and Mexican migration.

was the appropriate seating for a woman on horseback. Riding in this fashion allowed a woman's long riding skirt to fully cover her legs that were resting to the left, her right leg set slightly higher than her left. For a working woman on horseback, the saddle and the skirt limited her mobility and comfort

In the later part of the 1890s, attitudes were slowly changing toward the expectations of women in society. Nevertheless, women who chose to ride astraddle for work and for pleasure did cause a stir. The terms themselves— "astraddle, astride, clothespin style"—took on sexual connotations. The medical community considered the position a strain on women's reproductive organs and a catalyst for uterine prolapse. Medical journals also claimed that women's rounded thighs were not strong enough to grip the saddle and, overall, it was unattractive to see a woman in this position.

Despite public reactions, riding women in the West went on with business. With the change of saddle, the divided skirt became popular. First, it featured the same long, full flare as the riding skirt but with a seam up the center. In 1895, Evelyn Cameron, rider and Western photographer, rode through Miles City, Montana, in this divided skirt. She documented in a letter, excerpted in Teresa Jordan's *Cowgirls*, that even though her outfit was as full as the traditional skirt, she was given a warning against wearing such attire in public and if she persisted she might face arrest. Not long after Cameron's run-in, divided skirts were seen regularly in Miles City as well as in other Western locales. The skirts became shorter and more tailored until the World War I years when jodhpurs and pants made their way into the Western woman's riding habit.

Lizzie Johnson, Cattle Rancher, and Molly Dyer Goodnight, Manager and Conservationist

The shifts in clothing and riding style are tangible examples of freedoms offered to ranching women. Less noticeable but immensely valuable examples of women's independence can be found in the life and ranching career of Lizzie Johnson and in the conservationist thought of Molly Dyer Goodnight. In 1865, at age twenty-four and unmarried, Johnson was teaching school and keeping the books for local cattlemen in Lockhart, Texas. She continued both careers in several different Texas towns and, reportedly as a counter to boredom, she wrote pulp fiction for newly mass-marketed dime novels and series. Although she wrote under a nom-de-plume, several of her stories are known to have appeared in *Frank Leslie's Illustrated Newspaper*. With her bookkeeping experience and her association with prominent cattle brokers whom she had known through family connections, she began investing her money in cattle industry stock. Her investments grew quickly, and by 1871 she had purchased land and cattle and had registered her own CY brand in central Texas. By 1879, she had a crew of cowboys and was regularly sending her herds up the trail for sale. That year she married Hezekiah Williams, a widower and a former preacher who had taken up the cowboy life. In an unprecedented agreement, prior to her marriage Lizzie Johnson had Hezekiah Williams sign a premarital contract stating that all of her assets, including any future equity, belonged to her. He entered the cattle industry at her urging but as a couple they maintained separate business accounts. In addition to her independent financial arrangements, she was the first woman to take her own brand up the Chisholm Trail. At least twice, possibly a third time, riding in a horse-drawn buggy, she and her husband drove her cattle into Kansas.

In the early 1880s, Molly Goodnight settled with her husband Charles Goodnight on their JA Ranch in the Texas Panhandle's Palo Duro Canyon. Not only did she manage business transactions for the ranch she also served as the only medical doctor for the local area. For five years, until a trained physician was encouraged by the Goodnights to build a practice nearby, Molly Goodnight prescribed a creative combination of available medicinals and folk remedies to her family, staff, and neighbors. Outside of this work, Goodnight took a strong interest in the shrinking buffalo herds in the region. Almost as soon as she had settled in the Panhandle, she began to adopt abandoned buffalo calves and bottle-feed them. In the next several years more calves as well as mature buffalo were added to her domesticated herd. Her buffalo came to be known as the Charles Goodnight Herd. Despite carrying her husband's name, it was her forethought, in part, that was instrumental in saving the Southern Plains buffalo from extinction. Today, many of the descendants of these animals live in Caprock Canyons State Park in the Texas Panhandle.

Although women, for the most part, were not an itinerant labor force, there is no lack of evidence in placing women as working partners in the cattle ranching culture. Their positions as managers and investors as well as their riding and animal husbandry skills add new facets to the character of the pioneer woman. Instead of being understood only as a mother, wife, or a saloon-style prostitute, women played key roles in the development of the land and the nation's economic growth.

The End of Open-Range Ranching

The cattle ranching boom that carried so many men and women to the West came to an end not thirty years from its outset. Ranching had promised wealth and into the early 1880s investors were seeing rapid return. At that time, cattle were pulling in $35 a head. However, by 1884 the success of the beef market had crowded the range and created a surplus of cattle. Trade prices dropped rapidly to $8 a head at the end of 1885. Already taking severe losses investors, ranchers, their seasonal laborers, and their cattle met with the extremely severe winter of 1885–1886. Hundreds of thousands of animals died. Cattle shipped the next year were in poor condition and brought in even lower prices. From Texas through Montana, overgrazed grassland and then the depletion of the herds dramatically changed the lives of cattle ranchers and their crews. As the ranching world began the process of reparation, several concurrent events brought a sure end to the open range culture identified by seasonal round ups and trail drives.

Joseph F. Glidden, a farmer from Illinois, received a patent in 1874 for his specialized design for barbed wire. Although not necessarily the first to consider wire barbs as fencing material, he held the first patent and was the first to produce it on a mass scale. Originally it was used to keep open range cattle from wandering into homesteaders' cultivated fields. Western ranchers, on the other hand, were wary of the sharp device. Injured animals were more susceptible to infections and the strands of wire limited movement across grazing land. For a time, ranch land remained unfenced.

After the winter of 1885–1886, the structure of the range took a new shape. To slowly nurture meat back into a competitive market and to let the range recover from earlier overgrazing, ranchers kept smaller herds. Barbed wire fencing was used to control the movement of the herds away from new growth and into secured pasture. To supplement the animals' diet, sections of ranch land were fenced and cultivated for feed. With cattle contained and crops to support, wells were dug and windmills raised to provide on-site access to water.

Cowboys' tasks went from riding the round up and trail to digging wells, growing and harvesting hay, and setting fences. Many carried bandage kits out into the field when stringing wire fences. Wire barbs could cause injury even through long sleeves and leather gloves. The fenced ranges met mixed reactions from those working the smaller ranches. One Texas cowboy commented in 1884 that he was sickened by the thought of potatoes growing where animals should be grazing. Farms, enclosed pastures, and fenced water holes, he felt, were the ruin of the country.

The expansion of the railroad industry also had direct effect on the ranching world. As ranching territory moved farther north into Colorado, Wyoming, and Montana, rail lines also reached farther across the West and into the mountain regions. Although cattle were still pushed on foot to rail hubs, the trail drives from ranches to rail access were much shorter. The semi-nomadic life of the cattle driver shifted to a more ranch-based culture within the boundaries of fenced ranges.

Cowboy Reputation

During this same time, when ranchers were pushing the limit of capacity of the Western grasslands and the dynamics of the range were in flux, the public impression of the working cowboy was at an all-time low. In Lincoln County, New Mexico, in 1878 cowboy ranch hands representing local ranchers were pitted against a posse organized by a wealthy and politically influential mercantile and banking house. After one young, prosperous ranch owner was murdered over debt issues, allegiances were tested. Later known as the Lincoln

County War, the cowboys, including Henry McCarty—sometimes known as William H. Bonney or "Billy the Kid"—were overwhelmed by a coordinated effort between the merchant's gunmen and U.S. troops. Though many escaped alive, including Billy the Kid, their actions against the U.S. military coupled with public action against powerful money-holders made them outlaws and forced them to disperse. News of this event only deepened a negative image of cowboys already being reported in popular journals. In an 1875 *Lippincott's* article, journalist Laura Johnson had called cowboys, "rough men with shaggy hair and wild, staring eyes."

Only a few years later in fall 1881, cowboys faced off with local law enforcement in Tombstone, Arizona Territory. Allegedly disturbing the peace and breaking a local ordinance that prohibited possession of firearms, a cowboy named Ike Clanton was arrested by local sheriff, Wyatt Earp. After his release, Clanton threatened retaliation on local law officials. In what is now infamous as the "Gunfight at the O.K. Corral," Earp, his two brothers, and J.H. "Doc" Holliday were on the defensive against Clanton and five other men. Newspaper coverage reported "A Desperate Fight Between Officers of the Law and Cow-Boys." Earp's two brothers and Holliday sustained injuries but three of Clanton's men were killed, including his brother. The others ran. No doubt this incident, so closely following the conflict in Lincoln County, perpetuated an image of the cowboy as renegade and violent. In his first Presidential Address presented on 6 December 1881, President Chester A. Arthur drew attention to the disruption of the peace in the Arizona Territory by "a band of armed desperadoes known as 'cowboys' [who] have been engaged for months in committing acts of lawlessness and brutality."

The cowboy's reputation as dangerous and fearsome was replaced only a few years after President Arthur's pointed remark. In 1885, as a recognized historian, Theodore Roosevelt explained the rowdy cowboy's behavior as a celebration at trail's end. In the following year Joseph Nimmo, chief of the United States Bureau of Statistics, wrote in a *Harper's New Monthly Magazine* article that cowboys possessed courage and physical alertness, were skilled horsemen, and, despite a rough appearance, a majority of them were "true and trusty men." An 1887 British newspaper reported the cowboy to be "a gentleman." The shift from outlaw to honorific reflects the growing nostalgic and romantic perception of Western life consciously promoted in Eastern media. While Western men and women were experiencing the realities of the end of open-range ranching as well as increased violence between the U.S. Army and Indians, urban Easterners were looking toward a fictionalized West to diffuse tensions associated with rapid industrialization.

Eastern Economic Collapse and Urban Anxiety

The decades flanking the Civil War were marked by rapid economic and social change. The young American nation went from being a land-based agrarian society to an industrialized, financially sound player in world markets. In under a century, the swift rise of industrial capitalism in the East built a system of manufacturing and factory labor. At the same time the country doubled in size, eradicated the original occupants of the Western plains—the American Indian and the buffalo—and replaced them with cattle, ranches, and railroads. The Jeffersonian ideal of an agrarian, egalitarian republic of white farmers was overshadowed by real private investment, big business, and a hierarchical labor system.

Although Eastern factory conditions were poor and advancement opportunities for the working class very low, American economic prosperity, as a whole, sustained its upswing over the course of the Civil War. In the years between 1868 and 1873 Southern agricultural reconstruction proceeded, rail tracks were nearly doubled, and a new immigrant work force labored for the lowest wages while still maintaining high production of material goods. Attesting to the continued flow of money, in the early 1870s, Eastern investors took note of the large sums of cattle money passing through Western banks. The National Live Stock Journal of 1871 documented that the prior year had brought $3 million into Kansas City banks. At that time, seven railroads passed through Kansas City, where stockyards, livestock exchange, and meat packing operations secured the wealth in the region.

In an early attempt to attract Eastern and European investment in cattle ranching, the Union Pacific Railroad in Omaha published the first how-to stock raising guidebook, *Trans-Missouri Stock Raising: The Pasture Lands of North America*. Then, just as rail corporations and the stock raisers began joint promotion, the bottom dropped out of the railroad market. On 18 September 1873, the Philadelphia banking house of Jay Cooke & Co., over-extended to the Northern Pacific Railroad, declared bankruptcy. The next day, nineteen other banking firms collapsed. The New York Stock Exchange closed for ten days. With the Panic of 1873 in full swing, prices fell, bonds defaulted, and credit became difficult to obtain.

Although Eastern industries felt the effects of the 1873 economic depression for over six years, Western cattle ranching and the railroad rallied significantly faster. Only a year after the crash, American and European investors again saw promise in Western cattle raising and innovations in railcar refrigeration were also well under way. Flush with new capital, cattle ranching became a cattle industry. But as soon as the vast herds again took over the West, open-range ranching was hindered by overgrazing and severe winter weather. As a result, cowhands were pushed into different lines of work. At the same time, Eastern working-class urban men and women were facing crowded domestic conditions, labor strife, new immigrant populations, and racial tensions as well as the social constraints dictated by Victorian society. To counter urban anxiety, popular culture was finding entertainment and diversion in mass-marketed dime novels and in the theatric interpretations of the West suggested in new melodramatic stage productions.

The time was right, according to folklorist Beverly J. Stoeltje, for a unifying, national symbol of American identity. By the early 1880s, an image of the cowboy emerged on the East Coast. Built concurrently on popular literature and performance, the cowboy image underscored American freedom and self-sufficiency as well as white authority and virility. Through the cowboy ideal, the congested white, middle-class, urban population could indulge in a fantasy of a Western life of space and free agency.

FICTIONALIZATION OF COWBOYS AND COWGIRLS

The Dime Western and Buffalo Bill's Wild West

The emergence of the cowboy, and eventually the cowgirl, as illustrations of virtue, strength, and independence were hinged on the introduction of new, mid-century printing technology as well as a chance meeting in 1869 at Fort McPherson, Nebraska, that brought together two very different men.

The steam-powered cylinder printing press of the antebellum era reduced labor expenses and could print 1100 sheets per hour. At the same time, paper costs were cut with the introduction of inexpensive wood-pulp production and upgrades in transportation systematized delivery and dissemination, allowing printed materials to reach a wide audience. These advancements made the mass-production of books possible, and in doing so, promoted the act of reading as a popular middle-class activity.

In 1860, the New York publishing house of Beadle & Adam used the steam-powered press to print the first dime novel. The house of Beadle was already known for its inexpensive pocket-sized paperback handbooks including *Beadle's Dime Letter Writer* and *Beadle's Dime Book of Beauty*. The first novel, *Maleaska or the Indian Wife of the White Hunter*, written by Mrs. Ann S. Stephens, set a sentimental and sensationalized plot of miscegenation in the familiar landscape of the James Fenimore Cooper's Hudson River valley. Advertised as the first of a series and offering a controversial subject, the novel sold 65,000 copies in its first few months and continued to sell into the next century. Ingeniously marketed as series, dime novels promised more than each issue actually delivered therefore securing the purchase of future installments. Beadle & Adam took full advantage of this by diversifying into many similarly named series including *Beadle's Dime Novels, Beadle's New York Dime Library, Beadle's Half-Dime Library,* and *Beadle's New Dime Novels.* Beadle & Adam published twenty-five series, and the other companies produced even more.

As popularity of the format grew, the dime novels took on a standard presentation. Foregoing the pocket design, the dime novel became a quarto booklet—its broadleaf pages folded four times to measure 12.5 inches tall and 9.5 inches wide. Typically 100 pages (or fifty pages in the *Beadle's Half-Dime*

Library series) with woodblock cover art and a formulaic plot often featuring historic characters, dime novel publishing houses including Beadle & Adams, Street and Smith, and Frank Tousey provided the general reading public, for over sixty years, with action-packed stories filled to the brim with dangers, romances, and opportunities for heroism.

William F. "Buffalo Bill" Cody

When Edward Zane Carroll Judson met William F. Cody, acclaimed hunting guide and a U.S. army scout, at Nebraska's Fort McPherson, he was well aware of the success of the dime novel format. Judson, who was more often known as Ned Buntline, had been a Know-Nothing Party activist and a temperance lecturer. Eventually, he found his niche as a writer. In fact, he was an extremely prolific writer of pulp fiction and sensationalized journalism. Buntline's writing had appeared in the New York literary magazine *Knickerbocker*, and in the early 1840s, he started his own paper, published in Kentucky, called *Ned Buntline's Own*. He made it known that he could produce six dime novels a week and could pull in $20,000 a year.

The Know-Nothings

The Know-Nothing Party was the popular nickname for the American Party, a short-lived political movement that supported a strong anti-immigrant and anti-Catholic platform. It formed in New York and was most active between 1852 and 1856, at one point representing one million members. Its reactionary stance toward immigrants aimed to place only native-born Americans into public office and its reformist, middle-class foundation pushed temperance and Bible study in public schools. The movement split over slavery issues and by 1860 was a nominal political force. The "know-nothing" moniker reflects the exclusive and secretive origins of the movement. If a member was asked about his political associations, the proper response was "I know nothing." In American vernacular today, the term "know-nothing" is used in political arenas to criticize anti-immigrant and xenophobic directives.

When the two men met, Cody was returning from an excursion as a hunting guide and scouting for the army. Buntline may have been returning from a temperance tour or he may have been there specifically to gather material for his fiction. Although Buntline's purpose at the fort is historically unclear, the upshot of the interaction was a dime novel, published in December 1869, in which Buntline used Cody's personal moniker Buffalo Bill and was loosely based on the scout's frontier life. The story, *Buffalo Bill, King of the Bordermen*, exalted Cody's life in the army and as an Indian fighter. In a plot that resembled nothing like an authentic scout's experience but advertised as truth,

Buffalo Bill and Wild Bill Hickok rescue Cody's mother and sisters from out-laws and their Indian accomplices. In the style of dime fiction, the story was understood as both sensationalized journalism and entertainment.

Wild Bill Hickok

James Butler "Wild Bill" Hickok was born in Troy Grove, Illinois, in 1837. He served in the Union Army during the Civil War, and then made a living as an Indian scout before earning fame as a Kansas lawman and a gunfighter. In the only "quick draw" fight on record, in 1865 Hickok killed Davis K. Tutt Jr. in a duel over gambling debts. As sheriff and marshal in several Kansas towns, he was involved in a series of gunfights, one in which he accidentally killed a friend. In 1876, in a saloon in Deadwood, Dakota Territory, he took the last available seat at a poker table, with his back to the door. He was shot from behind and killed. His poker hand of two Aces, two 8s, and a Jack, became known as the "Dead Man's Hand."

At the same time the novel left the reader curious about the dangers and possibilities of the West it also drew attention to the authentic Cody and amplified real press coverage of him as a guide and scout. As interest in the West and in Buffalo Bill grew, New York playwright Fred Maeder adapted the novel for the stage as a play called simply *Buffalo Bill* in early 1872. It was staged at the Bowery Theatre, a popular venue with the working-class Irish and other immigrant populations. Cody himself was present on opening day and he was invited to the stage to speak. In a cataclysmic moment, when the audience met the real Buffalo Bill, the actor's version and the real man's character were difficult to distinguish.

Meanwhile, Buntline had maintained connection with Cody. After the success of *Buffalo Bill,* he encouraged Cody later that year to come East to take the role of Buffalo Bill in his new play, *Scouts of the Prairie.* Cody eventually assented and went to Chicago with a young, light brown–haired, blue-eyed cowboy-turned-scout, John Burwell "Texas Jack" Omohundro Jr. The two men were joined by a group of other actors including Italian dancer Giuseppina Morlacchi and actress Elve Carfano. Both Cody and Omohundro were cast as themselves in a plot that included Irish, German, and Mormon negative stereotypes; Indian dancing and fighting; the daring rescue of a white woman; and, more important, featured Texas Jack as a scout with impeccable lassoing skills. For the first time, Eastern audiences were introduced to a "real cowboy."

Melodrama and plays about the Western frontier were new in the 1870s. Buntline's original novel, his play, and the stylized performances of historical characters reflected a working-class turn toward theatrical interpretation of popular issues and demonstrated commercial medias that could capitalize on the public's particular curiosity of frontier life. Additionally, popular reviews reported both Cody and Omohundro as exceptionally handsome men whose "bearing and glances mark their long familiarity with the free life of the prairie." Riding this crest of popular culture, Buntline saw means to promote his theater troupe by using his stage characters in his serialized dime novels. Cody and the recently married Omohundro and Morlacchi performed in three more of Buntline's plays. Buntline underscored their stage personas in print, taking special interest in Omohundro's cowboy skills in *Texas Jack; or, Buffalo Bill's Brother* and *Texas Jack, the White King of the Pawnees,* and *Texas Jack's Chums; or, The Whirlwind of the West.* Both a promotional tool and an entertainment in its own right, the dime novel offered a mass readership an image and an invitation to see an authentic cowboy hero of the West.

Cody was not a cowboy. However, prior to his theatre experience he had honed a reputation as an elite hunting guide and frontier showman. He had designed a series of celebrity buffalo hunting tours that included army escorts, staged Indian participation, and riding and shooting lessons as well as lavish accommodations, fine food, and evening entertainment. In this fashion, by 1872, he had already led several groups of American businessmen and political leaders as well as the European royals Lord Adair, Earl of Dunraven, of Britain and the Grand Duke Alexis, son of Russian Tsar Alexander II, on well-publicized big-game hunts. The hunts delivered an impression of the West that had all the features of dime novel excitement. The press, however, reported the events as true to Western life and in doing so, confirmed Cody's authority of the region. He even began to distribute photographs of himself in full frontiersman's regalia with his hunting trophies or with groups of hunters who wanted to remember their Western adventure. By the time Buffalo Bill Cody was cheered to the Bowery Theatre's stage, the audience already understood his image of the West as truth.

Over the next decade he built a successful theater troupe of his own, "The Buffalo Bill Combination." His performances repeated the common melodramatic theme of the capture and daredevil rescue of a white, virtuous woman and always featured Cody as Buffalo Bill. The shows met packed, typically male, audiences ready to cheer and applaud the actor's heroism. Cody's popularity encouraged further dime novel tales. He produced several of his own and Ned Buntline offered a few more issues, but a prolific Beadle & Adams writer, Prentiss Ingraham, pushed out Buffalo Bill tales and later cowboy dime Westerns well into the 1890s.

The Wild West

Cody took full advantage of the popularity of his persona. Proving both a keen sense of business as well as showmanship, he created a new form of traveling public entertainment that combined the melodrama of theater and the thrill of dime novel action. His show took place in an outdoor arena that emulated the authentic intrigue, dangers, and tribal mystique of the Western frontier. With the help of talented performer Nate Salsbury, who eventually became his stage manager, Cody introduced an outdoor variety show called the "Old Glory Blowout" on 4 July 1882 in his hometown of North Platte, Nebraska. The original show featured hundreds of cowboy contestants in shooting, riding, and bronco-busting events and a small herd of buffalo was used for a mock hunt. On the heels of the success of this event and his stage career, Cody aimed to package his show as authentic, educational entertainment.

In 1883, the show opened in Omaha, Nebraska, as "The Wild West." Quickly becoming "Buffalo Bill's Wild West," it featured a range of acts meant to demonstrate Western life. Although the show's souvenir program underscored the performance's realism, Cody's production employed working cowboys to act in renditions of Western conflicts in which they would rarely, if ever, have participated. In "The Deadwood Stagecoach Attack" and in "The Attack on the Settler's Cabin," Buffalo Bill and a band of cowboys fought off Indian attackers and in another act, "Cowboy Fun," cowboys exhibited their riding and roping skills but without cattle. All three of these acts remained in the program over the course of the show's phenomenal nearly thirty-year run.

In Cody's fictionalized arena, the popular perception of cowboys as renegade and violent was replaced with an image of a hardworking and just hero who helped to extend civilization across the country. Cody purposefully separated his performers from the reigning negative national stereotype. In print, in his first program he included an article written earlier by Texas Jack Omohundro that insisted the cowboy had been "little appreciated" and misunderstood as a cattle rustler and instead was truly a hardworking, honest man who deserved respect. In action, cowboys conquered wild, raiding Indians and were staged in skits that set white cowboys against vaquero-style cattle rustlers.

The process of making the cowboy an appealing champion of the arena dramatically distanced him from his authentic working ancestry. The cowboy hero became racially white, and instead of cattle he protected the physically weak but socially and economically powerful westerly march of Eastern culture. Cody's production gave flesh to the action hero depicted in dime novels in the form of the cowboy. As a group, his cast represented a national guard. In a stirring presentation, as the show's finale, Cody and his cast would gallop around the arena beneath a banner that claimed them as "Rough Riders of the World." In individual skits, the audience saw the cowboy as defender of civilization. At one point, Cody hired a striking six-foot-five Texas cowboy, William Levi "Buck" Taylor. In the show, Taylor was promoted as "the Centaur Ranchman of the Plains" and then "King of the Cowboys." Taylor became the first cowboy star from Buffalo Bill's Wild West Show to be featured in a dime novel series. Prentiss Ingraham wrote the first issue, *Buck Taylor, King of the Cowboys; or, The Raiders and the Rangers*, in 1887.

The Cowgirl Makes Her Entrance

For Cody, his audiences readily received his rendition of a cowboy as a general character or as a celebrity like Taylor. In 1885, when he hired a young woman sharpshooter from Ohio who called herself Annie Oakley, he was in the position to formulate a popular image for Wild West women as well. Oakley joined Cody's cast when she was twenty-five and remained in the program for the most part of sixteen years. Her headlining performances as an expert shooter and as a skilled rider suggested a new position for women in the arena. In Cody's original acts, women were vulnerable matrons or young, screaming victims of Indian savagery. Oakley's stand-out skills placed her, instead, alongside the male heroes of the show. However, it was the combination of her risky athleticism and her on- and offstage emphasis on femininity, clean living, and devotion to her husband Frank Butler that led to her rapid popularity. At the same time she represented the virtues expected of women of the era, she called to mind the courageous women who were truly invested in the West as homesteaders and ranchers.

In performance, Oakley would girlishly skip and wave into the arena and throughout her career continued to wear modest calf-length dresses. Offstage she rarely drank, kept up a daily fitness routine, and on occasion gave tea parties and practiced needlepoint. On public record she promoted women's health through athletics and encouraged women's participation in "arenic" sports but openly remained outside of women's suffrage efforts. To both the women and the men in the Wild West audience her mastery of a traditionally male skill balanced with an unerringly feminine presentation made her an easily admirable figure. Oakley's overall appeal did enlarge Wild West audiences. She was a petite woman who ably handled the staged chaos of the show. Her presence gave the impression of safety and control, and, in turn, invited more women and families to enjoy the Wild West Show. Inspired by heightened publicity and the commercial return, Cody and stage manager Nate Salsbury hired more skilled women performers. For a short time Lillian Smith, another sharpshooter known as "the California Girl" rivaled Oakley in the arena. Unlike Oakley, she was flashy and flirtatious. After only two years, in 1889 she left Buffalo Bill's Wild West for a similar production. Georgia Duffy joined the cast in 1887. As a bronc rider she was billed as a "rough rider" from Wyoming but like Oakley, remained firm in her more traditional appearance. She wore a long dress with a corset but did dress up with boots and hat.

Bronc Riding

Bronc riding was a typical task for the open-range cowhand. Broncs, or horses that had never been saddled, tended to reject riders by arching and bucking. The perseverant cowhand could break the bronc by remaining on its back for consecutively longer periods of time. Wild West shows featured bronc riding as entertainment. American rodeos include bronc riding as a competition.

Let any normal healthy woman who is ordinarily strong screw up her courage and tackle a bucking bronco, and she will find the most fascinating pastime in the field of feminine athletic endeavor. There is nothing to compare, to increase the joy of living, and once accomplished, she'll have more real fun than any pink tea or theater party or ballroom ever yielded.
— May Manning Lillie

Over the course of the program, Cody advertised women participants under a variety of different names. Women were "Wild West Girls," "Prairie Women," "American Frontier Girls," and, at one time, "a bevy of beautiful Rancheras." Della and Bessie Ferrell were "frontier girls" and Emma Lake Hickok, stepdaughter of Wild Bill, demonstrated an "Exhibition of Fancy Riding." She amazed audiences with her riding skills as she performed in the horseback version of the traditional quadrille dance the Virginia Reel. Eventually, *cowgirl* became the most popular term for women in Wild West–style performances.

Wild West Shows Beyond Buffalo Bill

Buffalo Bill's Wild West Show was the first to present Western reenactment entertainment. His program set the tone and created parameters for "Western arena realism." His success encouraged other promoters to offer similar productions. Over the last decades of the nineteenth century and into the twentieth, there were countless small traveling shows and local reenactment celebrations. There were some that did reach similar popularity as Cody's design. In 1888, Gordon Lillie launched "Pawnee Bill's Historic Wild West" with his wife, sharpshooter and rider May Manning Lillie.

Gordon Lillie had been an agent and teacher at the Pawnee Indian reservation in Kansas. He had also been an avid dime novel reader. When William Cody came to the reservation in 1883 to recruit Pawnee for his show, Lillie signed on as an interpreter. When he opened his own show he maintained Cody's white cowboy versus outlaws or savages scenario though he pushed the scenes to a new limit of staged realism that often included circus-like gore. His acts included "Catching and Hanging the Horse Thief by Cowboys and Mexicans," and an Indian cremation ceremony. In another skit, a cattle rustler was dragged behind a team of horses. Lillie added further flair to his show with Chinese, Japanese, and Arab performers. Pawnee Bill's Historic Wild West failed as a large production but provided entertainment for smaller audiences. Lillie stayed in business into the nineteen-teens. His final venture was a merger with Buffalo Bill's Wild West in 1908 when Cody's show was flagging. The two Bills staged a show that combined Cody's heroic ensemble with Lillie's more exotic images. As "Buffalo Bill's Wild West and Pawnee Bill's Far East" the production continued until 1913.

Another successful Wild West show opened in 1905 when the Miller Brothers of the 101 Ranch began to produce large-scale Western reenactments on their 110,000 acres in the Oklahoma Territory. Their project, specifically designed as a tribute to what was perceived as a passing phase of American history, went on the road in 1907. The Millers were dedicated to an already nostalgic image of the cowboy and the West. The show carried a strong anti-Mexican sentiment and foreign-born, non-white actors were not welcome. Despite this apparent whitewashing of the West, or on account of it as a sign of the times, the 101 Ranch caught President Theodore Roosevelt's attention—he acknowledged their show as a realistic portrayal of the ranching life.

The Miller's show attracted cowboy and cowgirl performers from all over the country. By the 1880s, cowboy work was much less in demand. For men, traveling performance with steady pay was an attractive option over seasonal ranch work or laboring in the stockyards and meat-packing plants. For women in the early twentieth century social restrictions were relaxing. The advantages for women suggested in Buffalo Bill's production could be more easily played out. Women leaving home for Miller's Ranch were looking forward to their own incomes, the chance for travel alone or with husbands, and a life-style beyond the domestic sphere. Lucille Mulhall was a headlining performer with the 101 Ranch at the same time she was proving herself a champion on the early Western rodeo circuit. Mulhall had learned her roping and riding skills on her family's Oklahoma ranch and, at age twelve in 1897, she began appearing in public. In 1900 the press proclaimed Mulhall as "America's First Cowgirl."

Other women headed for the adventurous life that Miller's promised. Originally a rodeo contestant, at the turn of the century Lulu Belle Parr chose to focus all her attention on Wild West shows, including the Millers' production. She was one of the first cowgirl champion bronc riders and was known for her unique and elaborate riding outfits. Twins Juanita and Etheyle Parry from Riverhead, Long Island, made their way west in the early nineteen-teens. They performed as trick and fancy riders with the 101 Ranch company. Unfortunately, Juanita Parry was killed in a riding accident in New York City's Madison Square Garden during her performance in the Wild West segment of the Barnum and Bailey Circus.

Rodeo

At the same time Wild West shows were building a fictionalized world through inspiring and reassuring Western images, the parallel development of rodeo was offering a celebration of authentic ranching skills through competition. Key to the success of the Wild West shows was the notion that through the enactments they provided public historical education. In this light, the shared experience of spectators built a collective mythologized knowledge and memory of the West. Rodeo, on the other hand, began outside of the public sphere. It was originally a forum for ranch hands to socialize and prove their expertise. However, as rodeo evolved into a spectator sport, it took on some of the Wild West show's glamour as well as a sentimental tone of nostalgia. As it became more of a commercialized, consumable product, it offered outsiders an exaggerated glimpse of the physical prowess and open-air freedoms considered characteristic of the cowboy and cowgirl's trade.

Early rodeo-style competition can be traced back to eighteenth century vaquero traditions. After a day's work or during slow seasons hacienda vaqueros would informally compete. More structured steer-roping and bronc-riding competitions have been documented through the 1830s and 1840s in Mexican Texas and California. After the Civil War ranch crews were staging competitions across the American Southwest. Cowboy Teddy Blue Abbott remembered looking forward to the round-up season for its social aspects. Round-up season was a time for cowboys not only to work but also to catch up on gossip, gamble, compete in horse races, bronc riding, and roping contests. Testament to its Mexican and round-up origins, the term "rodeo" comes from the Spanish *rodear* or "to surround." In 1888, Prescott, Arizona, held the first rodeo on record to charge admission and award trophies to its winning contestants. Among countless local and regional rodeos, two of the largest events, Cheyenne, Wyoming's "Frontier Days" and Pendleton, Oregon's "Pendleton Roundup," begun in 1897 and 1911 respectively, are still major competitions and well-attended events.

Rodeos became a combination of traditional skills, sport, and theatrics. Some early male rodeo contestants had experience as working cowboys although women who had not traditionally been hired cowhands honed their skills in ranch chores and demonstrated them at local fairs. This was the case for Lucille Mulhall who succeeded both as a rodeo steer-roping champion and Wild West headliner with Miller's 101 Ranch. Later, in the 1912 Pendleton Roundup, another 101 Ranch star Tillie Baldwin amazed audiences with bulldogging and other rodeo feats.

Bulldogging

Bulldogging became a rodeo event that mimicked a bulldog's herding instinct. Bulldogs, specially bred with flat noses and extended under bites, could follow roaming cattle into hard-to-reach thorny areas. The dog menaced the cow until it lowered its horns to fend off its small attacker. Once in this position the dog could latch onto the soft tissues of the cow's face and subdue the animal until a cowhand with a rope could reach the stray.

Bill Pickett, an Oklahoma cowboy of black and Indian descent, performed with the 101 Ranch and was integral in the formation of rodeo competition. In 1905, Pickett was the first to demonstrate a technique called "bulldogging" in which a contestant brought down a steer by leaping onto its back from a running horse, twisting the animal's head then biting its lip or nose to bring it to the ground. This technique was modified, especially in women's events, to using only the twisting motion to bring the animal down. In the early 1900s, a young Pennsylvania-born hopeful joined Miller's company and formed himself into both a Western showman and rodeo contestant. Later, Tom Mix would take his cowboy persona to the silent screen and become one of the most renowned cowboy performers of all time.

Women and Rodeo

Interestingly, at the turn of the century rodeo offered men and women the same opportunities. In her informative text *Cowgirls of the Rodeo*, Mary Lou LeCompte points out that the equal treatment received by women in rodeo reflected the same family-run ranch ethic in which everyone, regardless of gender, participates. Rodeo cowgirls competed against men in bronc riding and steer roping and entered relay racing, trick riding, and trick roping contests. Women's events were popular. They were featured at the major rodeos and usually a part of smaller-scale functions. Rodeo cowgirls were the first American women athletes to receive pay for their participation. It is estimated that from 1890 and into the 1930s, more than 450 women held professional careers in rodeo.

Rodeo changed for women during the Depression years. With decreases in financial backing, rodeos cut women's events. In 1924 at the Pendleton Roundup a group of champion cowgirls including steer-roping record-setter Eloise "Fox" Hastings and one of the first Cheyenne Frontier Days cowgirl bronc riders, Prairie Rose Henderson, petitioned to compete in all the same events as cowboys and for the same prize money. Their request was denied. Additionally, in 1929 at Pendleton, bronc rider and crowd favorite Bonnie McCarroll was trampled to death in the ring. Her death, following others that were equally tragic, spurred a movement to eliminate women from all bronc-riding competitions. Pendleton complied and others followed. Rodeo women experienced further setbacks when that same year the Rodeo Association of America formed and neglected to set rules that would allow women to continue to compete. Finally, in 1936, the Cowboys' Turtle Association, later the Professional Rodeo Cowboy's Association (PRCA), formed and excluded women entirely. Without a place in the professional organization of the sport, by the early 1940s women's participation as contestants was at a low. Through the World War II years, women were less active in the arena as contestants and more often presented as "sponsor girls," who, often chosen for their appearance, took part in exhibitions and other supportive aspects of the rodeo. After the war, women in rodeo pushed to return to the arena. In 1948 the Girls Rodeo Association, later the Women's Professional Rodeo Association, was established. The group succeeded first in placing women's barrel-racing competitions into the programs of larger professional rodeos and by 1967 had secured barrel racing as an event at the most prestigious rodeo competition, the PRCA's National Finals Rodeo. Today, barrel-racing women are some of the highest rewarded rodeo contestants and women's participation in other PRCA events, though not without obstacles, is on the rise.

Barrel Racing

Barrel racing is a women's event designed specifically for rodeo competition. The rider and horse loop in a cloverleaf pattern around three barrels placed in a triangle. With the clock as the judge, the contest requires exquisite riding skills, a sure-footed horse, and practiced communication between horse and rider.

THE COWBOY CAPTURES THE AMERICAN IMAGINATION

At the end of the nineteenth century and into the twentieth, Wild West and rodeo cowboys and cowgirls headlined across the nation. In a single generation, the signature characteristics of open-range ranching had become traditions of the past. The men and women who experienced the closing of the range also witnessed the introduction of a mythologized interpretation of the West. As national concerns changed, it was the image of the fictionalized rugged cowboy that replaced the Indian fighter and scout as a public protector. Popular culture had reinforced the West as a place that required physical strength, industriousness, and knowledge of the land. More important, the West was also understood as the antidote to the reformist and domesticated urbanized East. It was a masculine realm that upheld silence, space, and free will. Popular imagination saw the cowboy as embodiment of these qualities. Needless to say, women's authentic and fictionalized experiences on the range were eclipsed as the cowboy became the heroic provider of safe passage across the rough Western land.

The Cowboy and Literature

To a nation dedicated to the extension of Eastern cultural thought across the West, the image of the cowboy as part of the West and as an escort across it was indispensable. When historian Frederick Jackson Turner announced, at a meeting of the American Historical Association held at the World's Columbian Exposition in Chicago in 1893, that the frontier had been pushed as far west as possible and was now closed, the academic world turned toward this cowboy image for reassurance.

Turner's frontier was a westward-moving geographic line that lay between "savagery and civilization." Turner stated that the frontier's "existence, its continuous recession, and the advance of American settlement westward, explain[ed] American development." To Turner and other theorists who saw the American national character to be a result of a Euro-American settlement process, the closing of the frontier put American national identity in crisis. In response, American elite educated circles elevated the cowboy from his popular image into more sophisticated cultural expressions. Although artists Frederic Remington and Charles Russell centralized the cowboy in both celebrations of the West and in melancholy images of its passing, author Owen Wister went further. More than featuring the cowboy as the human actor on the range, in his 1902 publication of *The Virginian*, he imbued his cowboy character with the archetypical qualities understood to be the range.

Very loosely built on the tensions of the Johnson County, Wyoming, Range Wars *The Virginian* is primarily a romance. Wister's cowboy, the Virginian, who is never named, is strong, silent, and quick-witted. His pursuit and courtship of the recently arrived Eastern schoolmarm drives the story. *The Virginian* sold 50,000 copies in the first two months. The popularity of the novel was integral to the shift that turned the cowboy of popular culture from a Western hero to a national icon.

The Johnson County War

At its height in 1892, disagreements between small homesteaders and large, wealthy ranchers in Johnson County, Wyoming, had escalated into armed civil conflict. Smaller ranchers accused of rustling cattle from the larger operations chose to retaliate by driving their cattle to market instead of participating in the big-business marriage between wealthy ranchers and the railroad lines. Larger ranchers, already determined to acquire homesteaders' land and further angered by their effective efforts to organize, hired a band of mercenaries to remove the local ranchers from the area. Known as the Johnson County War, murders, hangings, and shoot-outs ensued between the hired killers and a local sheriff's posse until President Benjamin Harrison sent the U.S. Cavalry to intervene.

Beyond his romantic motivations, the Virginian exemplifies the transformation from the limited future of the Southeast to the realized masculine potential on the Western range. Strains of the Virginian's Southeastern birth are retained in his slow drawl and courteous air but he has fully dedicated himself to life in the West. Although striking good looks and a fine physique firmly establish him as the cowboy hero of popular culture, his ease of movement across the wilderness, loyalty to his rancher boss, and his own plans for acquiring land expand his character. Moreover, his perseverant and controlled passion for the schoolteacher and ability to disarm his adversaries with a sharp wit and cool demeanor underscore a current of virility admired by both men and women.

In an era that upheld geographic expansion and revived masculinity as crucial to American national identity, the Virginian became a vessel to hold and demonstrate these Western ideals. Late-nineteenth-century medicine had identified a nervous condition brought on by anxieties of the urban life called "neurasthenia." Studied and publicized by "nerve doctor" Silas Weir Mitchell, his prescription for a cure was based on gender, overtly supporting the Victorian premise of male and female spheres. For neurasthenic women, he recommended the return to domestic life including bed rest and removal from public life. For men, however, he suggested Western travel, grappling with nature, and self-discovery through literature and exploration.

Among many late-nineteenth-century Western travelers, Wister was diagnosed as a neurasthenic. His travels became the foundation for his writing and it was not a coincidence that he created his exquisitely male cowboy character at the same time as the theoretical closing of the West. For those concerned about the loss of the frontier, the Virginian—the "young giant, more beautiful than pictures"—preserved its revivifying qualities. In the "Letter to the Reader" that serves as the novel's introduction, Wister writes that he tells a story of "a vanished world," one that has succumbed to the inevitable transformation from agrarianism to industrialism. This imagined emasculation by the loss of the frontier is reversed through Wister's exaltation of the cowboy, the "last romantic figure on our soil." In this figure, the potency and promise of the open range remains accessible.

Owen Wister firmly established the image of the cowboy as a heroic and intrinsically American character. Western fiction that followed Wister's cowboy took cues from the Virginian's rugged masculine grace. Like Wister, Clarence Mulford was an Easterner who was known for his well-designed Western tales that centered on courageous cowboy heroes whose riding skills and gunslinger natures drove the storylines. Most remembered for his Hopalong Cassidy cowboy hero, Mulford was at the helm of the new genre of Western fiction. Using popular cowboy autobiographies and other published information that offered images of life in the West, he published over forty Westerns. In 1912, Zane Grey secured his position in the Western written genre with *Riders of the Purple Sage*, in which his virile, gun-savvy, romantic, and sympathetic cowboy protects Protestant America against corrupt Mormon forces. Close to two million copies were sold and Grey went on to write fifty-six more top-selling Western novels. With similar swagger, Frederick Schiller-Faust, also known as Max Brand, pushed the cowboy-against-villain scenario into the modern era of the 1920s. Other early Western writers chose to illuminate the cowboy's connection to his environment. Although the cowboy's trail-riding life and pioneering experiences were exalted by Emerson Hough and Frank Spearman, the poetic prose of Harvey Fergusson and former cowboy Eugene Manlove Rhodes offer further romantic impressions of the cowboy's labor and his place in nature. The many-faceted cowboy hero of the early Western genre provided foundation for modern interpretations of his place in society. Later twentieth century writer Louis L'Amour often placed his cowboy in defiant stance against the decadence and amoral directives of big business while Larry McMurtry, in his 1985 Pulitzer Prize–winning Western *Lonesome Dove*, removed the glamour of the West, making his cowboys susceptible to the nuances and dangers of the range.

Less well known are the early twentieth century Western literary selections written by women that feature ranching women. Essentially a subgenre of the standard Western novel, women authors began producing domestic Westerns. In 1908 Bertha Muzzy Bower launched her *Flying U Ranch* series that upheld competent ranching women and other professionals. Bower wrote for thirty years. Her works, including this fifteen book series as well as over fifty other novels and 150 shorter stories, reached a readership of two million. As a best-selling author, her novels matched the success of some of the more popular male writers.

Bower's domestic Westerns rarely featured a truly independent female character. Writing from a modern perspective, most of her women were professionals and often associated with ranch management. Other women authors of domestic Westerns featured more specifically riding, roping, shooting cowgirl characters equally adept at leading wagon trains and running ranches as they were with household tasks. However, the heroines' competence in these novels was emphasized as a support structure for her male counterpart. Most of these female characters were married or planned to marry and honored the traditional domestic relationship.

After World War II, the premise of the domestic Western was revised. Reflecting the rising number of women in the workforce, domestic Westerns featured business-minded women who maintain their individuality as single people or within marriages. Among many women writers who developed this new image for female characters, Vingie E. Roe set an original example in *The Golden Tide* (1940) and Lillian Bos Ross followed with *The Stranger* (1942). Roe's novel features a group of Western women who find strength in their numbers and, although many wish to marry, they are all more interested in personal exploration and career opportunities. Ross's heroine is a mail-order bride who challenges her husband's expectations of marriage and eventually changes his mind.

In spite of the legacy of women writers who pushed the edges of the Western literature, there is no doubt that male authors dominated the genre. The social concerns and theoretical projections of the day extolled a male hero in a male environment. Overshadowed by ideology, fictionalized Western women heroines would remain characters confined to text while the male cowboy hero's Western life became integral in the definition of the American experience.

The Cowboy in Early American Film

At the same time that Wister was elevating the cowboy from the melodramatic and inflated heroism of the Wild West and rodeo arenas, the nascent

American silent film industry presented the first on-screen narrative. *The Great Train Robbery* produced in 1903 was a Western. Although it was filmed in rural New Jersey, it featured cowboy heroes who fought off train robbers. The film's popularity was an opportunity to transfer the popular and new literary Western genres immediately to film. The first decades of the twentieth century were filled with Western action-adventure film cowboys. Typically performing in non-stop demonstrations of athleticism and bravery, among many early silent Western actors, Max Aronson (who became Gilbert "Broncho Billy" Anderson), William S. Hart, and Tom Mix offered a range of heroic cowboy swagger.

Max Aronson as Broncho Billy created the first film cowboy hero. After a small role in *The Great Train Robbery*, Aronson changed his name to Gilbert Anderson and co-founded the Essanay production company. Despite his average appearance, he cast himself as the lead character in most of the company's 375 films. In the role of Broncho Billy he attracted an ardent following as the good-bad cowboy or the hard living man who finds reason to change his ways permanently or temporarily to help a less fortunate.

William S. Hart refined Anderson's character. As a trained Shakespearian actor he brought subtlety and emotional projection to the good-bad cowboy. He also was devilishly handsome by the standards of the era. His real acting ability and physical appeal resonated well with popular understanding of the cowboy hero. Hart quickly became one of the first idolized movie stars. Cowboy and memoirist Charlie Siringo admired Hart for his honorable portrayal of a "bad cowboy turned good." In a unique exchange between the authentic cowboy and his fictionalized counterpart, the two became friends. In 1924, Hart hired Siringo as a consultant on Western life for his final film, *Tumbleweeds*.

Tom Mix followed Hart's film success but departed from the well-established good-bad man. Hardly a trained actor, Mix began with Miller's 101 Ranch and rodeo competition. In exaggerated Western attire he played a straightforward action hero and he did his own stunts. His cowboy character appealed to a younger audience, especially boys. In response, Mix's films focused on the chase over actual violence and scenes of the seedier side of cowboy life were reduced. Eventually appearing in over 300 films between 1909 and 1935, he became a true superstar. As an actor and public persona he was featured in a comic book series and on cereal boxes. By the end of his film career, he leased his name to a weekly radio series and to the Tom Mix Wild West Circus.

Anderson, Hart, and Mix were the reigning cowboys of the silent screen. By the late 1920s, a new type of on screen cowboy hero appeared. After World War I, the hero of Western melodramatic silent film gave way to a less flamboyant, more controlled cowboy. He was built on Wister's Virginian, Grey's Lassiter, and other literary heroes as well as the masculine worlds of influential wilderness writers Jack London and Ernest Hemingway. The new on-screen cowboy was pensive and lean. He was cool yet simmered with masculinity.

With the exciting onset of sound film his silence was emphasized by limited dialogue. Actor Gary Cooper launched his career as this cowboy, successfully portraying the Virginian in a 1929 film adaptation of Wister's novel. John Wayne carried this character in over 200 films over the course of his thirty-year career. From his early star appeal in the classic film *Stagecoach* (1939) to his seasoned leadership in *Red River* (1948), and from his loner attitude and aggressive perseverance in *The Searchers* (1956) to his paternal presentation in *The Cowboys* (1972), Wayne's cowboy character and the actor himself dominated as a symbol of mental agility and physical prowess.

During the World War II years, the cowboy image took on a moralizing component. During the Depression movie houses felt the pinch as attendance dropped. In an effort to make cinema more enticing, the double feature was introduced. Inexpensively made "B-Westerns" were churned out to supply second films. By the 1940s, actors had played the same role so often their characters, like Buffalo Bill Cody experienced a half century before, blurred with their real identities. In this light, singing cowboy characters Roy Rogers and Gene Autry picked up where Tom Mix had left off. The actors themselves were seen as the squeaky-clean characters they played. Appealing primarily to young boys, teenage girls, and family audiences, through the 1940s and into the 1950s these actors set aside the grit of the West and instead promoted health, hygiene, and the upstanding life.

The cowboy of film is perpetually reincarnated. As the image moved into the later twentieth century, its formulaic parameters became less rigid. In Robert Altman's *McCabe and Mrs. Miller* (1971), more complex issues obstruct a standard plot of heroic shootout and rescue. In Clint Eastwood's version of *Unforgiven* (1992) the central character mocks his own imperfect skills, and in Kevin Costner's *Dances with Wolves* (1990) the central cowboy-type character faces his loss of patriotism. Challenging traditional perspectives even further, the characters and audiences of both John Schlesinger's *Midnight Cowboy* (1969) and Ang Lee's *Brokeback Mountain* (2005) are asked to face sexuality issues. The cowboy in film still resonates as a hero but one built with facets of human fallibility, not simply formed on mythologized masculine inclination.

The Cowboy in American Politics

Although Wister was boosting the cowboy into more literary circles and *The Great Train Robbery* was amazing cinema audiences, the cowboy hero was making its way into national politics as well. Theodore Roosevelt went west in the 1880s for inspiration after the sudden loss of both his wife and mother. He spent time as a ranch hand then as a rancher in the Dakota Territory. As a historian, he upheld the buckskin-wearing cowboy as an extension of the heroic frontiersman who began the advance of white civilization across the continent. In his own frontier thesis, he found the cowboy to be an essential part of building the economic viability of the West. Ultimately, as an American male in search of vigor, Roosevelt found value in the hard work and outdoor life of the herdsman and adopted the cowboy's style as his own.

In addition to his personal experiences, Roosevelt recognized the mass appeal of the heroic cowboy image. During his tour with the U.S. Cavalry during the Spanish-American War, he borrowed from Buffalo Bill's Wild West when he led his "Rough Rider" regiment of Western cowboy recruits in Cuba in the Battle of San Juan Hill. When he became president after the assassination of William McKinley he continued to hone his Western persona. On his presidential trips back west he publicized his horseback rides, hunting expeditions, and rodeo attendance. As a result Roosevelt was well received by cowboy communities who treated him to "chuck wagon" breakfasts and provided escort in presidential parades and through populated areas. At his 1905 inauguration, Roosevelt honored the group of fifty cowboys who celebrated his election with invitations to the White House where he greeted them along with a group of Harvard graduates and a few former Rough Riders.

Roosevelt became the first "cowboy president." His association with authentic cowboys coupled with his Western-style presentation had a lasting impression in the Oval Office. Roosevelt had successfully combined the qualities of the popular and more sophisticated character into a national image that unexpectedly drew political support. As a Rough Rider he emulated the Wild West cowboys who paved the way for civilization, as a political candidate he represented the competitive spirit of rodeo, and as an ersatz Westerner who found value in the "strenuous life" and promoted "virile qualities necessary to win in . . . actual life" he reflected the nostalgic and romantic cowboy-master of the range.

At first, Roosevelt's association with the West was met with a negative public response. The cowboy image had only recently been recognized in more elite social circles and still implied unrefined recklessness. When Roosevelt took office, Republican senator Mark Hanna of Ohio expressed a concern held by many with his near-legendary comment, "Now look! That damned cowboy is president." However, it did not take long for Roosevelt's personality and evident political competence to earn him praise. A *New York Times* editorial found him unique, energetic, and equally capable as a soldier, a Western cowboy and rancher, and a distinguished scholar. By the time Wister's *The Virginian* became a national bestseller, Roosevelt's cowboy persona took on new meaning as a symbol of the charismatic American everyman. For publicity and personal interest, presidents that followed Roosevelt maintained a connection to Western imagery. A judge and man of letters, President William Howard Taft expressed an interest in horseback riding. Despite his 300 pounds, he spent vacation time at his half-brother's Texas ranch. Former university professor Woodrow Wilson enjoyed Western films and the sharp-witted political commentary of cowboy comedian Will Rogers.

Later twentieth-century presidents followed the trend. Texan Lyndon B. Johnson celebrated his ancestral connection to trail-riding cowboys. He brought his saddle to the White House, used his Texas property as a political retreat, and often appeared in public wearing informal Western attire. At the end of the Cold War it was Ronald Reagan, former cowboy film star and skilled rider, who took the cowboy image back to the height of Theodore Roosevelt. As president during the collapse of the Soviet Union, Reagan epitomized the heroism of the freedom-loving, independent American cowboy. Most recently, amid bipartisan concern over the image suggesting an overly simplified perception of hero and villain, George W. Bush has taken on the cowboy persona in a similar manner as Johnson. Bush has upheld the image especially following the 11 September 2001 terrorist attack in New York City and Washington, DC, during the Republican National Convention in 2004 as well as throughout the U.S. military offensive in Afghanistan, Iraq, and across the Middle East.

In only half a century, the American cowboy was transformed from an itinerant laborer to an internationally recognized symbol of power and freedom. The iconic American cowboy emerged from the conflation of the mass-marketed dime novel with Wild West show reenactment and from the convergence of literary interpretation, political posturing, and the theoretical closing of the frontier. The cowgirl is absent from this lasting mythology. Although popular expression pushed the cowgirl image into view, she remained a novel, or at times exotic extension of the masculine, fictional West. It is the ideologically driven image of the male cowboy and his Western world that took root at the core of American identity. Today, the specialized worlds of women's rodeo, country music, and women's activist groups separately celebrate the cowgirl as a subculture heroine of independence and equality. On a broader scale, as both an icon and a device, the cowboy remains a powerful image that reflects the concerns of the nation and suggests idealized, romanticized solutions.

FURTHER READING

Brown, Bill (ed.). *Reading the West: An Anthology of Dime Westerns* (Boston: Bedford Books, 1997).

Dary, David. *Cowboy Culture* (Lawrence: University of Kansas Press, 1981, 1989).

Hine, Robert V., and John Mack Faragher. *The American West* (New Haven, CT: Yale University Press, 2000).

Laegreid, Renee M. *Riding Pretty: Rodeo Royalty in the American West* (Lincoln: University of Nebraska Press, 2006).

LeCompte, Mary Lou. *Cowgirls of the Rodeo* (Chicago: University of Chicago Press, 2000).

Massey, Sarah R. *Texas Women on the Cattle Trail* (College Station: Texas A&M Press, 2006).

Reddin, Paul. *Wild West Shows* (Chicago: University of Illinois Press, 1999).

Savage, William W. *Cowboy Life* (Norman: University of Oklahoma Press, 1975).

Wallman, Jeffrey. *The Western* (Lubbock: Texas Tech University Press, 1999).

Warren, Louis S. *Buffalo Bill's America* (New York: Alfred A. Knopf, 2005).

Watts, Sarah. *Rough Rider in the White House* (Chicago: University of Chicago Press, 2006).

Wood-Clark, Sarah. *Beautiful Daring Western Girls, Women of the Wild West Shows* (Billings, MT: Buffalo Bill Historical Center Artcraft Printers, 1991).

General George A. Custer. Courtesy of Library of Congress.

George Armstrong Custer

Shannon D. Smith

Long after this generation has passed away, long after every vestige of the merciless Sioux has passed from the continent, long after this Yellowstone country has become the seat of towns and cities and a prosperous civilization, the name of Custer and the story of his deeds will be fresh in men's memories. The story that comes to us to-day with so much horror, with so much pathos, will become a part of our national life.
—*New York Herald*, 12 July 1876

George Armstrong Custer was an officer of the United States Army during the Civil War and Plains Indian Wars. The flamboyant, ambitious officer was famous, and infamous, well before his last fatal conflict with Indians on 25 June 1876 at the Battle of the Little Bighorn that is universally known as "Custer's Last Stand." For decades after his death, Custer was lionized by the American public, and his image as an exceptional officer and perfect Victorian gentleman was jealously guarded and managed by his wife Elizabeth "Libbie" Bacon Custer. She published three major books and countless articles lauding her husband's life in the fifty-seven years she survived him. Custer is a Western icon not only for the reality of his actions in the Civil War and on the Western frontier, he is iconic because his romanticized, larger-than-life story—one that has evolved from over a century of myth-building—has come to represent America's changing perception of the U.S. expansion into the West. He remains one of the most fascinating, controversial, and recognizable characters in Western history and is a prominent subject of military scholars, Western historians, fan clubs, historical reenactors, and the popular media. Writers frequently point out that more books and articles have been written about Custer than any other American, with the possible exception of Abraham Lincoln.

EARLY LIFE

Custer's parents, Emanuel Henry Custer and Marie Ward Kirkpatrick, were married in 1836. They were both widowed and their marriage merged his three children with her two to form the new family. Emanuel Custer was a blacksmith and farmer of Pennsylvania Dutch background who followed family members from his birthplace in Maryland to New Rumley, Ohio, a frontier town laid out by his uncle two decades earlier. The Custers had two children who died as infants before George Armstrong Custer was born in New Rumley on 5 December 1839. The blended family was not unusual in that era and Custer later said of his older siblings that he could not recall who was his mother's or his father's. After George, who was called "Autie" because that was how he pronounced his middle name as a toddler, the Custers had four more children: Nevin, Thomas, Boston, and Margaret. Biographers agree that the Custer family was playful and fun-loving, an unusual characteristic among the normally prim, formal, even harsh, German-descended Pennsylvania Dutch. His father frequently played practical jokes on his children that became a trait of the entire Custer family, especially George who was a notorious prankster throughout his life.

Upright men in frontier communities belonged to local militias and Emanuel Custer was no exception. He took four-year-old George to the meetings of the "New Rumley Invincibles" where the boy wore a velvet suit with showy buttons made by his older sister Lydia. Soon he was marching and holding a weapon exactly as described in the manual of arms, and the militiamen were said to have called him "a born soldier." Custer's father was religious—he helped found the community's Methodist Church—and a man with strong political opinions that he voiced freely and frequently. He was proud to be a well-known Democrat in a region of Whigs where he enjoyed debating the political issues of the day with anyone who would listen. When Custer was still quite young, his family moved a farm outside of New Rumley where Emanuel kept up his blacksmith business. Growing up on a farmstead in the middle of ten children shaped George into a strong and vigorous young man. He and his brothers wrestled, fought, teased, played hard, and worked hard. When he attended school a few months every year, Custer was known as a good athlete with a happy disposition, though not necessarily a great student.

Democrats versus Whigs

During Andrew Jackson's presidency (1829–1837) the first well-organized political parties came into existence. The Democratic Party, with Jackson himself as the rallying point, brought about radical changes, including a presidency that for the first time threatened to overshadow Congress. Prior to Jackson, the presidential veto had been interpreted as something the president could only do if he considered a bill unconstitutional, but Jackson eventually established the precedent that the president could veto a bill on basically any grounds.

The Whig party was formally organized in 1834, bringing together a loose coalition of diverse groups united in their opposition to what they called the tyranny of the president, "King Andrew" Jackson. For most of its history, the party was concerned with promoting internal improvements, such as roads, canals, railroads, deepening of rivers, etc. This was of interest to many Westerners in this period, isolated as they were and in need of markets. Abraham Lincoln was a Whig for most of this period.

On the other hand, Democrats of this era supported states' rights and were generally opposed to limitations on slavery in the south. The Whig Party ultimately broke down as a result of sectional antagonism over slavery and states' rights and by 1854 most northern Whigs had joined the newly formed Republican Party and southerners joined the Democrats.

When he was ten, Custer's oldest sister, Lydia, married David Reed and moved to Monroe, Michigan. Lydia soon became homesick and convinced her parents to send George to live with her. Unlike the Custer family's relative prominence in New Rumley, the Reeds were not considered part of the upper-class society of Monroe. This made a lasting impression on Custer. While doing yard work and other odd jobs for one of the town's most powerful and wealthy citizens, Judge Daniel S. Bacon, he met Elizabeth Bacon, known by everyone as Libbie. Custer hung around the Bacon house as much as possible but was never received or allowed to formally meet Libbie because he was not of the Bacon's social class.

At fourteen, Custer entered Alfred Stebins's Young Men's Academy. By now, he had developed the ambition and drive for which he would later become famous; he finished at the top of his class when he graduated two years later. He then obtained a position teaching in a one-room schoolhouse not far from New Rumley, where his salary included room and board with a well-to-do farmer. There Custer fell in love with a farmer's daughter, Mary Holland. Acutely aware that social standing was a major factor in life—reinforced by his experience with the Bacons and Holland's father's apparent disapproval of his relationship with Mary—Custer decided to apply to the United States Military Academy at West Point. There he could get a free education and his position as a soon-to-be officer would give him immediate social standing—a necessity if he hoped to marry into the Holland family. Custer had to overcome long odds to get the appointment, for he was the son of a prominent Democrat and the local congressman, John A. Bingham, was a Republican. Fortunately, Holland, who seems to have wanted distance between Custer and his daughter, was a powerful Republican and pulled strings with his friend Bingham and Custer received one of Ohio's appointments for 1857. His mother was not happy at the thought of her son being a soldier, but his father was extremely proud and supportive and sold the farm so he could give Custer $200 for expenses to travel to the academy in New York. Upon completion of his five-year program at the military academy, he would be an officer in the army and would be welcome in the highest society functions and received in homes where he was previously shunned. More than the desire for battle and military acumen, Custer desired status and social prominence.

WEST POINT

Custer was seventeen in 1857 when he entered West Point. Though he was younger than his classmates and weaker academically than many of his East Coast counterparts, Custer had more life experience. He had lived away from home, earned his own keep, and traveled more than most of the incoming class of cadets. He was physically fit, handsome, and meticulously groomed; indeed, his flamboyance was immediately evident to all who met him. But Custer's greatest strength was his personality and ability to make friends; he had a ready smile and was playful and constantly on the lookout to pull off a practical joke.

My career as a cadet had but little to recommend it to the study of those who came after me, unless as an example to be carefully avoided.

Much has been made of Custer's lackluster performance at the academy. He was last in his class, he barely graduated, and he was always in trouble. To remain at West Point, cadets were required to maintain their grades and were under constant observation to ensure strict adherence to military discipline. If a cadet acquired more than 100 demerit points—known as "skins" to academy insiders—in any six-month period, they were expelled. Custer is famous for having gone semester after semester with demerits in the high nineties. Typical skins for Custer were things like being late to supper, throwing snowballs, using a "loud and boisterous voice," and trifling in ranks while marching from parade. Famous for his wavy blonde hair, which he kept longer than his fellow students—he was called "Curly" or "Cinnamon" for the scented oil he used to groom it—Custer's long locks once cost him two demerits for "hair out of uniform at a guard meeting." Many have wondered how a student who was, to all appearances, undisciplined and completely indifferent to his studies and rank in class, became the man whose name is synonymous with ambition, determination, and drive for glory. However, recent evaluations suggest Custer was a very controlled jokester who knew exactly how many skins he had accumulated at any given time. In one six-month period he received ninety demerits within the first three months and went the remaining three months without a single one—a tremendous accomplishment for even the most diligent, focused cadet. His last semester he came closer to the limit than any previous period with ninety-seven skins, a feat demonstrating the control for which he had "trained" during the previous four years.

As for his studies, Custer did the bare minimum required for passing. Of 108 candidates for admission the year he entered West Point, only 68, including Custer, passed the entrance exam. Of the 68, only half graduated—22 cadets resigned to join the Southern cause at the start of the Civil War, and a dozen were expelled for academic or disciplinary causes. Of the remaining 34, Custer came in dead last. While his low rank might be attributed to sub-par preparatory education as compared to cadets from larger East Coast cities, it appears more likely Custer exercised the same amount of self-control demonstrated in his disciplinary highjinks. He always knew where he stood and did just enough to ensure he would not flunk out. His West Point years did, however, launch a lifetime of writing and it seems as if he knew he would be famous one day, for most of his prolific outpourings on paper were about himself and his adventures.

Although Custer was at the bottom of the class academically, he was at the top when it came to popularity. He was irrepressibly jovial and exuberant.

I knew Gen. Custer well; have known him intimately from boyhood, and, being on opposite sides during the late war, we often met and measured strength on the fields of Virginia, and I can truly say now that I never met a more enterprising, gallant or dangerous enemy during those four years of terrible war, or a more genial, whole-souled, chivalrous gentleman and friend in peace, than Major General George A. Custer.

—Brigadier General (Confederate States Army) Tom Rosser, Custer's West Point Classmate in "A Word for Custer. By Gen. Rosser, of Minneapolis, Formerly of the Confederate Army," *Daily Columbus Enquirer*, 13 July 1876

His classmates, above and below, loved him. Though the national polarization over slavery divided the academy, he was perfectly positioned to have friends from both sides of the political divide. Custer was a pro-South Democrat from Ohio and he believed that the greatest threat to the Union was the new Republican Party's hard-line stance on abolishing the expansion of slavery. However, he was thoroughly pro-Union, and though he counted many Southern cadets as his closest friends and he was not opposed to slavery, he believed secession was treason. Because he was so fun, outgoing, and happy-go-lucky and was friends with both Northern and Southern boys, he was one of the most popular cadets to come from the academy.

THE CIVIL WAR

When Custer entered West Point, cadets underwent a five-year program, but everything changed as Southern states started to secede the union. Soon, Southern and Northern cadets were faced with a daunting choice. Southern boys could resign their future commission with the army to return home and join either their state militia or the Confederate Army, both of which offered a substantially higher rank and pay scale than the cadets would have after graduation. A similar option was open to the young men from the North, their state's hastily assembling volunteer forces needed officers and they could enter higher ranked and higher paid than they could hope for in the regular army after graduation. Most grappled with breaking the oath of allegiance to the United States they took on entry to the academy as well as abandoning the years of sacrifice and hard work they had under their belt. Slowly but surely, however, the Southern boys, many of them Custer's closest friends, left to join the Confederate cause.

Cadets leaving for the war were exhilarated and eager to get to the battlefields. The boys who remained, including Custer, were miserable. They all believed this would be a quickly settled conflict and viewed it as an opportunity for recognition. The class ahead of Custer immediately petitioned the Secretary of War to be graduated a few months early, which was granted, and Custer's class followed suit. The War Department desperately needed officers to recruit and command the rapidly filling ranks of enlisted men, so permission was granted and on 24 June 1861 his class graduated one full year early.

A few days after their commencement, while waiting for their official orders and assignments to arrive, Custer was serving as Officer of the Guard when two younger cadets got in a fight. Rather than break up the ruckus, Custer ordered the boys to have at it in a fair fight. The Officer of the Day came upon the melee and immediately arrested Custer for neglect of duty. The next day, his classmates departed for active duty in Washington, DC, while Custer sat in the guardhouse waiting for his court-martial. Several of his classmates had powerful contacts in government who intervened on Custer's behalf and two weeks later he was released with a reprimand and orders to report immediately at the nation's capital.

THE BOY GENERAL

Custer's Civil War service launched his name into the public eye and into the world's history books. Even if he had not gone on to infamy in the Indian wars of the Great Plains, he would still be famous for his achievements and escapades on and off the field of battle. To understand the Custer of the West one needs to understand his Civil War experience—it shaped his every move during the last decade of his life on the frontier. Probably the greatest factor that influenced his decisions and brought him the fame and glory he sought was that he was so young—he was just twenty-one when the Civil War broke out. His excitement and enthusiasm for battle reflected the sense of immortality that accompanies youth. The fact that he remained unscathed while leading men in some of the most violent and chaotic battles of America's bloodiest war only served to increase his confidence. His audacious battlefield antics, coupled with the astonishing number of times he was in the right place at the right time, bolstered the young officer's reputation on and off the field and became known as "Custer's Luck."

From his first day of service, Custer was exposed to the war's highest commanders. In Washington, DC, he waited for hours in the chaotic halls of the frenzied war department before he finally met with the officer who would determine his assignment. The officer casually asked Custer if he would like to meet General Winfield Scott, the general-in-chief of the army, who had a well-known soft spot for West Point cadets. Of course, Custer was thrilled to meet the old general who was in charge of the entire army on his first official day as a commissioned officer. Like all of Custer's future commanders, Scott liked what he saw in the confident, high-spirited young man and offered him the opportunity to go directly to the front lines to deliver a personal dispatch to the commander of Union troops in Virginia, General Irvin McDowell. So, instead of drilling new recruits as he later found out his classmates were doing at that time, Custer rode to the front lines and was temporarily attached to McDowell's regiment and participated in the Battle of Bull Run, the first

*This officer is one of the
funniest looking beings you
ever saw, and looks like a
circus rider gone mad!*
—Lt. Col. Theodore Lyman, Gen.
George Meade's aide-de-camp,
describing Custer in a letter
to his family

major battle of the war. Although Bull Run was a complete defeat for the Union forces, battlefield reports mentioned the newly commissioned second lieutenant (commonly referred to as a "shavetail" in the army) and his outstanding leadership and bravery displayed on the field. The shavetail did not remain so for long, as Custer was soon promoted to first lieutenant. While his fellow cadets remained in the capital city, the student who came in dead last in their class and was awaiting court-martial when they left for duty had already made his name.

Custer's famous "luck" had more to do with his ability to take advantage of the frequent opportunities for recognition that came his way than simple happenstance. One day, Gen. George McClellan and the entourage of staff and dignitaries that accompanied him at all times were astride their horses on the bank of the Chickahominy River when McClellan said, as much to himself as any of his fellow travelers, "I wish I knew how deep it is." Custer was at the back of the column when the general's question passed down the line and immediately drove his horse into the river and, after crossing and returning, yelled, "That's how deep it is, General" and rode back to his place in line. McClellan is said to have called Custer forward on the spot and offered him a position on his staff. Working directly for McClellan, Custer continued to take every opportunity to distinguish himself. When the general could find no one willing to go up in a hot air balloon to observe enemy positions, Custer gladly volunteered for the dangerous duty. He earned a reputation as a decisive, courageous man who could be depended on, characteristics that were greatly appreciated by the six generals on whose staffs he served during the first two years of the war. He also built a name for himself as a great leader in battle. Custer's critics point out that his units suffered high casualties and suggest his successes were more a result of dumb luck than his tactical or leadership skills. However, Custer was never considered to be careless about the lives of his men, and his battlefield casualties were comparable to other units that saw a lot of action. The ghastly death counts in the later battles of the war were more attributable to the "total war" annihilation strategy implemented by the senior command of the army—as time progressed, they began to view the huge casualties as the unfortunate cost of victory.

If serving under Custer was dangerous during the Civil War, it did not seem to affect the morale of his men who were nearly universal in their admiration and confidence in him—particularly his fellow cavalrymen. Throughout the war Custer's troops were devoutly loyal to their notoriously brave commander. He shared in every danger that his men faced and the victories, recognition, and prestige they earned under his command generated a strong sense of pride. Custer was regarded as one of the hardest working—and hardest playing—officers in the army. He was certainly one of the most ostentatious. Custer's uniform reinforced his flamboyant, devil-may-care image. He had studied Napoleon's military tactics, where he learned that extravagant uniforms distinguished the light cavalry and impressed soldiers and civilians. Shortly after he took command of his first cavalry unit, his outfit began to evolve until by the time he led troops in Gettysburg he always wore a conspicuous crimson kerchief at his neck and a huge, floppy hat and oversized boots—both Confederate-issued prizes he picked up on the field and wore for their symbolism and flair more than comfort. Soon his men began to sport the same crimson kerchiefs until it was a proud feature of his entire command. Custer's shoulder-length hair was perhaps his most recognizable feature, which coupled with his unique style and his flair for the dramatic quickly attracted war correspondents and the public eye.

COURTSHIP

During the first two years of the war Custer returned to Monroe several times—either on sick leave or on furloughs. Custer was frequently recognized on the streets and received in the social circles where he was formerly excluded and he finally managed to catch the eye of Elizabeth Bacon. But he also caroused like most young soldiers and was known to get quite drunk. In late 1861, after a full day of revelry, Custer staggered home on the sidewalks of Monroe, getting sick, falling down, and generally making a spectacle of himself. Unfortunately, he happened to walk past the Bacon residence in this inebriated condition while both Libbie and her father were at the window. Custer's image was damaged nearly beyond repair, especially in Judge Bacon's eyes. That night, Custer's sister, Lydia, took him aside and convinced him of the shame he was bringing to his and his family's name. The twenty-one-year-old pledged then and there to abstain from alcohol—a pledge he honored for the rest of his life. Custer knew, however, that it would take more than a pledge of abstinence to redeem himself to the Bacons. Several months later, when her father caught on that she and Custer were mingling at social events, the Judge shipped Libbie off to visit friends in Toledo. For the next two years Custer and Elizabeth Bacon carried on a surreptitious written relationship while Custer pursued the glory and promotion he would need to be able to ask the judge for her hand in marriage.

When Custer returned to active duty in February 1862 he had more motivation than ever to garner a name for himself—he desperately wanted to win the love of Libbie and needed the approval of her father. After several victorious cavalry raids against Confederate positions in northern Virginia and conspicuous successes in the Peninsula Campaign, General McClellan made Custer his aide-de-camp and promoted him to the rank of captain. In 1862 and 1863

Custer distinguished himself in several major battles and became known as one of the cavalry's best commanders. In June 1863, newly appointed general-in-chief of the army George G. Meade reorganized the Cavalry Corps. That opened three new brigadier general commander positions and on the recommendation of his immediate commander, Custer received one of the generalships and command of the nearly 2000 men of the 2nd Brigade of the 3rd Division of the Cavalry Corps. At the age of twenty-three, the cadet many considered to be one of West Point's worst graduates ever became the youngest general in the Union Army.

Though it was an appointment in the volunteer ranks—he remained a first lieutenant in the regular Army—Custer's promotion was highly publicized, especially back in his hometown of Monroe. After leading his brigade in the Battle of Gettysburg, Custer's achievements were published in newspapers throughout the Union. Following a stunning victory over Confederate General J.E.B. Stuart's cavalry in which he had his horse shot out from under him—one of a dozen such unlucky mounts during Custer's Civil War service—he rode up to his commander, who had seen the whole skirmish, and cavalierly stuck out his leg to show where his boot had been torn by the bullet that killed his horse and glibly asked for a fifteen day leave-of-absence. The general gave him twenty-five. So, in September 1863, the proclaimed "Boy General" whose picture had recently appeared in the most read paper in the nation, *Harper's Weekly*, returned to Monroe to see if he had made an impression on Judge Daniel Bacon. Within a few weeks Custer convinced Libbie to accept his proposal of marriage, but it took several months and many letters for Custer to convince her father he was mature enough and held enough promise to be worthy of his prized daughter. When his promotion to brigadier general was confirmed in Congress, Custer finally won the judge over and on 9 February 1864, in a large wedding said to be the most splendid in the state of Michigan, George Armstrong Custer married Elizabeth Clift Bacon. As they discussed in detail in their correspondence prior to the wedding, Libbie retained her maiden name and would forever be known as Elizabeth Bacon Custer.

MARRIED TO THE ARMY

Custer's marriage to Libbie shaped his future, and his legacy, even more than his Civil War experience. The newlyweds began their army life in Custer's brigade headquarters near enemy lines in Virginia. There, Custer introduced his young wife to his two servants, a young boy named Johnny Cisco who tended the general's horses and many pets, and Eliza, a "contraband," or slave who escaped and found work with the Union army. Eliza served the Custers for the next five years, freeing Libbie of all household chores and enabling her to join her rambunctious husband on an adventure at a moment's notice—a request Libbie insisted her husband made throughout their married life. As the wife of one of the most well-known and successful officers in the army, she soon found herself in the best circles both in the field, where she regularly enjoyed Custer's various commanders' elegant six-course meals, as well as when they visited the nation's capital. Indeed, the Custers enjoyed many privileges that officers of similar rank rarely attained. Unlike the horse-drawn wagons, called ambulances, in which other officer's families traveled, Libbie wrote to her father that she and her Autie rode in a fashionable carriage with two magnificent matched horses and a silver harness the general had captured the previous summer.

Ambulance Wagons

Ambulance wagons, or wagons especially designed for the transport of sick and wounded, evolved rapidly during the Civil War in response to the massive casualties incurred in battle. There were many types of designs, but the essential nature of the wagon was the ability to reconfigure the inside to accommodate as many injured men as two horses could pull and to transport medical equipment and supplies to the battlefield. Most had many drawers and benches that could be shifted around the box of the wagon and a tent to attach to the rear for doctors to perform triage or field surgeries. During and after the war, the ambulance became the primary means of transporting civilians attached to the army. Officers' wives traveled by ambulance along with all their worldly goods, the space and number of ambulances assigned depended upon their husband's rank and the number of wagons available to the unit.

Libbie was instantly one of the young general's greatest assets. Shortly after their marriage the couple rode to Washington on a train specially prepared for the army's newly appointed general-in-chief, Ulysses S. Grant. This opportunity to connect with power was not lost on either of the Custers, both of whom were exceptionally sociable and confident in the presence of the most important of people. Libbie would later write that she found Grant talkative and funny though many saw him as quiet, shy, and even sullen. Luck continued to follow Custer, for within the first two weeks of their arrival in the capital he was featured twice in *Harper's Weekly*, giving the Custers even more visibility as they entered the social circle of Washington's elite. The flamboyant general received so much attention Libbie wrote to her parents, "I find it very agreeable to be the wife of a man so generally known and respected." Mrs. Custer was in her element as the elegant and attractive wife of the army's most dashing officer and decided to take a room in a boarding house while her husband returned to the front.

Grant quickly began to implement changes in the Union military strategy and replaced Custer's commander with Major General Philip H. Sheridan—who remained devoted to Custer throughout the remaining years of his life. Sheridan was eager to place more emphasis on cavalry operations—where Custer was clearly the army's star—and "Little Phil" had his eyes set on neutralizing Jeb Stuart's Invincibles, the Confederate Army's famous cavalry unit. After several months of cat-and-mouse skirmishes, Custer met Stuart on the battlefield on 11 May 1864, and in another stroke of Custer's famous luck, Sheridan came upon the field just as the Boy General led his men in a charge Sheridan called "brilliantly executed." During the course of the battle, Jeb Stuart—the South's equivalent to Custer in popularity and success—was mortally wounded. Sheridan sent congratulations to Custer while he was still on the field, and thus began a lifelong relationship of mutual respect and support between the two celebrated cavalrymen. Meanwhile, Libbie also made lasting impressions on the political and military elite. While accompanying a powerful Radical Republican congressman—whose favor she was cultivating on behalf of her husband—to an event at the White House, she was introduced to the president. After they shook hands, Lincoln recognized her name and asked if she was married to the officer who "goes into a charge with a whoop and a shout?" When she affirmed, the two joked about whether marriage would make her husband more cautious—Libbie insisting that it would not be so. Shrewdly, before she left the affair she told one of Lincoln's secretaries to tell the president if women were allowed to vote he would have hers.

In April 1864, Grant began to implement his new strategy—later called the "total war" strategy. There would be no occupations; in his mind the only way to bring the war to a close was to completely annihilate the Confederate armies on all fronts. As long as the Union could maintain the will to win, he could replace the Union's huge losses of men where the South, on the other hand, could not. During the Wilderness Campaign in May, Custer lost nearly 800 men, one-third of his brigade, demonstrating to Grant that the young cavalry leader was a good fit for his total war strategy. Custer's exuberance and ferocity in battle was unmatched. Leading his cavalry, standing in his stirrups with saber raised and his band playing in the background, the Boy General's antics made for great victories and even greater publicity. The war-weary Northern populace, reeling from the staggering numbers of casualties, was eager for good news and Custer was just what Lincoln and Grant needed. In October, after another classic Custer charge drove back a last-ditch attack by the weary Confederate cavalry in the Battle of Cedar Creek, Sheridan nominated Custer for another promotion—a "brevet" position of major general.

CUSTER'S "GLORIOUS WAR" COMES TO AN END

After the battle of Cedar Creek, Custer received his promotion in a grand ceremony in Washington where he presented the captured Confederate flags

Brevet Promotions

Brevet promotions were extremely common in the U.S. Army during the nineteenth century. In recognition of their gallantry in battle or to fill higher positions until receiving formal authorization from army headquarters, an officer would be awarded the right to wear the insignia of the brevetted rank, but would not receive the corresponding pay or authority. During the Civil War almost all senior officers received at least one brevet and they frequently held several different ranks simultaneously, such as the case of Custer at one point being a brevet major general of volunteers, an actual brigadier general of volunteers, a brevet lieutenant colonel in the regular army, and an actual regular army captain.

to the secretary of war, Edwin Stanton. Major General Custer returned to the front lines and soon sent for Libbie to join him in the palatial tent that served as his home base. Sheridan probably noticed that Custer became melancholy almost to the point of distraction if he was away from Libbie for too long and not engaged in battle. He wanted to keep his successful protégé happy and productive, so Libbie became a fixture in Custer's headquarters on the front. In spring 1865, Libbie was back in Washington where she attended another ceremony in which her husband's captured flags were once again handed over to the secretary of war.

In April, Custer captured the train station and nearly thirty major artillery guns at Appomattox, effectively cutting off Confederate General Robert E. Lee's desperately needed supplies and shortly thereafter the beleaguered commander requested terms for surrender. Custer himself accepted the flag of truce. In the Appomattox Court House, General Lee and General Grant negotiated the South's surrender and afterward officers purchased items as souvenirs from the room where the generals had signed the peace contract. Sheridan paid twenty dollars for the table on which the document had been signed and gave the table to Libbie Custer along with a personal note honoring her husband's contributions to the surrender. By early May the war was over and on 23 May the 80,000 men of the victorious Army of the Potomac paraded through Washington. Custer, resplendent and flamboyant as usual, was at the front of his division where he dramatically reared his horse in front of the presidential reviewing stand.

A DIFFICULT TRANSITION

Custer's extraordinary Civil War experience could be called an American fairy tale. Although Custer as a historical figure has drawn a tremendous amount of criticism over the years, most agree his overall performance in

My Dear Madam, — I respectfully present to you the small writing-table on which the conditions for the surrender of the Confederate Army of Northern Virginia was written by Lt. General Grant, and permit me to say, Madam, that there is scarcely an individual in our service who has contributed more to bring about this desirable result than your very gallant husband.

—General Philip Sheridan to Libbie Custer, 9 April 1865

the North-South conflict was spectacular. It also determined his future because every decision he made was based on attempting to either recreate the thrill of battle or regain the prestige and success he lived during the war. His phenomenal rise in ranks at such a young age left an indelible impression on his, and his wife's, psyche. They would forever assume their elite and celebrity status—which would sometimes cause them great difficulty. Custer also came to the West having led mostly professional cavalrymen and having held a rank and recognition factor that commanded authority. With a super-abundance of confidence, a large and devoted staff, and plenty of victories, he kept his men's morale fairly high and rarely faced major disciplinary problems. That was all about to change.

Custer's first postwar assignment was to join his mentor, General Sheridan, in the Department of the Gulf to put down defiant Confederates in Texas, enforce Reconstruction policies imposed by Congress, and to protect the Mexican border from invasion by forces loyal to the French-backed Emperor Maximilian of Austria. The Custers traveled to Alexandria, Louisiana, where he took command of his newly assigned volunteer troops to prepare for their march into Texas. The Confederates in Texas had already surrendered so Custer's mission would be primarily one of occupation to control Southern sympathizers to ease slaves into the free world being defined for them. His forces would also serve as a demonstration of power to the puppet Maximilian's Mexican government.

The Emperor of Mexico

The Archduke Maximilian of Austria was proclaimed Emperor of Mexico in April 1864 with the support of a group of Mexican conservatives and Napoleon III of France. The United States refused to recognize his government and once the Civil War ended in May 1865, U.S. leaders, uncomfortable with a French monarchy as a southern neighbor, manned posts along the border and supplied weapons to opposition forces led by Benito Juárez who eventually deposed and executed Maximilian in 1867.

From the start, Custer's command was in trouble. His troops were all volunteers who served in the Western theater during the war and they were ready to be mustered out and go home. Under normal circumstances volunteers were not inclined toward regimented discipline—something Custer had never experienced before. When the twenty-five-year-old West Pointer marched in, pompously demanded their abject obedience, and began to make examples of insubordinates through excessive and extreme discipline—punishments almost to the point of absurdity—the camp nearly erupted in mutiny. Desertions, which plagued Custer throughout his Western assignments, began to mount, so the general began to apply even more stern punishments. After he executed a farm boy from Illinois with no previous record of insubordination for attempted desertion, Custer hoped he had laid down the law and stemmed the flow of runaway soldiers. Instead, it appears his actions in Alexandria and on the subsequent hellacious march into Texas drove many of his men to risk everything, including their lives, to get out from under his apparent tyranny.

When he marched the division through the humid, subtropical piney forest of east Texas in the heat of July, Custer forced his men to wear their wool uniforms because his quartermaster had not ordered enough cotton shirts and pants. He also demanded they march in close formation to prevent desertions and raiding and foraging in the farms and towns they passed. While his wife rode in a custom-outfitted ambulance or on one of Custer's many horses, men were dropping like flies. Of the seventeen ambulances on Custer's 240-mile march to Texas, ten were eventually filled to capacity with men sick from dysentery, heat stroke, and other ailments. Custer's staff used the remaining seven, five for equipment, one to transport Libbie, and one hauling the Custers' menagerie of dogs. While the officers carried enough quinine to keep the nasty and virulent "breakbone fever" virus at bay, the enlisted men were forced to suffer the excruciating symptoms through the long hard march. It is easy to see how Custer earned the reputation of mistreating his enlisted men—a charge that would follow him through the rest of his days.

The haggard, worn-out column finally reached Camp Hempstead, Texas, where Custer and his division settled in to await orders. Conditions for the enlisted barely improved in camp, and many men wrote home urging their families to pressure their state governments to intervene. Soon newspapers in Iowa and Wisconsin—home of the volunteer units Custer now commanded—featured stories of the one-time hero's abuse of their state's valiant solders. When their governors and legislators complained to Stanton and Sheridan, Custer's devoted commander remained loyal to his protégé, stating that the disciplinary measures were all necessary and appropriate. Sheridan apparently failed to notice the numbers of men who had yet to recover from the trip. The regimental returns for one Wisconsin unit recorded twenty-six of eighty-three men were ill a few days after arriving in camp.

While in Hempstead, Custer received notice he had been brevetted major, lieutenant colonel, and brigadier general in the regular army, and Sheridan assured his favorite officer that he was pressing hard for him to receive a permanent rank of major general. By now, the army was well into the demobilization process—nearly one million volunteers needed to be mustered out of service during the first twelve months after Appomattox. The first step in re-garrisoning the regular army was to rebuild the officer corps and a frenzy of veteran regular and volunteer army officers vied for the commissions that were about to become available. But there were more high-ranking volunteer and brevetted officers than there were available positions. Regular army officers, like Custer, who had held high rank in the volunteers reverted to their regular grades, while volunteers who now aspired to a regular army career applied for the percent of vacancies apportioned to them. All contended for brevet grades in recognition of wartime services, which were not empty honors because an officer could be assigned to commands based on brevet rank. By early 1866, officers who were generals at the close of the war a few months earlier found themselves as colonels, majors, and sometimes even captains, while colonels and majors found themselves lieutenants. Probably because of the bad publicity covering Custer's treatment of his soldiers in Texas, Sheridan was unable to secure his appointment as major general and on 31 January 1866 the Boy General received notice his rank had reverted to his regular grade of captain, his salary of $8,000 per month dropped to $2,000, and he was ordered to return to the East Coast.

The Reconstruction Controversy

Reconstruction is the term for Congress's attempt to resolve the issues of the Civil War, especially how to return secessionist Southern states into the Union and enforce the new legal status of the freed slaves. Violent controversy erupted all through the south and the Union Army served as an occupying force to enforce Reconstruction policies. "Reconstruction" is also the common name for the entire era of U.S. history from 1865 to 1877.

In early March the Custers moved in with Libbie's parents in Monroe. Custer left his wife in Michigan and went to New York and Washington, DC, where he was wined and dined by wealthy businessmen and powerful politicians while exploring his career options. Many pressed Custer to enter politics, while others encouraged him to join their businesses—they all wanted to cash in on his fame. It didn't take long to determine that an elected office was not going to pan out for him in the current political environment—his pro-slavery stance did not sit well with the Republicans in power—and a Wall Street position that would afford him and Libbie the lifestyle to which they had grown accustomed did not materialize. Watching unemployed volunteer officers hang around army headquarters desperately seeking an appointment of any grade, Custer came to believe his commission and reputation to be his most valuable possessions. Sheridan did not give up on his campaign for Custer. He found a sympathetic ear in Secretary Stanton, who had a personal affinity for both Custers, and though Sheridan sought at minimum a colonelcy, on 28 July Custer was appointed Lieutenant

Colonel of the Seventh Cavalry. After five more months of exploring career opportunities, he finally accepted his appointment and joined the Seventh Cavalry at Fort Riley, Kansas, in January 1867.

CUSTER'S FIRST INDIAN WAR

A few weeks after the close of the Civil War, General of the Army Ulysses S. Grant appointed fellow Civil War hero William Tecumseh Sherman to command the Military Division of the Missouri, essentially the territory between the Mississippi River and the Rocky Mountains north of Texas. Sherman's main concern was to protect the construction and operation of the transcontinental railroads from attack by Indians, who were surrounded and pressured by white expansion and were preparing to fight for the land they had left. Sherman ultimately implemented the total war strategy that brought the Union victory in the Civil War. The goal would be to not only defeat the enemy's military, but to also destroy the resources that enabled the enemy to continue warfare. For the Plains Indian nations, this would mean elimination of their primary source of food, shelter, and clothing—the buffalo. Sherman knew that the intercontinental railroad would be completed in about a year, speeding up the settlement of the West, improving military efficiency, separating the large buffalo herds, and ultimately sealing the fate of the nomadic Plains Indians. By the time Custer arrived in Kansas, the Union Pacific and Kansas Pacific Railroads were nearing completion and buffalo hunters had begun the systematic destruction of the Plains Indian's way of life. But the so-called "Indian Problem" was just heating up.

Custer reported at Fort Riley in early January 1867 just as news of a disastrous battle near Fort Phil Kearny on the Bozeman Trail in Wyoming Territory made it to the post. Brevet Lieutenant Colonel William Fetterman and eighty men were overwhelmed and killed by a superior force of Lakota, Northern Cheyenne, and Northern Arapahoe warriors led by Lakota Chiefs Red Cloud and Crazy Horse. Sherman wanted to take on the northern Indians but Washington was attempting to settle the dispute through treaty negotiations. So he decided to focus attention on the southern Plains tribes—he would drive them out of the way of white travel and onto reservations by force or by bribery, and if war was required then Custer was the man Sherman wanted. Sherman appointed General Winfield Scott Hancock commander of the Department of the Missouri, and ordered him to launch a large-scale campaign in Kansas and Nebraska. Sherman believed that Hancock's leadership and Custer's tactical skills would bring about a quick victory and demonstrate that the Fetterman debacle was an anomaly. Unfortunately, none of these men had experience

First clear off the buffalo, then clear off the Indian. For the gold, we must act with vindictive earnestness against the Sioux even to their total extermination, men, women and children.

—U.S. Army General William T. Sherman in a telegram to President U.S. Grant fighting Indians. Discounting the Fetterman incident as being caused by an incompetent commander, they all brought an inflated view of their own—and their army's—superiority against their new foes, especially Custer who received so much glory and adulation at such a young age. It is not surprising, then, that the subsequent mission was an unequivocal fiasco.

Hancock immediately launched a campaign to move Indians away from the railroads. When negotiations with Pawnee Killer, a Cheyenne chief and the first Indian leader he encountered, broke down, Hancock refused to listen to the advice of the local Indian agent and marched his entire division of 1400 men to Pawnee Killer's village to force his people to move next to Fort Larned in south-central Kansas. The agent explained that this dramatic and uncalled-for action would terrify the Cheyennes—mostly survivors and relatives of the Sand Creek massacre by volunteer forces just three years earlier. But Hancock did not relent. When the column neared the village, Hancock ordered Custer to surround it to prevent any Indians from escaping. Custer and his men crawled to the edge of the camp only to find the entire village abandoned. Hancock was furious and ordered Custer and his cavalry to give chase. But soon the tracks spread in all different directions and Custer learned his first lesson in Indian warfare: Given a head start his opponents were nearly impossible to catch, even with women and children along. For several more days Custer pursued small war parties but they all managed to elude him while running amok up and down the stage line. Hancock could not believe Custer had been in pursuit so long and found no Indians. Beside himself in anger, Hancock decided to burn the abandoned village of over 250 tipis. Hancock and Custer had set off a war and soon Indians were attacking whites all along the Kansas frontier.

THE COURT-MARTIAL

The utter failure of his first frontier mission and the moribund situation at his headquarters in Fort Hays, Kansas—a pitiful, poorly supplied outpost—brought on a desperate melancholy and Custer wrote to Libbie, "Come as soon as you can . . . I did not marry you for you to live in one house, me in another." Foretelling future troubles he wrote, "I almost feel tempted to desert and fly to you." While waiting for Libbie to arrive from the East, Custer spent the month of June wandering the plains of western Kansas seeking to engage a significant force of Indians to repair the damage to his ego and his reputation. As he moved farther west, and farther from Libbie, he became morose. His need for her at this time was almost an obsession. Disregarding specific orders to proceed as far as Colorado in pursuit of hostile bands, Custer decided to make a temporary camp halfway to the state line and send small detachments out looking for Indians while he sent word to Libbie to meet him at Fort Wallace, a few miles south of his camp. He sent a detachment to the fort and another to scout the area. For the next week, in a comedy of errors, Custer moved around the region, looking for Libbie or at least a letter from her, while searching for Indians. After a grueling, sixty-five-mile march north through barren, waterless land in which several dogs and mules died of thirst, his column arrived at the Platte River, near the stage coach and telegraph line, but still there were no signs of Indians. Custer telegraphed back to Fort McPherson and found out Sherman was livid that he had not gone west as planned and ordered Custer to return to Fort Wallace which was practically under siege by the Indians Custer could not find. Though he was in trouble, Custer was glad to head back to the fort. He was concerned about his wife traveling through hostile territory and also worried about a unit of ten men Sherman mentioned in the telegraph that were trying to bring him his new orders. That night, he ordered his men to prepare to return to Fort Wallace the next morning, across the same desolate and dangerous landscape they had just barely survived. Thirty-five men deserted in the middle of the night rather than face the journey; they were close to the roads leading to the Montana goldfields and the temptation was too much. Custer, desperate to get to Libbie, did not give chase and that noon, about fifteen miles into the march, thirteen more soldiers turned back north—deserting in broad daylight. Realizing that the remaining men were likely thinking the same thing, Custer had his officers chase down the deserters with orders to shoot to kill. Only three men were finally caught and were brought back gravely injured and thrown in a wagon—one would eventually die. Custer soon faced more problems when his company found the detachment Sherman sent to find him and deliver his orders, all ten men had been killed and mutilated after what appeared to be a lengthy chase by Pawnee Killer and his warriors. Custer learned another lesson in Indian warfare: It was futile to try to outrun their faster horses; soldiers should turn and fight if they wanted a chance.

The next day, Custer led a weak and weary column into Fort Wallace, a post that was under nearly constant attack and could barely supply Custer's division's needs. He had covered nearly 1000 miles and had not killed an Indian, while more than 200 whites in his territory had fallen to the warring Cheyennes and their allies. But, more important to Custer, he finally heard from Libbie—she was clear across the state at Fort Riley. Claiming he had to get to Fort Riley to order supplies, he turned right around and raced 100 tired men and horses 150 miles in a nonstop mission to the next post to the east, Fort Hays. Some of his soldiers could not keep up and two stragglers were picked off by Pawnee Killer's men, but Custer did not return to support them or retrieve their bodies. He left ninety-four of his exhausted men at Fort Hays and continued his reckless dash to Fort Harker, where, after 500 miles and almost no sleep, he caught the 3:00 a.m. train to Fort Riley and nine hours later walked into Libbie's room. They quickly prepared to return to Fort Wallace. Before they could depart, however, Custer received a telegram informing him that he was under arrest for deserting his post while it was under attack.

Generals Sherman, Sully, and myself, and nearly all the officers of your regiment have asked for you . . . Can you come at once?

—Telegram from General Philip Sheridan to Custer, 24 September 1868

He was also charged with excessive cruelty and illegal conduct for ordering his officers to shoot the deserters, for leaving the two men who were killed by Pawnee Killer, and for pushing his men beyond human endurance. He was eventually found guilty on all counts, and suspended from rank and command for one year—without pay—and in June 1868, the Custers returned to Monroe. There, Custer wrote his Civil War memoirs and hunted and fished and generally relaxed while contemplating his future.

Meanwhile, Sheridan assumed Hancock's command of the Division of the Platte and had no better luck on the Kansas frontier than his predecessor. His search-and-destroy missions proved ineffective against the Indians who had killed hundreds of settlers in the previous few months. Buffalo killers had reduced the southern herd and the army and the agents for the southern tribes were pressing hard to bring them onto a reservation one way or another. In the north, Red Cloud's Lakota allied with Northern Cheyenne and Northern Arapahoe bands, defeated the U.S. Army, and brought the United States to terms; the army agreed to abandon the forts on the Bozeman Trail in return for Red Cloud's acceptance of peace. When the soldiers marched out of the posts later that fall, Red Cloud would "touch the pen" to the Fort Laramie Treaty of 1868. The southern tribes hoped to duplicate Red Cloud's success by launching an all-out war—but Sheridan was about to apply the full force of the army's total war strategy on the Kansas Indians and the central Plains were about to erupt. Sheridan needed his point man, the man who helped him burn through the Shenandoah—he needed Custer. The general secured a reduction of Custer's sentence and on 24 September 1868, Custer received a telegram from Sheridan imploring him to return to the front as soon as possible.

WASHITA

Custer, of course, was ecstatic and raced to the frontier. Sheridan wanted to execute a winter campaign and Custer was eager to take on the challenge. Sheridan gave him free reign "to act entirely on your own judgment," and Custer moved to Fort Dodge, Kansas, to assume command of his Seventh Cavalry. He spent a month preparing his men for the mission and departed in November for the Oklahoma panhandle. After establishing a base camp, he began to reconnoiter the area. On 27 November 1868 Custer's Osage scouts located a trail, and Custer followed it without stopping until dark. There was enough moonlight to continue their pursuit and the unit eventually reached the village of Cheyenne chief Black Kettle. A survivor of Sand Creek,

Black Kettle sought to protect his people by coming to the Washita to join the peaceful tribes away from the railroad. But many of his young men continued to raid white settlements.

Crawling through snow in the bitter cold, Custer crept up on the camp and, after hearing a baby cry, determined that this time his targeted village was not empty. He ordered his men to surround the village and launched the attack at daybreak. Drawing on his Civil War successes, he charged in with sword in hand and his omnipresent band playing in the background and caught the sleepy village off guard. Witnesses claim around 150 Cheyennes were killed, including Chief Black Kettle. Custer set about burning every last item in the camp and ordered a unit of soldiers to kill the village's 800 Indian horses. Twenty of his men, under the command of Major Joel Elliott, were missing, but seeing a growing number of mounted warriors on the hills in the area, Custer decided to march back to Sheridan to report his grand victory. Custer's name would soon be back in the Eastern papers; this time the Boy General was called a great Indian fighter. Just like his Civil War experience, Custer's panache and charisma made for great reporting—his Western exploits would keep him in the limelight through the few remaining years of his life.

The incident at Washita was controversial from the beginning. Custer's men were divided between those who supported their commander and enjoyed the public accolades for their victory and those who resented Custer for abandoning Elliott and his men, who were later found to have been surrounded and killed. This rift between officers in the Seventh Cavalry would remain. Some contemporaries, including humanitarians back East and soldiers who were sickened by the slaughter, labeled it a massacre, as do most historians, but most newspapers proclaimed it as a great victory after several years of army debacles on the Plains. The fact that the Cheyennes had killed several white captives when Custer's attack began justified the attack in many Americans' minds. Custer relished the attention and didn't seem to mind the criticism— with the exception of an unsigned letter from one of his officers published in the *St. Louis Democrat* that accused him of abandoning Elliott's group. When confronted, Captain Frederick Benteen freely admitted to writing the letter; he had resented Custer for quite some time.

The Custers spent the next two and a half years at Fort Hays. Custer's star was shining again, perhaps even more brightly as an exotic Indian fighter. He was an avid hunter and entertained numerous dignitaries as they passed through. He especially loved hunting buffalo, claiming it was as exciting to chase buffalo as Indians, and became a well-known guide for the rich and powerful who came west to hunt the great animal before they disappeared. Libbie wrote a romantic and detailed account of their idyllic years at Fort Hays in *Following the Guidon*. Custer, however, became bored with commanding a post in a peaceful region and, after toying with resigning, he took a leave in spring 1871 to see what prospects there were for him in the East.

He spent several months in Washington and New York and discovered he was as popular as ever—even more so it appeared. Though he received several offers, he could not shake the lure of the West and returned to the Seventh Cavalry. His command was sent to Kentucky in September and Custer became even more bored than he was up in Kansas. He read of the conflicts with Crazy Horse and Sitting Bull of the Lakota bands on the northern Plains and he longed to secure an appointment to bring these last "hostile" bands under control.

A Cross-Country Tour with the Grand Duke of Russia

In January 1872, Sherman asked Custer to guide a buffalo hunt for the Grand Duke Alexis of Russia. The two men had many common interests and soon became fast friends. The Duke invited Custer to continue on his tour and Sherman readily agreed. For the next month the men traversed the West by horse, train, and steamship, always in the most lavish style possible and at the expense of the royal tourist. They road on top of railcars and shot dozens of buffalo as the train passed through the Plains at twenty miles per hour and spent hours playing cards and racing horses. They met Libbie in Louisville, and the couple enjoyed Alexis's generous hospitality as they steamed down the Mississippi to New Orleans where they spent a week enjoying opulent balls and dinner parties.

THE YELLOWSTONE EXPEDITION

In February 1873 Sheridan assigned Custer the duty he had so desired: He was to take the Seventh Cavalry to Fort Abraham Lincoln in North Dakota to protect the Northern Pacific Railroad as it inched westward just as her sister lines had done a few years earlier. The rail line was soon to enter territory that had been promised to the Lakota in the Treaty of 1868 Red Cloud had so successfully negotiated. Though Red Cloud's and many other bands had moved to agencies on reservations, Crazy Horse and Sitting Bull led bands that were still roaming the territory the United States was conveniently calling "unceded Indian Territory." Sheridan wanted Custer to protect the developing railroad—just as he had done in Kansas. Indians who had agreed to the 1868 treaty believed their lands stretched to the Canadian border, but American negotiators had left the northern boundary intentionally unclear. This land was called "unceded" territory where the United States did not recognize Sioux ownership but did not deny their hunting rights. Both "treaty" and "non-treaty" Indians—groups who had not signed the treaty—held fast to the belief in their exclusive rights to this land. Politicians and businessmen interested in expanding into northern Dakota Territory, however, rationalized that

Indian lands ended on the southern border of the Yellowstone and demanded army protection for the westward-moving rail line. Sherman and Sheridan, having seen the southern and central railroads solve their "Indian problems" on the central Plains, were happy to oblige and attached Custer and his Seventh Cavalry—their Indian fighting division—to the 1873 Yellowstone expedition led by Colonel David S. Stanley.

The huge expedition consisted of nearly 2000 men with Custer's Seventh leading the way. The column spent the summer supporting a team of Northern Pacific engineers who surveyed the future route of the railroad. Custer enjoyed every moment of the entire trip—even without Libbie at his side. He wrote hundreds of pages of letters to his wife describing the magnificence of the land and his exciting adventures in exquisite detail. He fell in love with the "perfectly delightful" land where he had never seen better hunting. On 31 July, Custer had his first encounter with the Sioux when a small group of Lakota under the leadership of Crazy Horse attempted to lure Custer and twenty men into a trap. Both parties had learned from the Fetterman fight: The Indians hoped to duplicate their success with decoys luring the army into a trap; the cavalry were not about to fall for the trick. A few days later, Custer's scouts discovered the trail of a large Lakota village on the move between their regular summer encampments. Custer took off with his cavalry, and after a two-day march, caught up with the Lakota who had just crossed the Bighorn River. The current was too much for the cavalry's horses and after a humiliating day of attempting various strategies at crossing, Custer gave up and set up camp. The Lakota, who had no trouble crossing with all of their families and possessions in tow, watched from across the river and decided to attack the next morning. At daybreak, Indians began to shoot at Custer's camp from across the water and warriors began to ford above and below to circle the cavalry. Seeing his predicament, Custer formed his men in ranks, pulled out his sword, struck up his ever-present band, and charged at the pressing warriors who were so surprised they took off in all directions. Both sides had casualties but both could claim victory. The Lakota, bands who were loyal to Crazy Horse and Sitting Bull, assumed they had repulsed their enemies, while Custer was confident that he had cleared a path for the railroad and taught his new opponents a lesson. The Indians, following the last of the Lakota leaders who refused to accept life on a reservation, moved on to their regular winter camp. Custer and the Yellowstone Expedition wound their way back to Fort Abraham Lincoln where a spacious new home—the first one of their own—was awaiting the happy officer and his wife.

Libbie joined her husband at Fort Lincoln in fall 1873 just as the depression, or "Panic of 1873," engulfed the nation. Northern Pacific construction ground to a halt as the economy and the railroad company's stock value plummeted. Custer, who had befriended many executives of the Northern Pacific during the summer's expedition, became a spokesperson for attracting settlers to Dakota Territory. The company had massive tracts of land granted by the government that could be sold to potential settlers if they could be convinced of the prospect of a better life. Custer wrote articles for Eastern magazines expounding on the fertility and beauty of the region. Meanwhile, Grant, who was now president, was desperately seeking a solution to the nation's economic woes. The most promising solution was to pump money into the economy by adding to the treasury's gold reserves. For years the Black Hills—in the heart of the Sioux reservation—had been rumored to be filled with vast deposits of gold, but the government actively prevented potential miners from entering the Indian's legal territory. The Panic of 1873, however, changed the federal government's position. General Sheridan proposed sending a column into the Black Hills to establish a fort and quietly look for gold—under the pretense that non-treaty Indians had attacked settlers in Nebraska. Indian agents and others with close ties to the reservations pointed out the "remarkable quiet" throughout the territory for the previous year and vehemently protested this explicit violation of the treaty. But Grant needed to bring an end to the depression, and if a gold rush couldn't solve the problem it could at least divert the

Crazy Horse

"Crazy Horse" is the somewhat confused English translation of Tasunke Witko (Tah-Shoonkeh Weetko), the name of the Oglala Lakota warrior and spiritual man who became famous for his successful military tactics and his determined resistance to the white man's invasion of the northern Great Plains. Tasunke Witko was an important family name handed down from Crazy Horse's father and grandfather. Crazy Horse led the decoys in luring eighty soldiers to their doom at the so-called Fetterman Massacre on 21 December 1866. This and other successes in the Lakota's siege of the U.S. Army posts along the Bozeman Trail forced the United States to abandon the trail and negotiate the Fort Laramie Treaty of 1868. Crazy Horse steadfastly refused to join the growing numbers of Lakota bands moving to the treaty-defined "agencies" on the reservations where the people depended on rations from the government for their existence. His leadership attracted many followers to remain in buffalo country, where they continued to hunt, fish, and wage war against enemy tribes as well as whites. He ultimately united with Chief Sitting Bull to fight U.S. encroachment into treaty-defined unceded territory, including the Black Hills. He was involved in all of the major battles with the U.S. Army in this war, including Custer's famous last fight. The army eventually stepped up their pursuit of Crazy Horse's bands and in winter 1877, his tribe, weakened by cold and hunger, finally surrendered at the Red Cloud Agency in Nebraska where he attempted to negotiate for a special reservation for his people. A few weeks later, he was murdered in a scuffle with soldiers who were trying to imprison him in a guardhouse.

nation's attention. Sherman's proposal was publicized throughout the country, and Custer quickly asked for and received command of the entire expedition.

THE BLACK HILLS EXPEDITION

On 2 July 1874, Custer started out from Fort Lincoln with a force of over 1000 men. Scientists, geologists, and newspaper reporters accompanied the column. The mission was to explore the Black Hills, locate a potential site for a fort on the western side, find a route to connect the post to Fort Laramie on the south, and report back to Fort Lincoln by the end of August. Of course, the unofficial charge was to determine if there was gold in the Black Hills. The expedition arrived on the western side of the hills in the vicinity of present-day Custer, South Dakota, on 22 July where the army explored and the accompanying miners looked for gold, which they found in small quantities in French Creek. The Expedition eventually covered much of the western and north-central Black Hills before returning to Fort Lincoln at the end of August as ordered. A historian wrote of Custer's highly publicized report on the Black Hills, "It would be difficult to frame language better calculated to inflame the public mind and excite men to enter this country or die in the attempt." News of gold found in French Creek eventually attracted tens of thousands of miners to the Black Hills. In response to protests made by those seeking to protect the Indians' legal claim to the land, Custer countered that the Indians weren't using the land so they should make way for the whites who would. The army made a few half-hearted attempts to hold back the gold-seekers from the treaty-guaranteed land, but eventually they were unable to quell the vast numbers of would-be miners on their way to the goldfields. The government eventually determined it would be much more practical and probably a lot easier to suppress the Indians than the miners and thus set the stage for Custer's famous "Last Stand."

Claiming Lakota Lands

The Lakota arrived in the Black Hills in the 1700s after a gradual migration from Minnesota. They ultimately drove other tribes from the region and claimed the land, which they called *Paha Sapa*, for themselves. After the final Plains wars brought the defeated Lakota onto reservations, the United States claimed that terms of surrender included a purchase of the Black Hills, but the Lakota never accepted the validity of this purchase and the area remains under dispute to this day. In 1980, the Supreme Court of the United States ruled that the Black Hills were illegally taken and over $100 million was owed to the Lakota. The Lakota Nation refused the settlement, as they wanted the return of their land instead, and they still demand the return of the Black Hills to this day.

THE LITTLE BIGHORN

For the next two years the United States lobbied the Lakota to sell the Black Hills, which created a great amount of dissention among the many bands throughout Lakota territory. Some believed that it was already lost so they supported the idea of negotiating as high of a price as possible out of the government. Others, mostly followers of Sitting Bull and Crazy Horse, were steadfast in their refusal. In summer 1875, Red Cloud and Spotted Tail, a peace-supporting chief who had brought his people onto a reservation to save them, traveled to Washington, DC, to meet with the president. The Lakota leaders believed they were going to present their grievances to the "Great Father," but all President Grant wanted to discuss was selling the Black Hills. The leaders would never agree to a deal of this magnitude without the consent of their people so they returned to their reservations. That fall, the government attempted several times to negotiate a sale but the Lakotas who were willing to negotiate made such unreasonable demands that no deal could be brokered. Plus, the so-called "hostiles," Indians living off the reservation mostly in unceded territory north of the reservation, were threatening the pro-sale Indians. With nearly 15,000 whites living in the Black Hills and no treaty or sale in sight, Grant called a confab with his military and administrative leaders to come up with a solution, which was announced in early December 1875. Grant announced that the hostiles in the unceded territory were the barrier to U.S. access to the Black Hills so he was ordering that all Indians were to move onto reservations by 31 January 1876 or he would send his military to bring them in by force. Indian agents on the Lakota reservations knew that the order would not bring in Crazy Horse and Sitting Bull and they were right. January 31 came and went and the army began to plan a spring campaign to force the hostiles to the reservations.

As plans were developing, Custer was called to testify before a congressional investigation that ended in an indictment of President Grant's secretary of war. The "Sioux expedition" was scheduled to commence in a week, and Custer believed this was going to be the greatest, and probably last, Indian campaign; he told his brother Tom he would "rather have died than missed it." But the embittered president believed Custer's testimony was politically motivated and that he may have even been harboring thoughts of running on the Democratic ticket in the next presidential election—an idea that prominent Democrats floated past Custer on several occasions. For many reasons, not the least of which being he was angry with Custer, Grant would not authorize him to return to Dakota to lead his men. Typically, Custer simply convinced someone in the War Department to write him out an order and left town without Grant's approval. Custer was stopped in Chicago on 3 May and placed under arrest, and General Alfred Terry was placed in charge of the campaign. For days Custer groveled and begged and implored his superiors—Sheridan, Sherman, and Grant—to release him. Terry, who knew he needed

Custer's Indian-fighting experience, finally interceded and Grant relented. Custer was not, however, allowed to command the entire expedition, only his Seventh Cavalry division, but he didn't care as he knew he would have free reign once out in the field.

The expedition would entail a three-pronged attack. Custer's column, with Terry in command, would head west from Fort Abraham Lincoln and follow the Yellowstone River. Another column, led by General George Crook, who led a disastrous winter campaign just a few months earlier, would try again by moving north from Fort Fetterman to the Little Bighorn River. Major General John Gibbon would lead the third column coming down from Fort Ellis in Montana. Because all of the officers involved were certain that any one of their groups were capable of conquering the Indians in the region, they did not incorporate much more tactical or strategic planning into the mission.

The Terry-Custer column departed from Fort Lincoln on 17 May 1876. The Crook column made the first encounter with the Lakota and their allies on 17 June in a six-hour clash on the upper branch of Rosebud Creek. Though Crook claimed victory, he lost twenty-eight men and had fifty-six wounded to contend with so he retreated to his base camp on Big Goose Creek. The other two columns had no idea where Crook was and would not hear from him until mid-July—weeks after the Battle of the Little Bighorn. Meanwhile, Terry, who had never been on the Plains or fought Indians, was exhausted from the month-long overland journey and decided to manage the conflict from the comfort of a steamboat on the Yellowstone. After confirming there was significant Indian activity in the area, Terry drew up detailed orders for Custer and Gibbon—they could have used information from Crook regarding the size of their opponent's forces but it isn't likely that the officers would have changed their plans. Gibbon and Terry would go back up the Yellowstone and come into the Little Bighorn Valley from the north. Custer would take the Seventh Cavalry up the Rosebud and block Indians from leaving the valley to the east.

On 25 June, Crow Indian scouts informed Custer of a large encampment of Lakota. Based on all of his previous experiences, Custer decided to attack the village immediately. Custer knew he was outnumbered—though he did not know by how much—but he was confident in the superior force of his cavalry over an unsuspecting village of warriors and their families. He split his forces into three battalions—one led by Major Marcus Reno, one by Captain Frederick Benteen, and one by himself—and left a company to guard his supply wagons. Custer sent Reno to attack the village from the south and Benteen was ordered to go west and engage any hostiles he encountered, and Custer would go north and come down into the village to support Benteen in a classic pincer strategy, much like was originally planned with the three large columns.

Reno ran into serious resistance and was forced to retreat after losing nearly a quarter of his command. Meanwhile, Custer came upon the Lakota camp and commenced his own strategy. Evidence suggests he was attempting to capture women and children like he had done in his Washita attack. When Custer saw the size of the village he sent a message to Benteen to come as quickly as possible and to "bring packs, p.s. bring packs!" meaning mules packed with ammunition. Benteen, however, ran into Reno and the two units were engaged in a defensive position on the other side of the village where they remained besieged for nearly two days and lost over one-third of their men. This freed many of the Indians in this skirmish to join the forces fighting Custer's battalion. From this point on Custer experts speculate that he may have attempted a diversionary attack on the village and deployed other companies to scale ridges above the camp to buy time for Benteen or Reno to relieve him. But relief never came and what was left of his column retreated to higher ground. After a lengthy defensive battle, the cavalry companies on the hills eventually collapsed and fell back together on what is now called "Custer Hill" where the few remaining soldiers exchanged fire with the Indians until the last man fell. Custer, two of his brothers, his nephew, and his brother-in-law were among the 225 soldiers who were killed in the course of about twenty minutes.

THE CUSTER MYTH

Custer as a man and his demise in his so-called Last Stand would have made America's history books and his name would have lived on in perpetuity, but he is a true icon of the West because of the way the nation, and the world, has reacted to his story. Immediately after his death, what has come to be known as "the Custer myth" began to take shape. Myths are powerful stories, beliefs, or traditions that grow up around something or someone and come to represent the ideals and institutions of a society. In essence, a myth embodies how a people view themselves. As a society's worldview changes over time, so do the versions of its myths. Custer's myth is no exception. As one Custer expert wrote, the Custer myth was "built like other myths, upon the actual deeds and events, magnified, distorted and disproportioned by fiction, invention, imagination, and speculation." The story became a reflection of America's view of the West.

For decades, due to the extraordinary and prolific efforts of his wife, the Custer myth was built around heroic and valiant soldiers fighting heathen savages. Living fifty-seven years after her husband's death, Elizabeth Custer published three books and lectured extensively to defend and embellish his reputation and promulgate an idealized and romanticized home life with her hero. Her image as a devoted wife and respectable upper-class lady—and a widow to boot—was reinforced by the Victorian values of the day. Proper women were considered morally unimpeachable and no honorable man would challenge her integrity. Thus most of her husband's critics were kept at bay for half a century out of respect for the widow's devotion. As one future investigator complained, "All who stood in the way of her appraisal were made to appear as cowards or scoundrels."

Because most of the previous publicity surrounding Custer romanticized him as a nearly invincible warrior, the defeat at Little Bighorn was a major shock to Americans. They needed an explanation. Were previous portrayals wrong? Had he changed? Who or what was to blame, the officers who did not come to his rescue, or the unfair advantage in numbers of the Indians? For decades, Custer remained America's popular Boy General, martyred at an early age while advancing the nation's civilizing agenda. The nation needed to believe that the actions taken to pacify and control the Indians were justified and Custer represented that rationalization. However, over time, facts began to leak into the story and the myth changed. Gradually, shifting attitudes toward American Indians and U.S. treatment of them also impacted the myth. People began to revisit his actions from Washita to Little Bighorn and argue that he represented the U.S. agenda to eradicate the Indian. The ideas that Custer made serious tactical and strategic mistakes were woven into the myth. People began to question Custer's actions and motivations during the battle of the Little Bighorn, claiming they were impulsive and foolish and reflected his desperate desire for adulation and his aspirations for glory. Was he planning on running for president and seeking another wildly successful battlefield victory to elevate his image so he could easily defeat the scandal-ridden Grant administration? After all, he had a Democrat-owned newspaper reporter along to cover his mission. Others continued to praise him as a fallen hero who was betrayed by the incompetence of his subordinate officers. The controversy over who is to blame for the disaster at Little Bighorn rages to this day and will continue to captivate the attention of people around the world.

FURTHER READING

Ambrose, Stephen E. *Crazy Horse and Custer: The Parallel Lives of Two American Warriors* (New York: Random House, 1996).

Barnett, Louise. *Touched by Fire: The Life, Death, and Mythic Afterlife of George Armstrong Custer* (New York: Henry Holt and Company, 1996).

Custer, Elizabeth B. *Boots and Saddles* (New York: Harper, 1885).

Custer, Elizabeth B. *Following the Guidon* (New York: Harper, 1890).

Custer, Elizabeth B. *Tenting on the Plains; or, Gen'l Custer in Kansas and Texas* (New York: C.L. Webster, 1893).

Custer, George A. *My Life on the Plains. Or, Personal Experiences with Indians* (New York: Sheldon and Company, 1874).

Dippie, Brian W. *Custer's Last Stand: The Anatomy of an American Myth* (Lincoln: University of Nebraska Press, 1976).

Graham, William A. *The Custer Myth: A Source Book of Custeriana* (New York: Bonanza Books, 1953).

Leckie, Shirlie A. *Elizabeth Bacon Custer and the Making of a Myth* (Norman: University of Oklahoma Press, 1993).

Scene in Geronimo's camp, before surrender to General Crook, 27 March 1886.
Courtesy of Library of Congress.

Geronimo

Vanessa Gunther

There are few young children in America who have not made a leap of faith while shouting out the name of one of the Apache's greatest war chiefs—Geronimo. As a symbol of defiance and bravery few can match the almost bulldog expression Geronimo affected in Ben Wittick's 1887 picture. Like all icons there are often discrepancies between what we perceive and what is real. In truth the image that is most often remembered of the great Chiricahua chief was taken the year after he had surrendered to U.S. forces and was being held at Fort Pickens in Florida, separated from much of his family and his home in the American West. To further cloud this image, Geronimo, or *Goyathlay*, translates as "one who yawns," hardly the proper moniker for generations of thrill-seeking prepubescent children, or one of the Apache's greatest leaders. It is uncertain where the name Geronimo was derived from; it was not the name given to him by his parents when he was born into the Bedonkohe band of the Chiricahua Apache near the Gila River in what is today Arizona sometime around 1829. There is speculation among historians and Geronimo's contemporaries that his name was the mutilation of his Apache name by the Mexican soldiers and traders who occupied the land of the Apache until the middle of the nineteenth century. Other reports claim that Mexican soldiers would call out to St. Jerome before entering battle with the fierce war chief in order to build their confidence. Over time Geronimo took to shouting the name himself to unnerve his opponents whenever he entered into battle against them. While each tale is possible, it is more probable that Geronimo's name was mangled by the Mexicans since St. Jerome is more known for his scholarly attributes than his military talent. Whatever its root cause, the name stuck and in his later life was adopted by members of his own tribe.

The Chiricahua Apache are generally divided into four related bands, although some historians and Geronimo himself identified six. For modern discussions, two of the bands have been integrated into larger bands and the number is generally agreed to remain at four. The Chokonen, or central Chiricahua tribe, controlled territory in southeastern Arizona near and within the Dragoon, Dos Cabezas, and Chiricahua Mountains in the west, the Gila River in the north, the Sierra Madre Mountains in the south, and portions of New Mexico in the east. The Southern Chiricahua, Janeros or Pinery Apache, controlled the mountains along the modern Mexican and American borders. The Eastern Chiricahuas, also known as the Mimbres or Mogollon Apache, lived along the Rio Grande in New Mexico in the various mountain ranges that dot the region. Lastly, there were the Bedonkohe, the tribe into which Geronimo was born. The smallest of the Chiricahua tribes, their territory was northeast of the Chokonen lands near the Gila River and the Mogollon Mountains. Each band was supported by sub-bands, which were identified largely by the landmarks of the area in which they lived. Many of these smaller bands would suffer almost total annihilation at the hands of Mexican and later American soldiers during the middle decades of the nineteenth century. The Bedonkohe would be one of these bands. In the early 1860s the Bedonkohe were adopted into the other Chiricahua tribes when their numbers fell to levels that could not adequately sustain their people. Geronimo and his followers were adopted into the Chokonen tribe and followed one of the Apache's greatest chiefs, Cochise.

In his autobiography, dictated in 1905–1906, Geronimo stated that he was born in June 1829 into the "mountainous country which lies west from the east line of Arizona and south from the headwaters of the Gila River." Today this area would be part of Gila National Forest in New Mexico. Other historians, most notably Angie Debo, identified his date of birth as 1823, and the place near what is today Clifton, Arizona. Debo largely determined this site because "the Gila does not head in Arizona," and because of the traditions of the Bedonkohe themselves, wherein the site of an individual's birth was considered sacred and would be visited throughout their lives. It is possible that Geronimo, a man well versed in the traditions and religion of his people did not want the place of his birth defiled. Of his early life, Geronimo described an almost idyllic existence of warm sun, gentle breezes, and the shelter of trees. To his parents Tablishim and Juana he was the fourth of eight children. Such a large family would have been highly unusual among the Apache and it is possible that Geronimo's designation of siblings also included his cousins because there is no distinction in the Apache language between the two. As he grew he helped his parents toil in the fields where they grew corn, beans, melons, and pumpkins. The early childhood memories of Geronimo were recorded when he was between the ages of seventy-six and eighty-two, and almost twenty years after he had been removed from his homeland by U.S. authorities. Although Geronimo's memories of agricultural toil may be accurate, there is considerable debate among historians over whether the Apache ever engaged in agricultural activity of the intensity that Geronimo described in his autobiography. Though they did engage in some agriculture, it was limited in its scope. However, the Bedonkohe lived in relative isolation in the mountains and perhaps found greater reward in agricultural pursuit than did their cousins.

Geronimo was born at a time when the relationship between Hispanics and the Apache was changing. By the late eighteenth century, Spain's policy in the Southwest had evolved from attempts at colonization to eradication of the Apache. After a series of futile and destructive wars the Spanish came to realize the limitations of their attempts at elimination. In 1786, Spain adopted the *Instruccion*, a cohesive plan to disrupt the Apache's traditional food gathering and cultural patterns, by providing food and other goods to them. In time it was hoped the Apache would forget their old ways and adopt the more sedentary lifestyle of a peon. For forty years this policy kept the Spanish and the Apache at relative peace. However, when the war for Mexican independence broke out in 1810, Spain was incapable of devoting many resources to its northern territories. The overall Hispanic population declined dramatically and those who remained were mired in poverty. Soldiers often went without pay, food, or even adequate clothing. The limited rations that many of the

Indians had come to depend upon was reduced or eliminated. By the end of the Mexican struggle for independence in 1821, the Apache had returned to raiding the settlements and driving off livestock to sustain themselves. Faced with what could easily prove to be a widespread war, the government asked the villagers to donate cattle to feed the Indians, and forestall further raiding. For the Mexican villagers this request highlighted their considerable weaknesses and added to the growing animosity between the Apache and the Mexicans.

By the time of Geronimo's birth, the ration system developed under the *Instruccion* had declined to the point of near nonexistence due to the disastrous policies of the early Mexican government. Within a few years, the Apache had returned to raiding the Mexican villages and depredations abounded on both sides of the conflict. The Mexican military responded with a series of punishing attacks that forced the Apache to sue for peace in 1832. In the ensuing treaty between the two nations, the Mexicans offered no rations to the Apache, but instead limited their territory and expected the Indians to sustain themselves with hunting and agriculture. In the arid Southwest, this hard-line treaty was destined to fail as the land proved incapable of producing an adequate food supply for the Apache people. Within a year the raids had begun again. It was during this time that Geronimo's earliest recollections of farming began. Over the next several years the various bands of the Apache and the Mexican army engaged in a series of skirmishes that killed hundreds. Mexican troops often resorted to trickery to gain an advantage over the Indians by luring them into negotiations for peace, but then slaughtering those who came to talk. By 1842, the bloody conflict was largely ended when another treaty was signed that called for rations to be given to those who agreed to peace. However, the years of conflict had resulted in little trust between the parties and the wealth generated by the raids would prove to be hard to overcome for Indians and unscrupulous traders alike. For Geronimo these negotiations occurred at a time when he was coming of age, but his autobiography does not mention the raids. Since most Indian men went on raids only after securing the safety of their families, it is possible that Geronimo's recollections of this time were absent of the conflict that raged around him because his father had died when he was "but a small boy" and his mother never remarried. Although it was traditional for the bounty from these raids to be shared among the people of the tribe, Geronimo's experience with the raids of the early 1840s would have been only peripheral.

By 1846 Geronimo was a young man of seventeen and had entered into the council of warriors. This process normally began when a boy was about the age of seven. A male relative would give the boys their first bow and arrows and thus began their tutorial in the ways of the Apache warrior. With his mentor's approval and direction, a boy would be encouraged to join with other boys in hunting small game. Over time new tasks and activities were introduced that would hone their hunting, riding, and fighting skills. Each of the tasks was intended to teach obedience and responsibility. Once a boy had proven himself capable of these tasks, he would be allowed to travel with a group of warriors as part of a raiding or war party. These initiates would not fight, but would serve the warriors and learn from them. After several such outings, those boys who had distinguished themselves would be admitted into the warrior class. Only after joining the ranks of the warrior could a young man marry and enjoy the freedom afforded to the adults in the band. In 1846, Geronimo reached this milestone in his life and as a member of the council of warriors was able to marry the "fair" Alope, a young woman who had captured his heart. However, the price for his transition to manhood was steep; the bride price set by Alope's father was a small herd of horses. Geronimo paid the price and took his new bride home. Within a short period of time they would have three children, and Geronimo's family would expand to include the care of his aging mother.

While Geronimo's autobiography does not mention the conflicts that occurred between the Mexicans and the Chiricahua Apache following his induction into the council of warriors, raids and massacres continued to characterize the relationship between these two people. Though it cannot be said with certainty that Geronimo was involved in the raids, as a young man ready to distinguish himself in battle it would be have been unusual for him not to have participated. Geronimo himself was quiet on the subject; his autobiography characteristically underplayed or ignored his role in most of the conflicts he was engaged in throughout his life. However, it would be folly to believe that events such as occurred at Galena in 1846 would not have made the young warrior thirst for revenge. At the Mexican village of Galena, James Kirkner, a trader and former ally of the Indians, enticed them to come into the village to negotiate a peace between the warring factions. Mescal flowed freely and soon the Indian warriors were drunk. With their adversaries incapacitated, Kirkner and his men began the systematic slaughter of most of the Indians present. Reports indicated that as many as 130 Chiricahua Apache were murdered in this massacre. Mangas-Coloradas, chief of the Bedonkohe, was present but escaped the slaughter. The loss of his leadership would have robbed the Apache of another of their great chiefs. Geronimo could well have been among the warriors present—this would have been around the time of his initiation. Although his presence at the Galena massacre is in question, his participation in the revenge raids by the Chiricahua that fall is not. According to Nah-delthy (Jason Betzinez), who fought with Geronimo and was imprisoned with him in Florida in the 1880s, Geronimo was one of several legendary Apache warriors, including Cochise, Mangas-Coloradas, and Benito who "increased their reputations in the (following) battle" at Galena.

During the Mexican-American War (1846–1848) a raid and retaliation pattern characterized the relationship between the Mexicans and the Chiricahua. However, the necessity of fighting two foes at the same time left Mexico at a distinct disadvantage. By the time the hostilities between America and Mexico had ended and the Southwest was annexed into the United States, the Indians had gained the upper hand. Following the conclusion of the war in 1848 American troops were stationed near the border of Chiricahua territory. However, the entry of these new players into the world of the Apache would have little initial impact on the Chiricahua. The inhospitable terrain of the Southwest enticed few Americans to settle in the region; subsequently, the Apache continued their raids into Mexican territory. In his autobiography, Geronimo reported that he did not see his first white (American) man until 1858; however, it is widely believed that he most likely confused the date. Geronimo recounted his life story some fifty years after the events took place and an infallible recollection of his early life would be unheard of. Additionally, the Chiricahua were a non-literate culture, the timetables that governed the white world would have meant little to them. The Bedonkohe, under the leadership of Mangas-Coloradas, met with American military forces during the Mexican-American War and peacefully traded with them. The Apache took pains to establish friendly relations with the Americans to preserve their traditional way of life. It is possible that Geronimo was present at some of these exchanges, but because he was only a young man, he would not have taken part in any of the discussions. Because the meetings were subdued they may have had little impact on the young warrior. By 1851 American surveyors had entered into Chiricahua territory and again they were met by the Apache, including Geronimo.

When the American surveyors came into Chiricahua territory, Geronimo reported in his autobiography that they peacefully traded with the Bedonkohe, and even shook hands and "promised to be brothers." This clearly European custom gained widespread use among the Western tribes when dealing with non-Indians. Geronimo's mention of this practice in his autobiography may have been intended to portray the Apache as innocent victims in the events that he would recount next. At the time of his contact with the American surveyors Geronimo also reported that the Chiricahua were at peace with the Mexicans. Geronimo's recollection that peace existed between the Mexicans and the Apache fifty years after the fact has been questioned. His memory was clouded either with the passage of time or because the Bedonkohe made their home in remote mountain areas and their contact with the Mexicans was limited. Whether age or proximity was the cause, reports of Indian and Mexican depredations continued throughout the late 1840s and into the 1850s. However, because the Bedonkohe believed they were at peace, in 1851, the entire band traveled into Mexican territory with the intention of trading. The presence of women and children in this trek lends credence to Geronimo's contention that they were at peace. The goal of the tribe was to reach Casa Grande in the state of Sonora. However they stopped off at a place the Indians called Kas-ki-yeh to trade. While the men were engaged in trade, Mexican troops surrounded the lightly defended Indian camp and attacked. They easily overwhelmed the few warriors who had been left to guard their possessions and their families and then began the slaughter of the women and children. When the main trading party returned to the camp, they found the gruesome remains of their loved ones. To compound the tragedy the troops had destroyed their supplies and weapons; the Bedonkohe found themselves defenseless in hostile territory and vulnerable to further attack. For Geronimo the impact of the slaughter at Kas-ki-yeh was profound—killed in the attack were his wife Alope, their three children, and his aged mother. Geronimo swore to revenge the loss of his family and thus began the most personal of wars, waged at times almost single-handedly by Geronimo against the Mexicans and one that would last for almost the next twenty years.

Over the next year the Bedonkohe regrouped and solidified alliances with other Chiricahua Apache tribes. By 1852, Bedonkohe, Chokonen, and Nedni warriors left their homelands in Arizona and slipped into Mexico. Outside the Mexican village of Arispe the warriors killed several men who had been sent to speak with them, sending a clear message that this was a war for revenge. The following day the Chiricahua engaged in a pitched battle against Mexican troops. By the end of the afternoon the Mexicans troops were routed and the massacre of Kas-ki-yeh had been avenged. For Geronimo, the battle marked his elevation to war chief within the Bedonkohe. The battle however, did not assuage the hatred he felt toward the Mexicans, and almost immediately after returning home he was again on the warpath. Geronimo's hatred of the Mexicans was a mostly singular affair, no one else had lost as much as he had at Kas-ki-yeh, and few felt the same burning need to continue to exact retribution. Because of this, only a few warriors agreed to accompany him on his forays into Mexico. The early years of this personal war bore little fruit for Geronimo as he was often the only warrior who returned from these raids. Within his own tribe many held him personally accountable for the loss of these warriors, and he was rewarded with the enmity of some members of his tribe. However, Geronimo's desire for revenge also earned him the enmity of the Mexican soldiers and villagers to whom his name became equally synonymous with death and established him in the minds of Mexicans and later Americans as the iconic image of the savage Indian, and of native defiance.

During the time Geronimo began his personal war, his band merged with the Mimbres, most likely because the profound losses they had incurred in the previous years left them vulnerable to attack. The leader of the combined tribes would be Mangas-Coloradas who better than most could remember the horror of Galena and sought peace for his people. To forestall any hostilities that might erupt between the Americans and the Indians several Chiricahua leaders including Mangas-Coloradas agreed to a treaty of peace that allowed for the free passage of Americans through their land. Since most white men were merely using the Apache land as a conduit to get to California, their presence had little impact on the day-to-day lives of the Chiricahua. As such the treaty was little more than a goodwill gesture between the two groups; this goodwill would not last. Though Geronimo was not a signatory to this treaty, as a member of the combined tribes he honored the agreement with the Americans but continued raiding into Mexico. Following the loss of Alope, he married two women, Chee-hash-kish and She-gha, and began to rebuild his shattered life.

By 1855, the government had persuaded some of the other Apache bands to agree to land cessions. As with the Chiricahua treaty, its impact on the daily lives of the Indians in the Southwest would be minimal because of the limited white settlement. Geronimo's band was not involved in these negotiations; however, in 1858 he and his band met with American soldiers and agreed not to commit depredations in the region. The following year that agreement would be tested when Americans resumed the mining of copper in Mimbres territory, and the year after that gold was discovered near Santa Paula. A rapid influx of Anglos and Mexicans into the territory followed, along with a concomitant rise in violence against the Indians and a sharp reduction in the game on which they depended for survival. With their survival threatened bands began raiding the settlements, but Mangas-Coloradas continued to push for peace. An all-out war with the Americans would result in further hardship for his people and would further reduce their numbers. In summer 1860, Mangas-Coloradas was at Pino Alto offering assurances of the peaceful intentions of the Chiricahua when he was seized by the miners, tied to a tree, and whipped mercilessly. This foolish action resulted in a bloody war that demonstrated the combined might of the Chiricahua bands.

The outbreak of the Civil War in 1861 forced the United States to reallocate most of its soldiers to the East, which left the Southwest with few trained soldiers for defense. Although the Confederacy attempted to seize the Southwest early on in the conflict to gain access to ports along the Pacific and the mining resources, their attempts were thwarted by military volunteers from California. By 1862, the Confederates had been pushed out of the Arizona territory and Union forces, led by James Henry Carleton, moved to control the warring Indians, either by annihilation or forced confinement on reservations. Carleton's limited forces found themselves hard pressed to achieve their mission and the situation began to spiral out of control. As conditions deteriorated, duplicity on the part of the Union forces became common and the results predictably disastrous. In early 1863, American forces approached Mangas-Coloradas with a proposal for peace. When the peace proposal was presented to the tribe, Geronimo opposed it, but to test the sincerity of the Americans the tribe was divided into two factions. One led by Mangas-Coloradas would accept the American offer of peace, and the other would remain in their homelands until they were sure the peace treaty would be faithfully adhered to. The Chiricahua were wise to be cautious, once Mangas-Coloradas was within the control of Union military forces, General Joseph Rodman West, a subordinate of Carleton's, arrested him. Later that evening the military reported that Mangas-Coloradas was shot while trying to escape. The army surgeon then removed his head, boiled it, and sent the skull to the East for study. To the Chiricahua such betrayal under a banner of peace was, according to Geronimo, "Perhaps the greatest wrong ever done to the Indians." The murder of Mangas-Coloradas elevated Geronimo to a leadership position within the tribe, and only inflamed the hostilities between the Chiricahua and the American.

The murder of Mangas-Coloradas resulted in a fury of depredations against settlers in the Arizona territory. Allied with the Chokonen band, led by Cochise, the Bedonkohe, now led by Geronimo, and other Chiricahua bands raided with impunity until the end of the Civil War. Once the war in the East had ended however, troops and settlers returned to the region, this further incursion into Chiricahua territory only escalated the violence further. By 1870, it became apparent that the government would need to approach the situation differently if the region was to be settled safely. Under president U.S. Grant's celebrated but ultimately disastrous peace policy, the government dispatched Special Agent William Arny to negotiate an end to the hostilities. After meeting with various bands of the Apache, Arny persuaded several of the Chiricahua bands to agree to live on reservations of land if rations and other support were provided. Geronimo while aware of the negotiations did not take part in the treaties, but did move with the tribes to the designated areas. In 1871, the United States approved $70,000 for the purchase of rations and supplies, but also sent General George Crook into the region to oversee the transition of the Indians onto reservations.

For George Crook, Grant's peace policy was both carrot and stick. The government would provide the rations and the land to those Indians who agreed to the terms of the policy. Those who refused the peaceful overtures of the government would confront the might of the military. Crook sent word to the various tribes that they were obligated to be on their reservations by February 1872 or face retribution. To the chagrin of Crook and the benefit of the Apache, the government dispatched Brigadier General Oliver Otis Howard on a mission to evaluate the conditions in the Southwest. Howard reevaluated the suitability of the lands that had been set aside for the Indians and conferred with the bands that had failed to heed Crook's warning to move to the reservations. He pointedly sought a meeting with Cochise to encourage a peaceful resolution to the conflict that had raged for too long. Cochise and the leaders of his allied bands, including Geronimo, met to discuss the issues and on 13 October 1872 a final agreement was made. The Chiricahua would remain on their homeland and would receive support from the government to offset the loss of game and land that would be given over to settlers. In exchange, there would be peace between the Chiricahua and the settlers. By spring 1873, the Southwest was largely at peace. Although reports of depredations still filtered in, most were the result of outrages perpetuated by Americans and the predictable retaliation by the tribes. The peace held until 1875 when the government changed its tactics in dealing with Native Americans to open up more lands for settlement and embarked on a new policy, concentration.

The policy of concentration called for the government to collect onto small tracts of land several tribes of Indians, many of whom were traditional enemies. This policy would be carried out despite the promises and treaties made by the government that had guaranteed the Indians access to their traditional lands in perpetuity. For the Americans, the promise of the wealth held in the lands and the desire for increased settlement outweighed the desire to honor the treaties. These new reservations were universally dismal, poorly supplied, and grossly overcrowded. Predictably the change in policy resulted in conflict. At the center of the conflict would be Geronimo.

By 1876, it was time for the removal of the Chiricahua. Cochise, the primary chief of the Chiricahua, had died in June 1874, and his demise had restructured the authority within the tribes. While Cochise had designated his son, Taza, as the new leader of the Chokonen, his leadership was contested by members of his own band. This internal conflict allowed Geronimo to assume greater authority among the Chiricahua tribes. When presented with the new policy of concentration Geronimo and his followers left the reservation and hid out in the Alamosa. Instead of seeking a mutually beneficial agreement to deal with the Chiricahua, in June 1876 the Chiricahua reservation was closed. For the Chiricahua, this meant their traditional lands would be given over to white settlement; there was nowhere for them to go except to crowd onto reservations with other Southwestern tribes. Since these new reservations were overcrowded and barren, the life the government now proposed for the Chiricahua would be one of poverty and despair. The job of convincing the Indians to relocate fell to Agent John Clum, a man who would prove to be ill suited to the position entrusted to him. When he was unable to persuade the Chiricahua to relocate, he began a prolonged campaign of character assassination, with Geronimo as his target. To Clum and the other Americans gathered in the small settlements of Arizona, Geronimo became the convenient target for any depredation that occurred in the region. As a result his name became synonymous with a war that would rage for the next decade.

Using the Warm Spring Agency in New Mexico as a base, Geronimo and other "renegade" Indians raided into Arizona and across the Rio Grande into Mexico from 1876 to 1877. Reports indicate that he drew rations, and brought stolen horses into the reservation. In early spring 1877 the Commissioner of Indian Affairs issued orders for Geronimo's arrest and removal to the San Carlos Reservation in Arizona where he was to be held under a charge of murder and theft. Indian police on the Warm Springs Reservation complied with the commissioner's order and Geronimo along with several of his followers was arrested. To compound the matter, additional orders were given for the Warm Springs Chiricahua who were under the leadership of Victorio to also be removed to the San Carlos Reservation. By late May 1877, Geronimo, his sub-chiefs, and the Warm Springs Apache had been removed to the San Carlos Reservation. Once there the civil authorities failed to take control of Geronimo and he remained a prisoner of Agent John Clum. By June 1877,

Clum resigned his position as Indian agent over a salary dispute. When the new agent arrived on the reservation he ordered the release of Geronimo and the other chiefs. The chaos generated by the commissioner's order had resulted in little more than further confusion and ill will.

By spring of the following year, conditions on the overcrowded and arid San Carlos Reservation had become intolerable. On 4 April 1878 Geronimo, his immediate family, and Juh, the leader of the Bedonkohe, and several followers quit the San Carlos Reservation. Within a year, missteps on the part of the government agents pushed several more Indians away from the agency. Without a safe haven and denied access to their traditional homelands, these Indians had little choice but to raid to feed their families, the cycle of depredations had begun again. As before the government proved largely incapable of managing the crisis. Eighteen months later, the government sued for peace and Geronimo and Juh again returned to the San Carlos Reservation. Although Geronimo had temporarily agreed to stay his hand, his agreement for peace was not binding on the other Chiricahua bands. Raids by the Warm Springs Chiricahua under the leadership of Victorio continued to plague Mexico, Arizona, and New Mexico. Victorio's rampage forced retaliatory action by the Mexican and American authorities. On 14 October 1880 a Mexican army force led by Colonel Joaquin Terrazas ambushed Victorio's band at Tres Castillos in the Mexican state of Chihuahua, killed seventy-eight including Victorio, and enslaved sixty-eight women and children. Of the original band, less than twenty survived the attack. The following year the decimated band sought assurances from the Americans for their safety if they returned to the reservation. None were given.

Rebuffed by the American authorities, the Warm Springs Apache, now led by their war chief Nana, joined with warriors from the Mescalero Chiricahua band and returned to the warpath. Fear of the rampaging Indians meshed with the rise of a messianic figure named Noch-ay-del-klinne who promoted the eradication of the white settlement on native lands and combined to create near-hysteria in some Southwestern communities. Despite the devastation brought on by Nana and the marauding Chiricahua, Geronimo remained peacefully on the San Carlos Reservation until 1881 when the U.S. military began to flood the area with soldiers. Centuries of betrayal and duplicity convinced Geronimo and Juh that a trap was being set, and he fled with his band to the Sierra Madre Mountains. A short while later they were joined by Nana and his band. Convinced that another band of Warm Springs Indians led by Loco needed rescuing from the San Carlos Reservation, on 19 April 1882 Geronimo led a small army of warriors and forced the reluctant Indians to join with their renegade forces. With their numbers now swelled to between 400 and 500, mostly women and children, the Chiricahua fled to Mexico to escape the troops that would certainly follow. In their path they left a swath of death and destruction. A week later they had crossed the international boundary and rejoiced in their deliverance. Their celebration would be premature.

Combined U.S. and Mexican military forces dogged the slow moving bands and forced them into several engagements. The most devastating was at Aliso Creek in Mexico when seventy-eight Indians were killed and thirty-three taken into slavery. Believing they had devastated the Indians' fighting ability the Mexicans did not pursue the Indians and ordered the American forces to return to America. This small grace allowed the Indians to make their way into the Sierra Madre Mountains where they were reunited with Juh and the rest of the Chiricahua. Despite the tremendous losses they had incurred on their journey, the renegades still had a large force with which to defend themselves within a mountain hamlet that had up to then been impregnable. So comfortable was Geronimo in this mountain fortress that he married his fourth wife, Zi-yeh, possibly as a replacement for Chee-hash-kish, who had been among those captured by the Mexicans.

The Chiricahua raided into both Mexico and southern Arizona, at times with seeming impunity. However, the unity they enjoyed would be short-lived; many of the Warm Springs Chiricahua they had rescued feared an all-out attack by the Americans and wished to return to the reservation. Additionally, Juh removed his band from Geronimo's camp to return to Arizona, and though the bands would meet periodically over the years, Geronimo was left with a band of eighty warriors and their women and children. Although the reduction of his fighting force did not immediately portend problems for Geronimo, the reassignment of General Crook to the territory of Arizona would.

As an experienced Indian fighter, Crook was well aware of the military prowess of Geronimo and the Chiricahua. At the same time he was aware of the purpose of his reassignment: to remove a band of Indians who were an impediment to settlement in the region and whose persistent raiding had strained the relationship between the United States and Mexico. Crook's assignment notwithstanding, he also knew that many of the complaints leveled by the Indians against the American settlers had merit. In summer 1883 Crook and his forces boldly entered Mexican territory to capture Geronimo and return the escaped Indians to the San Carlos Reservation. Wary of the precarious situation with a population, both American and Mexican, that wanted nothing less than the blood of the Indians and his trespass across an international boundary, Crook proceeded cautiously. Under a banner of peace he managed to convince Loco's band to return to San Carlos in July, and Geronimo had given him assurances he would round up his forces and come in soon after.

However, Geronimo would not present himself to the authorities at the U.S./Mexican border until late February 1884, a full seven months after his agreement with Crook. His surrender had been delayed by more raiding in Mexico to secure the livestock his people would need to sustain themselves and the death of Juh, the co-leader of the Bedonkohe people. When he finally arrived Geronimo's band consisted of twenty-six warriors and seventy women and children. They settled along the banks of Turkey Creek under the watchful eye of Captain Wirt Davis. However, it seemed conflict would be inevitable.

Stung by army regulations that prohibited their consumption of intoxicants or the right to deal with tribal members according to their own traditions, Geronimo abandoned the camp in 1885 and returned to Mexico and the Sierra Madre Mountains. The U.S. military crossed the international border in hot pursuit. Despite negotiations and another agreement to surrender, in March 1886, Geronimo slipped away from the Americans and with forty followers, twenty warriors, fourteen women, and six children. The group would eventually divide into even smaller bands to decrease their chance of capture and to increase the speed with which they might travel. Eventually, Geronimo was left with a core band of six men and four women. Geronimo's escape prompted the army to assign General Nelson A. Miles, who had recently defeated the Nez Perce in the Northwest as the new commander of the Arizona territory.

Geronimo believed that the American and Mexican military only pursued him for the purpose of killing him. Subsequently, he and his band were "reckless with their lives" and intentionally killed all Mexicans they came in contact with. While Geronimo was wreaking havoc throughout Mexico and the American Southwest, General Miles, with an eye toward his legacy, called for a new policy to remove all the Chiricahua to a location outside the Southwest. This would remove the Chiricahua from their home territory, and once they were gone settlement could proceed as planned. Miles's proposal would become policy for the War Department; however, no suitable location had been suggested for the Chiricahua relocation. With this new plan in place Geronimo found himself relentlessly pursued and with few options. At one point almost a quarter of the U.S. military troops—5000 men—were engaged in the hunt for Geronimo. By late August 1886, Geronimo had simply run out of places to go. While being pursued by Lieutenant Charles B. Gatewood in Mexico, Geronimo met with his tormentors under a flag of truce. Impressed with the young lieutenant and weary from the constant need to flee, Geronimo agreed to return to the United States and surrender. After an anxiety-ridden week, Geronimo did as he had promised and gave himself up to Nelson Miles on 4 September 1886. A series of missteps and broken promises followed as the Chiricahua and their leader were transferred from their homeland to various locations—San Antonio, Fort Marion, and Mount Vernon Barracks—before they were finally settled at Fort Sill in Florida in October 1894. For the next twenty-seven years the Chiricahua would be prisoners of the U.S. government.

Geronimo would be taught to range cattle and raise crops, which he successfully did and sold much of his surplus to the post. Over the years, Geronimo adapted to, but it can never be said accepted, his confinement at Fort Sill. His repeated requests to "go home" went unheeded, and it can be imagined that some sympathy was due this aging man who longed only for the comfort of his native lands. In time he was afforded considerable freedom within the fort and allowed to leave for occasions such as the Trans-Mississippi and

International Exposition in 1898, the Pan-American Exposition in 1901, and the Louisiana Purchase Exposition in 1904. It seemed the government had found Geronimo, the prisoner, was a marketable commodity, proof of the nation's conquest of the Wild West. Geronimo's movements were limited only by his occasional reluctance to conform to the rule prohibiting the consumption of alcohol. In 1904, Geronimo's wife Zi-yeh died of consumption and the following year he married for the fifth time at the age of seventy-six to a woman named Sousche (Mary Loto). Their marriage, however, lasted only a year before the couple separated. Sometime between 1905 and 1906, Geronimo married for the last time to a woman named Sunsetso. After several years as a prisoner he converted to Christianity, but continued to practice elements of his native religion as well. The lifelong battles of Geronimo would come to an end on 17 February 1909. After several years of decline, the once-feared warrior fell from his horse after a night of heavy drinking. Unable to move he lay on the cold ground until he was found the following day. By then the cold had seeped into his chest and within a week he was dead from pneumonia. Although Geronimo's imprisonment at Fort Sill lasted from 1894 to 1909, the Chiricahua would not be free to leave the fort until 24 August 1912 when their status as prisoners of war was lifted and they were allowed to leave. However, the Chiricahua Apache were still not allowed to return to Arizona because of public sentiment against them there. Despite the passage of more than a hundred years, Geronimo remains an iconic image of the Indian warrior. These images belie the role he also played in the conflicts that rocked the Southwest for almost thirty years, that of peacemaker.

FURTHER READING

Debo, Angie. *Geronimo: The Man, This Time, His Place* (Norman: University of Oklahoma Press, 1976).

Deloria, Philip Joseph. *Indians in Unexpected Places* (Lawrence: University Press of Kansas, 2004).

Geronimo. *Geronimo: His Own Story* (New York: Dutton, 1906, 1970).

Johnson, Virginia Weisel. *The Unregimented General: A Biography of Nelson A. Miles* (Boston: Houghton Mifflin, 1962).

Wooster, Robert. *Nelson A. Miles and the Twilight of the Frontier Army* (Lincoln: University of Nebraska Press, 1993).

"We have it rich." Washing and panning for gold in a stream. Courtesy of Library of Congress.

Gold Rush to California

Susan Badger Doyle

James Marshall's discovery of gold in California in 1848 was a critical turning point in American history. His inadvertent discovery impelled hundreds of thousands of people from around the world to rush to California in search of instant wealth in one of the largest migrations in history. The California Gold Rush was the five-year period from 1848 to 1852. In this brief period, anything seemed possible. It was a time of boundless enthusiasm when individuals with the simplest tools had equal access to gold. From the beginning, the excitement that gripped the nation and the world has been called a fever, a mania, and a contagion, but "gold rush" perfectly describes the phenomenon, as men rushed by the thousands, then hundreds of thousands, to get to California as fast as they could. It was like a giant lottery for anyone who could get there. And getting there became a significant part of the gold rush experience. The California Gold Rush was unprecedented in history, and its consequences still resonate today.

GOLD DISCOVERY

At the end of 1847 California was an isolated, distant region occupied by the U.S. military and awaiting the signing of the treaty ending the war with Mexico so that civil government could be established. Colonel Richard B. Mason was the military governor at Monterey, the capital. Monterey was the largest settlement in California with 1000 residents. It was also the commercial center of the region, but San Francisco was fast becoming a serious competitor. Formerly named Yerba Buena and renamed in January 1848, San Francisco had 800 residents and many new businesses and buildings.

Until the Mexican War, California was a thinly populated peripheral province of Mexico that was connected to America by the New England shipping trade. Beginning in the 1820s, Americans came by ship or overland on southern trails and settled in California in towns or on ranches, often marrying local women. The first American emigrant party to travel overland to California over the route that later became the California Trail was led by John Bidwell in 1841. From that tenuous beginning through 1848, the total number of emigrants who traveled the California Trail was 2700. At the end of 1848, the non-Indian population of California was about 7000 Spanish-speaking Californians, called Californios, and 6000 Anglos, mostly Americans. The Indian population is unknown but certainly exceeded the number of whites. California might well have continued its slow growth and marginal status but for the discovery of gold that changed everything.

In January 1848 James W. Marshall was in charge of a work crew of Indians and Mormons recently discharged from the army's Mormon Battalion who were building a sawmill for his partner John Sutter. The site of the sawmill was on the American River at Coloma, about forty-five miles east of Sutter's Fort at Sacramento. During the construction of the mill, the ditch or tailrace under the mill that carried water from the waterwheel back to the river needed to be deepened. Each night the workers diverted the river through the tailrace to scour it out, and in the morning the flow would be stopped for construction to continue.

In the morning of 24 January Marshall went to the tailrace to inspect its progress. He saw a few flecks and pea-sized pieces of yellow metal shining in the shallow water of the drained ditch. He reached into the icy water and picked one up, then another and another. Soon his men found more pieces. Suspecting it was gold, but not certain, they tested the metal. They pounded pieces with a hammer, and they flattened but didn't crumble. The camp cook placed some in boiling lye, and they didn't tarnish. A few days later Marshall took some nuggets to Sutter, who looked gold up in an encyclopedia and tried the recommended tests. Confirmation that the metal was gold only upset Sutter, who didn't want his workers distracted or goldseekers invading his property.

Sutter wanted to keep the discovery a secret until he could obtain official title to the mineral rights, but by then it was too late. Within weeks Marshall's and Sutter's men left their jobs to search for gold along the American River and its tributaries. The two weekly newspapers in San Francisco, the *Californian* and Sam Brannan's *California Star*, published the first announcements of the discovery in March. The *Californian* printed a short item on the back page on 15 March, and the *California Star* followed with a skeptical response on 25 March. The reports gained strength when the *California Star* published a six-page "extra" issue promoting the advantages of California on 1 April. The section on gold declared it could be "collected at random and without trouble." Brannan organized an express mule train to carry 2000 copies of the extra issue back to Missouri, in hopes of generating overland travel to the goldfields and business for his expanding miner's supply stores.

Although people in San Francisco had been hearing, reading, and debating about the gold discoveries for nearly two months, the spark that finally ignited the gold rush in California was on 12 May when Sam Brannan walked up Montgomery Street to the plaza, holding a bottle filled with gold pieces over his head and shouting that it was gold from the American River. Seeing Brannan's gold was the proof it took to convince people that the rumors were true. The next issue of the *Californian* on 17 May described the "considerable excitement" sweeping through the town as "gold fever."

THE ONSET OF GOLD FEVER

Gold fever spread like wildfire across the region. By mid-June most of the men in San Francisco had gone to the mines. Most businesses and churches closed, crews abandoned their ships, and a majority of the soldiers and sailors stationed in San Francisco and Sonoma deserted. The city was so vacant that the *Californian* temporarily suspended publication on 29 May, as did the *California Star* two weeks later. The papers were publishing again by late August, and they merged in the fall, but in July San Francisco was like a ghost town.

News of gold on the American River reached Monterey, 100 miles south, at the end of May. At first most were disbelieving. But slowly convincing reports and samples came in, and most of the residents rushed to the mines. From Monterey gold fever spread south to Santa Barbara, Los Angeles, and San Diego. However, southern California was predominantly Mexican, composed largely of native Californios. In spite of the distance and knowledge they would possibly be an unwelcome minority in the goldfields, more than 1000 made their way north in the fall.

As men from all over California flooded into the mountains, gold strikes were made on other rivers. John Bidwell made one of the richest strikes of the gold rush on the Feather River, not far from his ranch. Rich strikes were made on the Yuba River, Bear River, Weber Creek, and the Trinity River. Two thousand miners were in the goldfields in June, and the number doubled in July. By fall 5000 men and a few hundred women and children were scattered along the rivers, streams, and dry gulches from the Trinity to the Tuolumne, a distance of 400 miles.

Meanwhile, two government officials investigated the escalating events in California and sent reports to Washington. The first, Thomas O. Larkin, U.S. consul in San Francisco, traveled to the mines on the American River and was impressed by the quality and amount of gold being found. He sent two letters to Secretary of State James Buchanan in June. Knowing his news would be hard to believe, he included considerable facts, statistics, and assessments. The military governor of California, Col. Richard Mason, also decided to visit the mines. Accompanied by Lt. William T. Sherman, later the famed Civil War general, he started from Monterey on 17 June. They arrived at Sutter's Fort on 2 July. They visited the lower mines at Mormon Diggings, and then went up the river to Coloma. They spent several days examining mines in the area with James Marshall before returning to Monterey. Mason, too, anticipated skepticism and disbelief among his superiors in Washington when he wrote his official report. As supporting evidence, he sent 230 ounces of gold along with his report by special courier who traveled via Panama to Washington. Two weeks later he sent another courier with a duplicate of his report, but without any gold, via Mexico.

Word of the rich gold mines spread at first by sea and reached ports in the Pacific Ocean months before it reached the eastern United States. Orders for supplies urgently needed in California went by ship to Hawaii in July, and immediately ships headed to San Francisco with eager miners and whatever goods could be found. When the news reached Oregon in August, thousands of men, some with their families, left on ships or by wagon for California. Most of these went to the Trinity River mines in northern California. Another rush came from Mexico as thousands from the state of Sonora reached the southern mines during the summer and fall. In the fall ships began arriving from Peru and Chile. In December word reached Australia and China, although the first goldseekers from those countries didn't arrive in San Francisco until spring.

At the end of 1848, California had radically changed. The non-Indian population of California had increased from pre-gold discovery level of 7600 to nearly 20,000 at the end of the year. One of the most intriguing aspects of the gold discovery is that it happened in a foreign country. James Marshall's discovery on 24 January was nine days before the Treaty of Guadalupe Hidalgo was signed on 2 February, by which the United States acquired California and large parts of the Southwest from Mexico. When the news that it had been signed finally reached Monterey, the capital of California, on 6 August, the ensuing celebrations were somewhat anti-climactic in the frenzied atmosphere of the gold rush and rapidly changing character of the population.

ALERTING THE NATION

The first communications about the discovery of gold in California reached Missouri at the end of July, carried in Brannan's express mule train. St. Joseph and St. Louis newspapers printed excerpts, particularly the mention of gold being collected "at random and without trouble." Newspapers across the Eastern states began printing more letters and reports "from the gold regions," and any other news they could get from California. Many newspaper editors downplayed the stories about gold, others discounted them as too unbelievable, and some warned readers that the California promoters were merely trying to increase migration to the region. As a result of the conflicting reports, public interest was slow to overcome skepticism. To most Americans, California was a distant and relatively unknown place that had recently been acquired by an unpopular war. There was too little hard evidence to support the astounding claims appearing in the newspapers.

Earlier in the summer, the U.S. military dispatched several couriers to carry news of the discovery to Washington. The first, famed mountain man and scout Kit Carson, arrived in Washington on 2 August with letters and a copy of Brannan's *California Star* "extra." But no mention was made of gold in his extensive press coverage along his journey or in Washington. Navy lieutenant Edward F. Beale was also sent to Washington with a small amount of gold and official reports. He went by way of Panama and arrived on 18 September. Two days later he met with President James K. Polk. He told Polk about Marshall's discovery, but Polk didn't believe him. However, publication of the letters he brought from U.S. consul Thomas O. Larkin and Monterey mayor Walter Colton in New York and Philadelphia papers sparked a great deal of public interest, particularly Colton's statement that the California streams "are paved with gold." Finally, the first of two messengers sent by

Governor Mason, not the one bringing gold, arrived 22 November. By then Polk apparently realized the importance of the reports from California.

A dramatic shift in public opinion came when President Polk delivered his annual State of the Union message to Congress on 5 December. He spoke confidently and authoritatively about the "abundance of gold" in California. The gold also offered him a way to defend the Mexican War that resulted in the acquisition of California, saying the reports indicated the mines were more extensive and valuable than anticipated, as if he'd known about the gold all along. Two days later the second courier from Governor Mason arrived with the 230 ounces of gold, and Polk put it on display at the War Office. In the end the president's confirmation, the gold on display, and the full details of Governor Mason's enthusiastic report published throughout the country convinced the public that something extraordinary was happening in California. The national reaction was immediate and tremendous. Unrestrained exuberance pervaded the press. Foreseeing the momentous events about to unfold, *New York Times* editor Horace Greeley proclaimed the dawning of "the Age of Gold." The rival *Herald* described the atmosphere in New York as "gold mania."

WORLDWIDE GOLD RUSH

The news of unlimited gold in California, free to anyone who could get there, sent shockwaves around the world, setting off the greatest international gold rush in history. When President Polk's message reached London on 22 December 1848, it was published in the *London Times* along with "gold fever" stories from American newspapers. In January 1849 a report in Liverpool stated "the gold excitement . . . exceeds anything ever known or heard of." Thousands sailed for California from England, Ireland, and Scotland, joined by thousands more from across Europe, predominantly from France and Germany. Goldseekers from Sonora, Mexico, continued coming to the southern mines, and ships from Chile and Peru sailed into San Francisco. In the spring ships began arriving from China and from Australia in the fall. The first ships reached San Francisco in April. Hundreds more arrived by year's end. In total, 41,000 passengers landed at San Francisco in 1849.

AMERICAN GOLD FEVER

In the eastern United States, the effect of the news of gold in California was electric. Through winter and spring 1849, articles appeared in virtually every newspaper in the country about immigration to California. A nine-part series titled "The Golden Chronicles" in the January to April editions of the *New York Weekly Tribune* typifies the wild fervor in these articles. On 20 January the first article in the series announced that gold fever "exceeds anything of the kind ever witnessed in this country." Even more than editorial enthusiasm about the prospects in California, printed letters from the 1848 gold miners inspired Easterners. A letter from Peter Burnett, who led a wagon train from Oregon to the goldfields, raved, "The gold is positively inexhaustible."

A significant characteristic of the goldrushers is that most of them did not go to California to settle there but rather to find wealth. Their journey was an adventure rather than a commitment to a new life. They called themselves "argonauts," after the mythical Greek heroes who sailed on the *Argo* with Jason in search of the Golden Fleece. In the same way, they perceived themselves as adventurers engaged in a dangerous but rewarding quest. They called California "El Dorado," the mythical land of gold, or more often, the New El Dorado.

An expression that gained popularity during the gold rush is "seeing the elephant." Although it was used in America as early as 1834, the expression came to symbolize the uniqueness of the gold rush. Its meaning is difficult to precisely explain today, but it was understood by all goldrushers. It roughly meant "to have seen it all," but it was also used more broadly to express the uncertainties and difficulties of the journey and life in the mines. Many different references to the elephant were common. Those going to California were "going to see the elephant." During the journey travelers reported seeing "the elephant's tracks" or "the elephant, from the tip of his trunk to the end of his tail." Overlanders who turned back reported they "had seen enough of the elephant."

GETTING THERE

The California Gold Rush began in the eastern United States at the beginning of 1849. The immediate problem was getting there. Goldseekers from the East followed three main routes: by sea, around Cape Horn or by way of Panama, or on Western overland trails. The sea routes from New York, Boston, and other East Coast ports were the most popular at first because ships left long before conditions on the Plains allowed overlanders to begin traveling. The sudden surge of goldrushers wanting to go by sea routes in early 1849 created an unprecedented demand for passenger ships. Steamers, schooners, brigs, and even old whaling ships hurriedly announced sailing dates to carry passengers and cargo to San Francisco.

Few women and children made the voyage, and the men who sailed were usually well off. The cost of passage on a ship was high, as much or more than most men made in a year. For those who took goods to sell in California, the price was negligible compared to the profits that could be made. Those who couldn't afford an individual fare or wanted to economize joined a joint-stock company. The cost of joining one of the hundreds of companies that set sail in

1849 ranged from $300 to $700, and for one Boston company it was $1000. Companies usually had thirty to fifty members, although larger associations that bought ships had as many as two hundred. The members usually agreed to bylaws, articles of association, or a constitution and elected officers, which often disintegrated under the rigors of the journey.

Sailing to Central America and crossing the Isthmus of Panama was the quickest sea route. The average time from New York to San Francisco was three to five months, but later the travel time was reduced to two months or less. The first leg of the trip was a voyage of 2000 miles from East Coast ports to the landing at Chagres, Panama, at the mouth of the Chagres River. There they hired native boatmen to take them and their baggage forty miles upstream in dugouts to one of the small settlements in the middle of the isthmus. From there they rode mules on winding trails twenty-six miles through dense jungle to Panama City on the Pacific Coast. Travelers risked contracting malaria, yellow fever, or other tropical diseases in the trek across Panama. Once they reached Panama City they had to wait—many for six weeks or more—for a ship to take them 3500 miles to San Francisco.

Sailing around Cape Horn was a voyage of 17,000 miles that took five to eight months. Accommodations on the ships were crowded and uncomfortable. Violent storms off the cape were a constant threat. In part because the uninterrupted route around the cape allowed passengers to take more gear and even trading goods, more forty-niners chose it over the Panama route. Also because it was the older, established route for the New England whaling and trading ships, it was more familiar.

Although thousands left on ships in winter and early spring 1849, most California-bound forty-niners traveled overland on two major routes during the spring and summer. The central route, the main overland route, left from jumping-off places along the Missouri River. Known today as the Oregon Trail, California Trail, or Mormon Trail—depending on the destination—it went up both sides of the Platte River, up the Sweetwater Valley, and over South Pass. Routes to California departed from the South Pass route at various points and crossed the Sierra Nevada into Northern California. The trail was 2000 miles and took four and a half to five months. Thousands of gold-seekers also traveled on southern routes, on either the Santa Fe Trail or routes from Arkansas and Texas. These routes then crossed New Mexico and Arizona to destinations in southern California.

THE OVERLAND JOURNEY

The most popular way of getting to California in 1849–1852 was on one of the overland routes. Traveling by wagon was more affordable and convenient for most mid-nineteenth-century Americans than ship passage. It also carried on the tradition of American westward expansion that began in Colonial times.

In 1849, 30,000 goldseekers traveled the Platte River route—the California Trail—and another 20,000 went on the southern trails. After that traffic dropped off sharply on the southern routes but continued strong on the Platte route. In 1850, 45,000 emigrants traveled the California Trail but dropped to less than 10,000 in 1851. A peak occurred in 1852, when more than 50,000 emigrants crowded the trail. More families traveled in 1852, as the newly created state of California became more attractive as a place to settle. Thereafter the numbers of overland travelers declined and the pattern of predominantly family migration in the 1840s resumed as overlanders traveled to settle on the Pacific Coast and regions in between.

The California Gold Rush initiated a new form of migration that overshadowed the agricultural and religious migrations that characterized earlier overland travel to Oregon and Utah. Goldrushers went to California for the economic opportunities in the goldfields. In contrast to the extended families who were the basis for agricultural migration to Oregon, more than 80 percent, and at times 95 percent, of goldrushers were men. They were predominantly young, and they tended to travel alone, in single family units, or with acquaintances. Initially most of the men going to California did not perceive their destination as the place to establish a new life. Rather, they went to accumulate property that could be brought back home. The move was seen as temporary, and once sufficient money or gold was obtained, the adventurers intended to return home. If they stayed, they usually turned to other occupations and sent for their families to join them.

White, middle-class Americans dominated the gold rush as they had in agricultural migration, but in contrast to the more homogeneous rural and small-town emigrants in the 1840s, goldrushers were ministers, doctors, lawyers, craftsmen, merchants, store clerks, as well as laborers, farmers, former soldiers, and even gamblers. They were a cross-section of typical Americans. Although the majority were native-born, a large minority were born outside the United States. Goldrushers also came from a broader geographical area of the country, and more were from urban Eastern areas. Many were immigrants, mostly from northern Europe and Canada. A number of blacks made the overland journey, and though their presence was not considered unusual, very little information is available about them. As a result, the gold rush overlanders comprised a broader range of age, class, and ethnicity than agricultural emigrants.

Raising the money to make the journey wasn't always easy. Many goldseekers mortgaged or sold homes and farms, used their life savings, or borrowed from friends or family to buy a share in a company or an outfit of their own. For those with families, making the decision to go to California also wasn't easy. It often meant hardship for the family left at home. Special arrangements had to be made, and the social and economic life of communities was disrupted when great numbers of men left. Although it is evident that an unprecedented number of men decided to go, we will never know how many stayed home in response to the opposition of family and community members.

Once the decision was made to go to California, almost all men going overland joined an organization. One type was the joint-stock company, in which each man contributed an equal share to fund the purchase of wagons, teams, and provisions. Names like the Boston and Newton Joint Stock Association, Pittsburgh and California Enterprise Company, Washington City and California Mining Association, and Waterford Mutual Mining Association indicated groups of ambitious businessmen, not merely adventurers, in contrast to those like the Buckeye Rovers or the Experiment Club. Others traveled in more loosely organized traveling companies in which property was individually or jointly owned. Still others worked for their passage as hired hands or purchased fare on one of the few commercial passenger lines that were organized during the gold rush. The hired teamsters usually made the trip successfully, though most passengers on the commercial lines had a disastrous experience.

Those starting from home had to assemble a wagon and team, food supplies, bedding and clothing, firearms, and other essentials. Wagons used on the Western trails were smaller and lighter than the big Conestoga wagons used in earlier periods in the East. Emigrant wagons were composed of a box with bows and a cover that sat on running gears. The majority of wagons throughout the emigrant-trails era were drawn by oxen, but during the gold rush the use of mules increased dramatically. As trail animals, oxen were slower, but they had greater pulling power and performed better in rough uneven terrain than mules. They also required less training, needed simpler equipment, and generally had more endurance and patience. Mules were faster than oxen but not as strong and needed special feed. Despite their sometimes bad temper, mules were popular with forty-niners because speed was their main priority. Another enormous advantage was that mules could be used as pack animals. A great number of goldrushers resorted to packing when their wagons broke down, trail conditions deteriorated, or just to gain additional speed.

THE CALIFORNIA TRAIL

California Trail travelers left their homes in early spring and headed for the departure points on the Missouri River known as jumping-off towns. Before 1849, nearly all wagon trains departed from Independence, Missouri. St. Joseph was the center for gold rush travelers in 1849 and 1850. By 1852, the favored jumping-off town was Council Bluffs, Iowa, which continued to hold the lead thereafter. The reason for the shift in popularity from Independence to Council Bluffs is that the Missouri River bears westerly as one goes upstream, so that the jumping-off points upstream were closer to the trail along the Platte River.

Although many brought their own wagons and provisions from home, a large percentage of goldrushers in 1849 and 1850 came from towns and cities rather than farms and reached the jumping-off towns on steamboats from St. Louis. Individually or in a company, they needed to purchase most or all of their equipment and supplies. Outfitting overland travelers was the main business in Independence, Weston, Kansas City, St. Joseph, and Council Bluffs. Merchants sold wagons, animals, equipment, provisions, and all types of articles needed for overland travel, but often at exorbitant prices. Some overlanders outfitted by buying animals, wagons, and supplies for bargain prices at street auctions that flourished in these towns.

The earliest overlanders began arriving at the Missouri River towns in March to wait for the grass on the trail to be high enough to meet the animals' needs. The optimal time to start from the Missouri River jumping-off points was mid-April to mid-May. Each spring thousands of people camped on the outskirts of the towns while they waited to cross the river, creating instant tent cities that just as suddenly evaporated when all had departed. Ferries operated at several places from Independence to Council Bluffs. St. Joseph had two ferries, one in the town and the other a few miles upstream. Long lines of wagons waited at these ferries during the peak crossing times. Newspapers carried daily reports of trains arriving and departing, as well as the latest ferry and steamboat information.

Once across the Missouri River, feeder routes from the ferry crossings came to the Platte River and continued up both sides on what has been called the Great Platte River Road. The trail passed notable landmarks, first Jail Rock and Courthouse Rock, then Chimney Rock, the most recognized on the entire trail, and Scotts Bluff. The trail next came to Fort Laramie, a fur-trading post that was converted to a military fort in June 1849. Fort Laramie was the most important supply post on the Western trails prior to 1849 and continued to be during the gold rush. West of the fort the trail entered foothills the emigrants called the Black Hills and began a gradual climb toward the Rocky Mountains.

Travelers left the North Platte in the vicinity of present Casper, Wyoming, after crossing at one of the fords or ferries. A dry, alkaline stretch of trail brought them into the Sweetwater Valley and to Independence Rock, one of the most anticipated landmarks on the trail. Thousands of overlanders carved or painted their names on Independence Rock or nearby Devil's Gate. From there the trail gradually gained elevation to South Pass, a wide shallow pass on the continental divide. South Pass, the pass that Lewis and Clark searched for but never found, was the key to the entire central overland route and marked its halfway point. The ascent to the pass was so gradual that most travelers could not identify where they crossed the continental divide. But a few miles further at Pacific Springs they noticed the waters flowing toward the Pacific Ocean.

Not far to the west, travelers began facing an array of forks in the trail, shortcuts, and cutoffs leading to California. At Parting-of-the-Ways, the right fork went by way of the Sublette Cutoff due west to the Green River, then on to the Bear River and Fort Hall, a Hudson's Bay Company trading post on the Oregon Trail. It was a shorter trail but crossed desert and mountainous terrain. The left fork was the easier, established trail to Fort Bridger, Jim Bridger's well-known supply post. From Fort Bridger, routes went northwest toward Fort Hall or southwest toward Salt Lake City. Most forty-niners traveled the Sublette Cutoff, although many turned off on the newly opened Hudspeth Cutoff beyond Soda Springs that went west and intersected the California Trail near Raft River, bypassing Fort Hall.

The California Trail went south from Raft River to City of Rocks and then entered the dreaded Great Basin. Most of the travelers who went to Fort Bridger and Salt Lake City took the Salt Lake Cutoff back to the main trail at City of Rocks. From City of Rocks the California Trail went south and struck the headwaters of the Humboldt River, then followed its winding course for three hundred miles until it disappeared into the alkaline Humboldt Sink. The Humboldt River, then also known as Mary's River, offered the only practical route for wagons across the Great Basin. The long tedious trek, choking dust, temperature extremes, poor water, and harassment by Indians wore down the already exhausted emigrants and their animals. In disgust, many called the Humboldt River the "Humbug" River.

After the grueling weeks of traveling down the Humboldt, the goldrushers came to Big Meadows, the last place with grass and water before crossing the Forty Mile Desert. By this time they were in generally poor condition for the desert crossing. Although many were relatively better off than others, countless travelers had already abandoned most of their property and wagons, lost their animals, and had little or no food left. Most stayed at the meadows a day or two to rest themselves and their animals and prepare for the crossing. The plight of the forty-niners was alleviated in 1850 when enterprising traders from California brought wagons to Big Meadows loaded with provisions to sell at exorbitant prices.

From Big Meadows the trail skirted the edge of the Humboldt Sink, which in wet years was a shallow lake. At the southern end of the sink the trail forked. Two routes crossed the Forty Mile Desert, one to the Truckee River and the other to the Carson River. The two routes paralleled each other across the desert and trail conditions were similar. The difference between them was their route through the mountains on the other side of the desert. The Truckee route was older, but it crossed the river numerous times and was a more difficult mountain passage. After the easier Carson route was opened in 1848, it was overwhelmingly preferred.

The desert crossing was all that the emigrants feared it would be. There was no water on the desert, and mirages tormented them. Virtually all emigrants made the desert crossing in one run of twenty-four hours or more, stopping occasionally to feed and rest their animals. Most started in the late afternoon and traveled all night to avoid the heat of the day but had to travel through scorching heat and hot sands the next afternoon. The last ten miles on both routes were the worst. Here they hit deep sand, and many had to leave their wagons and lead livestock on to the river, then return. As they approached the river at the end, animals stampeded to the water. Those who crossed earlier in the season fared much better than later travelers. In 1849, relief parties were sent out from California to aid the last straggling emigrants, which saved hundreds of lives.

After getting across the desert, the Sierra Nevada presented the last great challenge before reaching California. Crossing the mountains was one of the most difficult parts of the entire journey. The passes were high, rocky, and steep. To reach the steepest ones, wagons were emptied and pulled up with ropes. From the summit of the passes it was still many miles over sometimes very rough roads to the mining camps and towns. As new camps and towns sprang up after 1849, entrepreneurs and civic boosters opened numerous new trails and routes across the mountains.

A number of goldseekers in 1849 and 1850 sought to avoid the Forty Mile Desert by turning off on the Applegate-Lassen Trail before Big Meadows. This route went north on the Applegate Trail leading to Oregon and then entered California on the Lassen Trail. The route was longer and crossed an equally forbidding desert, the Black Rock Desert. The Lassen Trail crossed the Sierras at Fandango Pass, a hundred miles north of the goldfields. This route proved to be as harsh and difficult as the Truckee and Carson routes, and many late stragglers also had to be rescued east of the mountains in 1849.

DAILY LIFE ON THE CALIFORNIA TRAIL

The overland journey was long, tedious, sometimes hazardous, and often un-comfortable. Daily life on the trail fell into a predictable pattern of breaking camp, traveling, nooning, traveling in the afternoon, and setting up camp in the evening. River crossings, deserts, mountains, and bad roads broke the monotony and challenged emigrants along the journey. The distance traveled each day varied with the kind of draft animals, the terrain, and the weather. Fifteen miles a day was the average for normal traveling conditions with oxen, at a pace of two miles an hour. Men with ox wagons walked alongside, driving the oxen from the left side. Wagons pulled by mules were faster, traveling at three miles an hour, could go farther, and the driver sat in the wagon.

Adequate water, fuel, and grass were important for evening camp. Most travelers used the same campgrounds and often depleted these resources with overuse. Water for people and animals and feed for animals were the most important requirements for the camp. In addition to the care and driving of animals and wagons, goldrushers traveling in all-male groups had to do every-thing from hauling water, gathering fuel, cooking, mending, washing, arrang-ing the tent and wagon, and other activities usually done by women. The men learned to distribute the domestic duties among themselves or hired a cook.

In the male groups of goldrushers, personality clashes, disagreements, and the absence of the social restraint of home and family often caused heightened tensions, occasionally erupting in violence. Quarreling, fighting, and homicide among emigrants were more common than violence involving Indians. The rate of homicide on the trail was comparable to that in their home communities, although accidental killings on the trail were more frequent than intentional homicide. As at home, most killings occurred between people who knew each other. "White Indians," white men disguised as Indians, and other white criminals were an occasional threat all along the trail.

More people died on the trail during the gold rush years than all other years in the emigrant trails era. Not only were there more travelers but also the gold rush coincided with the peak cholera epidemic years in the United States, 1849–1852. Cholera was the leading cause of all deaths on the trail. Other fatal diseases included dysentery, mountain fever, measles, and scurvy. The next significant cause of death was accidents. Most accidental deaths were the result of drowning, followed by accidental gunshot wounds. A wide variety of other accidents also caused fatalities. The third most common cause of trail mortality was homicide by fellow emigrants or Indians.

One of the remarkable sights along the California Trail was the enormous amount of supplies and property that travelers threw out to lighten their loads. Even before reaching Fort Laramie, the trail was littered with food, equipment, books, clothing, medicines, furniture, and wagon parts. One man wrote, "There has been enough thrown away on this trip to make a man rich." Another noted, "If I was going to start again, I would get a light wagon for mules, and gather up the rest of my outfit along the road." By the time they were on the Humboldt River, many overlanders reconfigured worn-out wagons or made new ones out of leftover pieces, while others abandoned their wagons and packed on what animals they had left.

The overland journey provided goldrushers opportunities for activities that interested them. Many men hunted game or fished at every opportunity. Some collected specimens of rocks, plants, and other natural objects. Some made drawings, and many kept diaries and wrote letters. Thousands carved or painted their names, often with dates and places of origin, on rocks, trees, and other surfaces at numerous sites along the trail. Evenings around the campfires were enlivened with talking, music, and games.

For many the overland journey was a memorable prelude to their gold rush adventure.

GOLD MINING

Whether they arrived in San Francisco by ship or traveled overland, goldrushers still had to get to the gold mines. There were two ways for those who came by sea to get to the mines: by boat to Sacramento and then over roads, or by land from San Francisco over primitive roads. Overlanders coming from the east had to make their way down the western slopes of the Sierra Nevada over rough roads. Men mined wherever they could. Among the first mining sites were sandy bars where the slower water flow dropped gold.

The source of the gold in California was the mother lode, one of the richest deposits of gold ever discovered. The mother lode was a four hundred-mile belt of gold-bearing quartz in the Sierra Nevada. During the years of the gold rush, virtually all of the gold mined in California came from placers. A placer is a deposit of gravel or sand along a stream or old stream bed containing nuggets and gold particles. The simplest process for placer mining is panning. The pan is used to wash the sand and gravel out of the pan in a stream, leaving the heavier gold particles. The basic tools used for panning are the gold pan, pick, and shovel. These essential tools were so ubiquitous that they became symbolic of the placer mining experience.

Because the fundamental activity in the California placer mines was digging with a pick and shovel, the mines were called "diggings." Placer mining was extremely hard work, involving intense physical labor under harsh conditions. A miner had to stoop or squat at the water's edge or in the water, and his hands were constantly in and out of the ice-cold stream. Washing "pay dirt" in pans was slow and tedious, and machines were used whenever possible. The first machines were rockers, or cradles, which were introduced in 1848. A rocker was a faster way of washing the dirt than using a pan. The long tom, or tom, was introduced in late 1849. It was an improvement over the rocker but took at least two men to keep the gravel and water flowing through the box. A year later the sluice, a series of long wooden boxes, was developed. These mining machines allowed men to pool their labor into larger units, and mining increasingly became a cooperative venture.

From 1849 to 1852 the diggings became more and more crowded. At the beginning of the 1849 season, there were 5,000 miners in the California gold-fields. The number grew to 50,000 at the end of the year, and doubled again by 1852. During these years as the number of miners increased, the claims got smaller, opportunities diminished, and mining became more complex and competitive. The rewards of gold mining were great for some, were decent for many, but the majority barely made a living. An ounce a day was considered a good return, but most made less than that. Still, a miner making $8 a day was doing eight times better than a coal-miner in the East. On the other hand, prices for everything were astronomical. A loaf of bread that sold for 4 cents in New York, sold for 75 cents in the mines. In Sacramento in 1849, eggs were $1 to $3 apiece, apples $1 to $5, coffee $5 a pound, a butcher knife $30, and boots $100 a pair.

As mining technology advanced during the 1850s, mining methods became more complex. Beginning in 1853, hydraulics, the process of directing a powerful stream of water against a hillside and washing it away through sluices, and hard rock quartz mining replaced individual placer mining methods. The shift from mining by individuals and small groups marked the end of the gold rush and the beginning of an industry based in expensive and complex mining machinery, heavy capital investment, and wage labor.

MINING LIFE

Although miners continually moved around to new strikes or diggings, mining itself was tied to place, which led to camps with stores, saloons, boardinghouses, and restaurants. Most stores in mining camps were makeshift structures, constructed of logs and canvas. The stores offered a variety of goods and services, sometimes selling merchandise, meals, liquor, and lodging in one place. Mining camps had colorful names such as Poker Flat, Red Dog, You Bet, Whiskey Town, Petticoat Slide, Rough and Ready, Skunk Gulch, and Angel's Camp. Camps were generally within a few miles of a town, to which most miners went weekly. These towns offered gambling houses, saloons, and brothels as well as theaters that presented plays, ballet, and dramatic readings. There were also churches, restaurants, and other stores in the towns.

Like the journey to get there, life in the goldfields was a matter of constantly adjusting to new circumstances and changing conditions. And just as the travelers found it more efficient to join with others, miners tended to organize into mining companies. These groups of men, usually six to eight, lived and worked together for mutual support and labor efficiency. Miners often cooked for themselves, but most camps also had public eating places. Miners' shelters were rudimentary, ranging from wagons or tents to crude frames with canvas sides and roof. Some even built log cabins. The population of mining camps was a heterogeneous mix of Americans, foreigners, and ethnic minorities. They were constantly changing, transient communities of mainly men thrown together under difficult circumstances.

The daily average earnings of placer miners may have been as high as $20 in 1848, but fell to $16 in 1849, the price of an ounce of gold. It declined to five dollars in 1852, where it stayed until it fell to three dollars in the late 1850s. It is difficult to calculate an annual income because of the wide variation in actual working days, which fluctuated widely due to illness, traveling about, and weather conditions. Extremely high costs for food, tools, recreation, and transportation further reduced the net value of a miner's earnings. With so many miners in the goldfields, the placer gold that individuals could find was soon depleted. The net earnings of most miners fell so low that a great many of the goldrushers were barely able to make enough to live on and were forced to remain there because they did not have enough money for transportation back home.

THE COMMERCIAL RUSH

Many goldrushers realized that the way to make money was not to work in the mines but to sell something or provide a service to the miners. The mining camps provided a ready-made opportunity. Entrepreneurs, freighters, and mule packers made huge profits bringing supplies to the mining camps.

These commercial opportunities were made possible by the ships that brought goods to California from around the world. The phenomenon of finding more profit in commerce and services than mining has been called "mining the miners." While very few miners became wealthy, the entrepreneurs were the lucky ones and many made huge fortunes. Notable successes whose products are still well known include Levi Strauss, J.M. Studebaker, Philip Armour, James A. Folger, and Henry Wells and William Fargo. In particular, Wells Fargo and Levis have become popular symbols of the West's frontier past.

Levi Strauss was born in Bavaria in 1829 and immigrated to New York when he was sixteen. In January 1853 he became an American citizen, and a month later he left for California via Panama. On his arrival in San Francisco he established a successful wholesale business that imported all kinds of dry goods—clothing, underwear, umbrellas, bolts of fabric—and sold them to small stores all over the West. In 1872 he formed a partnership with Jacob Davis, a tailor in Reno, Nevada, who made work pants stronger with metal rivets at the points of strain. In 1873 they patented the copper-riveted "waist overall," the original name for jeans, made from cotton denim.

John M. Studebaker came overland in 1849 to Placerville, where he made enough from making and selling wheelbarrows to miners to return home and build up the renowned Studebaker wagon company in South Bend, Indiana. By 1875 it was the largest wagon builder in the world, with over $1 million in sales. From 1902 until 1963 the company manufactured Studebaker automobiles. Philip Armour began as a butcher in Placerville and later became the foremost meat supplier in the nation.

James A. Folger, a Nantucket native, came to San Francisco via Panama with two of his brothers in 1849. His brothers immediately went to mine gold, and James Folger and his partner William Bovee bought a mill to grind roasted coffee beans and spices. They founded the Pioneer Steam Coffee and Spice Mills in San Francisco in 1850. Folger traveled through the California gold camps selling their products, and he took over the entire business in 1859 when his partner left for the gold mines. The company grew, survived the 1906 earthquake, and eventually became the leading coffee brand west of the Ohio River. The spice business was sold to A. Schilling & Co. in 1929. The Folgers Coffee Company was sold to P&G in 1963.

Henry Wells and William Fargo established Wells, Fargo & Co. in 1852 in New York to provide express and banking services in California. The company quickly built up a network of express lines and obtained a monopoly of the express business in the mining districts by 1860 and offered miners secure, honest banking services as well. In 1866 a consolidation of all the major express and stagecoach lines west of the Missouri was negotiated, and several companies, including Ben Holladay's extensive interests, merged into Wells, Fargo & Co.

Charles Crocker was born in Troy, New York, in 1822. When he was fourteen his family moved west to Iowa, where young Crocker struck out independently, doing farm, iron forge, and sawmill work. Swept up in the gold rush, he led a party of forty-niners overland to California, arriving in Sacramento in 1850. Two years of gold mining convinced him that opening a dry goods store in Sacramento would be a better way to make money. By 1854, he was one of the wealthiest men in town.

Collis P. Huntington and Mark Hopkins opened a miners' supply store in Sacramento and made fortunes from selling shovels and blasting powder. Later, together with shopkeeper Charles Crocker and grocer Leland Stanford, they became the financing partners of the Central Pacific Railroad. Known as the Big Four, they were the first great Western railroad barons and played a prominent role in California's rapid economic development from the 1850s onwards. Stanford University, Crocker National Bank, Mark Hopkins Hotel, and The Huntington Library are embedded in California's cultural landscape.

Another successful entrepreneur was Sam Brannan, the owner of the *California Star* who started the gold rush in San Francisco in May 1848. Brannan led a party of Mormons who sailed from New York around Cape Horn in 1846 to San Francisco Bay. He began establishing businesses in spring 1848 to take advantage of the rapid changes taking place in San Francisco, Sacramento, and Coloma. When he flagrantly used Mormon Church tithe money for his own investments, he was expelled from the church. Through his diverse businesses he soon became California's first millionaire.

Although the gold rush was mainly an opportunity for men's labor or commercial business, women played an important yet often underestimated role during the period. Women were scarce in the mining camps, and many realized the entrepreneurial opportunities that existed for their much-needed domestic skills and made huge profits. It has been noted that the less rigid social setting in the gold rush that allowed women more economic opportunities was the beginning of the women's movement.

INSTANT TOWNS AND CITIES

San Francisco emerged as California's most important port and city in 1849. San Francisco's economic growth was astonishing. In just one year, its population exploded to 25,000. By 1856, San Francisco was a complex city of 50,000 people, the largest on the West Coast. From 1848 to 1858, San Francisco went through several cycles of boom and bust brought on by a series of disastrous fires, declining gold production, a surplus of imports, and a shortage of warehouse facilities. Unfortunately, there were more bust than boom years. The erratic economic cycles in San Francisco were also influenced by its reliance on the shipping trade, seasonal fluctuations in commerce, and the tendency of merchants to oversupply and glut the market.

At the beginning of the gold rush, hundreds of ships in the harbor were abandoned when the crews deserted to the mines. The bay looked like a forest of masts. While the empty ships were clogging up the harbor, the rapidly growing downtown business area needed room to expand. Some of the ships were salvaged for their wood to rebuild the city after major fires. Others were towed onto the beach, grounded, and then converted into warehouses, dwellings, and other buildings. One was used as a hotel, until it burned in one of the fires. Another served as a jail.

San Francisco was literally built on the shipping industry. In summer 1851, workers began extending land into the large, semicircular curve of land in the northeast part of the city that was once Yerba Buena Cove. A steam excavator dug soil in the sand hills above the downtown and loaded it into railroad cars that deposited it along the wharves stretching out into the water. Hundreds of the abandoned ships were sunk intentionally and covered with the landfill. In the late 1860s, what remained of the cove was enclosed by a seawall, running roughly along the Embarcadero. In recent decades, as developers have demolished old buildings, excavated sites, or tunneled beneath San Francisco, many of the gold rush ships have been unearthed.

The largest inland towns were Sacramento and Stockton, which developed as distribution centers for the inland valleys and mountain mines. Sacramento supplied the northern and central mines while Stockton was the supply center for the southern mines. Towns sometimes developed from temporary mining camps when they became commercial centers for a district or when large numbers of miners congregated at an unusually rich strike. Placerville, strategically located on the main overland trail, was one of the best-known towns that grew out of a camp in the mining district. Nearly half of the mother lode population lived and worked in the mining district towns.

THE GOLDEN STATE

Mexican War hero General Zachary Scott Taylor replaced James K. Polk as president in early 1849, just as the gold rush was taking off. By that fall, Taylor agreed with those who wanted California to become a state without the usual process of obtaining territorial status first. A territory needed to reach a population of 60,000 to be granted statehood, and California had far surpassed that already. Partly because Congress was deadlocked over the question of slavery in states that would be created in the Mexican cession territory, many felt it was crucial to admit California as a free state. In September 1849 a convention at Monterey drew up a state constitution that prohibited slavery, not for humanitarian reasons but because most of the gold miners feared that slaves would be used in the mines and would compete with the white miners.

California applied to become the thirty-first state, but its admission to the Union would make sixteen free states to fifteen slave states. The proposed admission of California was also complicated by other unresolved slavery issues in the vast Southwestern territory ceded to the United States by Mexico.

After much debate between opposing North and South supporters, a compromise was passed by Congress, known as the Compromise of 1850, to settle the slavery issue and avoid a threatened dissolution of the Union. The compromise had five important measures: California was admitted as a free state; slave trading was made unlawful in the District of Columbia; a harsh fugitive slave law was enacted; the Texas-New Mexico boundary dispute was settled; and New Mexico and Utah territories were organized with popular sovereignty, so that when the territories became states the citizens living there could vote on their slavery status.

Zachary Taylor died from typhoid fever in July 1850 and was succeeded by his vice president Millard Fillmore, who supported the principles of the compromise. Congress admitted California as a free state on 9 September 1850, as part of the Compromise of 1850. It was a spectacular achievement. Less than two years, and two more presidents, after Polk announced gold in California in December 1848, California was a state. Although the compromise was a temporary solution forced by California's explosive growth as a result of the gold rush, it had an important consequence. The admission of California as a free state gave the Union the advantage over the next contentious ten years as the nation irrevocably headed toward the Civil War.

The character of California as a state was also a direct consequence of the gold rush. The 1850 census showed that two-thirds of the population in California was born in America and 24 percent were foreign born, compared to 10 percent in the rest of the nation. The majority of foreigners in California were from Latin America. The same census also found that 73 percent of California's population were between the ages of twenty and forty, and 92 percent were men. In 1852 at the end of the five years of the gold rush the population of California was 250,000. The U.S. population in 1852 was nearly 24 million, so 1 percent of the nation lived in California. An astounding amount of gold—more than $200 million—was mined in the five years of the gold rush. As a result of the gold as well as its popular perception as the land of opportunity, California has long been known as "The Golden State." The phrase was made the official state nickname in 1968.

GOLD RUSH LEGACY

The California gold rush was a revolution with worldwide consequences. The gold rush occurred at a fortuitous convergence of national events, happening at the precise moment the United States achieved territorial expansion from coast to coast and the American economy was in the beginning stages of industrial capitalism. Gold production in California during the gold rush and subsequent years as mining industrialized contributed nearly 45 percent of the world's total output. As a result, all countries of the world were affected by inflation. The gold rush also led to tremendous growth in shipping and trading.

More important, the desire to link California with the rest of the nation led directly to the development of the transcontinental telegraph and railroad. The construction of the railroad was the largest construction project of the time and impacted capital, commodity, and labor markets worldwide. Upon its completion, the transcontinental railroad created the largest unified market in the world. Together, the transcontinental telegraph and railroad mark the beginning of modern America.

The brief period of 1848–1852 was characterized by "gold rush society" in California. It was an unstable period of intense optimism, mobility, and opportunism. The spirit of gold seeking based on hope, opportunity, and luck conformed to the ideals of an urbanizing American culture much better than earlier rural values of pride, thrift, and hard work. Transition to permanent, stable society inevitably occurred within the next decade, but the effervescent gold rush social and economic environment can be seen as a precursor of twentieth-century California, a state with the reputation of being on the cutting edge of high-risk ventures and technological advances. The development of the aerospace industry, Hollywood, Silicon Valley, and the beginning of the biotechnology industry all share the limitless, optimistic atmosphere of the gold rush.

The spirit of the forty-niners is still with us. An enduring legacy of the California Gold Rush is the words and phrases embedded in our popular culture today. "Strike it rich," "lucky strikes," "mother lode," "make a pile," and "pay dirt" reflect the sense of immense wealth. "The golden years," "good as gold," and "solid gold" signify high value, while the term "gold digger" is demeaning. Most of all, the gold rush was the beginning of what has been termed the American dream: the freedom to find personal happiness and success. The goldrushers did not go to California to build a new life or found a new state, they went seeking personal betterment. Whether they found it or not, goldrushers changed the world.

FURTHER READING

Brands, H.W. *The Age of Gold: The California Gold Rush and the New American Dream* (New York: Doubleday, 2002).

"The Gold Rush: California Transformed" [June 2007]. Available online at California History Online on the California Historical Society Web site www.californiahistory.net/goldFrame-main.htm.

Holliday, J.S. *Rush for Riches: Gold Fever and the Making of California* (Berkeley: Oakland Museum and University of California Press, 1999).

Holliday, J.S. *The World Rushed In: The California Gold Rush Experience* (New York: Simon and Schuster, 1981, 2002).

Jackson, Donald Dale. *Gold Dust* (New York: Alfred A. Knopf, 1980).

Levy, Joann. *They Saw the Elephant: Women in the California Gold Rush* (Hamden, CT: Archon Books, 1990).

Owens, Kenneth N. (ed.). *Riches for All: The California Gold Rush and the World* (Lincoln: University of Nebraska Press, 2002).

Paul, Rodman M. *California Gold: The Beginning of Mining in the Far West* (Lincoln: University of Nebraska Press, 1947, 1965).

Rohrbough, Malcolm J. *Days of Gold: The California Gold Rush and the American Nation* (Berkeley: University of California Press, 1997).

Hetch Hetchy Dam in Yosemite. Dreamstime.

Hetch Hetchy

Kenneth W. McMullen

The biggest environmental fight in the American West concerned building a dam at the mouth of the Hetch Hetchy Valley. John Muir considered this valley second only to Yosemite in its beauty and ability to refresh the soul. The valley's location, in the western part of Yosemite National Park, became the cause of years of legal fighting, hearings in the House of Representatives and the Senate, and finally an act of Congress to finally settle the matter—somewhat. This fight between Western urban interests against a combination of Eastern and Western preservationists lasted almost fifteen years, and in the process created the modern environmental movement.

The valley lies in the Sierra Nevada Mountains and is part of the Tuolumne River watershed. The Central Miwok tribe used the valley for gathering food and as a temporary summer residence to escape the heat and humidity of the San Joaquin Valley. The name may possibly be derived from *hatch-atchie*—an edible grass seed—or from the idea that the main path into the valley went between two trees—tree being *Hetchy* in the Central Miwok tongue. In the latter case *Hetch Hetchy* meant "the place of two trees."

In the maneuvering that occurred during the wrangling over the valley, both sides failed to mention, or perhaps even realize, the original natives had already altered the landscape through fire, more than once, to suit their needs long before the white men arrived. The natives periodically burned the brush on the floor of the basin to make it easier to travel. Such burnings increased the grasses and ferns, drawing game animals such as deer. The Miwoks also harvested the seeds, as well as the acorns from the large oak trees.

Later, during the 1880s, as landscape painters discovered Yosemite, some, including William Keith, a friend of John Muir, moved on to Hetch Hetchy, possibly shying away from the competition in Yosemite. Muir sometimes dropped in to see the works based on Hetch Hetchy being painted. If the painting did not resemble the view as Muir remembered it, or if he thought the work did not show enough intensity, he badgered the artists to make the canvas match Muir's mental image of the scene. Others besides the artists appreciated the scenic quality of the valley. Harriet Monroe waxed eloquent concerning Hetch Hetchy's beauty, both in her testimony before the Senate's Public Lands Committee and in a poem. She, and several others, had experienced the valley close up while participating in Sierra Club camping trips held in 1908 and 1909.

Although the valley had scenic value to some, the narrowness of the western end of the valley attracted San Francisco's engineers, because at that spot the valley narrowed to a steep "V." This narrowness of the river's exit from the valley sometimes caused the basin to flood and create a temporary lake—if the runoff from the snowpack was heavier than normal. Some engineers, after investigating the suggested construction site, thought that narrow passage looked as if it had been created for the specific purpose of a dam.

From early on the city had locked its attention to Hetch Hetchy in spite of its possible legal troubles. One attraction of the river for the city came from the lack of downriver preassigned agricultural water rights. Many of the other water sources suggested by Hetch Hetchy opponents had potential problems because of the agricultural uses downstream from the projected dam sites.

Harriet Monroe

Harriet Monroe was an acclaimed poet of the early twentieth century and publisher of *Poetry, a Magazine of Verse*, which featured first-time poets including Robert Frost and Ezra Pound. Monroe loved the American West and became a central figure in the battle to save Hetch Hetchy Valley.

In 1899 Monroe visited Arizona, where she became enchanted with the Western landscape. Trips with John Muir and the Sierra Club to Hetch Hetchy in 1908 and 1909 made equally deep impressions. When San Francisco officials obtained a permit to dam the Tuolumne River and make a reservoir of Hetch Hetchy Valley, Monroe joined Muir's Society for the Preservation of National Parks in rallying national support for the valley's protection. She wrote repeatedly to the Public Lands committee, insisting that no government officer who visited Hetch Hetchy would deprive America of it.

As placation, San Francisco offered the government Hog Ranch on the edge of Yosemite in exchange for Hetch Hetchy Valley. Monroe decried the proposal. She also gave powerful testimony before the Senate Committee on Public Lands on 10 February 1909, vividly describing Hetch Hetchy's irreplaceable beauty and questioning why San Francisco should receive this water access without compensating the government or national parks. In 1910 she made similar arguments in a lengthy written statement to Secretary of the Interior Richard Ballinger, who had visited the valley and begun to question San Francisco's plan.

Ultimately the process became delayed into the administration of Woodrow Wilson, whose secretary of the interior favored the dam. Congress passed the Raker Act in 1913, granting San Francisco authority to flood Hetch Hetchy.

No one but John Muir had fought harder to save Hetch Hetchy. Even in later writings Monroe would longingly recall the splendor of the valley and lament America's great loss.

The city began looking for alternative water sources because the city officials, and the public, wanted to remove their dependency on the private water company—Spring Valley Water Company (SVWC)—that held the monopoly on the closest water resources. A reform-minded mayor, James D. Phelan—elected in 1900—spearheaded the drive for a publicly owned water supply. Many in the city seemed to feel that graft and corruption surrounded the water company and its owners. The city officials and boosters felt that SVWC had committed the "sin"—in the eyes of these self-same San Franciscans—of gouging the city's residents with its high water prices over the years. Being typical businessmen of the times, the directors of SVWC had taken advantage of unregulated capitalism in extracting a profit from their water company. The San Francisco Charter of 1900 mandated a municipal water system, and civic reformers, led by Phelan, saw Hetch Hetchy as the lynchpin for that system. Because of the way Congress created Yosemite National Park there remained a few private holdings within the Hetch Hetchy basin. Phelan and a few other concerned San Franciscans bought up these private lands; they then deeded the land over to the city. This maneuver allowed the city to file claim to water rights from the valley.

Phelan saw his city as a noble city with its favorable position: on the west the Pacific Ocean and Asia; to the east a potential commercial empire. The mayor envisioned San Francisco creating a domestic imperial presence throughout California and into Nevada. Phelan recognized that for the city to grow it needed water. The city had access to water on three sides, but the salty ocean liquid did not satisfy the thirst. Early on, Phelan fixated on Hetch Hetchy; there were other, perhaps closer, and perhaps better, Sierra Nevada rivers to provide the necessary water, but Phelan only had eyes for Hetch Hetchy and he never deviated from his purpose of obtaining the valley for his city.

In the 1880s, before Phelan became mayor of San Francisco, the state of California commissioned a study of possible water resources that might serve municipal needs. The engineer in charge of the study looked into Lake Eleanor—west of Hetch Hetchy—and at a higher elevation. Later another engineer re-surveyed the Lake Eleanor site and its creek, but passed over Hetch Hetchy. At the same time John Wesley Powell—chief of the U.S. Geological Survey—had engaged in his study of Western water resources. Powell indicated that he wanted no part of a plan to dam the Hetch Hetchy Valley to create a reservoir. Later, with the passage of time and a different administration, the Geological Survey's representative had no hesitation in recommending the valley as a potential water source.

Additionally, the city engineer of San Francisco undertook a two-year study of possible water sources. His recommendations to the city council suggested the Tuolumne watershed with dams at either Lake Eleanor or Hetch Hetchy. Significantly he included the idea that the untamed Tuolumne River with dams at Lake Eleanor and Cherry Creek, plus the SVWC watershed resources, was enough for the city.

In spite of all the other possible locations for the city to get its future water, the San Francisco officials continued to advocate for the dam at Hetch Hetchy. One possible additional factor in their focus on Hetch Hetchy lay in the elevation of Hetch Hetchy—it would facilitate the creation of hydroelectric power.

It needs to be remembered that national park land did not have the same cachet in the late nineteenth century and early twentieth century that it has today. If a public body did not control the natural resources, then they might fall prey to privately held, for-profit companies. Based on the city's experience,

San Francisco's officials had a great fear that if the city did not get permission, then SVWC or even the nascent Pacific Gas and Electric might obtain rights to the basin. If that did occur, then the city would remain in the grip of a monopolistic utility corporation.

In January 1903, Secretary of the Interior Ethan A. Hitchcock rejected the city's request to build a dam. He based his decision of the fact that the land lay inside of Yosemite National Park. The city countered that the lake created by the dam would make a scenic attraction leading to more tourism.

When Congress created Yosemite, the bill did not take into account property lines and watershed drainages. In the Yosemite Act of 1905 Congress attempted to rectify this oversight by realigning the boundaries and shrinking the overall acreage of the park. Yet the bill added a little over 100 square miles to the northern part of the park. The report, from which Congress based its action, said the land was needed to protect water rights. The question then asked by both sides was, "Whose water rights?"

A year later the San Francisco Earthquake of 1906 added more pressure to the issue. The city claimed that the SVWC could not, or would not, deliver the water the city needed to fight the blazes that erupted after the quake. The papers published reports that said that at times the fire fighters had insufficient water pressure to combat the fires. The quake and reported water problems in fighting the fires reenergized the dam supporters to submit their petition to Washington, DC, because Secretary Hitchcock had left the position. They expected a favorable decision because the new secretary, James R. Garfield, appointed by President Theodore Roosevelt, counted among his close friends U.S. Chief Forester Gifford Pinchot.

Pinchot, one of the leading conservationists of the time, sided with the city because he appeared to feel that Hetch Hetchy provided a splendid place for a reservoir for the city. Pinchot's progressive conservationist outlook came with a touch of utilitarianism: the greatest good for the most people. The city hoped, with reason, that if Pinchot supported their petition, Roosevelt might also.

Soon after his appointment, Secretary Garfield traveled to San Francisco to meet with city officials and other promoters of the reservoir; no opponents had been invited and none attended this meeting.

In the petition submitted to Garfield the city stated that it would develop Lake Eleanor first before building the dam at Hetch Hetchy. It also said the city planned on building the dam at Hetch Hetchy only when the populations had grown to the point where the city actually needed the water from the proposed reservoir. But the petition's language did not absolutely bind the city to do so. Once the city received approval from the interior department, the decision-making powers passed from the federal government to the city. San Francisco alone then had the power to determine when it became necessary to build the dam.

Shortly after receiving the city's petition, Garfield approved the plan. Within a brief period of time after Garfield's decision, Congress took on the Hetch

Hetchy issue when it investigated the idea of swapping of land between the city and the federal government. The city proposed exchanging some private land, which then would become part of Yosemite, for Hetch Hetchy, which then would be non-park land. This issue never came to fruition, but it became part of the congressional debates about Hetch Hetchy.

As Congress held hearings about the proposed dam, William H. Taft became president and Garfield left the interior department. Taft appointed Richard A. Ballinger to the position of Secretary of the Interior. Taft also traveled out West, but he met with Muir in Yosemite. Because of Muir's eloquence during their discussions, Taft suggested that Ballinger meet Muir in Hetch Hetchy. Ballinger then traveled to Hetch Hetchy and spent several days with Muir. Afterward Muir told friends that he believed that the valley itself won Ballinger over to their side.

To help with the fight for preserving Hetch Hetchy, Muir and some of his supporters created a new national organization, the Society for the Preservation of National Parks. This organization aimed to create a more national support base than that of the Sierra Club. The advisory council included people from: Appalachian Mountain Club (Massachusetts), Mountaineers (Washington), American Scenic and Historical Preservation Society (New York), *Poetry Magazine* (Illinois), Mazamas Mountain Club (Maine), and former Secretary of the Interior John Noble (from Missouri).

In addition, the General Federation of Women's Clubs became another effective ally for Muir. The clubs had a membership of approximately 800,000 women. Its members flooded the House of Representatives and the Senate with mail and telegrams opposing the building of a dam in Hetch Hetchy. The records of the House and Senate hearings have copies of the multitudinous mail the representatives and senators received, the vast majority of which argued that Hetch Hetchy needed to be saved.

Some small opposition arose even in the city itself. The prestigious Commonwealth Club of San Francisco appointed a committee of its members to investigate the issue in 1909. Their response was that the city should use the Lake Eleanor and Cherry Creek water resources first, and save Hetch Hetchy until some future time when the size of the city's population demanded the expenditures to obtain the needed water.

The new secretary ordered a study by the U.S. Geological Survey (USGS) on San Francisco's petition. The USGS report recommended—like the Commonwealth report—the Lake Eleanor and Cherry Creek approach to obtaining water for the city. The report added that if the city needed more water, the city could dam Poopenaut Valley—located about a mile below Hetch Hetchy on the Tuolumne River—for the additional water supply.

Upon reading the USGS report, Ballinger became convinced that the city did not need Hetch Hetchy; it could get by on Lake Eleanor and Cherry Creek. He then demanded the city "show cause" as to why their petition should be approved and set a date for a hearing.

At the hearing Ballinger required the city to report back to his office with a new study that looked at all other possible water resources, and evaluate how the reservoir would impact the national park. Muir and his supporters asked that the Garfield grant be revoked, and that the city be limited to the Lake Eleanor and Cherry Creek water storage resources. The opponents of the dam left disappointed that Ballinger did not completely eliminate Hetch Hetchy from possible use by the city.

In response to Ballinger's demand for a new report and to counter the growing opposition, which had begun to make headway against the efforts of the city officials, San Francisco hired, as a consultant, John R. Freeman. Freeman, a nationally recognized expert on hydro-systems, had assisted William Mulholland on the Los Angeles aqueduct. Getting a delay of several months, Freeman produced a large, very impressive report—the size of which dismayed the Sierra Club members because they did not have the financial wherewithal to research and present their position in like manner.

In his report for the city, to be forwarded to Secretary Ballinger, Freeman argued that Hetch Hetchy had very few visitors—countering Muir's tourist argument—partly because of the mosquitoes. Once the flooding from a dam established the reservoir, the mosquito problem would be gone and the overall tourist experience would be that much better. Freeman also argued that there were no roads to Hetch Hetchy, but after the dam was built there would be a road to the area that would facilitate access by tourists. Part of his report suggested that the creation of a lake by the dam had the potential to augment the beauty of the park and draw many people for water-related recreation.

While Freeman worked to create his report, a controversy developed between Pinchot and Ballinger over issues not related to Hetch Hetchy. The dispute lasted from 1909 through 1911. At the end of the dispute, President Taft had fired Pinchot and Ballinger had resigned. Taft then appointed Walter Fisher to the position of Secretary of Interior.

After a hearing with Fisher during which the city presented the Freeman report, the secretary ordered a survey by the Corps of Engineers. The Corps of Engineers performed their survey and wrote their report with complete objectivity—which did not benefit Muir and his supporters. The engineers were not mentally equipped, nor did they attempt, to consider the national park status of the land. They only examined its potential use as a reservoir. They also did not take into consideration any cultural issues. The report favored the San Franciscans and their future need for water.

After reading the report, and despite its contents, Secretary Fisher ruled that the Department of the Interior did not have the authority to grant the city petition. Thus he let stand Ballinger's "show cause" order.

In 1913 newly elected President Wilson appointed Franklin Lane to the office of Secretary of the Interior. Lane previously worked as a city attorney for San Francisco and had lived in the city. One of his first actions as secretary involved notifying the opponents of the dam that he had decided in favor of the dam. Additionally he told them that the Interior department would now place all of its resources at the disposal of San Francisco to help the city obtain the necessary approval for the construction of the dam. However, former secretary Fisher's decision that the Secretary of the Interior did not have the authority to grant the petition tied Lane's hands. The matter now had to be resolved by Congress.

The city lined up support among the Progressives in Congress, and, with Secretary Lane's support, succeeded in having Congress pass the Raker Act of 1913 that authorized the city to begin construction of the dam. The act also allowed the city to create and distribute hydroelectric power, but under restrictive conditions. Several lawsuits have been brought against the city in the latter half of the twentieth century accusing the city of violating the Raker Act in regards to the possible reselling of electric power to Pacific Gas and Electric. The construction of the dam began in 1915. Completed in 1923, it did not begin supplying water to San Francisco until 1934. Because the water is delivered unfiltered to San Francisco, no water recreational sports are allowed on the reservoir—eliminating one of the benefits Freeman argued would derive from having the large body of water.

Under the charter amendments of 1900, the voters mandated that the city purchase the SVWC. During the fight, and well afterward, the city and the SVWC negotiated—off and on—trying to agree on a purchase price. When the transaction was complete the city then built the aqueduct.

A few years after passing the Raker Act Congress seemed to have second thoughts about using national park land for municipal water projects. In 1916 Congress passed the Organic Act that created the National Parks Service, in part to try to make sure nothing like Hetch Hetchy happened again. The act requires that the Parks Service conserve the natural scenic beauty, the historic objects, and the wildlife in the national parks. The bill also charges them with making sure that the parks remain undamaged for the enjoyment of future generations.

FURTHER READING

Primary Sources

"Hetch Hetchy Reservoir Site. Hearing Before the Committee of Public Lands, United States Senate, on the Joint Resolution (S. R. 123) to Allow the City and County of San Francisco to Exchange Lands for Reservoir Sites in Lake Eleanor and Hetch Hetchy Valley in Yosemite National Park, and for Other Purposes (2-10-1909)," in *Hearings Held Before the Committee on Public Lands of the Congress of the United States and Related Reports, December 1908 to March 1909.*

"San Francisco and Hetch Hetchy Reservoir Hearings Held Before the Committee on Public Lands of the House of Representatives, January 9 and 12, 1909, on H. R. Resolution 223," in *Hearings Held Before the Committee on Public Lands of the Congress of the United States and Related Reports, December 1908 to March 1909.*

Secondary Sources

Righter, Robert W. *The Battle of Hetch Hetchy: America's Most Controversial Dam and the Birth of Modern Environmentalism* (New York: Oxford University Press, 2005).

Simpson, John W. *Dam! Water, Power, Politics, and Preservation in Hetch Hetchy and Yosemite National Park* (New York: Pantheon Books, 2005).

Wolfe, Linnie Marsh. *Son of the Wilderness: The Life of John Muir* (New York: Alfred A. Knopf, 1945).

James Bridger, American frontiersman, trapper, and scout. Image 1866, from the only known portrait. Eon Images, www.eonimages.com.

Mountain Men

Adam Pratt

The names of the hardy mountain men have become forever linked with the American West and the frontier. Jedediah Smith, Kit Carson, and Jim Bridger seem to tower above the other heroic figures of the West. Serving as trappers, explorers, army scouts, and guides west of the Mississippi River, the mountain men became folk heroes in their own times and part of the pantheon of American myths surrounding the frontier that have persisted for generations. With the exception of a few brave soldiers, several brave Native American warriors, showmen, outlaws, or a wealthy tycoon or two, mountain men had a monopoly on capturing the imagination of those who lived outside of the West. Before they faded into obscurity by the end of the 1840s, mountain men had become synonymous with the frontier, the American West, and the masculine qualities associated with those who lived in the West. Their self-reliance, ruggedness, and independent lifestyle came to define, for those in the East, the qualities of all Westerners.

From the year 1807 until the mid 1840s, mountain men worked primarily as trappers in the newly acquired and sparsely settled Louisiana Territory. A majority of the trappers worked for fur companies that supplied European hat makers with highly sought-after beaver pelts. Working primarily in the Rocky Mountains and the headwaters of the upper Missouri River valley near the Canadian border but also in mountainous areas of the Southwest, ranging from Santa Fe all the way to California, mountain men worked and trapped over a huge swath of territory. After 1840, mountain men turned to new professions so they could stay in the land they called home. Acting as guides, frontier diplomats, traders, and army scouts, mountain men used their knowledge of wilderness survival and mountain geography to safely incorporate a new generation of Americans into the Western landscape. Just as trappers stalked and captured their prey over such an expansive and varied country, so too did the experiences, motivations, and adventures of the individual mountain men differ from one to the next. Despite the assortment of experiences associated with the mountain man, historians and other students of the fur trade have sought to classify or generalize the different types of characteristics associated with the mountain man.

MOUNTAIN MEN STEREOTYPES

Stereotypes abound concerning the nature of the mountain men. Each attempt to define the mountain man is also an attempt, in some fashion, to define the West. The first Americans to study the trappers saw the mountain man through a romantic lens. For these early students of Western and frontier lore, mountain men could do no wrong. They sought a more simple existence, one free from the constraints of civilization, and spent their days not behind a plow but wandering through pristine wilderness communing with nature. Their many skills allowed them to survive in the wilderness as well as to find profitable employment with the fur trading companies. This interpretation, first attributed to the writer Washington Irving, does little to expand any understanding of the motivations or desires of mountain men but did firmly ensconce the mountain man in a layer of myth. Certainly some trappers did yearn for the freedom associated with living a more simplified life, free from the confines of civilization and society. Yet just as certain, other mountain men saw themselves not as enlightened individuals whose relationship with nature remained pure but as men who struggled against nature to earn a living.

This overly sentimental picture of trappers in the West probably had more to do with Irving's romantic notions of nature and the unsullied purity of the West rather than how any of the mountain men pictured themselves. For these individuals, the West was a natural treasure and those who lived in such a paradise must have taken on the traits of the place they called home. However, despite the mythic qualities associated with this version of mountain men, it became their most popular portrayal especially after their quarry, the beaver, had all but disappeared by the 1840s. With the disappearance of their primary source of income, the mountain men, too, began a slow disappearing act. They survived only in frontier myths and legends perpetuated by Irving and others who sought to glorify the mountain men for their willingness and ability to defy social customs and carve out their own niche in the wilderness.

Another generalization surrounding the mountain man suggests that most of the Western trappers had few redeeming qualities. Mountain men, because they could not find acceptance in civilized society, sought camaraderie from other loners in the wild. Lack of morals in the entire lot of trappers resulted in a class of men so degraded in character that they had reverted back into a stage of barbarism. Rather than an enterprising employee, this version of the mountain man held that the complex market forces driving the demand for beaver pelts were beyond the simple understanding of their primitive minds. Furthermore, the zeal and skill with which trappers sought their quarry ensured the ruin of their profession: The lack of regulations imposed on the fur trade resulted in trappers exhausting their only supply of income by depleting the beaver population faster than it could replenish itself. Their willing participation in the destruction of their livelihood all but proved to the mountain man's detractors that these men could not see beyond the present and were not worth the amount of praise given in the past. Most popular among environmentalists during the 1960s and 1970s, these individuals saw the mountain man as symptomatic of the destructive and wasteful nature of American culture. They also saw within the story of the mountain man lessons for future generations of Americans: Without government protection of wildlife and the environment, they argued, endangered American wildlife would go the way of the beaver and the buffalo.

Most recently, the more popular overview of the mountain man has been one that describes him as a highly motivated individual searching the West for a way to make a decent living. This interpretation of the mountain man's motives places him squarely within the spirit of the burgeoning American nation and the economic explosion that occurred after the conclusion of the War of 1812. Not only did he seek fortune in the West, but the mountain man also looked to the future and saw the land as an opportunity to spread civilization and American society. Instead of trying to commune with nature or live like an Indian, mountain men understood the expansion of civilization as a positive progression and consciously sought a means of aiding this process. Acting as the vanguards of American civilization, trappers served as frontier diplomats, guides, and traders, acting as intermediaries between the burgeoning American nation and the native populations. Their conscious attempts at nation-building facilitated the ease with which settlers could move to the frontier, expel the natives, and begin clearing land. But the mountain men, according to this view, always understood their role as trappers as a temporary one. The skills learned in the backcountry afforded them the opportunity to begin lives anew in any number of new occupations: farmer, scout, shopkeeper, and even politician. Most understood their occupation as mountain man as temporary, albeit profitable; a profession that would help secure a small nest egg and a reputation to boot. Mountain men thus had little reason to care about the survivability of beavers as a species, just as long as they survived long enough for the mountain man to earn enough money to start his own endeavor. But they did have a large stake in the expansion of the American nation. Mountain men desired the growth of the American nation because with it, mountain men would be assured of their property's protection and prestige in frontier communities.

Through these three generalized views surrounding the mountain man, a composite image of the Western trapper emerges. Certainly they were brave, familiar with the ways of nature, and able to survive in the wild. To a certain extent, they had ambition that drove them to the edge of the map and beyond. They often successfully negotiated, traded, and integrated into the native population. But mountain men also exhibited negative traits as well. They often lived by loose morals and their wanderlust often had the effect of tearing apart families as the mountain man went in search of quarry. They drank away too much of their meager pay and probably lived a violent life. But even these broad strokes do not perfectly define any one mountain man.

THE LIFE OF A MOUNTAIN MAN

Though still romanticized by many, mountain men lived harsh lives in the wild. Despite being able to range freely over land that few or no whites had ever seen, the lives of mountain men were unhealthy, dangerous, and turbulent. Having to rely on skill and their understanding of nature to find and trap beaver, Western trappers had to face the elements in their continual quest to trap game. Throughout the span of the fur trade west of the Mississippi, trappers had to contend not just with the elements but with hostile Native Americans who resented white incursions onto native lands. Mountain men faced the many dangers of the wilderness because beaver pelts had become very valuable in the eastern United States and Europe. Though usually only the fur company owners—those who could sell large quantities of pelts to hat makers—made large profits. Mountain men could make a decent living depending on their skill as trappers, the types of contract they negotiated with their employers, and how much of their pay they spent on whiskey. Though most never did make enough money to retire, trappers seemed to believe that another season would take them out of the red.

At its heyday in the 1820s and 1830s, about 1000 mountain men actively engaged in trapping. Most of the trappers, almost three-fourths, were of French-Canadian or Creole ancestry. The French had always played an important role in the North American fur trade, but once the French had been expelled from Canada and sold the rest of their land to the United States, their traders worked for both American and British companies, easily alternating their alliance based on who paid the highest wages. The small American minority of trappers usually hailed from Kentucky and Tennessee before moving closer to the Mississippi and then into the Western mountains. The American trappers worked solely for American companies. Eastern Indians, mostly Delaware and Iroquois, comprised another significant minority population in the Western fur trade. The Native American trappers also had few qualms about switching allegiances from one season to the next.

Most mountain men adorned themselves in buckskin outfits and tried to mirror the dress of Native Americans as closely as possible. Because store-bought clothes rarely lasted an entire trapping season, trappers often resorted to wearing the hides of the animals that they had caught. Often depending on strength of arms for their survival, mountain men carried rifles, knives, pistols, and tomahawks. They also carried a "possibles" sack that contained an assortment of essential gear—spare moccasins, blankets, flint, and tobacco. Most trappers also owned at least two horses, one to ride and the other to use as a pack animal to carry furs, traps, and other supplies. Their diet consisted mainly of buffalo meat, a few vegetables, and for many, frequently imbibed whiskey.

Most company trappers worked in teams of two. One man would paddle a canoe or pirogue filled with the men's supplies and traps, while the other trapper had the unenviable task of wading through cold mountain streams so as not to leave a scent, all the while looking for signs of beaver activity and for suitable locations to place traps. Traps weighed nearly five pounds apiece, constructed of steel with two powerful jaws and a metal spring that when stepped on would snap the jaws shut. Placed four inches or so below the surface of a fast-running stream, the trap was set and then anchored by a chain to a stake planted firmly in the deeper part of a stream. For bait, trappers used a stick covered with castoreum, an excretion from a beaver's sex glands, protruding from the bank over the submerged trap. When a beaver investigated the bait and stepped on the trap, it would spring, locking the leg or tail of the creature within the trap's sharp jaws. The captured beaver could swim off but the weight of the trap would inevitably drown the creature. After setting all of their traps, the trappers would return to the traps, remove the dead animals, skin them, and set the traps again. At camp, the mountain men would remove any remaining flesh from the pelt, stretch it on a circular hoop, and dry it. Once dried, the harvested pelts were bundled into bales of almost sixty pelts, ready for sale. This circuit of laying traps, skinning, drying, and resetting traps would continue until they had enough pelts to transport to the trading post or rendezvous.

The best hunts occurred in the spring, when the beaver still had their glossy and full winter coats. The spring hunts usually brought the trappers the most money because of the high quality of the pelts. The fall hunt, though important for both the trappers and their employers, produced furs of lesser quality because the beavers had shed most of their excess fur during the warm summer months. Summer, after 1825, had been reserved solely for rendezvous. In winter, the slowest season, the trappers remained in winter camp. This cyclical schedule soon dominated the trapper's life and the fur trade itself.

Throughout this entire process of laying traps, harvesting pelts, and bringing their haul to a trading post, trappers had to constantly remain wary of their surroundings. Severe mountain storms, especially in fall and winter, could strand trappers in the wild, away from food or shelter. Unwary trappers could also fall prey to Indian attacks or even assaults by wild animals. But a trapper's line of work also suffered from the fierce competition of the fur trade itself. Paid low wages for back-breaking and dangerous work, trappers could ill afford not to work because of hostility toward their employer. Fur traders could easily enough find replacements for disgruntled employees. In the wild, mountain men often resorted to base means to get a leg up on their competition. Theft of traps or pelts left in traps or worse, the outright destruction of traps were the most common forms of sabotage, though oftentimes trappers resorted to violence if one man felt that another was infringing on his territory. International rivalries, especially between American trappers and those employed by the Hudson Bay Company, could also turn violent.

William Ashley revolutionized the fur trade industry when he began engaging trappers to work for his company. Three levels of engages existed; the lowest, manguers de lard, usually applied derisively to rookie trappers. These men tended camp, butchered and cooked meat, and performed other menial tasks about camp. Equipped by the company and paid an annual salary, engaged hunters either hunted meat for the other trappers or directly participated in trapping beaver. The final group, called sharecroppers, also received supplies from the company in return for a share of that hunter's catch at a previously agreed upon price. The sharecropper eventually evolved into the pinnacle of mountain men, the free trapper. Not employed by any company, free trappers equipped themselves but could hunt with a company expedition for the added security. At the end of the season, the free trapper would sell his catch to the highest bidder. Most trappers, though they desired to turn a profit, never did. Those who successfully navigated the many pitfalls of the fur trade and did wind up wealthy and could retire found it difficult to resist the lure of the mountains and many felt compelled to return to the dangers of trapping.

THE EARLY FUR TRADE AND THE FIRST MOUNTAIN MEN

Mountain men and fur companies formed a mutually beneficial relationship early in the history of European settlement in America. Mountain men provided the furs that companies wanted to sell to Europe, while the companies provided gainful employment and a source of income for the backwoodsmen. But the first mountain men did little of the trapping themselves. Rather, they traded with Indians for the furs that the Indians had harvested for goods. French trappers had a monopoly on the fur trade in the first half of the seventeenth century, ranging the length of the Mississippi and into Canada. In fact, two French trappers learned from Native Americans that the best fur-trapping lands existed far to the north of where they currently trapped. Gaining the support of investors in England and Massachusetts, the two Frenchmen formed the Hudson Bay Company (HBC) in 1670, which dominated the fur trade by the end of the century.

Many American colonists also trapped for the HBC, and after the American Revolution no American company formed to challenge the dominance of the HBC on the frontier. The relatively heavy settlement pattern on the American frontier and continued British presence hindered any American effort to create a large-scale trapping enterprise. However, in 1803, new lands opened to trappers west of the Mississippi River when Thomas Jefferson purchased the Louisiana Territory from France. Almost immediately, the vast potential of Louisiana became apparent. After purchasing Louisiana, Jefferson sent William Clark and Meriwether Lewis on an expedition to reach the Pacific Ocean, which departed from St. Louis in 1804. The company of hardy frontiersmen, soldiers, and even a slave, the Corps of Discovery returned to St. Louis in 1807 after nearly three years of continuous exploration.

Even though the Corps had not yet returned to St. Louis, Lewis and Clark had consistently sent reports back to Jefferson about the variety and abundance of wildlife in the Louisiana Territory. The news spread quickly throughout the nation and many individuals set out for the West on their own initiative to seek their fortunes, awaiting them, they believed, in the form of beaver pelts. John Colter, one of the members of the Corps, often ranged on his own, hunting, trapping, and learning the lay of the land. In the winter of 1806, Colter received permission to leave the exploration party and join two American fur trappers, Joseph Dickson and Forest Hancock, heading up the Missouri River for the Yellowstone. These three men became the first Americans to enter the fur trade west of the Mississippi River.

Upon his return trip down the Missouri River in 1807, Colter encountered a large party of trappers on the western bank of the river bound for the Rocky Mountains. The most important and influential organizer of the early fur trade industry in America, Manuel Lisa, a Spaniard from New Orleans, had organized the expedition. Lisa, a former Spanish agent in the fur trade for a number of years, became the first person to organize a large-scale trapping party to head west. Colter agreed to accompany the trappers as he had more knowledge of the West and its inhabitants than any living American. Lisa's expedition reached the mouth of the Bighorn River late in the year and immediately began trade with the native peoples living in close proximity to the camp he and his men constructed.

Lisa returned to St. Louis in search of capital and men to trap in the West. Forming the St. Louis Missouri Fur Company in 1809, the primary objective of the company was to construct a trading post at the Three Forks of the Missouri—prime real estate for fur trappers. Guided by Colter to the Three Forks, the expedition had no sooner set up camp than they encountered the first wave of native opposition. Unfortunately for Lisa and his fellow mountain men, the Blackfeet (also referred to as Blackfoot) Indians resided nearby and had no intentions of allowing whites into their territory. After several close calls, Colter escaped with his life and headed back East in early 1810. After Colter left the Three Forks encampment, another member of the Corps of Discovery and a seasoned trapper in his own right, George Druillard, died fighting the Blackfeet. With the loss of leadership, the remaining trappers at the post packed their belongings and floated back to St. Louis.

Colter and Druillard set the standard for the prototypical mountain man of the future. Strong, brave, capable of amazing deeds of stamina, and able to hold their own in a fight, the two mountain men blazed a path for others who wanted to follow in their paths. But strength and the capability to act violently did not solely define the early trappers or their successors. Colter and Druillard also understood nature and the elusive nature of the beaver they hunted. Furthermore, the two also brought many Indian tribes into the American economic network by offering to trade goods for furs. This greatly changed the scene of power relations in the West as weaker tribes could ally themselves and trade with the Americans for firearms along with metal tools and other weapons. For the mountain men, most important, the precedent had been set that would link the trapper to the fur company. Ambitious individuals with the know-how and drive to start a Western fur company stood to profit immensely. But without the mountain men doing the incredibly dangerous trapping, the company owners would not have been able to reap the rewards. Thus, a mutually beneficial relationship developed early in the history of the American fur trade: Company owners needed the services of the mountain men while the mountain men themselves needed an outlet where they could trade pelts for money. Though the company owners profited greatly from the work of the trappers, their wealth could not have been accumulated had it not been for the grisly work of the trappers. And if the mountain men were taken advantage of by company owners and paid low wages, they were still paid for living the type of life they chose to live.

THE ASTORIANS

Twenty-one-year-old John Jacob Astor arrived in New York from Germany in 1784 with grand ambitions of wealth and power. Entering the fur trade, Astor decided, would fully enable him to accomplish these goals. In 1808, he formed the American Fur Company and created a strategy to not just compete with the Hudson Bay Company, but to dominate the fur trade in North America. He planned to construct a series of trading posts from St. Louis all the way to the mouth of the Columbia River that would mirror Lewis and Clark's route to the Pacific. Unfortunately for Astor, no path had been blazed between the headwaters of the Missouri to the Columbia River nor had a feasible route through the Rockies been discovered. To secure a post at the mouth of the Columbia River before the British could move in, Astor hired a ship to sail several of his employees to the location so they could construct a fort and trading post. He also determined to send an overland party to find a more viable route through the mountains.

The overland party led by Wilson Price Hunt, who knew little of the wilderness or how to survive in it, somehow managed to arrive at the Pacific coast relatively unscathed. The party, consisting of nearly sixty trappers, left St. Louis in late October 1810. Originally planning to follow the exact route of Lewis and Clark, Hunt soon learned that the Blackfeet Indians had become particular about who could travel through their lands. Not wanting to provoke a conflict with potential future customers, Hunt chose a roundabout and often difficult path through the Rockies. By the time his expedition reached the mouth of the Columbia in February 1812, a journey of sixteen months, the sea-going party had already landed and had completed construction of a fort aptly named Astoria.

Astor's grand scheme envisioned Astoria as the keystone in a vast trading network that, he hoped, would eventually span continents. Signing a treaty with the Russian consul, Astor agreed to supply the Russian outpost of Archangel if the American company could market Russian furs; and both parties agreed to territorial agreements concerning trapping. Furthermore, both the Americans and Russians understood the magnitude of the competition offered by the British Northwest Company (soon to be annexed by the HBC), and planned on joining forces to pinch the British out of the lucrative fur grounds around the Columbia River. Astor also planned for Astoria to act as a trade hub with China, trading furs for even more valuable spices and silks that he could sell for an immense profit in New York. But the crux of his plan rested on the string of trading posts in the interior. These posts would harvest the furs brought in by trappers employed by the company, but, most importantly, the posts would rely on Indians to supply furs and trade them for goods. The furs would then funnel toward Astoria and would be sent by ship to the Orient or back to New York. Astor's dreams of a trans-Pacific trading empire rested squarely on the backs of the mountain men and their ability to trap and trade in relative safety. The mountain men probably understood little of Astor's scheme and probably could not imagine the wealth he stood to gain if his plan succeeded. Although not forced into labor, their contracts with the American Fur Company stipulated certain terms dealing with payment and length of service. Although a successful trapper stood to profit from his hard work and know-how, those who would gain the most remained Astor and his investors.

The trappers hired by Hunt to trap the length of the Columbia River and trade with the native tribes had little time to work for their employer before international relations changed the course of Astor's nascent trading empire. In 1812, the United States declared war on Britain and the tenuous peace in the Oregon country between the trappers shattered. The Astorians feared that at any time a British warship would arrive and open fire on their trading post. The leaders at Astoria decided to sell the fort in 1813 as well as their assets for a fraction of their market value. Allegiance among the mountain men usually came down to who could pay them more, and with the disappearance of the financial backing of the Americans, most of the Astorians hired by Hunt simply began trapping for the British—many in fact, were Canadian citizens to begin with and felt more loyalty to a British rather than an American company. Loyalty to the highest bidder became a seemingly distinctive trait of the trappers, and many cutthroat business practices emerged as competition between the fur companies became more intense.

The premature dissolution of Astor's trading empire did not completely destroy American trapping in the West, but it had been set back. Astor's venture, though, proved the feasibility of an inland trading network of posts connected by the vast rivers of the interior. Of particular importance, one of the Astorians, Robert Stuart, traveled a new overland route from Astoria to St. Louis in ten months (The route he discovered was seemingly forgotten about and did not see any use again by Americans until 1824). But Stuart's journey proved the viability of creating an overland string of trading posts that trappers could travel to and unload their goods. With each new voyage into the mountains, trappers learned more about the geography of the frontier and essentially helped fill in the map for westward American expansion.

WILLIAM ASHLEY, THE ROCKY MOUNTAIN FUR COMPANY, AND THE RENDEZVOUS

Born in Virginia in 1785, William Ashley's ambitions stretched beyond what he considered the limited horizons of just the fur trade. A major general of the

Missouri militia during the War of 1812, Ashley also acted as the state's first lieutenant governor from the years 1820 to 1824. Having whetted his political appetite, Ashley desired more power but first needed a source of income to fund his quest for authority. In the fur trade, he saw a means to that end. Over the course of his career, Ashley would personally lead four expeditions of trappers into the mountains in search of lands teeming with beaver. Ashley's greatest contribution to the fur industry, though, was the system he devised for supplying his company with pelts. Although previous companies had their own trappers, most relied primarily on Native Americans to arrive at trading posts and trade the pelts for goods. Deciding that this approach relied too heavily on chance, Ashley instead planned on hiring a large number of trappers to provide his company with furs. His employees, called *engages*, would receive part of their pay in equipment—rifles, traps, clothing, and other necessities—in exchange for half of their catch, while the trappers would be able to sell the other half of their catch to the highest bidder. This revolutionary step firmly cemented the ties between the mountain men and their employers.

Lacking investors, Ashley and his lieutenant Andrew Henry formed the Rocky Mountain Fur Company (RMFC). Ashley first advertised for 100 trappers in 1822 in a St. Louis newspaper and soon enough the ranks had been filled by a motley crew of trappers found in the rough-and-tumble bars and brothels that lined the St. Louis waterfront. Some of his first recruits would go on to have legendary careers as mountain men—particularly Jed Smith and Jim Bridger. The first expedition met with disaster in 1823, however, when some of the trappers snuck into a native village at night, lured by curiosity as well as the possibility of finding sexual partners. One of the trappers became engaged in a dispute and ended up dead. Wanting to expel the white trappers from their lands, the Arikaras then attacked the rest of the party who had to swim to safety to escape. Whereas many would count their losses and turn away from the fur trade after such a setback, the challenge seemed to energize Ashley. In 1824, Ashley organized another expedition that he would personally lead. He had received news that his primary trapper, Jed Smith, had discovered an easy path through the Rockies proved accurate. Ashley also desired an overland route rather than having to go by river and the prospect of facing Arikaras bent on revenge. Proposing an overland campaign to the Three Forks, Ashley successfully used Smith's discovery of the South Pass. After disembarking at the South Platte, Ashley and his men came upon South Pass in April 1825. Though the pass had technically been discovered in 1812 by Astorians returning to St. Louis, it had been forgotten about. Smith's rediscovery made the Rocky Mountains much less of a formidable obstacle, and for years South Pass acted as the only viable route through the Rockies for settlers making their way West. South Pass proved the efficacy of creating a fur trading empire that relied completely on overland travel, free from the constraints of post trading or the trading needs of the Indians.

After crossing the Continental Divide, Ashley divided his expedition into four smaller parties that could trap more territory than one large party. Ashley also had to find a meeting place for the four parties so they could reunite and return the pelts to St. Louis. From his simple instructions to meet later in the year at Henry's Fork west of the Green River in Wyoming, Ashley began the defining tradition of the fur trade. The practical purpose of the rendezvous was to provide a means for resupplying his trappers as well as facilitating the process of gathering for sale all of the furs his trappers had amassed. This also had the effect of keeping trappers in the field year round, so they would not have to return to St. Louis themselves. The longer they remained in the wilderness, the theory went, the more fur they could collect.

But the rendezvous was not just a call to the mountain men. Ashley wisely understood that the native tribes still wanted to trade with Americans. Rather than constructing a string of costly forts like his predecessors, Ashley also invited Indians to the rendezvous so that he could trade all of his goods to natives without having to fear competitor's lower prices. By inflating his prices so much, Ashley assured himself of profits not just from the Indians, but from his own trappers who, he reasoned, could not successfully resist the temptation of whiskey and other intoxicants. Over the next fifteen years, trappers, fur buyers, Native Americans, and not a few outlaws met to trade goods, furs, and tall tales. Although many attended the rendezvous for purely economically driven motives, most went for the camaraderie, drinking, and good times. Because of the hedonistic attitudes that surrounded the rendezvous, it soon earned a well-deserved reputation for notoriety. The men, trapper and trader alike, laid huge wagers on anything that involved competition, from horse races and fist fights to shooting and knife-throwing competitions. They consumed huge quantities of whiskey, sought out pliant native women, and fought anyone who got in the way of their revelry. For many trappers in the wild for so long, the gathering was their primary source of information from the outside world and a chance to reunite with friends. It provided an outlet for their aggressions and anxieties with others with similar concerns. But mostly, the rendezvous acted as an intense celebration that alleviated the boredom and constant wariness of living in the wilderness with minimal human contact. The intercultural contacts between American trappers and Native American peoples served to break down preconceived notions held by both groups, and made the rendezvous a diverse and lively gathering.

Ashley, however, also had the foresight to know when to get out of a business that had no future. After only his second organized rendezvous in 1826, he sold the RMFC and earned a small fortune. Ashley had begun to understand that real money could be made by supplying the trappers and selling their furs to Eastern buyers. Investing capital into the actual trapping expeditions not only drained him of money, but it also took him away from his first love, politics. The buyers of the company, Jed Smith, William Sublette, and David Jackson, all well-respected trappers, took over the business and continued the practices begun by Ashley with the hopes that they too could retire in style.

JEDEDIAH STRONG SMITH

Born in 1799, Jedediah Smith differed radically from his fellow mountain men. Smith, a pious Methodist, tried to live as godly a life as possible. When not trapping in the wilderness, he spent his days in close study and meditation of the Bible's lessons. Fortified by his faith, Smith could bear suffering, remain in control of chaotic situations, and provide excellent leadership for the expeditions he led. He never swore, drank, or used tobacco in any form. Whereas most trappers sought to exceed their comrades with tales and braggadocio, Smith allowed his actions to speak for him. Probably his most frightening moment occurred in 1823 on his first expedition for Ashley. While in camp, a grizzly bear attacked Smith, violently throwing him to the ground, which cracked several of his ribs, and swiping at Smith's head. The bear's claws nearly tore Smith's scalp from his head and one of the other trappers, James Clyman, had to sew the scalp back onto Smith's head with thread and needle. That Smith neither complained nor fell ill became a testament to his physical well-being and toughness.

First arriving on the fur trapping scene in 1822, Smith soon proved his efficacy as a trapper, but his primary motive for crossing the Mississippi and entering the Rockies was not simply to perfect his wilderness skills. He had an innate curiosity about the geography of the West, the rivers and mountains, and the people who lived there. He desired an occupation that would allow him the opportunity to explore the tramontane West and make money while doing so. In the fur trade, all of his desires coalesced into a job perfectly suited for Smith. Although he did not fit the majority of the mountain man stereotypes, Smith became one of the most important mountain men not only for his role as proprietor of the RMFC, but also for his many explorations in the West, which paved the way for American settlers to cross the Rockies.

After the incident with the Arikaras, Smith headed West in February 1824 with sixteen trappers under his command on a course for the headwaters of the Columbia River. When snow prevented his party from crossing the Continental Divide, Smith learned from Crow Indians that a much less formidable pass existed. Whereas Smith was credited for discovering South Pass in March 1824, his employer, William Ashley was attributed with popularizing the route. Having passed over the Continental Divide, Smith and his men ably trapped huge numbers of beaver on the Green River. By fall of that year, Smith and his men had collected more than 900 pelts. Smith's journey also brought him into the camp of British trappers employed by the Hudson Bay Company. Although the United States and Britain had agreed to jointly occupy the Oregon Territory, no American trappers had been active there since the Astorians had been expelled in 1814. Though surprised to see Americans in the Oregon country, the HBC could only take extralegal measures to defend their traditional hunting grounds. Smith and his companions did not linger long in Oregon, but their journey by land to the Northwest signaled a changing of the guard for the fur trade in that region.

Having returned to St. Louis in 1825 with Ashley after the rendezvous, Smith led another expedition into the mountains in November of that year. After wintering on the banks of the Great Salt Lake, Smith and his men had a successful season of trapping. The 1826 rendezvous at Cache Valley lasted at least a week and also marked a turning point in Smith's career. After this meeting, Smith himself would partially own the RMFC and would be responsible for the welfare of his employees and his company's profits. Although he was a part-owner of the company, his sense of wanderlust overcame any good business sense when he decided to travel west of the Great Salt Lake and trap unexplored lands. Unfortunately for Smith, the lands he chose to explore contained few beaver. Traveling all the way south to the Colorado River and then east through the Mojave Desert, Smith and his party finally reached Spanish missions in California where they could resupply and rest. Leaving the mission country in January 1827, Smith and his party headed north and trapped beaver all along the San Joaquin River and its tributaries. Returning East for the annual rendezvous without any beaver pelts, the Rocky Mountain Fur Company posted high profits mainly because the other company trappers had brought in large catches.

Returning to California after the meeting of the mountain men, Smith and his men came under attack by the Mojave Indians and suffered greatly. More misfortune befell Smith and his men when they aroused the suspicion of the Spanish governor of California. Placing them under arrest, Smith could not secure their release until December 1827. Finally able to sell his hoarded cache of beaver pelts that he had been harvesting for the past two years to traders in San Francisco, he purchased more than 200 horses and mules. Wanting to put as much distance between his expedition and suspicious Spanish officials as possible, Smith led his men north and they trapped for the next three months. Arriving on the Oregon coast in July 1828, Smith's contingent of mountaineers had become increasingly frustrated because of the rough terrain and constant harassment by Indians loyal to the HBC. Desperate to leave the rocky terrain of the coast, Smith scouted for a ford over the Umpqua River. While Smith had left, 100 Indians had entered the camp offering to trade with the Americans. Their ruse worked and the Kuitish Indians killed all but one of the trappers. Upon his return to camp, Smith barely escaped with his life. Thanks to the quick thinking of his native guide, Smith and his three companions found safety with the HBC. Making their winter camp with the British trappers, Smith returned East and organized an expedition into safer lands—the traditional home of the Blackfeet. Though he had organized a strong contingent of trappers, the Blackfeet eventually forced Smith and his men out of their lands and back toward St. Louis. Their catch, though, provided the company with more than $80,000.

In 1830, Smith and his business partners returned to St. Louis ready to cash out of the fur trading business. This decision only strengthened in his mind when he learned that his mother had died while he was trying to make his way home.

Causing a crisis for the deeply spiritual man, Smith felt guilty about not being at his mother's side and decided to settle down. Smith desired to publish the journals that he had meticulously kept in the field, and also desired to publish a map of the West, with particular emphasis on its rivers and mountain passes. Selling his share of the company, then, came at an appropriate time for Smith. Having made a sizeable profit at the last rendezvous, Smith and the other owners could retire from the fur trade with money in the bank. Selling their outfit to five partners, noticeably Jim Bridger and Milton Sublette, the RMFC again switched hands.

Bridger's role with the company, however, had not completely ended. Part of the contract required that the old partners supply the new company with equipment so that they could undertake the spring hunt in 1831. Smith and his former business partners Jackson and Sublette wanted to begin a new commercial venture that would supply travelers on the Santa Fe Trail. When the new owners of the RMFC did not arrive in St. Louis at the predetermined time to receive supplies, Smith and his associates turned south toward Santa Fe. When they did finally catch up to Smith and his business partners, both parties agreed to travel to Santa Fe together where the old owners would outfit the new. The baggage train became stranded on the Santa Fe Trail near the Cimarron River. While searching for water, Smith was surprised and surrounded by Comanche warriors. Shot in the back and stabbed by multiple lances, Jedediah Smith, perhaps the most skilled and influential mountain man, died in 1831 at the age of thirty-two.

JIM BRIDGER AND THE RETURN OF ASTOR

Born in 1804, James Bridger became one of the most revered of the mountain men. Beginning his career in the West at the young age of seventeen, Bridger joined William Ashley's expedition up the Missouri River in 1822. Though young, the other members of the brigade recognized his potential. His skill as a trapper only increased over the years, as did his understanding of the geography of the West. Whereas Smith was more of an anomaly among the mountain men, Bridger epitomized most of the trappers. Standing over six feet tall with a powerful frame and piercing gray eyes, Bridger had not just the physique of a man inured to harsh living in the wilderness but the typical hospitable personality as well. Most trappers deferred to his judgment during stressful and dangerous situations and when arguing over the fine points of the West's mountainous geography.

Most of the other mountain men remembered Bridger not for his skill in navigating through the mountains, but for his ability to tell a tall tale. Bridger's good nature became tested only two years after he had helped acquire the RMFC from Smith and his associates. The rendezvous system had grown so popular and so profitable that it was not long before other capitalists wanted a share of the profits. John Astor and his American Fur Company had returned to the Rockies after their failed attempt at the Columbia. Having come to dominate the trade of the Upper Missouri by the end of the 1820s, Astor turned his sights to the mountains. In 1831—the same year Bridger and his associates purchased the RMFC—Astor's trade empire began to pose a serious threat to the RMFC not because of the skill of its operators, but because of its sheer size and seemingly unlimited capital. Astor's fur trading empire became so vast, in fact, that most simply stopped calling the American Fur Company by its entire name and referred to it simply as "the Company." The experienced Bridger and his companions consistently brought in higher volumes for the first two years of competition between the two companies, but Astor's lieutenants proved fast learners as they followed the RMFC's trapping brigades, copied their methods, infringed on their territory, and committed outright sabotage. Many mountain men, seduced by the lure of higher wages, defected to the Company in the highly competitive era of the early 1830s.

The 1832 rendezvous, the first time both Company and RMFC officials shared the same grounds, ended successfully for Bridger and his partners. Their supply train arrived in Pierre's Hole before that of their competition. The free trappers and sharecroppers unloaded their pelts with the first caravan, while the other trappers, irrespective of company loyalty, bought Rocky Mountain whiskey. That year also proved memorable because of the fight begun by the mountain men with a band of Gros Ventres. After the trappers had returned to the mountains for the fall hunt, Bridger decided to forego his hunt in an effort to thwart as many of the Company trappers as possible. In late October, however, Bridger's attempts to sabotage the Company men ended when he came upon a party of Blackfeet. Shot in the back by two arrows, Bridger survived the wounds and continued the fall hunt.

The Rocky Mountain Fur Company would prove much less durable. The former owner, William Sublette, had become a devious businessman and planned a scheme that would make him a rich man. Sublette had formed a trading company that competed fiercely with the American Fur Company in the Upper Missouri. After the 1832 rendezvous, Sublette had acquired all of the RMFC's debts in exchange for their supply of pelts. The owners hoped that Sublette would be able to sell the pelts and place the company again on solid financial ground. However, with the growing competition for furs in the West, turning a profit in the fur trade had become increasingly difficult. Backed by the trader-turned-congressman William Ashley, Sublette brokered an agreement with Astor that spelled the demise of the RMFC. Basically, the Company would abandon the fur trade for at least one year and would turn over all of the trade to Sublette. After that time, Sublette would sell his string of posts to the Company. Sublette traveled to the 1834 rendezvous, supplied Bridger and the other Rocky Mountain trappers in exchange for that year's catch, and with the exchange, the Rocky Mountain Fur Company ceased to exist.

The former RMFC proprietors refused to abandon the fur trade and the mountains they loved. William Sublette, having swindled Bridger and his partners, was bought out by the Company, and then convinced Bridger and his partner Tom Fitzpatrick to acquire one of Sublette's trading posts, Fort William, in July 1835. However, at the 1836 rendezvous, the Company finally succeeded in destroying the last vestiges of the RMFC when it bought the strategically located Ft. William from Fitzpatrick. Most of the original trappers and proprietors that had begun working for William Ashley in the 1820s saw the writing on the wall. Many offered their services to the American Fur Company, while others abandoned the mountains altogether. Fitzpatrick turned to guiding missionaries through the mountain passes on their way to convert Indians in Oregon. Jim Bridger, however, stayed in the mountains and continued life as a free trapper. In late 1839, Bridger left the mountains for the first time in seventeen years and visited St. Louis. Gaining the support of influential suppliers in that city, Bridger organized an expedition to the 1840 rendezvous to trade goods for pelts. While at the gathering, Bridger encountered groups of parties—one a set of missionaries bound for Oregon, the other a group of settlers headed for California. At rendezvous that year, the West's past collided with its future. No longer the sole domain of natives and a few hardy trappers, the West had been opened, ironically enough, by the trappers and their explorations. Reports of the fertile valleys in California and the Oregon Territory lured settlers across the Rockies. Having discovered routes through the mountains and then popularizing those routes, mountain men played a role in the changing nature of Western settlement.

THE END OF THE FUR TRADE AND THE MOUNTAIN MAN'S NEW ROLE

The revelry surrounding the rendezvous lasted formally for only fifteen years. By 1840, the beaver population in the West had been reduced to a small fraction of its once abundant numbers. However, other factors outside of the mountain men's control acted on the decline of one of their favorite pastimes. Technology and fashion sense had caught up with the mountain man's trade. European and American fashion no longer desired hats made from beaver pelts; instead, hatters in the late 1830s and early 1840s began making hats from silk. The whimsical demands of fashion in faraway lands put an end to the fur trade. Prices for fur decreased by more than half in most Eastern cities, and the large fur companies could hardly stay afloat. The rendezvous system became an economic encumbrance rather than a profitable reaping of furs.

Understanding that the rendezvous system could no longer turn a profit, Bridger turned his energies to trading with Indians. On the western bank of the Green River, Bridger began constructing a fort to facilitate trade between his venture and the Shoshone. Quite fortuitously, a large party of emigrants arrived at Bridger's post in July 1821. Accompanied by both Catholic and Protestant missionaries, the settlers found that some of the trappers associated with Bridger could supply their wagon train with necessary goods and provisions, albeit at a steep price. This encounter provided a new direction for the mountain men to take: With the beaver gone, their future lay not in exploiting the mountains' resources further but by aiding (and exploiting) settlers who wished to cross the mountains. Bridger abandoned the fort he had been constructing and returned into the wild to hunt in spring 1842. On his return East to sell his furs in the summer, Bridger came to Fort Laramie and encountered another party of settlers heading for Oregon. Fitzpatrick and Bridger guided the settlers to Ft. Hall on the Snake River. Their skills as frontier diplomats paid off when the caravan came into contact with a large party of Sioux rumored to be out for white blood. Fitzpatrick and Bridger successfully negotiated with the Sioux and even commenced a friendly trading session between the two peoples. The settlers, guided by the two seasoned mountain men, would become the first group to successfully navigate the entire length of the Oregon Trail.

Bridger soon enough realized that gainful employment in the future could be found in guiding and trading with settlers, but still found it hard to abandon trapping. In 1842 he partnered with Louis Vasquez and they built Fort Bridger on the banks of the Green River squarely on the route travelers would take to cross the mountains. Taking on the role of trader only reluctantly, Bridger found it difficult to resist the call of the mountains and continued to trap. In 1847 he briefly aided Brigham Young and other Mormon settlers on their way to the Great Salt Lake. With the cession of California to the United States at the conclusion of the Mexican War coupled with the discovery of gold, the "forty-niners" poured into the mountains on their way to California.

With the increased number of settlers in the West, the army also beefed up its number of troops to protect the settlers from Indian attacks. Despite previous friendly relations with the Mormons, Bridger felt betrayed when Brigham Young and his church expanded their territory west to include Bridger's fort on the Green River. In 1853, the Mormons, who believed Bridger had stirred up the Shoshones against them, sent a posse after the mountain man. Barely escaping, his fort was confiscated by the Mormons. Seeking revenge, Bridger acted as the guide for Albert Sidney Johnston's column in 1857 when it sought to impose federal authority on the Mormons. Though peaceful negotiations had concluded before the army could arrive at the Great Salt Lake, Bridger felt like he had been cheated because he never recovered his property. Bridger acted as a guide for several other military expeditions, including the Raynolds Expedition in 1859. Serving in the army for eight additional years, Bridger retired and spent the rest of his days on his farm in Missouri, where he died in 1881.

KIT CARSON AND JOHN C. FRÉMONT

Just as Jim Bridger and the rest of the mountain men had to diversify and shift their focus from trapping to guiding by the early 1840s, so too did Christopher Houston Carson. Having already trapped with Bridger and Fitzpatrick for nearly nine years before the 1840 rendezvous, Carson understood that trapping had no future before many of his other colleagues. By accident, Carson met the army officer John C. Frémont on a steamboat bound for Independence, Missouri, in 1842. Frémont had been commissioned by the Corps of Topographical Engineers to explore and survey the areas surrounding South Pass. Though it had been used by settlers for many years and Frémont could have found his way without Carson, the mountaineer managed to talk his way into Frémont's expedition. Much of the expedition required Frémont to take scientific measurements, record the flora and fauna, and to make contact with the native tribes. Though most of the information Frémont gathered amounted to much of anything new, his greatest attribute lay in self-promotion and his reports made it seem like he, with the help of Carson, had accomplished an impressive feat. Frémont's reports garnered fame for both explorer and guide, and the two became fast friends.

Most of Frémont's and Carson's future expeditions would take the tone of their first. Carson remained fiercely loyal to Frémont even after it became obvious that the officer had grander ambitions and his self-aggrandizement was merely a means of achieving those goals. The expedition in 1843 nearly proved disastrous for Frémont and his men. Frémont, convinced that quicker passage existed from the Plains to the Green River, led his party on a voyage. When stymied by the mountains, Frémont moved further north to try another attempt at crossing the Rockies at the onset of winter. Rather than turn around, Frémont decided to cross the Sierras in January 1844. Barely surviving the trip, Frémont and his party reached California and safety. Satisfied that no other route through the mountains existed, Frémont, though he did not discover the Great Basin, popularized it as a land with no outlet to the sea. This meant that the Columbia River was the only river to span the Rockies, and securing it became all the more important for the burgeoning United States.

Frémont's expedition of 1845–1846 met with trouble when it arrived in a politically turbulent California. Still part of Mexico, Californians had recently rebelled against the central authority in Mexico City and had placed a native Californian in charge. Frémont's arrival, or rather the arrival of an armed American military expedition, caused further tensions. Granted permission to make winter camp away from the coastal settlements, Frémont and his band were also allowed to tour those villages on their way north. The Californians instantly became suspicious of Frémont's actions due to his group's rude actions toward the civilians. The Mexican military commander reneged on his permission for the Americans to camp in California and told them to leave.

Feeling betrayed, the Americans constructed a makeshift fort on top of a hill and Frémont even planted the American flag. With rumors of war between Mexico and the United States already spreading, the situation grew tense. The Mexican authorities, though, realized they could not dislodge the Americans, while Frémont came to see the egregiousness of his actions. Able to retract his small band without a serious international incident erupting, Frémont retreated back to the east to continue his scientific measurements of the mountains.

When President Polk did declare war against Mexico in May 1846, Frémont wasted little time in exploiting the confusion in California for his own advancement. Creating four companies of troops with himself in command, Frémont began a campaign of filibustering in California against Mexican troops. Though the Americans did not experience much action, Carson and his friend made a name for themselves by resorting to brutality and outright slaughter. With American victory in California as well as Mexico, the war ended in less than two years. The United States had secured territory spanning the entire continent. Acting as a courier between Frémont and his supporters in St. Louis and Washington, Carson carried important dispatches to the capital. His return trip spanned the entire continent and pioneered not just the concept but the practicality of an overland mail route connecting the two coasts.

Carson's journey from Washington to San Francisco secured his place in the memory of the American West. Yet without the pioneering spirit and physical endeavors of the mountain men who had come before him, Carson's journey would have been impossible. What began as a career to hunt beaver in the relatively pristine wilderness west of the Mississippi in the early nineteenth century evolved into one of the most important professions in the history of the West. Mountain men acted not just as trappers and soldiers, but explorers and guides as well. Their acquisition of knowledge during their years of trapping translated into practical and useable knowledge for those who desired to make their way to the Pacific. Mountain men not only discovered the paths that would lead Americans to the Pacific Ocean, but they guided these individuals, protected them, and often served as mediators between whites and native people. Though many trappers continued to serve the army during the 1860s as Indian agents and translators, even that role soon disappeared as the government herded Native Americans onto reservations.

Having explored the reaches of the Rocky Mountains and the river valleys of the Pacific Coast in search of valuable beaver pelts, having guided travelers overland to their new homes, mountain men became relics of a bygone era. But the mountain men were partially responsible for their own demise. Their zeal and skill at trapping nearly resulted in the extinction of beaver. Likewise, their wanderlust and hardiness allowed them to explore even the most remote locations. When the news of each new discovery filtered to the East, settlers could ably travel west with a relatively accurate picture of Western geography and a route through the wilderness. As the map filled in, the need for explorers dwindled. Once again, mountain men had themselves destroyed their own purpose. Taking on the new roles of guide and trader, mountain men sought to eke out a living in the land they knew and loved. Although partially responsible for their own demise because of the skill and tenacity with which they undertook their work, mountain men also succumbed to outside forces. Western expansion, the discovery of gold, and Manifest Destiny in particular propelled Americans, determined to carve out their own existence, across the continent. Though mountain men had been the forerunners of the Western settlers and gold miners, the sheer volume of settlers undermined the need for guides. Routes became popularized, wagons rutted the ground, and settlers filled the valleys where the trappers once hunted, and mountain men disappeared from the landscape.

FURTHER READING

Ambrose, Stephen E. *Undaunted Courage: Meriwether Lewis, Thomas Jefferson, and the Opening of the American West* (New York: Touchstone Books, 1996).

Cleland, Robert Glass. *This Reckless Breed of Men: The Trappers and Fur Traders of the Southwest* (New York: Alfred A. Knopf, 1950).

Goetzmann, William H. "The Mountain Man as Jacksonian Man," *American Quarterly* 15 (Autumn 1963): 402–415.

Rawling, Gerald. *The Pathfinders: The History of America's First Westerners* (New York: Macmillan, 1964).

Smith, Henry Nash. *Virgin Land: The American West as Symbol and Myth* (Cambridge, MA: Harvard University Press, 1973).

Utley, Robert M. *A Life Wild and Perilous: Mountain Men and the Paths to the Pacific* (New York: Henry Holt & Co., 1997).

Wishart, David J. *The Fur Trade of the American West, 1807–1840: A Geographical Synthesis* (Lincoln, NE: University of Nebraska Press, 1979).

John Muir. Courtesy of Library of Congress.

John Muir

Kenneth W. McMullen

By the time of his death, John Muir had become one of the most well-known figures in the young movement to save the Western wild lands from destruction. Although, starting in 1868, he lived in the West, as he fought to save the lands of the West he found himself, more often than not, fighting Westerners over the best use of the land in contention. The West had been conquered by people who forced the land to give up its resources. They saw no need to set aside land that happened to have some scenic value to urban dwellers. Since Yosemite Valley lay in fairly close proximity to California's gold country, some people thought the land had been taken by the national government because of some supposed huge deposits of gold. Why else would anyone want claim to the mountainous land?

Muir arrived in the West already a man enamored of the natural world, and although he started out in his youth loving the outdoors, another path also opened for him, a path for which he had superior talent and which for a time seemed destined to take Muir away from the wild lands.

Muir was born in 1838 in Dunbar, Scotland, the third of eight children. His father, Daniel Muir, owned and operated a small store. His father brought the family to the United States in 1849. Daniel's move to the United States grew out of his joining the Disciples of Christ denomination. The group was somewhat new in Scotland, and the founder had already emigrated from Scotland to America to start new communities of believers there. Daniel hoped to join with one of the newly established Disciples of Christ settlements. Instead Daniel Muir settled in Wisconsin where few Disciples had yet settled. In addition to his work at farming, Daniel Muir became an occasional speaker at the Sunday services, as the Disciples in the area did not have regular clergy.

Even before he moved to America, John had fallen under nature's spell. In Scotland, he and his brothers escaped from studies and chores to roam the area investigating the natural phenomenon of the local landscape. Muir eventually put aside the fundamentalist religious beliefs he received from his father and replaced them with a new calling: extolling and documenting nature, and its scenic wonders. Muir also rejected other viewpoints of his father. Daniel Muir refused to have any adornments in his homes. He called such things "pagan idols." John, on the other hand, loved to fill his home with pictures, fine rugs, nice linen, and embroidered items.

During this time in Wisconsin, two neighbors exerted a powerful influence on him. They opened up to him the world of literature, the world of Milton and Shakespeare, of poetry and prose. Before this his readings came primarily from the Bible because his father distrusted any other writings.

As he grew up on the farm, he frequently devised small versions of water wheels and mechanically moved lumber saws. Ironically, he created inventions designed to cut down and destroy forested areas, the very things he spent most of his adult life trying to save. A part of inventiveness, John also built various one-of-a-kind clocks, some of which remained working for over fifty years. He additionally created thermometers, devices to measure humidity, and barometers. His devices attracted enough attention that his reputation spread throughout the surrounding countryside.

In 1860, another neighbor encouraged John to take his creation to the State Agricultural Fair with the hope that an owner of a machine shop would hire him. At the fair he won an award that carried with it an honorarium of fifteen dollars. Afterward he worked for several months as a mechanic in the Madison locale. By this time John had decided that life on a Wisconsin farm had no appeal for him.

He sought and gained admittance to the University of Wisconsin, where he studied for two and a half years. His course of study included chemistry, botany, and geology. His interest in botany remained with him his entire life. At one point, moved by the sick and wounded soldiers at the Civil War hospital at nearby Camp Randall, Muir planned to study to become a doctor to serve his fellow, suffering human beings. But the natural world still held sway over Muir and he never pursued this career.

With the support and encouragement of one of his professors, Dr. Carr, John studied glaciation through the writings of Louis Agassiz. In addition, Increase Lapham, a regent of the university, influenced John through Lapham's own conservationist activities. Lapham recognized the danger of forest depletion and campaigned throughout the state of Wisconsin arguing for the need to save the forested areas. A few years later, Muir made the same arguments supported by his observations taken during his travels throughout the United States and Canada. While at the university Muir read the writings of Alexander Humboldt. These writings influenced him so greatly that he sought, at various times in his life, to undertake some of the same journeys that Humboldt took.

He left the university in 1864 without receiving a degree. The uncertainty of the Civil War draft helped prompt this move. He spent several months with his family, and when he did not get selected by the draft, went to Canada to wander through its untamed lands. He did not return to school to finish his degree.

During these Canadian travels he traversed the Holland River swamp in the province of Ontario. There Muir came upon a *Calypso borealis*—the rare lady-slipper—for which he had been searching. This incidence of beauty surrounded by the rank bog seemed to Muir such a sublime moment that he sat down and wept. The singular beauty of the *Calypso* helped to serve as a catalyst for him. He came to believe that he could read the matchless goodness and omnipotence of the Creator through the beauty of the natural world. This occurrence sealed within him the conviction to spend his life devoted to the propagation of the gospel of nature. He completely turned away from the Christian faith of his father and found his spiritual meanings in the natural world. As part of his convictions, Muir came to believe that wild things are worthwhile for their own sakes.

Already he had begun to keep journals of his impressions of what he observed during his meanderings. He filled his journals with sketches of the special plants he encountered on his travels. Besides plants, Muir also made drawings of especially striking landscapes such as the ones he made of the rocky mounts in Yosemite Valley.

After leaving the *Calypso*, John went to visit with his brother who lived near Niagara Falls. Lacking funds to continue his journeys, John worked for several months in a factory making broom handles and wooden rakes. Then he moved onto Indianapolis where he found employment in the manufacturing of wheel hubs, spokes, and other carriage parts. At both locations he invented mechanisms that speeded up the manufacturing process. He never patented his inventions because he felt that all such work belongs to the whole human race, and no one person should make a profit from it.

Also at both locations Muir taught classes to children about nature and what he knew of the sciences. This duality of love—for mechanical design and nature—created an internal struggle for Muir. He loved the inventive process, but he loved to be out in nature exploring and botanizing. An injury to his right eye as he worked in the Indianapolis factory convinced him to devote his life to the natural world.

In 1867 he left Indiana and headed south to tramp through the wild places on the way to the Gulf of Mexico. He had in mind, as Humboldt had, to travel all the way to South America. However, he became ill when he reached the Gulf Coast, and although he recovered enough to reach Cuba, his illness forced him to abandon his trip to South America. He booked passage for New York City, and upon arriving there boarded another ship for the Isthmus of Panama. From Panama he went to California and arrived in San Francisco in March 1868.

He spent that first summer in the Golden State working odd jobs in the San Joaquin Valley while observing the flora of the Sierra Nevada Mountains. He later took a job in a sawmill in Yosemite Valley. The mill was unique in that the owner and Muir chose not to cut any live trees but only use naturally fallen timber. There had been a great storm in 1867 that blew down so many trees that Muir reckoned the downed trees would keep the mill busy for many years.

While still working in the mill, in 1871, Muir met Ralph Waldo Emerson. Muir tried to convince Emerson to leave his party and go hiking and camping in the mountains, but Emerson, due to the objections of his friends, declined. Later Muir came to the conclusion that Emerson and the Transcendentalists only accepted nature as something for human beings to use. Muir never became a Transcendentalist although he did hold some similar philosophical beliefs. Through these years of working in the mill and taking other jobs in the vicinity, Muir continued to explore the mountain range.

His observations made during his explorations led him to challenge the current belief that Yosemite Valley came into existence through a subsidence of the valley floor as expounded by Josiah Whitney. Muir believed that the action of glaciation formed the valley. To buttress his arguments, Muir collected evidence from the valley floor and took measurements of the snow pack, and tracked the movements of the glaciers he found within the boundaries of the park.

The strong association of John Muir with Yosemite Valley and the national park has caused many to believe that Muir played a role in the formation of the park itself. Although Muir became an active defender of the park and sought publicity for it, he had little to do with its formation. President Abraham Lincoln created the park in 1864 when federal legislation set much of the current park acreage aside and passed control over to the state of California. The state had governing authority over the park while the land still remained in federal ownership. Frederick Law Olmsted, in California during the late 1860s, became on of the first state commissioners, and helped develop policies and long-range goals for the park.

While living in the valley Muir began to write articles concerning Yosemite and its beauty. Many of these published works appeared in nationally known publications. Horace Greeley published one of Muir's first major pieces, titled "Yosemite's Glaciers," in the *New York Tribune*.

Due to personal problems, Muir left Yosemite in 1873 and moved to San Francisco. He never lived in Yosemite again, although he made many trips to the valley and surrounding mountain ranges in the remaining years of his life. He continued to read and became influenced by John Ruskin, the English art and social critic, and George Perkins Marsh's book *Man and Nature*. Ruskin's work led Muir to believe he needed to be more proactive toward the preservation of the wild lands he loved. Muir paid special attention to Marsh's book because of it conclusions. George Marsh had traveled extensively as an American diplomat, and his observations led him to the judgment that over-harvesting of forested areas and lack of replenishment led to the destruction of arable lands with deleterious effects on civilization. The book came to be regarded as the cornerstone of the conservation movement. It popularized the concept, to which Muir subscribed, that society had the responsibility to intelligently use and renew the natural resources in the United States.

While he resided in the San Francisco Bay area Muir spent much of his time writing. He wrote both articles and books, always striving to awaken America to the need to protect the scenic beauties of the natural world. After a period of writing, Muir often left for an extended Western trip—up to and around Mt. Shasta, through Utah, or up to Alaska. After each trip he returned to the Bay area and wrote of his travels and discoveries.

As he stayed in the Bay area Muir made many friends, including the Strentzel family. The family made their living from their orchards in Martinez, near the eastern end of San Francisco Bay. He had many discussions with the father, Dr. John Theophile Strentzel, but after some time his attention became focused on the daughter Louie. After an extended time of letter writing and courtship, John and Louie married in 1880. Muir's family grew to include two daughters, Wanda and Helen. John and Louie lived in a house on Dr. Strentzel's land.

In the 1880s, Muir became concerned with the widespread abuses of privately held forested lands. He began to favor federal ownership of wilderness lands that possessed exceptional scenic regions. In the spring of 1889 Muir met Robert Underwood Johnson, publisher of the *Century Magazine*, which had already published some of Muir's articles. Johnson expressed interest in the Yosemite area and accompanied Muir on an extended camping trip in the park. During the trip Johnson became enamored of Yosemite and pressed Muir on how to save it from being despoiled. The men agreed that the federal government needed to take possession of more of the land around the park. They reached an agreement whereby Muir would write two articles for *Century* to publish and Johnson would join Muir in a campaign to protect Yosemite. As part of Muir's fight to save the wild lands, he organized the formation of the Sierra Club in May 1892. The club selected Muir as its president, a position he held until his death in 1914.

Several times, various governmental agencies and commissions invited Muir to join their organization. Muir always refused. He recognized that remaining a private citizen, one with no aspirations for political office, allowed him to be both advocate and critic. Additionally he probably realized that if he joined a commission, he ran the risk of being co-opted by the political maneuverings of the other people involved.

In participating in the wilderness preservation activities, John Muir became friends with Gifford Pinchot. Pinchot rose to public awareness as a member of the National Forest commission, and two years later he obtained the appointment to be the head of the Department of Agriculture's Division of Forestry. He later spearheaded the formation of the National Park Service.

During the late 1800s Muir and Pinchot worked in tandem for the common goal. While Pinchot worked from within the governmental Forest Commission, Muir, through his writing, agitated from without. In this manner Muir proselytized the general public on the desirability of saving forests and wilderness areas, while Pinchot guided the government's decision-making process in setting aside the desirable tracts of land for preservation and conservation.

At the end of the nineteenth century disagreements arose between conservationists and preservationists. Conservationists believed in a scientific use and management of the nation's natural resources, especially the large tracts of Western land. They approved of controlled livestock grazing, a better approach than the unfettered grazing practices of the time. The preservationists wanted as close to no use of the land as possible. The conservationists' approach carried with it some small aspect of utilitarianism: the greatest good for the greatest number. Muir differed with Pinchot in that Muir believed that some lands must be preserved in pristine condition with no logging or grazing. Muir further believed that sheep grazing constituted a greater danger to the natural areas than logging, because trees could be replaced but the grazing habits of sheep destroyed habitat almost beyond recovery. (His attitude toward sheep grazing may have been influenced by the fact that one of his earliest jobs in California consisted of shepherding sheep. He called them "hoofed locusts.")

The relationship became further strained as Muir changed his opinion of federally managed forests. After 1900 Muir became disenchanted with how the federal government managed the forestry reserves. He came to the conclusion that allowing the forests to be used—no matter how carefully—was incompatible with wilderness. This belief hardened through the early years of the twentieth century. To use Yosemite as an example, Muir believed that it should be preserved as a wilderness just for the sake of it being a wilderness, as opposed to Pinchot who would try to save the natural world but would put human needs above the natural.

However, it is important to note that by preserving the land as wilderness, Muir did not necessarily mean in a pristine condition. He saw nature as a wilderness vacation spot, a place of contemplation; he favored building a small number of roads into scenic areas so people could enjoy them. This Muir felt would save the lands from "commercialism."

As an activist for preserving nature, Muir involved himself in several environmental issues, such as control of Yosemite National Park acreage, the size of the park, and the proposal by the city of San Francisco to build a dam within the boundaries of Yosemite.

Although Muir came to distrust the national government's policy toward forested reserves, he had greater concerns toward the politicians in California and the interests of the Southern Pacific Railroad. Fearing that eventually the railroad, through the state politicians it controlled, would gain access to the resources inside the park, Muir led a fight to have the state of California release its governing authority, which then allowed the control to pass back to Washington, DC. This he accomplished in 1905.

During the American Civil War, when Congress first created Yosemite Park, Congress made no attempt to lay out the boundaries in a practical manner in light of privately held lands. Instead the Conness Park Bill stated the boundaries in terms of the grid lines of latitude and longitude. By doing so, many private holdings became part of the park. This allowed timber and various grazing interests to start logging and grazing the herds within the park—on public land, not just on the private lands.

The secretary of the Interior convened a commission in 1903, which, in 1904, recommended that over 542 square miles be removed from the park, mostly on the western, southern, and eastern boundaries. The commission recommended adding some land to the north to keep the Tuolumne watershed from despoilment. Congress adopted these measures in the Yosemite Act of 1905. Muir fought the removal of land from Yosemite National Park for any purpose. He remained skeptical of the motives of those who wanted to change the boundaries. He believed that Western commercial interests sponsored such acts to somehow obtain access to the natural resources residing in the mountainous region. But the biggest fight for Muir concerned San Francisco's petition to build a dam across the Tuolumne River and flood Hetch Hetchy Valley to create a reservoir to meet the future fresh water needs of the city.

Muir and his supporters felt outrage at the suggestion of building a dam at the end of Hetch Hetchy because the valley resided within Yosemite National Park. He rejected the concept of using park land to satisfy the thirst of San Francisco. It must be noted that although he fought vigorously against the dam in Hetch Hetchy, Muir did not fight against the dam that created Lake Eleanor—eventually part of the whole water system built for San Francisco—even though that land also fell within the park boundaries. The beauty of Hetch Hetchy had taken hold of Muir's soul and he fought to keep the valley wild.

Muir fought against the dam with all the vigor and rhetoric of an evangelical preacher—which he was—of the gospel of the wilderness. He believed that Americans focused on materialism and ignored the more meaningful aspects of life—nature untouched by human hands, or at least only a little touched. His passions may have actually hindered his efforts—he felt too deeply about Hetch Hetchy to explore a compromise whereby San Francisco could develop Lake Eleanor first and hold Hetch Hetchy in reserve for later. Muir did not have it in him to compromise and thus gain time for later maneuvering.

The Hetch Hetchy Valley held a special place in Muir's life. His trips there tended to reinvigorate him. During the fight over the dam he visited the valley several times. Although he appreciated the efforts of artists to publicize the beauty of Hetch Hetchy, he believed that the individual must visit the valley to truly appreciate its worth. This belief had validation. Of the four men who held the position of secretary of Interior during the fight, the two who visited the valley in person ruled against San Francisco and against flooding the valley.

Recognizing the scope of the fight, Muir worked to build a constituency to assist him in the saving Hetch Hetchy—the various nature clubs and walking clubs throughout the country. Muir and Robert Underwood Johnson also convinced J. Horace McFarland to join the fight to save Hetch Hetchy. McFarland had become famous for helping to stop Niagara Falls from becoming a hydroelectric facility. The well-known poet Harriet Monroe also became another ally in the fight. She had camped in Hetch Hetchy while attending one of the extended camping trips to the valley sponsored by the Sierra Club.

Although the vast majority of the membership of the Sierra Club supported the fight against building the dam, a few supported the city's efforts—including Warren Olney, one of the founders of the Sierra Club who resigned from the club over this issue. The meeting that founded the Sierra Club took place in Olney's office. After Olney announced his decision to support the dam, Muir regarded him as a Brutus.

Pinchot also supported San Francisco's efforts, seeing them as a beneficial use of natural resources. This support seemed to be the breaking point in the relationship between Muir and Pinchot. Muir felt betrayed by Pinchot; because they had worked together on so many issues before, Muir supposed that Pinchot felt as he did. Muir argued that the park land needed to be preserved as a wilderness just for the sake of its wildness. Pinchot wanted to save the natural world whenever possible but he placed human needs above the natural.

Although many national newspapers and periodicals supported Muir, the Western publications—especially the San Francisco ones—did not. They saw him as someone who refused to help out the needy people of the city whose water supply was in the hands of a greedy private monopoly—the Spring Valley Water Company. The city's papers portrayed Muir as a wild, impractical nature lover, or an uncompassionate human, or, worse, a tool of the water company.

As an example of the local pressure on Muir and his supporters, the Sierra Club attempted to hire an engineer, who also taught at the University of California in Berkeley, to refute the city's plans. After signing the contract and agreeing to assist the Sierra Club, the engineer asked to be let out of the agreement because the president of the university pressured him not to help Muir. The university president, Benjamin Wheeler, supported the efforts of the city and also happened to be a friend of Pinchot.

Although the club gained much favorable publicity nationally and made a positive impression with its supporters' testimony in the various hearings in Washington, DC, ultimately Muir and his supporters lost the battle. In 1913 Congress passed the Raker Act, which authorized San Francisco to build its dam and flood the valley. Many of Muir's friends thought that losing the battle for Hetch Hetchy took a lot out of him, and eventually contributed to his death. With failing health and a lung infection, John Muir died on 24 December 1914, a year after President Woodrow Wilson signed the Raker Act.

By the late 1800s, Muir had become a leading, if not the leading, spokesperson in the United States for the protection of America's wilderness regions against spoliation. Muir viewed the untouched mountain areas and forests as places of essential beauty that need to be preserved for their natural scenic quality. Muir primarily wrote to support the idea of preservation—although his concept of preservation has significant differences from that of the preservationists of today—of the wilderness and areas of natural beauty.

Muir, through his writings and attempts to save wilderness areas, strove to draw urban Americans out of their cities and into the untamed splendor of Nature in the American West. In his later writings, especially *Our National Parks*, Muir moved away from the idea that the wilderness is a spiritual area for an individual to the concept that exposure to the wild places had beneficial aspects for groups of people as well. The Sierra Club sponsored several extended group camping sessions, led by Muir, in the Sierra Nevada Mountains in general, and Yosemite in particular—specifically two trips to Hetch Hetchy during the battle to save the valley. He knew that city-dwellers needed to come to the mountains and forests to escape the stress of their modern, city life and to refresh themselves. In this, Muir faintly echoes the Transcendentalists of Emerson and Thoreau.

Even though Muir died in 1914, death has not stilled his voice. His writings remain popular and have been quoted to support the establishment of forest reserves and wilderness areas, and opponents to logging on federally owned land use Muir's words to buttress their cause.

FURTHER READING

Bunnell, Lafayette Houghton, MD. *Discovery of the Yosemite and the Indian War of 1851 Which Led to That Event*, 4th ed (Los Angeles: G.W. Gerlicher, 1911).

Cohen, Michael P. *The Pathless Way: John Muir and American Wilderness* (Madison: University of Wisconsin Press, 1984).

Fox, Stephen R. *John Muir and His Legacy: The American Conservation Movement* (Boston: Little Brown, 1918).

Miller, Sally M. (ed.). *John Muir: Life and Work* (Albuquerque: University of New Mexico Press, 1993).

Miller, Sally M., and Daryl Morrison (eds.). *John Muir: Family, Friends, and Adventures* (Albuquerque: University of New Mexico Press, 2005).

Righter, Robert W. *The Battle Over Hetch Hetchy: America's Most Controversial Dam and the Birth of Modern Environmentalism* (New York: Oxford University Press, 2005).

Wolfe, Linnie Marsh. *Son of the Wilderness: The Life of John Muir* (New York: Alfred A. Knopf, 1945).

Worster, Donald. *The Wealth of Nature: Environmental History and the Ecological Imagination* (New York: Oxford University Press, 1993).

Also see the home page of the Sierra Club Web site, www.sierraclub.org/history/key_figures.

Annie Oakley, ca. 1889. Courtesy of Library of Congress.

Annie Oakley

Glenda Riley

The renowned sharpshooter Annie Oakley was neither born in the West nor lived there. Yet her name and legend are an integral part of the mythical Old Wild West. With hard work, nerve, and luck, Oakley became a nationally known "Western" figure during the late nineteenth century. With the help of her husband and business partner, Francis E. Butler, and her employer, William F. Cody, she gave shape not only to the image of the receding frontier, but to that of its white women settlers.

Little in Annie's birth pointed to her future. On 13 August 1860, she was born Phoebe Ann Moses, or Mauzee, the fifth surviving child of a poor farm family in Darke County, Ohio. By the time Annie was four, she had two more siblings. When she was six, Annie's father died of pneumonia, leaving her mother with seven children under age fifteen. Feeding and clothing them was a daily struggle that kept Annie out of school. Instead, she worked with her mother Susan cooking, sewing, and farming. Annie also trapped and, with her father's old Kentucky rifle, shot game. She then spent time as a worker and seamstress at the Darke County Infirmary and with a farm family. After returning home as a teenager, Annie resumed hunting, selling the surplus to a local shopkeeper, who in turn sold it to Cincinnati hotels.

Later, in a 1926 autobiography, Annie remembered these years as happy ones. They culminated in two significant events. One, which filled her heart with "joy," was handing her mother enough saved nickels and dimes to pay off the farm's mortgage. The other was defeating vaudeville shooter Francis (Frank) E. Butler in a match probably held near Cincinnati in 1875. Butler, however, recalled the match as taking place in 1881 near the town of Greenville. Gallantly, the trounced Butler invited Annie and her family to the theater that night to watch him shoot. Thus began a courtship that led Annie to marry Frank, ten years her senior and a master of shooting and staging.

On 1 May 1882, Annie joined Frank on the stage of the Crystal Hall in Springfield, Ohio. She filled in for Frank's ill partner and was supposed to, she explained, "hold the objects as he shot." "But," she continued, "I rebelled;" she insisted on taking every other shot. This first appearance, which received what Annie called a "generous reception," led her to choose Oakley as her stage name, learn new shots from Frank, and sew her own modest costumes that concealed her slight frame. Standing five feet tall and weighing 110 pounds, Annie wowed audiences of men and women.

To escape the growing seamy side of vaudeville, Annie and Frank looked for new venues. They appeared with circuses, where Annie shot while riding horseback. In 1884, Frank, who increasingly dropped to the background where he handled business matters, noticed an advertisement for a new enterprise, a rodeo-drama called Buffalo Bill Cody's Wild West. But impresario William F. Cody refused to hire either Annie or Frank; he already employed the fine shooter, Captain Adam H. Bogardus, and his four sons. When Bogardus left the Wild West in March of the following year, Frank and Annie tried again. After watching Annie shoot, Cody's partner, Nate Salsbury, hired her on the spot.

THE "SHOW" BUSINESS

In 1885, Annie Oakley entered what she called the "show" business. She re-called: "There was I facing the real Wild West, the first white woman to travel with what society might have considered an impossible outfit." With Frank's careful management, Annie never compromised her modesty or her honesty. Although she now wore a cowboy hat with a six-pointed star, she continued to dress in blouses, skirts, and flat shoes. And every one of her growing reper-toire of feats was honest. When she shot a cigar out of Frank's mouth or an apple off their dog's head, no concealed wires pulled the cigar or the apple.

Even though Annie and Frank's first summer season with the Wild West was easygoing and prosperous, the second was problematic. The troupe spent the summer months at a new open-air arena and amphitheater erected by the Staten Island Amusement Company at a resort named Erastina near New York City. Here, Annie discovered that Cody had hired another woman shooter, Lillian Frances Smith. From California and supposedly fifteen, Smith appeared only two acts after Oakley. Unlike Annie, Lillian dressed immod-estly and fraternized with the men of Cody's troupe. The two women avoided each other at Erastina and during the subsequent winter season at Madison Square Garden. When the Wild West sailed for England in March 1887, both women were aboard. Through a summer season on twenty-three-acre grounds outside London, the two amazed audiences; performed for Edward, the Prince of Wales; and received press reports, which were always favorable to Annie and increasingly critical of Lillian, who was said to lie about her records and use deception in shooting. On 31 October 1887, Annie and Frank left Cody's Wild West. Neither Cody nor Butler commented on the reasons for the split.

During this period, Annie had become a consummate performer. The first season, Annie swung a rifle or a shotgun to her shoulder while Frank loaded traps and released clay birds, which she shot singly at first, then finally four at a time. With rifles and pistols, she shot glass ball after glass ball. Next, she lay down her rifle, threw glass balls in the air, retrieved her weapon, and smashed the balls before they fell. She concluded with a bow to the audience, a kiss blown to the stands, and a perky kick that became her trademark. Later, at the Garden, Annie tried some riding stunts, untying a kerchief from her horse's leg and picking her hat up from the ground, all the while perched precariously in a sidesaddle.

Annie's identification with the American West also emerged during these years. Although neither Cody nor the Butlers ever claimed that Annie came from the West beyond the Mississippi River, her audiences and fans associated her with Kansas, the Dakotas, and even Colorado. Route schedules of the Wild West during the 1890s indicate that Annie went West only with the troupe. In reality, the Wild West toured largely in Connecticut, Delaware, Massachu-setts, Maine, New Hampshire, New York, Pennsylvania, Rhode Island, and Vermont in the Northeast; in Illinois, Indiana, Michigan, Ohio, and Wisconsin in the Midwest; and in Kentucky, Maryland, Missouri, Tennessee, Virginia, Washington, DC, and West Virginia in the South. Cody was a savvy producer who realized that non-Westerners would provide the most enthusiastic audiences for his interpretation of the American West.

Undoubtedly, Annie appeared to be a Westerner because she performed with Cody's troupe, who were virtually all Westerners, but also she went along with romanticized publicity meant to attract non-Westerners. During Annie's time in England in 1887, for example, newspapers reported that Annie once had whipped a pistol out of her purse to chase a robber off a Greenville mail train. In addition, Annie dressed and acted like a Westerner, especially to Londoners who had gained their conceptions of Westerners through literature and other print media of the day. Observers who noted Annie's dress, hairstyles, and seat when riding in London's "Row," dubbed her a "western girl" and a "frontier girl." The *London Post* editorialized that although few would care to copy Annie, one had to admit that, "her get-up" was "that of the real wild West." Annie never demurred; instead, she let readers think what they might about her regional background.

Because Annie fit in so well with Cody's company, her separation in late 1887 must have been a jolt. She and Frank also gave up a good salary and a regular schedule. After their departure from the Wild West, they returned to New York City where they rented a small apartment. In trade papers, Frank placed advertisements for financial backers for a proposed stage play—*Little Sure Shot, the Pony Express Rider*—that would star Annie. In the meantime, Frank arranged shooting matches for Annie. One, held in mid-April of 1888 at the Boston Gun Club, proved that Annie was far more than a performer; she was an accomplished athlete as well. The *Boston Daily Globe* reported that at least half of the numerous spectators were "ladies."

The Butlers tried other venues as well. Frank booked Annie for performances in 1887 with Tony Pastor of Philadelphia, who presented family-oriented vaudeville shows. Reviewers loved Annie, calling her "a rattling shot" and a "decided acquisition in the vaudevilles." The following summer 1888, Frank placed Annie with Pawnee Bill's Wild West, where she got along famously with the other female shooter, May Manning Lillie. By fall, Annie and Frank talked about taking a touring company on the road performing *Deadwood Dick, or the Sunbeam of the Sierras*. Along the way, Annie also shot matches and exhibitions, winning and setting records even when competing against male shooters.

Although Annie and Frank made vigorous efforts to earn a living and build Annie's reputation, they missed Cody's Wild West. Meanwhile, Lillian Smith, now with a slipping reputation due to critics' charges that she used trickery and illusion in her act, left the Wild West. Shortly afterwards, Frank Butler and Nate Salsbury had a meeting, in which they agreed that Annie and Frank would sail to Europe with the Wild West in spring 1889. The European tour turned out to be wildly successful for the Wild West and for Annie. Her season in Paris flew by in a whirl of accolades, command performances, thousands of flowers, and hundreds of gifts. A circuit through Europe and a return to France followed.

1890 AS A TURNING POINT

In 1890, the Butlers returned to a United States increasingly bedeviled by such problems as urbanization, industrialization, and growing population. In that year, the U.S. Census Bureau declared that by virtue of population density the American frontier was closed, over and done, to be added to the chronicles of history. This declaration proved a turning point for such Western expositions as Cody's Wild West. Cody, who considered himself a historian of sorts and the Wild West far more than entertainment, seized the opportunity to broaden his presentation of the disappearing Old West. He and Salsbury created a series of dramatic sketches: "The Attack on the Settler's Cabin," "The Rescue of the Deadwood Stage," "The Pony Express," "The Buffalo Hunt," and "Custer's Last Fight."

At the same time, Cody recognized that his audiences included huge numbers of women and girls. During the historical skits, women were often hysterical victims or were invisible altogether. To offset this presentation of Western women, Cody turned to Annie Oakley, urging her to add additional exploits to her act, which he moved up to second spot on the program. Part of Annie's job was to reassure the female part of audiences by showing women that frequent and noisy bursts of gunfire were harmless to them. Annie began by shooting a pistol, gradually moving up to shooting full charges in a rifle and shotgun. Publicity agent John Burke noted that, "Women and children see a harmless woman there, and they do not get worried." Annie did more than this; she represented strong white women of the frontier who could face and conquer adversity. Cody reinforced Oakley's message by adding other women who performed complicated drills on horseback, did bareback tricks, and even rode untamed broncs.

As Frank and Annie honed her act, they incorporated five basic elements: guns, horses, heroes, villains, and the American West. First, it was clear that Annie was skilled with that Western symbol, the gun. She shot an apple off their dog's head, shot the ash off a cigarette Frank held in his teeth and a dime out of his fingers, shot holes in playing cards, and leapt over a table and shot two glass balls already in the air when she jumped. She also aimed her rifle over her shoulder and using a mirror, hit targets behind her back. Reviewers called her "marvelous," "superb," and "intrepid."

Second, Annie revealed her skill with horses. She became a female cowboy who could easily handle that mainstay of Western life, a horse. She trained one to follow her up flights of stairs, into theater freight elevators, and onto stages for performances. She trained another, a "difficult" horse, to kneel and bow and to shake hands. Yet another fractious horse would, at the least pressure of her rein, draw up a forefoot and drop to one knee in a salute.

Third, like a good Westerner, Annie was a hero, always acting in a clean-cut and honest manner. When, for example, a controversy arose over whether Oakley broke glass balls with bullets or with scatter shot, presumed by many to be easier, Frank made a public statement, explaining that she used shotted shells, containing about two hundred tiny pellets. These shells had a short range and fell harmlessly into the arena, leaving in safety audience members, performers and animals, and nearby buildings. But, Frank added, Annie fired real bullets at stationary targets with backdrops. He noted that neither he nor Annie ever used artifice in any act or stunt.

The fourth component of Annie's act was the presence of villainy. It was clear that Annie possessed power and could vanquish any villain who might appear. Explosions of gunfire, smoke and fire, and glass shards drifting from above convinced audiences that she, the hero, could triumph over any evil she faced.

The last factor, the West, united the above four into an effective package. Guns, horses, heroes, and villains appeared many places, including vaudeville and circuses. In the Wild West arena, however, they had a special twist; they were part of the legendary American West. Annie and Frank cooperated with this dramatization of the West. She wore a cowboy-style hat and dresses that, as one observer noted, "reminded one very forcibly of the wild West." She also adopted Western tack and Western-style guns, frequently ornamented with tooled silver, and she courted publicity that identified her with the American West.

These strategies proved very effective in labeling Annie a true Westerner. When the Wild West returned to England in 1891, the strains of a new song, "The Wild West Waltz," dedicated to Annie Oakley, filled the air. Stories abounded concerning Oakley foiling bank robbers, shooting crazed wild animals at close range, and shielding the defenseless against harm. Some people who spoke with Annie even reported that she spoke with a delightful "Western" accent. To the English, this simple Ohio farm girl was the model Western woman.

At home, a similar process occurred. A prime instance of such publicity concerned Annie's friendship with Chief Sitting Bull. The two had first met in March 1884. On a ten-day tour of St. Paul, Minnesota, Sitting Bull attended a variety show at the Olympic Theater that included Annie Oakley. When she skipped onto the stage, his bored expression changed. With interest, he watched her perform such stunts as knocking corks from bottles and snuffing out candles. The next day, Sitting Bull requested a meeting with Annie, but she initially refused. When the two finally got together, they liked each other immensely. She thought him a kindly "old man" and he thought her a wonderful little woman. Through an interpreter, Sitting Bull christened her "Watanya Cecilla," or "Little Sure Shot," and adopted her to replace a daughter who had died after the Battle of the Little Bighorn in 1876.

Frank quickly recognized the publicity possibilities in the incident. Frank fully understood the public appeal of the West to people caught between a waning frontier and the emerging machine age. His subsequent press releases established Annie as the "girl of the western Plains," as some reviewers already called her. He revealed that not only had Annie become friends with the most feared Indian chief of all, but that Sitting Bull had given her the pair of moccasins he had worn at the Little Bighorn.

In summer 1885, Cody's publicity agent John Burke enlarged on what Frank Butler had started. After complicated negotiations with the secretary of the Interior, Cody had gained permission for Chief Sitting Bull and several others from the Standing Rock reservation in Dakota Territory to travel with the Wild West for the summer season. Burke personally brought Sitting Bull to Buffalo, New York, boasting, "He is ours. I have captured him." Shortly, Annie marched up to Sitting Bull, asking if he had received some coins and a red silk handkerchief she had sent. He replied in the affirmative, adding that he was anxious to resume their friendship.

During that summer, Burke was able to capitalize on the "Little Sure Shot" name that the chief had given Annie years before. After Sitting Bull returned to Standing Rock, Burke described Annie as the chief's adopted daughter. When Sitting Bull was fatally shot in 1890, it was said that at the sound of gunfire the gray trick horse that Cody had given the chief sat down and lifted its front leg to shake hands. Both Cody and Oakley mourned the chief. Yet Cody retrieved the gray trick horse, which he rode in performances, and Annie frequently spoke of the chief to reporters and showed them the invaluable Indian artifacts he had given her when leaving the Wild West. Although they loved and respected Sitting Bull, their entrepreneurial sides saw that their stories were too useful to bury along with the chief.

There is little doubt that Frank and Annie were aware that every element of her act and her life would determine the numbers of people who would come to see her shoot with Cody's Wild West. As a result of their continuous work on what would now be called their "performance text," during the 1890s Annie and Frank were phenomenally successful. Annie's influence was felt in many ways. For instance, because Annie was an athlete as well as a performer, women emulated her by learning how to shoot and joining gun clubs. One commentator remarked that Annie constituted "another living illustration of the fact that a woman, independent of her physique, can accomplish whatever she persistently and earnestly sets her mind to overtake." Annie accomplished all this yet retained a "proper" Victorian persona. She never wore trousers, let her hair flow down her back, and always rode side saddle. She was a woman's woman, not a pseudo-man.

Despite their popularity, Annie and Frank were aging and were tiring of the relentless travel, training, performing, and conducting interviews and photograph sessions. A reporter friend of Annie's wrote that the rigors of the business were wearing Annie down; that Annie had told her, "It used to be fun, but I don't believe I care for it so much nowadays."

In addition, the "show" business was changing, inside the Wild West and out. In 1894, James A. Bailey replaced the ailing Nate Salsbury as manager of the Wild West. With his circus background at Barnum and Bailey, he introduced animal acts and sideshows. In the meantime, Cody's increased drinking and talk of divorcing his wife Louisa must have been repugnant to the Butlers. Too, Cody was falling deeper into debt, in part because he gave freely to his friends and partly because he founded a town in Wyoming named after him. On the larger scene, 1892 marked the beginning of basketball and the building of the first Ferris wheel for the Chicago World's Fair. The following year, Florence Ziegfeld introduced steamy acts to vaudeville. And Thomas Edison experimented with his phonograph, radio, and moving pictures. Edison even captured some of the Wild West troupe, including Annie Oakley, on film.

As the world of entertainment changed, discontented Americans of the 1890s were poised to flee to new forms of amusement. Many felt burned out from a series of cataclysmic national events: one of the worst economic depressions in American history in 1893, labor strikes and their repression in 1894, and the Spanish-American War in 1898. People wanted an escape, however temporary it might be. Unfortunately, the dawning of a new century did not promise much relief. In 1901, President William McKinley was assassinated.

At the Wild West, Cody relied upon Oakley to draw crowds. He issued a splendid new poster proclaiming Annie "The Peerless Wing and Rifle Shot," picturing her wearing medals and surrounded by such mementos as silver loving cups. Still, things did not go well for the Wild West. After a series of accidents, the troupe's train to Virginia collided with another unit. The crash threw Annie out of bed and slammed her back against a trunk. She was taken to a Newark, New Jersey, hospital where doctors who performed five operations declared that they had "never seen such fortitude displayed by any previous patient."

LEAVING THE WILD WEST

To Frank, the time was right to leave the Wild West. In an undated letter to Cody, Frank did not mention the accident. Instead, he expressed his regrets, adding that he and Annie had longstanding plans to try other pursuits. Frank planned to represent the Union Metallic Cartridge Company of Bridgeport, Connecticut. He would travel while Annie shot exhibitions and perhaps taught ladies to shoot. As it turned out, in 1903 the *Chicago Examiner* and the *Chicago American* erroneously reported, "Annie Oakley Asks Court for Mercy—Famous Woman Crack Shot . . . Steals to Secure Cocaine." Other newspapers picked up the story from the Publishers Press telegraph without checking its veracity. Although most apologized, beginning in 1904 Annie spent the next six years suing the fifty-five offenders. By 1910, she had either won or settled with fifty-four of them. This was not about money, for Annie's expenses were high and settlements modest. Annie strove to restore the wonderful reputation that she and Frank had worked for years to establish.

After years of trials, the Butlers felt they needed to change their lives. In 1909, Frank resigned from the Union Metallic Cartridge Company. Annie was about to make a comeback with Vernon Seavers's Young Buffalo Show. Between 1911 and 1913, the Butlers traveled with Vernon Seavers. In 1911 alone, they logged 8226 miles. With the exception of adding lariat twirling to her act, Annie proceeded as usual. Wearing a cowboy hat, a dress resembling buckskin, and her sensible flat shoes, she astonished audiences with her shooting abilities. Frank fell into his role as manager and publicity agent, now putting aside his usual modesty to proclaim Annie a "world champion" and "one of the highest salaried arenic attractions in the world."

The year 1913 was Annie's last in the Wild West arena. In that year, when Annie was to make a much-heralded appearance in Greenville, Ohio, the *Greenville Courier* urged every Darke County resident to attend, displaying their "love" for Annie, "one of our own." A few weeks later, on 4 October 1913, Annie played her last show in Marion, Illinois. Between 1885 and 1913, she had carved herself an enviable reputation as a performer, athlete, and person.

In 1913, Annie and Frank retired to a home in Cambridge, Maryland. Frank, age sixty-three, loved the place; to him, it was a "sportsman's paradise" only "two hundred miles from Broadway." But Annie displayed what her niece called "a restless spirit." At fifty-three, Annie had energy to spare. She hunted, shot, and wrote for hunting magazines, but it was not enough. In response, Frank organized an automobile tour in 1915. Along the way, they counted six stranded traveling shows. When they encountered Buffalo Bill Cody, who had sold the Wild West in 1913 to pay debts and now performed in shows he did not own, Frank pronounced Cody "quite feeble" and surely near his end.

During the next two years, Annie and Frank experimented with other retirement spots, including Leesburg, Florida, and Pinehurst, North Carolina. It was in Pinehurst that Annie and Frank learned of Cody's death. On 10 January 1917, Cody died at his sister's home in Denver. A lengthy funeral procession followed Cody's riderless white horse, with pistols and rifle hung from the empty saddle, accompanied by some 100 cowboys.

In her grief Annie wrote a stirring eulogy recognizing Cody's larger-than-life image and the effect it would have on people, especially Americans, for centuries to come. She wrote, "He was in fact the personification of those sturdy and lovable qualities that really made the West, and they were the final criterion of all men, East and West."

Even though Annie could see Cody's contributions to the evolving image of the American West, she was too close to Cody and the Western legend to recognize her own role. When she and Cody joined forces, the American frontier enjoyed a well-established image, but it was flat, appearing in literature, art, and popular print media. Cody's genius lay in dramatizing the romanticized Western frontier in three dimensions. His epic figures were of flesh and blood who acted out the Western saga in front of spectators' eyes. Noise and smell reinforced the aura of reality, and scenery transported the spectator to a Western scene. Annie Oakley added the female element, much appreciated by the women and girls in Wild West audiences. Oakley portrayed a Western woman who could handle guns and horses, yet maintain her modesty and femininity, thus appealing to audiences as a lady.

When on that important day in 1885 that Salsbury hired Oakley for Cody's Wild West, no one could predict that Oakley and Cody would be linking their careers for the next seventeen years. Perhaps a partnership of sorts was inevitable because Cody and Oakley shared numerous qualities. Neither was a native Westerner, an experienced actor, or an accomplished producer. Both came from the Midwest, both helped support their families after the death of a father, and as youngsters trapped and shot small game, leaving little time for schooling.

Cody and Oakley were a good match in other ways as well. Because of their impoverished childhoods, they dedicated themselves to earning a respectable income. They also supported such values as hard work, loyalty, honesty, and generosity to those in need. Unsurprisingly, Cody and Oakley liked and respected each other; he called her "Missie," and she addressed him as "Colonel." He even wrote in Oakley's autograph book that she was "the loveliest and truest little woman, both in heart and aim in all the world." Later, Oakley depicted Cody as "one of the nicest men in the world."

Moreover, Cody and Oakley were talented, attractive people with an instinct for what pleased audiences. Although Cody knew more about the West than Oakley, both became adept at portraying the West in a way that would please and impress viewers. Both were so highly attuned to their audiences that they did not hesitate to modify bits of their performances and even themselves to fit audience tastes and the times. Cody, for example, had to forego some of the historical points he hoped to make about Indian culture. Oakley, who was a sensational shot when standing on her head with her skirts strapped around her legs, refused to execute such an "unladylike" feat in public. Instead, Annie taught shooter Johnny Baker to do the trick. In 1893, Cody created the Congress of Rough Riders of the World. At the same time, Oakley learned more difficult exploits and even shortened her skirts as fashions changed.

Cody and Oakley were also instinctual showpeople. Cody strove for authenticity included convincing audiences they had been transported temporarily to the West. For a man of inventiveness, such as Cody, sounds and smells were easy. For example, the vignette known as "The Prairie" opened with Cody chasing real bison. In 1887, the Smithsonian ranked Cody's herd as fourth largest in the nation. Scenery was a bit more difficult. To re-create Western vistas, Cody used every artifice, including elaborate painted backdrops set up in the arena, to enhance the historical sketches played out in front of them.

Some of the backdrops were remarkable in size and detail, depicting a rocky terrain with old-growth forests, yet showing every rut and every leaf. Oakley, too, used props and elegant stage scenery when she appeared apart from Cody's Wild West. Because Oakley and Butler had to earn a living during the winter months, or the off-season of the Wild West, they produced a number of Western plays starring Annie. Of course, sounds and smells were less attractive in theaters than in open-air arenas, so Oakley and Butler relied on scenery and lighting to re-create the frontier West. One of their productions was *Miss Rora*, a melodrama that played American and English theaters the winter of 1896–1897 and was billed as "illustrative of life on the frontier." The West of *Miss Rora* was a domesticated place where guns were used in play and horses were pets. On theater stages, Annie shot glass balls thrown in the air, as well as a variety of other objects. Oakley even rode her horse Gipsy on stage, although Gipsy's hoofs sometimes broke through stage floors.

A later production, *The Western Girl*, opened in November 1902. In addition to guns and horses, Oakley and Butler incorporated lavish, spectacular scenery, painted on high-grade linen cloth, which advance publicity explained reproduced the "days of the wild and wooly West." One of the most spectacular scenes was the canyon of the Colorado River by moonlight, which, advertising noted, added a touch of realism to this "startling picture of the Wild West." Annie used her own horses on stage, especially Little Bess—whom she rode—and several others that pulled the old Leadville stagecoach, which looked like Cody's much-celebrated historic Deadwood stage that appeared in virtually every Wild West performance. Oakley and Butler had learned well from Cody, yet they went one step farther. Their West, presented indoors on a theater stage, seemed even more accessible than Cody's arena West.

Yet Cody and Oakley were far more than showpeople. Cody and Oakley were teachers who imbued millions of adoring fans—mostly white—with their performance subtexts, or tropes. First, Cody and Oakley became leading interpreters of Manifest Destiny and of its casualties, American Indians. Unwittingly, Cody and Oakley underwrote imperialistic principles and presented American Indians as primitive "others." Second, Cody and Oakley gave their audiences a clear visualization of the type of men and women who helped make the West part of the United States. By creating the cowboy and the cowgirl and characterizing them as living ideals of white manhood and womanhood, Cody and Oakley helped shape the Victorian era's debate concerning proper gender roles for men and women.

Because Cody's Wild West claimed to give a historically accurate picture of the development of the West, he, and later Oakley, had to address the prevailing philosophy of Manifest Destiny, meaning that God intended white settlers to "civilize" the West and its peoples. Because Cody and Oakley viewed the West as a frontier where white expansion fueled all action, their interpretation promoted the tremendously popular idea of white people struggling and eventually conquering the West, its earlier inhabitants, and its resources.

Always with their eyes on the bottom line, they tried to present what their audiences wanted—successful white conquest of the frontier.

Cody preceded Oakley in rodeo-drama performances by only a few years. After experimenting with rodeos and shooting shows, in 1884, Cody convinced stage entrepreneur Nate Salsbury to become a partner in "Buffalo Bill's Wild West—America's National Entertainment," to open that spring. Salsbury provided solid management and asked Cody to curb his drinking and to fight less with his wife Louisa. Although Cody agreed with the wisdom of these requests, he found them difficult to fulfill. Salsbury also recommended stronger themes, which pleased Cody, who now hoped to do more than just recreate an authentic West. In this and succeeding seasons, he presented what he called an "object lesson" that would inform and "instruct" audiences regarding the "nation's progress."

Cody intended to attract viewers and to help them develop a patriotic allegiance to white expansionism in the West. Clearly, Cody reflected his era, which was one of Manifest Destiny, a term first used in 1845 meaning that the movement of whites westward was a sign of progress and divinely inspired. According to this view, by "settling" the West (as if American Indians and Hispanics had not already done so), white immigrants developed American national character, including such qualities as persistence, hard work, and a kind of benevolence—that is, giving native peoples white religion, technology, and white values. Although Cody the individual opposed damaging policies toward American Indians, Cody the showman encouraged destructive actions by portraying Indians as a primitive and "vanishing" race.

In 1886, Cody and Salsbury adopted a new and enlarged format that made the themes of Manifest Destiny and declining Indian peoples even clearer. As was his policy, Cody included authentic Plains Indians who, in their buckskin, beadwork, and feather headdresses, were colorful and dramatic. Although Cody hoped the appearance of these Indians would be educational, he learned that to keep audiences interested he had to present them in a theatrical manner, representing them as inhibiting white "progress" and "civilization."

Cody was slightly more progressive regarding Western women. Annie's own emerging image, which leaned heavily toward the American West, fit Cody's agenda perfectly. From her initial season with Cody in 1885, Annie Oakley was the premier female shooting star, who carried out the Western theme in her costume, a buckskin-like dress (never trousers), and a cowboy-style hat with a star pinned to it. She also presented Westerners as family oriented. Although Western individualism counted for a lot, it was grounded in family. For instance, Annie always included Frank and their current dog in her act. When Annie shot a coin out of Frank's fingers or an apple off their dog's head, she emphasized the trust and love that could exist between family members. Too, in an era when one out of every fourteen to sixteen marriages ended in divorce, and with Cody chronically teetering on the brink of divorce, Annie and Frank demonstrated ideal harmony and a unity that would result in a fifty-year marriage. Moreover, in between show seasons, Annie and Frank spent time with her family in Darke County, Ohio. An 1892 newspaper notice announcing that the Butlers would "pay a somewhat extended visit to her mother" gave a characteristic view of Annie's and Frank's family relations.

In 1886, Cody and Salsbury decided to stage the Wild West for a long run at the recently constructed open-air arena and amphitheater at Erastina resort on Staten Island. The revised program proved so popular that the Wild West played at Erastina for a full six months. Within four weeks, the Wild West attracted 14,000 people a day to a 12:30 performance or a 7:00 show under artificial lights. Such crowds not only meant profits for the Wild West, but added up to millions of minds to absorb the Wild West's messages. To help audiences grasp Wild West themes, publicity agent "Arizona" John Burke wrote a "Salutory," which appeared at the beginning of program booklets. Burke claimed that the "pressure of the white man," especially in settlement and railroad building, worked with "the military power of the General Government" to destroy the "barriers behind which the Indian fought and defied the advance of civilization." In addition, during performances Cody repeated his slogan "An Enemy in '76, A Friend in '85," meaning that although Indians and whites had once been enemies, they could now learn to be friends.

Like Cody, Annie Oakley and Frank Butler thought of themselves as friends of American Indians. Their connection with Indians began in March 1884, when Sioux chief Sitting Bull saw Annie perform at the Olympic Theater in St. Paul, Minnesota. The next day he requested a meeting with her, during which he christened her "Watanya Cecilla," or "Little Sure Shot" and declared her his adopted daughter. Before Frank and Annie had even thought of seeking employment with Cody's Wild West, Sitting Bull had identified Annie with his West, the Plains of Dakota Territory. In return, Annie sent Sitting Bull coins and a red silk handkerchief, but she did not see the chief again until they appeared together in the Wild West in 1885. During that season, Annie listened to Sitting Bull's complaints and seemed to be the only person who could bring him out of frequent depressions. Sitting Bull's laments related to his people at Standing Rock. Army troops, he told Annie through an interpreter, had trespassed on Sioux hay and timber lands. He also talked about cattle ranchers who counted twice each cow intended for Sioux consumption and agents who gave Indians "half-and-half instead of sugar—the other half being sand."

In October, Sitting Bull announced his intention to leave the Wild West and return to Standing Rock. He said goodbye to Annie and gave her several Indian artifacts. Annie promised to write. In 1887, she commented that Sitting Bull had "made a great pet" of her. She added, "He is a dear, faithful, old friend, and I've great respect and affection for him." In 1890, after Sitting Bull's death, Annie defended him. "His disposition was neither aggressive nor cruel, nor would he have molested anyone if he had not been first molested." Years later, in 1926, Oakley was still upset by the way whites had treated Sitting Bull.

"Had he been a white man," she declared, "someone would have been hung for his murder."

During their sixteen seasons with the Wild West, Annie and Frank befriended other Native Americans. On one occasion, Pawnee Long John, who Annie said had been "shaking dice with a Mexican," gave her his money to hold so he could avoid gambling. Frank, too, spent time with the Wild West's Indians, even learning to speak a bit of Sioux. He told stories that placed American Indians in a favorable light and invented games for them to play in camp. Apparently, Annie and Frank liked a number of the show's Indians. Had they been told they acted in paternalistic ways, they would probably have been hurt. Had they been accused of exploiting Sitting Bull by allowing mention of him in advertising they might have responded that they did so with great pride and sympathy.

Yet Cody, Oakley, and Butler must have been aware of the national debate about "Indian reform" that was emerging. Many reformers—largely Eastern-ers and a number of former abolitionists—opposed the phenomenon of "show" Indians. In 1893, the board of managers for the World's Columbian Exposition in Chicago, who, like Cody, called exhibits "object lessons," denied Cody permission to perform on the fairgrounds. Board members objected to what they thought of as Cody's popularized representation of the history and culture of American Indians. In response, Nate Salsbury leased a fourteen-acre area outside the entrance to the fairgrounds and had bleachers constructed that would hold 18,000 people. To the seventy-four Sioux Indians from the Pine Ridge reservation already in the cast, Cody added another one hundred from Pine Ridge, Standing Rock, and Rosebud. He knew that recent white-Indian conflicts in the West had whetted people's curiosity about Indians. Capacity crowds at the Chicago site must have convinced Cody that Indian reformers and others who opposed the use of "show" Indians in Wild West performances were wrong in disliking what the Wild West taught people about Native Americans.

At the same time that Cody and Oakley developed a characterization of American Indians, they invented personalities for white Westerners as well. Another social issue of the day concerned proper gender roles and acceptable characteristics of manhood and womanhood. Cody and Oakley offered their opinion by casting the answers in the form of Western characters, notably the cowboy and cowgirl.

Cody worked on the cowboy's image, transforming him from a rough man-ual worker who engaged in low-paid, seasonal labor into an American hero. In an era when men, from office clerks to factory workers, wondered what had become of guns, horses, macho behavior, tough talk, and noble hearts, Cody offered a model of manhood—the American cowboy—to assuage men's fears and give them a historical image with which to identify. His cowboys dominated horses and cattle, used their guns to run off toughs, always tri-umphed over Indians, and won fair damsels.

At the same time, Cody and Oakley created the cowgirl. After all, if Cody wanted to attract female customers, he would have to include women in his Wild West. Because popular culture indicated that women in the West often fell prey, especially to Indians, Cody included female victims who screamed and wailed through such mini-dramas as "The Attack on the Settler's Cabin." But this was not enough for late-nineteenth-century viewers who saw assertive women everywhere they looked: in jobs, professions, politics, and reform activities. Even though American women had not yet achieved the right to vote, many of them found ways to metamorphose into what were then called "New Women," who went where they wished and did what they pleased.

Cowgirls were also appealing because Western women were very effective in expanding traditional female roles. Western women often rode horseback and handled firearms. During the 1890s, women went West as homesteaders; in Colorado they accounted for 11.9 percent of all homesteaders and in Wyoming numbered 18.2 percent. Some women ran ranches, wrangled cattle, and drove herds to market, whereas others worked in shops, for newspapers, and in factories. Also, 14 percent of Western women were in the professions, whereas nationally only 8 percent of women were professionals. In 1889, for example, Ella L. Knowles passed the Montana bar examination with distinction, began practicing law in Helena, and actively campaigned for Populist goals and for woman suffrage.

Even as early as the mid-1880s, Cody must have realized, as humorist Josh Billings later put it, that in the West "wimmin is everywhere." A male-dominated Wild West would not have the appeal or generate the profits Cody wanted. After Annie's hiring in 1885, Cody introduced Oakley to his all-male white cast as the "first white woman" to work for the Wild West. Although Cody had worried about Annie's ability to lift heavy rifles and feared that male cast members might heckle and take advantage of her, his fears were needless. Annie was a strong, talented shooter who, rather than becoming a disreputable "show" girl, wanted to preserve her "ladyhood." Even without Frank's considerable assistance, the intrepid Annie would have maintained her ladylike comportment and reputation.

Cody, too, wanted to stress femininity. Although in 1899 he stated that women should have the right to hold paid employment and to vote, he did not believe they should wear what he called "bloomer pants" or ride bucking horses. He also wanted to avoid irritating early audiences needlessly. Thus, he billed Annie and others he hired, such as Emma Lake Hickok, Lillian Smith, and Della Farrell, as *ranchera*, prairie beauties, and natural flowers of the American West, at the same time explicitly denying that cowgirls were "new women." Rather, they were spirited, athletic young women with exceptional riding and shooting skills. Only a few rode their horses astride. Annie Oakley refused to ride astride, which she declared a "horrid idea," but others did so, using men's light roping saddles.

As the first female cowgirl, Annie had a large task before her. For women ranging from shopgirls to wealthy matrons, Annie wanted to model what she saw as the best and most enduring of female characteristics. Consequently, she often surprised people. In 1888, for example, a reporter who expected to meet a "strong, virile, masculine-like woman, of loud voice, tall of stature and of massive proportions," discovered that Annie stood five foot tall, weighed just over 100 pounds, and spoke in soft, cultured tones. Annie cultivated her ladylike image by wearing her hair long and loose and by avoiding makeup, as well as jewelry and medals, which she put on only for publicity photographs. When other arena cowgirls adopted split skirts, bloomer outfits, and trousers, Annie wore her calf-length skirts, leggings, and sensible low-heeled shoes. Even when Oakley retired from Cody's Wild West in 1901 and later toured with Vernon Seavers's Young Buffalo Show between 1911 and 1913, she still wore her usual clothing, meaning no trousers or bloomers.

In all likelihood, Oakley's Midwestern and Quaker background encouraged her to think of herself as what Victorians called a "true woman." Certainly, she saw no gain to be had in perpetuating her image as an uncultured, gingham-clad farm girl from Ohio. Instead, she displayed the five characteristics associated with true women, who should be modest, married, domestic, benevolent, and a civilizing force. First, despite her fame, Annie was successful at remaining modest; she preferred that Frank handle her publicity. Second, Annie and Frank developed what was then called a companionate marriage, based on equality and pliable roles. In an era when the divorce rate had skyrocketed to about one out of thirteen marriages nationally—with the highest divorce rate in the Western states—Annie and Frank remained happily married for their lifetimes. Regarding the third characteristic, Annie tried to be domestic. She hosted tea parties and informal receptions in her tent, which she furnished with a Brussels carpet, couches, a rocking chair, and satin pillows. Between shows, Annie often sat in a rocking chair doing fine embroidery. But when it came to full-scale housekeeping, Annie admitted that her talents and interests lay elsewhere. Annie was far better at the fourth characteristic, benevolence, giving money and gifts to everyone from family members to orphans. Because of her own impoverished childhood, Annie was determined to share whatever she earned with others. Last, Annie was a civilizing force who refused to let even the roughest roustabouts or canvasmen get away with cursing, smoking, or drinking in her presence.

Obviously, Annie Oakley set high standards for women of the late nineteenth and early twentieth centuries. She entered a male domain and competed with men on their own terms, yet remained ladylike in appearance and demeanor. She was an athlete who watched her diet and exercised daily; people referred to her as tiny, dainty, or girlish. These depictions pleased Annie, who did not want to be thought of as a "new woman." Nor was she a supporter of woman suffrage because she feared that "not enough good women would vote." Perhaps her only regret was the she and Frank did not have children. As a good Victorian woman, Annie never talked about the topic, but she loved children and lavished attention on them, from relatives to strangers.

As the nation's first cowgirl, Annie answered questions that women of the era asked about femininity. She set a middle and just course, navigating between unusual achievements for a woman and all the trappings of what was then called a "woman's sphere." Oakley could shoot, ride, and perform a wide variety of authentic feats, yet she could also be traditionally feminine in appearance and conduct. As a result, she won respect from colleagues, friends, family members, and fans. She showed women how to capitalize on the opportunities opening to them during the late 1800s and early 1900s without totally deserting the world of women and becoming lost somewhere in between women and men. In other words, she subtly subverted customary gender expectations to serve her own ends, but was so graceful about it that most people applauded rather than criticized her.

Oakley's image of athletic ladyhood appealed especially to women attending colleges and universities that encouraged its female students to take part in such athletic games as tennis, basketball, and competitive shooting. Also during the 1890s, the bicycle craze hit. Oakley was partly responsible in that she brought an unassembled bicycle from England to the States. She also designed a modest outfit, in which unseen garters held down the skirt, and was soon riding and shooting from bicycle-back in the arena. Baseball followed—not for Annie, but for thousands of young women who played in amateur, semi-professional, and professional teams, such as the Bloomer Girls of Texas. It was women like these who emulated Oakley, believing she had just the right blend of athleticism and femininity. In England as well women applauded her; as one journalist said in 1892, Oakley "won the hearts of the ladies" with her singular shooting and feminine appearance.

Perhaps Oakley's ladylike demeanor was the reason that dime novelists, who generally preferred racier characters as prototypes, virtually ignored her. The one exception was the Dauntless Dell series by Prentiss Ingraham. Dell, like Oakley, could ride and shoot, yet she never cursed, never drank or smoked, and dressed modestly in a blouse, knee-length skirt, tan leggings, and "small russet shoes, with silver spurs at the heels." Although the adventures of Dautless Dell now sound old-fashioned and melodramatic, they were an important part of the emerging cowgirl image. Dell idealized feminine virtues in a time of wrenching change, whether it be on the Western frontier or the Eastern urban frontier. Dell, alias Annie, modeled bravery, assertiveness, ladyhood, and loyalty. She never let down a friend, and she always triumphed over evil. This was the way Cody and Oakley wanted Western women and their counterparts in the Northeast and South to think of themselves.

Clearly, by the early 1900s, Cody's and Oakley's Wild West was more fantasy than reality. The Wild West was now often referred to as the Old Wild West, indicating that its time had come and gone. At the turn of the twentieth century, the real Old West was giving way to an increasingly urbanized and industrialized "new" West.

Cody's and Oakley's Wild West was a social construction that fit its times. During the late nineteenth and early twentieth centuries, the romanticized Wild West appeared widely to be a carefree and promising region, an image that had many adherents and few critics. It was in that milieu that Cody and Oakley became historians of sorts, presenting their version of westward settlement and instructing white citizens, immigrants, and children in the American national ideology. They also reinforced in peoples' minds the erroneous image of a largely homogenized West, its harmony disrupted only by supposedly wild and disappearing Indians who gave way to cowboys and cowgirls, all with idealized attributes of manhood and womanhood. Although Cody's and Oakley's rendition of the West was not as "authentic" as Cody had hoped, it was highly usable, meaningful to many Americans at the turn of the twentieth century and still meaningful during the early twenty-first century.

THE FINAL YEARS

Although Annie Oakley followed Cody's lead in life, she had no intention of doing so in old age. When in January 1917 a *New York Tribune* reporter described her as a little old lady who sat and knitted, Annie was beside herself. She fired off a letter saying she had never knitted. Rather, she had spent her adult years fighting an "uphill battle" in the arena "to live down" widespread prejudice against female performers. She thanked the many "good American people" who had given "their approval and applause." Annie concluded that she hoped her story would encourage those who were "just beginning the great battle of life."

When on 11 February, almost four hundred people watched Annie shoot at Pinehurst, North Carolina, not one of them could have thought of her as a has-been. She shot money out of Frank's fingers, split a potato sitting on Dave's head (their dog), scrambled five eggs in midair, cracked nuts, and shot over her shoulder by aiming in a mirror. When a reporter asked Annie for a copy of her program she replied that she and Frank had none; they put together "an impromptu shoot" and kept going as long as the audience wanted.

When America entered World War I in April 1917, Annie was ready to help. She offered, as she had during the Spanish-American War of 1898, to put together a regiment of volunteer women shooters to provide "home protection." When she got no reply from Secretary of War Newton D. Baker, she volunteered as an instructor of soldiers in proper weapon handling and shooting. Again rejected, Annie joked that she would go on the vaudeville stage, billed as the shooter the U.S. government turned down. She finally found her niche with the War Work Council and War Camp Community Service. Paying their own expenses and carrying their own supplies, Annie and Frank went from camp to camp, demonstrating shooting procedures to new recruits. Annie said that this service made her "the happiest woman in the world."

The Butlers also enlisted Dave, who raised funds for the Red Cross. During 1918, Dave searched out money that people wrapped in handkerchiefs and hid within one hundred yards of the performance area. Wearing a blindfold, Dave sniffed out the money, which all went to the Red Cross. Annie and Frank said that if Dave failed, they would give a like amount of money to the Red Cross. Not once did Dave miss finding the hidden cash.

After the war ended in 1918, Annie and Frank returned to The Carolina hotel in Pinehurst. Annie shot exhibitions for charities ranging from schools to tuberculosis asylums. She also taught women how to shoot. In 1921, the Pinehurst newspaper reported that since 1915, Annie had instructed 2000 women a year, including some 800 in 1921. Early in 1922, when shooting an exhibition, Annie hit 100 targets in a row, which the *New York Times* called a new world's record. Annie also continued such long-term regimens as exercising daily, eating nutritionally, and spending time with friends like comedian Will Rogers and vaudevillian Fred Stone and his family.

Annie's life might have continued this way had it not been for two horrendous events. The first was an automobile accident in Florida on 9 November 1922. A car in which Annie and Frank rode overturned, pinning Annie underneath. Annie had a fractured hip and a splintered right ankle. For the next six weeks, Frank lived in a room across from the hospital. When Annie returned home, she was fitted for a steel brace. The second disaster occurred on 25 February, when an automobile veered, hitting and killing Dave, the "Red Cross Dog," as he walked along the roadside with Frank. Both tragedies led to an outpouring of letters, telegrams, and flowers from fans who had not forgotten Annie Oakley, or Frank and Dave.

Life changed for the Butlers, who took up residence at the Lakeview Hotel in Leesburg, Florida. Although doctors had told Annie that she would never shoot again, she daily exercised her legs, enduring severe pain. In March 1923, Annie resumed shooting, wearing her steel brace and making some shots with her left hand. Shortly afterward, the couple traveled to Ansonia, Ohio, to spend the winter with niece Bonnie Blakely and husband Rush. Annie seldom spoke of her achievements and started to disperse her possessions and documents, including her medals and other memorabilia.

The following year, 1924, Annie and Frank, aged sixty-three and seventy-three, respectively, felt well enough to travel to North Carolina to help establish a gun club at the Mayview Manor in Blowing Rock. There, eighteen months after Annie's accident, she hit ninety-eight out of one hundred clay pigeons. Later, Annie and Frank moved to Dayton to be near her family. They still took interest in local shooting matches. They also thought about writing a will and Frank urged Annie to pen a memoir, which she finished in 1926.

When Will Rogers appealed to former fans to write to Annie, a deluge of letters and telegrams followed. Some thought of Oakley primarily as an entertainer. A Cleveland man wrote that he had first seen Annie with the Wild West in 1897 or 1898. Others remembered Annie as a sport shooter. A Florida man said that as a boy he had filled a trap with clay pigeons for a match where she, the only female competitor, had taken first prize. Others characterized Annie as a lady, one who spread her benevolence far and wide. A female well-wisher hoped that Annie's spirit would help her through hard times. Many more saw Annie as a Western woman. A California man commented that he first went West in 1881 and, like Annie, was "nearing the end of the trail."

During the summer of 1926, Annie and Frank returned to the Blakeley farm. When Frank spoke of going to Pinehurst for the winter, Annie urged him to go ahead, promising him she would follow when she felt strong enough. Feeling poorly himself, but wanting to please Annie, Frank first went to New Jersey but was too unwell to go on. He called Annie's niece, Fern Swartout, for help. Frank went to Fern in Michigan, where she put him to bed and cared for him, as Annie had asked when and if the necessity arose.

At home, Annie worsened. She gave away many of her remaining possessions and did not resist when her sister Hulda moved her to a house in Greenville, where she died in her sleep on 3 November 1926. In Michigan, Fern noted that when Frank heard of Annie's death, he stopped eating. Frank died on 21 November, eighteen days after Annie. Tributes and flowers poured in from fans and admirers. At a simple ceremony on Thanksgiving Day the two were buried in the family plot at Brock Cemetery near Greenville.

In the years since her death, Annie's story has taken on many dimensions, some accurate, some less so. Books, stage plays, motion pictures, and museum exhibits have interpreted her achievements in different ways. Most well known is the musical *Annie Get Your Gun*, which opened on Broadway in May 1946, with Ethel Merman playing Annie. In 1950, Barbara Stanwyck starred as Annie in a film version of *Annie Get Your Gun*. Since then, innumerable versions of the musical have played all over the United States and a good part of the world.

Today, in the early twenty-first century, Annie Oakley is primarily remembered for her immense contributions to Cody's Wild West and to the image of the Old Wild West. Despite Annie's Ohio background, she is thought of as a Western woman. Clearly, Annie Oakley became a Western icon not because of her origins, but in spite of them. Oakley looked like a Westerner and acted like a Westerner, thus the public accepted her as one. People at home and abroad also took in her rendering of Western women as strong, courageous, and able to defend themselves and others. In Oakley's case, representing the American West was a state of mind rather than a place of residence, allowing her to ably and effectively cast the Old Wild West into a form with widespread and lasting appeal.

FURTHER READING

Havighurst, Walter. *Annie Oakley of the Wild West* (New York: Macmillan, 1954).

Kasper, Shirl. *Annie Oakley* (Norman: University of Oklahoma Press, 1992).

Riley, Glenda. *The Life and Legacy of Annie Oakley* (Norman: University of Oklahoma Press, 1994).

Sayers, Isabelle S. *Annie Oakley and Buffalo Bill's Wild West* (New York: Dover Publications, 1981).

Sayers, Isabelle S. *The Rifle Queen: Annie Oakley* (Ostrander, OH: Sayers, N.p., 1973).

Swartout, Annie Fern Campbell. *Missie: An Historical Biography of Annie Oakley* (Blanchester, OH: Brown, 1947).

Cowboy on a Bucking Bronco, by Frederic Remington. Courtesy of Library of Congress.

Frederic Remington

Marie Watkins

I knew the wild riders and the vacant land were about to vanish forever. . . . Without knowing exactly how to do it, I began to try to record some facts around me, and the more I looked the more the panorama unfolded.

Close your eyes and most likely you will see this picture of the West: rugged cowboys, hard-riding bronco busters, fierce Indian warriors, and devil-may-care cavalrymen. This picture of the West is primarily derived from the late nineteenth-century artist Frederic Remington. His works, however, represented something beyond their purely formal qualities, both to his contemporaries, as well as today's audience. Likewise, his art assumed varying degrees of cultural importance. It is the cultural meanings of Remington's art that bestow value beyond its aesthetic appeal. This urbane Eastern artist took the morally flawed real West and made it heroic: a place and its peoples existing in the wild and unsettled frontier where time is forever suspended. He blended history and myth into an iconic image that was later appropriated by Hollywood filmmakers, television producers, and Wall Street advertising agents. Remington became the epic mythmaker of the American West.

By the 1880s the "winning of the West" was for all practical purposes accomplished. Thriving cities replaced frontier towns, Indians were banished to reservations, barbed wire fenced in the open range, and blue overalls displaced the jingling spurs of the cowboys. America's future became its past. The demise of the great Western drama now evoked nostalgic longing and regret. Remington enters the West at this point in time. Traveling to Montana in 1881, the nineteen-year-old Remington met an old wagon freighter who colorfully recalled the days of his youth as they sat around a campfire one night. The old man confirmed Remington's worst fears when he declared the West was gone. Years later, in 1905, the artist told a reporter he thereby resolved at that moment to preserve the past, and indeed his panorama of the West unfolded for all America.

At the time of Remington's premature death in 1909 at the age of forty-eight, his repertoire included over 3000 paintings and drawings, twenty-five bronzes, eight books, a Broadway play, two novels, and more than 100 magazine articles and stories. Remington towered as the most popular Western artist at the turn of the twentieth century, his Western imagery turning into a metaphor for the collective identity of America. From that time onward the American West became a place where life imitates art. Remington's West came to stand for America's Old West, and in particular the Wild West.

As early as 1892 Remington had clearly established his far-reaching influence as an artist-historian.

Eight years later, in 1900, the artist returned to the Southwest and Colorado. It was not the West he expected to see. Remington vowed he would never go West again because the West had failed to stay the same as the pictures he had painted. Remington had fallen victim to his own artistry, along with the nation.

Ironically, the New York–born Remington had limited experience of the "old West" that he wanted to depict so realistically in his art. He most often relied on what he had heard, not what he had seen. To be sure, he had served as an artist-correspondent in the last gasp of the Indian Wars. With brief excursions to Arizona and Mexico, he covered the Apache campaign and followed the trail of Geronimo. He had a short stint in Canada during the Metis unrest, and was in Dakota during the Sioux Ghost Dance War for the Battle of Wounded Knee that calamitously and tragically sealed the end of the Indian Wars. Unlike the life and death struggles that filled his art, Remington never saw action on these assignments. That would come with his posting to Cuba. With the Spanish-American War, his art and reality would mercilessly collide, forever tempering his visions of the glories of war. Nonetheless, his Western experiences alone were invaluable to his career. In particular, they enhanced his reputation as a recorder of history.

Writers and journalists repeatedly embellished Remington's life in the frontier and vouched for his reliable reporting. In essence, Remington had his own public relations firm with Eastern writers. For them, the artist had taken on the guise of the stock-type characters in his works, and he, too, was being packaged as a commodity. Remington became a positive brand image along with his art. For example, under the pen of Orison Swett Marden, successful author of motivational books in the early twentieth century, Remington became a cow puncher in Montana; a profitable mule rancher in Kansas; and a cowboy, guide, and scout in the Southwest. Another writer of the popular press added to Remington's growing legend:

In his pictures of life on the plains, and of Indian fighting, [Remington] has almost created a new field of illustration, so fresh and novel are his characterizations. . . . It is a fact that admits of no question that Eastern people have formed their conceptions of what the Far Western life is like, more from what they have seen in Mr. Remington's pictures than from any other source, and if they went to the West or to Mexico they would expect to see men and places looking exactly as Mr. Remington has drawn them.

—Art critic William A. Coffin, 1905

> [He] was once a ranger on the limitless prairies, a hard-riding, rough-living, free-fighting cowpuncher—for do not lose sight of the fact that Frederic Remington has put himself and his own experiences in very nearly every picture he has drawn or painted. "He rides like a Comanche," said one of his friends "He knows as much about horses and cattle as any man alive. And so he should, for he spent most of his youth in the saddle, rounding up mavericks, chasing and being chased by the red men, and hobnobbing with scouts, pioneers, miners, and picturesque freebooters of the plains." (Maxwell, 1907)

With twisted truths, Remington became larger than life. He was on his way to becoming a legend.

It would have been difficult, if not impossible for a reader to know how much was fact and how much was made up to fill the imaginations of Eastern readers. Perhaps it did not matter where the truth ended and the fiction began because by the turn of the century Remington and his art had become the Wild West. Rather than dry historical facts of Western history, the public preferred the meaning of the art and its artist. Even so, with conscientious chroniclers' biographical profiles like these how could anyone question the veracity of his Western art? Yet some did, mainly Westerners who had a bone to pick with an Eastern artist who was depicting their territory and challenging their views of artistic significance. They would dispute the factual accuracy of his art, especially the descriptive details.

Aesthetic quarrels such as these are not unusual in the history of Western American art, much less the history of art itself. One can readily turn to Renaissance Italy or closer to home in America with numerous vociferous artistic clashes. Although authenticity is a slippery concept, it has been and continues to be in some quarters a primary filter in assessing and interpreting Western American art. During Remington's era at the turn of the twentieth century, in a time of rapid transitions and the attendant loss of the frontier, many Americans found themselves seeking something both primordial and permanent. The concept of authenticity provided a means of defining such cultural values. Paradoxically, the standard of authenticity is culturally constructed and subject to constant change. Even more problematic is that it can only be defined in terms of its opposite. According to this binary structure, authenticity is indeterminate. On the one hand, the test of authenticity evaluates the work of art in terms of its truthfulness scale, or its qualities of documentation. On the other hand, as what is perceived as truth changes, so does its opposite. This paradox is endemic to the study of turn-of-the-century Western representations. The source of this conundrum lies in the origins of American art history itself.

Progenitors of Western American Art

America's frontier began in the East. The frontier was a dynamic process of expansion, a spasmodic imaginary line that continually moved westward on the continent, rather than a carefully delineated geographical region.

This shifting frontier took on different meanings and images, resulting in a vast array of art created and produced to fill imaginations and satisfy the curiosities of the public.

During the period of conquest and colonization in the sixteenth century, Europeans wanted to know what the New World and its inhabitants were like. Artists including Jacques Le Moyne (ca. 1533–1588) and John White (ca. 1540–ca. 1618) recorded the people, animals, and plants they encountered in precise detail. American art was thus born as an art of documentation. The need for understanding the New World and promoting colonization tempered, however, these artists' representations. Often they depicted native peoples with the body type and stance of Greek and Roman statues. In contrast to mainstream American art, their Western subject matter had the common threads of realism and truth running through it. Or so it seemed. It was assumed that Western representations must be accurate. More recently, however, art and cultural historians have questioned the accuracy of such representations. As they see it, such imagery is derived from the values of the artists, patrons, and viewing audiences of the East (and Europe).

Few people even know the true definition of the term "West," and where is its location?—phantom-like it flies before us as we travel, and our way is continually gilded, before us, as we approach the setting sun.
—George Catlin (1796–1872)

Rather than being categorized as narrative history painting or genre painting within the canon of American art, Western imagery was winnowed away from an encompassing American aesthetic. Western American art would seem a natural fit for history painting because history paintings do not necessarily portray an accurate or documentary description of actual events, for example Emanuel Leutze's *Washington Crossing the Delaware* (1851). Remington's works, in particular, portray the universal themes of the human spirit of which history paintings are so fond—heroic quest; struggle and sacrifice; virtues of courage, loyalty, and honor; the value of friendship; man against man; man against nature. However, this subject matter became consigned to records and interpretations of American history, essentially removed from aesthetic consideration. Authenticity and accuracy of detail became the core concepts of critical analysis (and remain for some today) for Western American art. Ultimately, authenticity was derived from firsthand Western experience: those who personally observed or lived in the West. The ability to determine authenticity was through the accuracy of detail. The details testified to the reality, that is, the documentary realism of the work of art. The rigor of factual accuracy as established by the New World artist-naturalists became the critical visual determinant among the artist-explorers (or pioneer artists), the progenitors of Western American art.

By the 1830s more and more artists began to explore the West and brought back visual proof of a dramatic new frontier to their patrons and an Eastern urban audience. They performed a heroic act in leaving the security and confines of the studio for the boundless West where they journeyed thousands of miles amid perilous terrain and unknown native peoples. George Catlin (1796–1872), Alfred Jacob Miller (1810–1874), and Karl Bodmer (1809–1893) were among the best known of the artist-explorers. These older established artists had a remarkable influence on later artists, including Remington. Through their paintings, especially those of Bodmer and Catlin, artists were encouraged to venture West and paint the Plains Indians. Moreover, these images became reference works for the illustrators who never left their Eastern studios, but hastened to meet the popular demand for Plains Indian imagery. Each artist shared a Romantic heritage but brought distinctive styles to their representations of indigenous cultures and Western lands. They argued unremittingly, with some theatrics thrown in, over the veracity of their pictures. By the time of Remington's generation, viewers were conditioned to look at Western American art as an instrument of information not cultural refinement, like stained glass windows for the medieval viewer.

In 1830, George Catlin, a former lawyer turned painter, was supposedly inspired to venture westward by a delegation of Western Indians traveling through Philadelphia. Catlin described how he zealously set out under his own volition to paint members of every Indian tribe in what he perceived as uncivilized country. In doing so, he believed he was documenting a dying race for posterity. The slap-dash technique of Catlin implied his urgent sense of mission to record one more face and likeness for posterity before fast-advancing civilization destroyed them. Catlin recognized his own limitations. Rather than stressing his artistic acumen, Catlin went to great lengths to promote the truthfulness of the ethnographic facts that he recorded in more than 600 paintings. Often he attached certificates of authenticity to his paintings. Official personages, including military officers and Indian agents, signed testimonials that they were not only present when Catlin painted the work but also vouched for the accurateness of the image. His best portraits capture sympathetically the individual's humanity as seen in *The Dog, Chief of "Bad Arrow Points" Band* (1832). On the whole, however, his interest was not primarily in individuals, but in a total record of Indian civilization.

Prefiguring Buffalo Bill's Wild West Show, Catlin took his Indian Gallery of paintings, artifacts, and sometimes Indian performers on the road in America and Europe. In his attempt to educate the public through his art, Catlin angered some Americans by his criticism of Indian policy. Wielding as much if not more influence than his paintings were Catlin's publications, such as the two-volume heavily illustrated *Letters and Notes on the Manners, Customs and Condition of the North American Indians*, published in London in 1841. Viewed as historical documents, Catlin's paintings and illustrations shaped public attitudes toward native populations and Western lands. His art became part of the visual iconography of the West. Remington would later read his books and study his art. Catlin's publications, including *Letters and Notes*, were part of Remington's library as reliable source materials.

Catlin's excessive attempts to fend off criticism of his art, however, were to no avail. Some detractors maintained Catlin chose his Western subject matter due to his inability to compete skillfully with other artists of his generation. The same charges would also be leveled at Remington decades later. Artistic egos flared as Catlin's paintings achieved acclaim for their historical and scientific value. Alfred Jacob Miller flatly stated that it was fortunate for Catlin that few had traveled westward because his works were filled with "humbug." Karl Bodmer seconded that view, calling Catlin a charlatan.

In 1837 Miller left the confines of a New Orleans French Quarter studio on Chartres Street to record the adventures of his patron, the Scottish nobleman Sir William Drummond Stewart. Miller traveled 1500 miles through partially uncharted territory from St. Louis to the heart of the Rocky Mountains to record Stewart's adventures as a dashing nineteenth-century romantic figure. Stewart was bound for the boisterous annual fur trade rendezvous at the Green River, Wyoming, where trappers and Indians came together to sell their furs to Eastern traders. Miller was among the first to depict the mountain man or fur trapper in his buckskin-clad adventurous lifestyle embodied in *Louis— Rocky Mountain Trapper* (undated), *Setting Traps for Beaver* (1837), and *Trappers* (1858). The mountain man, the first Western hero, lived in harmony with the exotic wilderness. Symbolizing courage, self-reliance, and individualism, he would become a type in Western iconography. This free-spirited, legendary loner was on his way to extinction, long gone before Remington made him part of his standard Western types. Initially the mountain man represented the frontier, but he would be supplanted by the cowboy by the end of the nineteenth century. Remington proved adept at rendering both cultural icons.

It's not hard to imagine the mountain man today. However, the image we have is of Remington's toughened stoic figures at bay in a perilous land, not Miller's lissome young men posed as classical gods at play in a pastoral setting. Firsthand experience did not necessarily represent truth. Remington's trappers were created from his imaginings, unlike Miller who had lived among the trappers. For example, when Remington saw the photograph of the real-life mountain man Henry Chatillon he was disappointed. Chatillon's physiognomy did not live up to his expectations. Remington had planned to use him as a model for illustrations in the respected historian Francis Parkman's reissued classic *The Oregon Trail* (1892). Nonplussed, he wrote Parkman that Chatillon looked more like a Boston fisherman than a wild rider of the Plains.

Parkman, who knew Chatillon, responded enthusiastically to the liberties Remington took in rendering the mountain man for his book and acknowledged that if the trapper were still alive he would be partial to the artist's portrayal. In this case, Remington's semblance of reality proved superior to the supposed truth derived from Miller's firsthand experience and observation. Reality could not measure up to his visual transformation of the ideal.

Among Remington's best representations of the trapper is the tension-filled twenty-eight-inch bronze *The Mountain Man* (1903) that fits Parkman's description. A trapper on horseback makes his way down a precipitously steep incline, where one false move would tumble horse and rider to their deaths.

The supporting function of the base dissolves into a steep rocky cliff uniting figures and landscape into a dynamic sloping movement. Survival in this forbidding terrain is a judgment of his character. Leaning back in the saddle the trapper grasps a tail strap, balancing with consummate skill as the horse cautiously makes its way over the narrow, sharply inclined, rock-strewn ground. Man and animal are one in their strength and endurance. In this work, Remington created the memorable icon of the mountain man: fearless, self-reliant, alone, rootless as the ground he traverses. He exemplifies Darwinian survival of the fittest, a man who survives on his senses, a breed of man larger than life. He is beyond the reach of Eastern civilization and its social control as the ground gives way at a sharp incline behind him. Only a being such as this, wearing the fur cap and buckskins made from the hides of the wild animals he has killed, could survive in a raw and unforgiving nature. His realistic character is conveyed through the artist's inclusion of a mountain man's basic accoutrements such as bear traps, axe, bedroll, and rifle.

Miller, too, portrayed the frontier with the romantic sensibilities of his generation. Unlike Parkman and Remington, who viewed Native Americans as more savage than noble, Miller represented them as the idealized "noble savage." It is the larger intellectual and social context of any given period that fosters perceptions of Indians and the West, or for that matter, any people in any region. For Miller, *Crow Indian on the Lookout* (undated) embodied the ideal primitive man embodying the virtues of wilderness life.

He described this individual as unaware of his natural elegance. Indian society was part and parcel of the frontier fur trade life Miller painted. He often represented Indian women partially dressed or nude, as playful woodland nymphs who had the appearance of dark-skinned Caucasians. *Snake Girl Swinging* (undated) is candidly erotic in the Rococo tradition of Watteau, while *Indian Girls Making Toilet*, *Scene of the River "Eau Sucre," Indian Woman Sleeping*, and *Waiting for the Caravan* (ca. 1837) are sisters to the odalisque and harem scenes in the Orientalist paintings of French artists Delacroix and Ingres, which Miller likely saw while in Paris in 1833–1834. Miller's paintings convey little of the impending doom of native cultures that he recorded in his diaries; rather they depict a land of romantic adventure, filled with nature's innocence.

There was little time for frolicking in Remington's West. Within his masculine domain that overflowed with violent life and death struggles, the "noble savage" and women have little place. Indians tended to be fierce adversaries and impeders of civilization. However, now that the Indian Wars had passed, he wrote of his respect for the Indians because they gave no quarter and asked no quarter. He admired their nobility of purpose to fight to their death for their land. His later works showed a change in attitude by empathetically depicting a quieter human nature as in the tender *The Love Call* (1909), and the elegiac *When His Heart is Bad* (1908). His West was never a place for a woman, possibly because, as Remington readily acknowledged, he didn't paint women because he didn't understand them, but not because they weren't there. An exception is the extraordinarily romantic nocturne *Waiting in the Moonlight* (1907–1909). This painting may be interpreted as a tragic romance set in the West rather than the love-triumphs-over-all cliché of the sweetheart riding off in the arms of her cowboy. A traditional adobe dwelling with support poles, a favorite prop of Remington's Southwestern settings, forms a backdrop in this barren land. Pale moonlight streams down on the apparitional couple in the nighttime tryst. The mounted cowboy leans from his saddle toward his standing lover who turns away. The fluid brushwork of narrow tonal range suppresses the details, creating a canvas of tension and mystery. The viewer is left to wonder if this is a love story of yearning, perhaps of the tragic love of star-crossed lovers. Or indeed, what has gone awry between the two characters?

It would be easy to denigrate Miller's romantic, misogynist, and racist practices, just as Remington's art abetted racial and cultural dominance, and leave it at that. But to be fair, the artistic results need to be placed in the context of their respective eras. These artists did not live in the multicultural times of today. Their art expresses the dominant ideologies of their respective time periods. Beneath the historical subject matter, the paintings' topical relevance would have been understood by the contemporary viewer. In particular, the popular magazines and journals in which Remington's illustrations appeared presented a tacit understanding of current national attitudes, trends, ideas, and events. It was art created for urban middle-class and working-class audiences. Western art has provided us with some of our grandest visions and some of our darkest dreams. It is the complexity and the ironies of this art that makes for interesting dialogue today, attempting to penetrate the imagery and understand the impact of the West both then and now.

In 1832, the twenty-four-year-old Karl Bodmer accompanied his patron, the German gentleman-scientist of Humboldtian tradition Alexander Philipp Maximilian, Prince of Wied-Neuwied, to document his explorations and observations in the Upper Missouri country that Catlin had recently traversed. While Bodmer's and Catlin's paintings shared similarities of peoples and places, Bodmer's superior European artistic training produced more precise renderings of anatomy and colorful material culture, hence a greater impression of the truth. Bodmer's representations were clinically executed records showing human specimens in ethnological detail. Works such as *Iron Shirt, Mehkskehme-Sukahs, Piegan Blackfeet Chief* (August 1833) accompanied studies of animal and plant life, as well as details of the geology and geography of the Upper Missouri. As directed by Prince Maximilian, Bodmer thoroughly recorded all aspects of their travels, which resulted in the widely acclaimed scientific publication *Reise in das Innere Nord-Amerika in den Jahren 1832–1834*. Parkman praised the accuracy of Bodmer's art to Remington. Unaware of the book, Remington went directly to a library and determined that Bodmer was a better draftsman and scientific source than Catlin.

Remington, however, opted to move from reporting to more complex constructions whether to create a national form of history painting or to contribute images to the American myth.

Catlin, along with other artist-explorers, gathered depictions of Indians in the manner that naturalists assembled plants, animals, and minerals. In this sense, the portraits served as cultural exemplars, not to be viewed as art but as scientific specimens like other natural phenomena. Perhaps that is why naturalist John James Audubon also entered the heated fray. Taking offense at Catlin's christening as "the Audubon of the Indians," he denounced Catlin's work as a fraud and nonsense. It was the accuracy of facts that drew the ire of his rivals, not his slap-dash artistry. And Catlin was not without blame. By promulgating the truth of his paintings, he downplayed their artistic merit. He explained his unrefined painterly technique as compliant with his urgent sense of mission to record one more face and likeness for posterity. For him, time was of the essence to capture the vanishing race. Moreover, he justified his style with the vagaries of working in the privations of the frontier. His challenging artistic process notwithstanding, Catlin painted each individual and captured their dignity of bearing. Nonetheless, a division was taking place between American artists: the art of Western artists was to be judged on its documentary elements, not its aesthetic ones.

Factual accuracy would continue to permeate Western subject matter, unlike that of other artistic schools. Like Catlin, Remington too would build his career on factual accuracy and take center stage in rancorous artistic rivalries within the Wild West school. It would also be his undoing in the later stages of his career, when he sought acclaim as a fine artist rather than a purveyor of historical records—a visual historian. Also like Catlin, Remington brought some of his troubles on himself.

Contemporary Artistic Rivals

Remington was proud of his artistic achievements, and deservedly so. Open the popular magazines of *Harper's Weekly, Outing, Century, Scribner's,* or *Harper's Monthly* from the mid-1880s through the 1890s and Remington was there. No less, his gripping illustrations played counterpoint to the prose of the best of contemporary Western writers, including William F. (Buffalo Bill) Cody, Bret Harte, John Muir, Frances Parkman, Theodore Roosevelt, and Owen Wister. Remington, too, wrote his own Western narratives. It is not without significance that his rise to the top was meteoric among the denizens of popular visual culture. Unequivocally, he attributed his achievement to his personal experience with typical bravado that he knew the West better than anyone else. It was Remington's West for a while. But by 1903, fellow Easterner Charles Schreyvogel (1861–1912) had moved into his artistic territory, and he had come to stay. Moreover, other up-and-comers, including Charles M. Russell (1864–1926) and Maynard Dixon (1875–1946) were trailing close behind from the West.

In 1891, after five years in the profession, Remington, now the sage illustrator, graciously offered guidance to the sixteen-year-old Dixon who wanted to
break into Western illustration. He had sent Remington, whom he admired above all other illustrators, his
sketch books. Remington's response to the rising young
artist is revealing not only in its genuine openness but also in his philosophy
of art and his attitude regarding the subject of popular illustration at this
time. Like a caring father to his son, Remington, fast approaching forty, wist-
fully wrote "your letter and books are here and I have quite enjoyed your
sketches. I hardly know what to tell you—I do not 'teach' and unused to giving
advice—the only advice I could give you is to never take anyone's advice, which
is my rule" (Hagerty, 1998). He kindly acknowledged that Dixon's technical
skills were better than his at that age. But straight away he counseled on the
challenges and frustrations of the profession, writing that "if you have the
'Sand' to overcome difficulties you could be an artist in time—no one's opinion of what you can do is of any consequence—time and your character will
develop that." Surprisingly, Remington recommended a formal artistic education, which he himself had rejected. "Most every artist needs 'schooling,'" he
encouraged, but "I had very little—it is not absolutely necessary—it is best to
have it" (Hagerty, 1998). Concerning artistic style, he insisted to "[b]e always
true to yourself—to the way and the things you see in nature—if you imitate
any other man ever so little you are 'gone'" (Hagerty, 1998). Remington followed his own advice throughout his career. For him, the subject matter was
a constant that he would not relinquish. But technically he would readily
attempt something new. One need only compare the loose, dappled impressionistic painting *Pool in the Desert* (1907–1908) with the hard-edged clarity
of color and form of *The Blackfoot War Party* (1887). It is hard to believe that
they are by the same artist, except for their figural subject matter of Indians.

By gad a fellow has got to race to keep up now days—the pace is fast.

Remington kept himself well informed of new developments in contemporary art through fellow artists, exhibitions, books, and lectures. He understood the competitive art world and the rapidly changing progressive art
movements.

He numbered members of The Ten, a rebellious American Impressionist
group, among his circle of friends. He keenly sought their guidance and criticism, especially that of J. Alden Weir, with whom he had studied at the Art
Students League. Remington also valued the opinions of Robert Reid, Childe
Hassam, John H. Twachtman, and Willard Metcalf. Of all the French Impressionist art that he saw, he appreciated and studied the work of Claude Monet,
whose paintings he had seen in Paris in 1893. Observing the works in the
same natural light in which they were painted enhanced his understanding of
Monet's technique. Remington also socialized with art critic and Tonalist
painter Arthur Hoeber, who critiqued his work and also kept him abreast of
the latest gossip in New York art circles.

Study good pictures—do not imitate them—read books and good literature and work work work.

—Remington to Maynard Dixon (1875–1946)

More of a maverick, Remington never felt the need to join a group, preferring to observe other artists' approaches and then place his own personal vision on his art. Supplementing Remington's drive to improve his technique and understanding of the material properties of the media was a strong work ethic. All through his life, on most days, Remington could be found at his easel from eight A.M. until mid-afternoon. He advised young Dixon to do the same.

As well throughout his career Remington fervently studied artworks independently, particularly that of European military painters Louis-Ernest Meissonier, Jean-Baptiste-Edouard Detaille, Alphonse-Marie de Neuville, and Vasili Vereschagin. Although some of Remington's works are derivative of their subject matter, it does not diminish him or his art at all. As Picasso once famously said, "Bad artists copy. Great artists steal." Remington, like other artists, would find a model, dissect it, analyze it, and reconstruct it. Under the time constraints of the commercial art market of illustration, models would be a vital resource.

Remington also warned Dixon of the capriciousness of the art market that he knew all too well. Although riding high at this time, he knew that he was at a turning point with his specialization in depicting the winning of the West. The military conquest had ended. As a result, imagery of the violent clash of cultures was on the way out, or so it seemed. He felt pressed to find other subject matter and new markets to offer to his publishers and public. He explained to Dixon that being an artist would not bring wealth, but perhaps happiness, because he was in control of how he spent his time. Most important, he admonished the young artist to respect the illustrator's art for it was as rewarding as that of the painter and most likely more financially secure. Soon, however, Remington would find illustrating others' narratives too narrow and displeasing. Showing in major art venues since 1888, he sought distinction beyond that of the foremost popular illustrator. It would prove to be a long hard trail to follow. But he obstinately pursued it to its end, in due course receiving limited critical favor as a sculptor and subsequently as a painter. Nonetheless, he remained practical. He reconciled that illustration was the bread and butter that provided the comfortable life he had achieved and enjoyed.

Dixon followed Remington's advice, and in many ways his career would parallel Remington's life choices. In 1893, Dixon's illustrations began to appear in the San Francisco *Overland Monthly*, to the pleasure of the public. In less than two years the publication proclaimed that Dixon now wore the mantle of the master. The young artist went into illustration because of Remington, but later he turned from storytelling imagery to that of the spiritual and introspective. Like Remington, he moved with facility from illustration to painting, experimenting with impressionistic and tonalist techniques. Dixon was also influenced by cubism and social realism, styles that Remington did not live to see. Dixon began to apply postmodern principles to Western landscapes, evident in *Study in Cubist Realism* (1925). The words cubism and realism are antithetical, but Dixon seemingly integrated them in his technical exploration. Although he used angular shapes, the work is not strictly cubist. Rather, the shapes are abstracted. A transition from the polarization of value and color eliminates the middle values, thus allowing an extreme contrast which is unlike analytical cubism, its stylistic model. The spaces in this painting clearly define a foreground, middle-ground, and background. The foreground shapes, which are larger and a little brighter, transition into the middle-ground to smaller shapes and slightly duller colors, and the background is a strip of sky plane. Two verticals create a frontal plane that put the landscape behind it.

The suppressed details, flattened space, and simplified and faceted forms, as in *Earth Knower* (1931–1932) and *Men and Mountains* (1933), are representative of Dixon's distinctive mature style. Akin to Remington, he never subscribed to a particular school of art, but Dixon lived long enough to develop his modernist style. His Western art predecessor had offered good advice and Dixon had taken it to heart.

An aesthetic pioneer, Dixon expanded the West. Intuitively, Dixon knew his destination, whereas Remington had difficulty trusting his own instincts. Dixon's growth as an artist was linear and direct, while Remington's vacillated more between realism and the new direction in art. In the end Dixon became the artist that Remington aspired to be. He was the true visionary. Ironically, Remington arguably ended up with the larger reputation.

With Remington's changing styles, one wonders whether if he had lived longer, he too would have eventually rejected Western drama for poetic formalism. He turned briefly in that direction with a series of *plein air* landscapes in 1908. Yet he was at odds with himself to create a personal style. He commented that "these transcripts from nature fellows who are so clever cannot compare with the imaginative man in long run" (Dippie, 2001). It was the subject matter that mattered most to Remington. As far as he was concerned, his landscapes were hardly ever beautiful. Nonetheless, he admitted how much he prized the work. Moreover, Remington himself doubted the marketability of his impressionistic and tonalist landscapes, especially as he saw that The Ten were lacking in sales, although their work met with the critical approval that he keenly wanted. He thought that one could not have seen a better modern showing than theirs in 1908. Yet several of them were in desperate financial straits as Remington noted in his diary. In fact, one member of The Ten, Reid, went bankrupt.

He faced the traditional schism between art and money. Remington was conflicted because he needed the income. He, too, knew his public wanted Western imagery.

Got me pigeon-holed in their minds, you see; want horses, cowboys, out West things, won't believe me if I paint anything else.

Perhaps typecasting was a boon for Remington in a manner, for he maintained recognition and salability in a precarious profession. The drawback was with the Eastern art establishment, who did not want to consider Remington beyond the role of an illustrator of Western subject matter, which they considered middlebrow. Even more so, the greatest drawback may have been Remington himself. He was too competent and too facile. Maybe with less ability he would have been a more visionary artist. Having reached the end of his skill, he was at a loss. Moreover, if he had not painted the West, he would never have achieved his iconic status. Given his competent but undistinguished manner of painting, if he had painted the subject matter of The Ten, for instance, he would simply be another name added to the list of American Impressionists.

In contrast to his support for Dixon, Remington had no warm words for Charles Schreyvogel, except in the heat of anger. Unintentionally, Schreyvogel hit one sore point after another where Remington was concerned. First, Schreyvogel was a latecomer to the world of the Wild West. He did not begin to paint Western subject matter until 1893, and second, it wasn't just any Western subject matter but that of Remington's action-packed narratives with charging cavalry, crackling gunfire, and resounding war whoops on the Plains. To have seen battles like these at this point in time, Schreyvogel would have had to buy a ticket to Buffalo Bill's Wild West, something he could have done that very year at the World's Columbian Exposition (the Chicago World's Fair), which was celebrating America's progress from its frontier origins. Remington, like half the nation, attended the fair where he exhibited fifteen drawings, along with writing and illustrating the article "A Gallop through the Midway" for *Harper's Magazine*. Sometime during the 1890s, when Schreyvogel visited the sensational Wild West productions, he became friends with its creator Buffalo Bill Cody. The artist used the Wild West performers as models for his art. Thus Schreyvogel came by his material secondhand, a flaw in the eyes of Remington.

Schreyvogel, like the fair-going public, had the rare opportunity to see an Indian in the flesh. Most Indians were confined to reservations and were removed from the day-to-day life of the majority of European Americans. Buffalo Bill's Wild West on the outskirts of the Chicago fair offered an alternative view to the exposition's ethnographic displays, although each maintained that they edified along with being entertaining. In Chicago, the Wild West performances repeatedly presented to packed crowds the unfolding drama of American civilization. Cody insisted the acts were exactly the way these events had occurred and as they were recorded in the annals of history. In truth, the shows suspended time and reenacted his vaudevillian version of the winning of the West, not unlike his artist counterparts Remington and Schreyvogel.

Cody paralleled Remington's ability to make Western icons. This showman's presentation of the Old West, however, impacted more immediately and more viscerally because of its theatricality and entertainment. Millions saw Buffalo Bill, but how many saw Remington's art or would be so inclined, especially to see his paintings? It would be impossible to record who saw Remington's illustrations and paintings, but it is implausible they numbered more than those who attended the Wild West performances. It was in the nature of his delivery to the public that Cody reigned supreme in creating his vision of the West. Looking at images is a passive engagement unlike the "real time" Wild West show.

Cody reinvented and reinvigorated the last frontier, perpetuating a continual renewal that enshrined and placed value on the winning of the West in the American consciousness. Ultimately, the program conveyed the same message as did the fair's ethnographic presentations—that the American Indians, heroic warriors of a vanishing race, must submit to a superior, progressive civilization. Their passing ignited a public longing for things Indian. Buffalo Bill and Remington, and now Schreyvogel, had tapped into a lucrative popular market that fed the public's nostalgic longing for the passing of the frontier and its inhabitants.

In Remington's eyes, the upstart Schreyvogel committed his second faux pas in painting *My Bunkie* (1899), which was clearly derived from Remington's 1896 sculpture *The Wounded Bunkie*. This painting portrayed bravery under fire as a mounted cavalryman rescues his fallen comrade. The painting won the esteemed National Academy of Design's Thomas B. Clarke Prize for figure painting in 1900, an honor that Remington coveted but never received. It gained further merit by being praised in the introduction to a collection of reproductions that included *My Bunkie*. Its author proclaimed that Schreyvogel had never worked as an illustrator, reproducing his imagery for the popular press. This comment of the divide between illustrators and painters hit too close to home for Remington, who was intently trying to transform his professional persona. Remington began to make a list of factual inaccuracies in Schreyvogel's art.

Schreyvogel continued to garner critical praise. Words that had been typically applied to Remington's work were directed toward Schreyvogel's paintings, as shown in the 1901 critic's remark that no one depicted the West more accurately. Then, in 1902 Remington's own publisher, *Harper's Weekly*, crowned Schreyvogel "The West's Painter-Laureate." Remington was bristling and contacted his friend Owen Wister, to condemn Schreyvogel in writing because he was confusing the public with a West he had never seen and could not understand.

In 1893, just as Dixon was beginning to make a name for himself as a Western illustrator, Schreyvogel embarked on the first of several trips to the West to make sketches, write detailed descriptions, take photographs, and collect artifacts that would enable him to bring a historical reconstruction to his studio paintings. In contrast to their opinion of Remington's work, other contemporaries, while acknowledging Schreyvogel's historical distance from his subject matter, applauded his painstaking research.

Fellow Western artists William Jones and Edwin W. Deming, on visiting Schreyvogel's studio in 1902, went one step farther. They directly compared him to Remington: "He does things western, especially where Indians and soldiers are fighting. . . . His pictures are like Remington's only far better. This statement has reference only to the pictures in action. In atmosphere, and cowboys and ponies, Remington is king" (Dippie, 1994). King or not, Remington was not about to tolerate any royal pretenders. Early in his career Remington established himself as the foremost American military artist. He remained enamored of the military his entire life, a legacy from his childhood hero worship of his father's military exploits. The very same year that James and Dewing praised Schreyvogel's military art, Wister championed Remington as the soldier-artist in his sole publication of poems *Done in the Open*, illustrated by Remington: "[Remington] with his piercing and yet imaginative eye has taken the likeness of the modern American soldier and stamped it upon our minds with a blow as clean-cut as is the impression of the American Eagle upon our coins in the Mint. Like the Mint, he has made these soldiers of ours universal currency, a precious and historic possession" (Wister, 1902). Remington coined the imagery and considered Schreyvogel's art counterfeit representations of the West.

Although Remington had moved on from military imagery to that of other Western subjects by 1895, not everyone had grown tired of soldiers in conflicts on the frontier. What was one to do with a royal pretender but crush him in his ascendancy? Remington had bided his time long enough and devised a plan to bury Schreyvogel: It would be in the details of his paintings. Remington believed that his personal version of Western reality was plainly dependent on realistic details and his cultural influence was wide and practically unassailable.

On 18 April 1903 the *New York Herald* pushed all the right buttons, igniting Remington's jealousy. The newspaper published a spread on Schreyvogel's latest painting with the heading: " 'Custer's Demand,' Schreyvogel's Latest Army Picture. Artist Made Famous by 'My Bunkie' Produces a Picture of a Historical Event in Indian Warfare." The journalist went so far as to hail Schreyvogel as "the Painter of the Western Frontier." Those were fighting words. Remington's moment had arrived. Nine days later in a letter to the *Herald*, Remington launched an all-out, vitriolic attack against the authenticity of his rival's painting *Custer's Demand* (1902), which depicted a peace parley between General George Armstrong Custer's staff and their Kiowa counterparts. No one loved controversy more than a newspaper and the *Herald* printed Remington's letter under the headline "Finds Flaws in 'Custer's Demand'/'Half Baked Stuff' and 'Unhistorical' Are Frederic Remington's Comments/Officers' Arms and Accoutrements Taken as the Basis for the Artist Attack." Conflict sold.

Remington was back in the headlines with the *Herald*, egging on a show-down. He stated the criticism was harsh but it all came down to who knew the West the best. Concerning the vital details of the painting as incorrect, Remington therefore regarded Schreyvogel's work inauthentic—one of the worst charges one could level at a Western painting and its artist. Remington charged that the painting was, in short, "half baked stuff" and filled with errors. He proceeded to list the faults, which were all details: pistol holders, ammunition belts, war bonnets, hats, boots, stirrup covers, saddlebags, saddle cloths, uniform colors, the height of Custer's horse. Remington viewed these pictorial details as wrong, and therefore judged the painting inauthentic, adding that Schreyvogel was hallucinatory.

A national controversy ensued over Western art. For Remington, the battle peaked when Elizabeth Custer, General George Armstrong Custer's widow, and the respected Colonel John Schuyler Crosby defended the authenticity of the painting. *Herald* headlines blared, "SCHREYVOGEL RIGHT, MRS. CUSTER SAYS." Crosby was actually present on that auspicious occasion with Custer and had advised Schreyvogel in his research. Moreover, Crosby's military trousers served as Schreyvogel's model. The aristocratic Crosby, of distinguished military and government service, did not stand quietly by, but counterattacked Remington with scathing commentary that included his knowledge of the details. "[C]ertain facts that I know, and Mr. Remington could not, because I was present at the moment Mr. Schreyvogel depicts on canvas and Mr. Remington was riding a hobby horse, which he seems to do yet" (*New York Herald*, 1903). Harsh words for a man who "knew the horse."

Crosby proceeded to take apart Remington's charges detail by detail. And who could doubt the word of the beloved widow who admired Schreyvogel's paintings? Remington retreated, expressing his regrets, although his last private words on the subject appeared in a letter: "I despise Schreyvogel." His rival, who never entered the debate except to remark publicly that Remington was "the greatest of us all," remained a gentleman to the end. He not only paid tribute to Remington's work when he was alive but also at his death when he sent a telegram to Eva Remington expressing, "My deepest sympathy for the great loss to you and to our nation" (Dippie, 2001).

The accuracy debacle proved the adage that there is no such thing as bad publicity. The prestigious art gallery M. Knoedler & Company in New York City, exhibiting *Custer's Demand* during the controversy, saw a considerable increase in gallery goers during the spring and summer. That fall the painting traveled to the Corcoran Gallery in Washington, DC. Again, it drew a large following, including veterans of the Seventh Cavalry and other Western commands who, according to the newspapers, viewed the painting, talking quietly in tones of veneration. Among the spectators were President Theodore Roosevelt and his wife, who intently scrutinized *Custer's Demand* with admiration on several occasions. Roosevelt extended a luncheon invitation to Schreyvogel to dine with him at the White House. They were then to view the painting at the Corcoran, so that, as Roosevelt wrote, he could applaud Schreyvogel's aesthetic, attention to accurate detail, and erudition of the historical event. At their meeting, Roosevelt confided to Schreyvogel that his friend Remington had behaved not only foolishly in his newspaper assault, but also was clearly wrong in his assessment of the painting's details. Roosevelt and Schreyvogel became friends. His artistic reputation continued to grow with much acclaim and respect, rivaling Remington in the first decade of the twentieth century (Horan, 1969).

What Remington did not consider was critiquing the painting for its artistic merit, where he may have had room for argument. The irony is that by the turn of the century, Remington had begun to leave behind his literal interpretation of the West. Primarily this was in response to the critics' dismissal of what they perceived as a dry, detailed, and unimaginative documentary aesthetic. Now focused on light and color, a more painterly approach that was without exacting detail, he arguably created some of his best works. He was devoting his efforts to pure painting rather than factual accuracy. One could argue that one factor that separates the illustrator from the artist is priority: For the illustrator it is the factual—technique is used to reinforce the "truth." For the artist the act of painting, the emphasis on the medium, is its own truth; subject matter may or may not be relevant. But where Schreyvogel was concerned he fell back on an older personal standard.

Visualization of the drama of the frontier proved to be a dynamically competitive artistic venue, whether in paintings, illustrations, books, magazines, or Wild West shows. Remington was reluctant to surrender any of his popularity and recognition. Although he was weaning illustration from his repertoire, he would never completely give it up. The Schreyvogel controversy also reveals that despite Remington's desire to be perceived as a fine artist, he still thought and looked with the eyes of an illustrator. This argument reflects the fluid nature of accuracy within the details of the paintings and calls into question the static, unchanging picture ideal of the West we are saddled with today. Though as his paintings were beginning to show, details would never be as important to him after this. His style was changing. Some, however, were still focused on the particulars of his past.

The standards to which Remington held Schreyvogel accountable would be held up to Remington with even more vehemence and malice. A contemporary of Remington, Emerson Hough, author of Western fiction and history, sarcastically put into perspective the influence of Remington's detailed works on a mass audience in 1908: "If Mr. Remington today wanted to add a cubit to the tail of the American bison, or to establish a Western horse with five legs, he certainly could make it stick" (Hough, 1908). This statement was a resounding backhanded slap, especially by someone who had only lived a year and a half in the West at this time and who implied only a real born and bred Westerner would know the difference.

Again, authenticity was derived from firsthand Western experience, namely those who lived in the West and inherently knew the real thing. Consequently, Remington's personal Western observations were sporadic at best, thus making him an outsider to his Western audience and critics. The ability to determine authenticity was through the accuracy of detail. The

The effete east has her Remington, but the glorious west has her Russell.
—*Butte Miner,* 11 October 1903

details testified to the reality, that is, the documentary realism of the work of art. Hough probed Remington's soft spot.

Hough teamed up with Texan photographer Erwin E. Smith, both itching for a fight with Remington. They connived to bring down the interloping Easterner who reigned as the most honored Western artist, not only with vehement criticism of his accuracy, but with the promotion of the up and coming Montana artist Charles M. Russell. In turn, they hoped to hitch their struggling artistic wagons to this rising star in the Western art firmament. Both Russell and Remington were unaware of this crafted competition. As Remington was leaving the world of illustration behind, Russell was making his entrance.

The Western press had already begun their own image management of Russell to differentiate the two artists in their native son's favor. In 1901, the *St. Louis Post Dispatch* anointed Russell "the Cowboy artist." Not only did the journalist laud Russell as a "realist" who knew "his Indians, his plainsmen, his broncho, and cayuse, and his cattle," but also his innate artistry, untainted by teaching, as if he sprung forth a fully-fledged artist like Athena from Zeus's head (Hassrick, 2000). This lack of formal training would continue to be a note of pride in Western critiques for both Russell and Remington. For critics, it was Russell's lack of artistic refinement that made his work believable. Both American and European artists influenced his imagery. Among these were Carl Wimar, from his hometown of St. Louis, Eugene Delacroix, and Horace Vernet. In particular, Russell studied art in public venues and from books and the popular press.

For Westerners, especially Montanans, Russell painted the West as it was. They saw him as the beloved "Cowboy artist" untainted by eastern art tradition.

Russell's distinction as a documentary artist perseveres. In the 1960s, a leading Russell authority affirmed that accuracy of the minutest element distinguished Russell's work from that of all other Western artists. Moreover, the author assured the details were exactly as Russell had seen because his memory was infallible. Although Russell may have had an unfailing memory, he wrote to a friend in 1918 that he studied Indians from pictures. Russell relied on other artists' work, including Remington, and Indian artifacts rather than firsthand knowledge. He established his authenticity through realism of ethnographic details, as in *Squaw Travois* (1895) and *Returning to Camp* (1901). Russell was very much a detail man. "You want to paint things

> *The west is still a great country, but the picture and story part of it has been plowed under by the farmer.*
>
> —Charles Russell

as they are, as you see them," he explained to a Montana reporter for the *Anaconda Standard* in 1901. "It seems to me that a painter can't have too much detail," he said, adding that "[h]e should have a mastery of it and make his pictures true" (Dippie, 2002). Russell and Remington never witnessed much of the West they painted so realistically. It had disappeared together with the pioneers of progress they now despised.

Although Russell and Remington seemed joined at the hip in the public mind's eye, their subject matter bears only a surface semblance. First and foremost, Russell was a Westerner. He celebrated his heritage, a lifestyle of the everyday and common that was more encompassing than Remington's episodic clash of civilizations and days of courage and valor played out on the Plains. Russell's art, as cultural historian Brian Dippie so perfectly describes, is like a lost lover lamenting the past.

His was a true yearning for days gone by. Perhaps in an attempt to heal his soul and spirit, his art came from deep inside himself. Russell, the former cowpuncher, knew his horses and lovingly painted and sculpted them in realistic detail.

Hough and Smith placed Russell's authenticating in counterpoint to Remington's "faking" as they assessed his art. In 1907, Hough penned to Smith that he personally relished the opportunity to expose Remington as a fraud in any way possible. They chose the image of the cowboy for Remington's denouement. In his 1908 *Collier's Weekly* essay "Wild West Faking," Smith pounced on Remington's inaccuracies of the cowboy, citing as an example *No More He Rides*, a cover illustration for the earlier 1901 *Collier's Weekly*. Hough cunningly chose to use the words from Russell's earlier assessment of the work. Russell had the reputation of not being critical of other artists' work. But in this instance, Russell incisively observed that he had never seen in real life ranching anyone able to rope with a quirt hanging from his right wrist the way Remington had depicted. Hough's poisoned barbs hit their mark dead center, temporarily bringing down Remington. He unburdened his heart in his diary: "There is one thing a man who does anything in America can figure on—a d____ good pounding. It seems to be one of the penalties of achievement" (Dippie, 1994). With his confidence shaken, Remington immediately burned a cowboy painting sitting on his easel that he was reworking. This, along with other works, he deemed failures. Remington was particularly vulnerable at this time because his aesthetic values had shifted from that of illustrator to fine artist. "My old enemies come to haunt me," Remington confided in his diary, "I am helpless. I would buy them all if I were able to burn them up" (Samuels and Samuels, 1982).

A year later, Smith followed suit, attacking another of Remington's iconic cowboy images—the highly acclaimed bronze *Broncho Buster* (1895)—for its erroneousness. Smith compared it to one of his own photographs, *A Pitching Bronc* (1907). He proceeded to list the mistakes, including inappropriate positioning of the cowboy's feet and hands, that a cowboy like himself and Russell would know better. Ironically, scholars have shown that various painted and sculpted bronco riders of Russell are similar to Rem-

The West is dead! You may lose a sweetheart, but you won't forget her.
—Charles Russell

ington's popular bronze, an artist he was known to use as a model. Nonetheless, Smith's expert observation of the details of the *Broncho Buster* was that the man who created the sculpture was indeed an artist, not a cowboy nor a rider. Inadvertently, Smith acknowledged Remington for what he was zealously seeking at this time in his career, recognition as an artist.

The controversy engendered by Remington's work and that of his contemporaries persists in our own time. In 1988 the exhibition *Frederic Remington: The Masterworks* concluded its national tour in the New York Metropolitan Museum of Art. Thomas Wolfe was certainly right in Remington's case: You can't go home again. Most critics ravaged the exhibition. The theme of the show was aesthetics as opposed to content. The hopes of having Remington's work taken more seriously as art than as a function of its subject matter was circumvented, however. *The New Yorker* warned its readers in "Goings On About Town" in an acerbic artistic assertion: "From the vague and documentary to the laughably impressionistic to the corny and moonlit, Frederick [sic] Remington's paintings of Indians chasing cowboys, his lackluster illustrations for *Harper's*, and his clichéd bronzes of riders on horseback are unworthy of serious attention by a major art Museum" (*New Yorker*, 1989). Although aesthetic judgments are arguable, Remington created those clichés, which hold a powerful sway over the emotions for some. As Dippie has clearly established, Remington's ability lay in creating the typical through invention, repetition, and refinement. His interchangeable imagery with illustrations, paintings, and sculpture realized a cultural resonance. Moreover, it is other artists who took Remington's art and turned it into clichés. And to be pedantic, the critic misspelled the artist's name.

Although he gave two of the paintings a lukewarm acknowledgment, John Russell—chief art critic for the *New York Times*—backed up this dismissal of the art works. He preferred, however, to attack Remington for his character, or lack thereof. He lambasted the artist: "Remington has traditionally been regarded as a popular favorite whose work is of no aesthetic interest whatever . . . as a man [he] was just awful . . . almost unfailingly ignoble" (Russell, 1989). "Bloated lout" and "poor blown-up barrel of nothing" rounded out the critic's character assassination. There was some truth in Russell's moral posturing. Physically, Remington had become extremely overweight in his forties, a contradiction for one who believed in the turn-of-the-century strenuous life ethic. Regarding his moral ethics, there is no question that he mirrored vehement racist attitudes of his generation. Writing to his equally prejudiced friend and sometimes employer Poultney Bigelow, who brought out the worst in him, Remington nastily ranted, "Never will be able to sell a picture to a Jew again—did sell one once. You cant glorify a Jew—coin 'loving puds'—nasty humans—I've got some Winchesters and when the massacring begins which you speak of, I can get my share of 'em and whats more I will. Jews—injuns—chinamen—Italians—Huns, the rubish of the earth I hate" (Samuels and Samuels, 1982). Remington adamantly subscribed to the public opinion that held immigrants responsible for the social unrest and labor problems of the period.

The ostensibly refined East, where Remington created nostalgic Western life-and-death scenarios in the comforts of his New York studio, was at this time far from quiet and peaceful. It was simmering with urban crises. Social conflict was spilling over as evidenced by class warfare, the Pullman strike, mass immigration, and Anglo-Saxon supremacy. Remington illustrated urban unrest in *Mounted Policemen Arresting Burglars Uptown in New York* of 1889 and he covered the Pullman strike in May of 1894 for *Harper's Weekly*, providing both copy and illustration. *Giving the Butt: The Way the Regular Infantry Tackles a Mob* is from the Pullman strike. In his accompanying article "Chicago under the Mob," Remington labeled the strikers as a "malodorous crowd of an archistic foreign trash" and lauded the military use of force to maintain order. Eva Remington wrote to a friend, "Frederic was in Chicago during the riots & enjoyed every minute of it. He is always happy if with the troops" (Samuels and Samuels, 1982). What his wife expresses and Remington depicts conform with the dominant political currents.

The Republican ideological response to America's crises was social Darwinism, emphasizing struggle as a necessary component of progress to civilization. Struggle meant progress. Moreover, the construction of national heroes was vital to the success of the Republicans at the close of the 1890s. In the process of constructing this Republican ideology, America's most recent past, the Western frontier, became the cultural ballast for the future. The struggle for the West took on mythic proportions and became a compelling national symbol. It evoked progress, the future, and spiritual renewal of the nation. Three forms of popular culture sustained this ideology: Buffalo Bill and his Wild West Show, Western dime novels that culminated in Owen Wister's *The Virginian*, and Remington's frontier imagery. These three forms of visual culture defined Western life for millions of Americans, both then and now. The Western hero was nationalized; the American identity formed.

Grasping the Western experience as uniquely American, Remington selectively chose Western subject matter for his imagery of America. He would ensure that "Old America," as he lovingly called it, would be seen by posterity as standing steadfastly against what he believed was a fast-crumbling America in the wake of mechanization and foreign immigration.

For his contemporaries, one could still enter the "authentic" Old America in Remington's realistic paintings and explosive bronzes. *The Intruders* (ca. 1900), a heroic last stand, exemplifies his early painting style while the bronze sculpture *The Outlaw* (1906) is one of his most daring technical achievements. In both of these works one could relive the heroic epic of death-defying adventures. The Western myth defined who we were as a people. Moreover, the dehumanizing effects of the Industrial Age could be forgotten for a few moments as one contemplated a Remington artwork. Remington took them (and us) from our uneventful mundane lives by elevating the mundane into the heroic. In Remington's "Old America" individual heroes existed where the common man made a difference. He was strong, self-reliant, honest, and independent—core American values still esteemed today.

> *I am going to do America.*

From Remington's artistic vision that depicted the theme of the winning of the West, a mythos took hold of the American psyche whose long-lasting effects are still debated today. The 1991 National Museum of American Art exhibition *The West As America*, which has taken on a mythic persona itself, drew the moral outrage of two polarized groups, the traditionalists and the revisionists. The show challenged traditional iconic imagery raising questions about the relationship between Western American art and myths and the meaning of history. In particular, the ideologies behind the production and consumption of the art were pressed forward. Many viewers did not like their Western history deconstructed and thought the interpretations historically inaccurate. In short, they were incensed. They were presented with a West that was less than heroic. The attempts to reconcile the mythical West to the reality of American expansion reached an impasse. The most controversial section of the exhibition quashed the big three's—Remington, Russell, and Schreyvogel—realism, exploding perceptions of historic fact not only into that of myths but also attitudes of cultural and racial superiority. Cherished heroic icons were toppled. A struggle over the meaning of the art ensued and continues today.

Images of the Old West are a vital part of American culture, as the repercussions from this exhibition demonstrated. Now that the pendulum of the analysis of Western art has swung between the extremes of historicizing the art to excoriating it, the question begs what will be the direction and significance of Western American art studies in the future. Remington continues to play a prominent role causing us to look at a more inclusive story that tells of both pride and shame. Remington's work, along with other Western artists, is an ideological lightning rod.

The Cowboy

Conflating history and myth, Remington's works celebrate individual valor, parts that made up the whole of a perceived national achievement in the conquest of the frontier. An ideological inventor, Remington innovated and reconstructed

With me cowboys are what gems and porcelain are to some others.

the tradition of America. His Western types, his men with the bark on, became American icons. In particular for the public, the inextricable iconic image is that of the cowboy. This popular relationship began with Remington's 1888 illustrations of Roosevelt's series on ranch life in the West in *Century Magazine*. Remington recalled that when he created these images "most people didn't know whether cow-boys milked dairy cattle or fought in the Revolution" (Maxwell, 1907). The public, however, would soon become experts. The cowboy, the low wage–earning common drover who lived a rough and unstable existence from 1865 to 1895, would become a mythic American folk hero. He represented the idea of freedom in the vast expanse of the West.

Unquestionably, Remington immortalized the cowboy. Remington's cowboys, however, were not of the glamorous Hollywood variety. They were not pretty faces. He found the faces of the men he met on his Southwestern travels unique from their sun-scorched exposure. Lined and worn faces are plainly visible in early illustrations of cowboys such as *An Arizona Type* (ca. 1888), *The Texas Type of Cowboy* (1888), *A Montana Type* (ca. 1888), *Old-Style Texas Cowman* (ca. 1888), *A Texan Cowboy* (ca. 1888), and *A Mexican Vaquero* (1890) and in paintings such as *The Puncher* (1895) and *The Cow Puncher* (1901). Remington easily transformed these stock characters into action-driven narratives of everyday chores that are fraught with danger where one misstep leads to death. Like characters from the *Iliad*, the cowboys continuously perform tasks of courage. For instance, in the painting *The Cowboy* (1902), a cowhand, precariously balanced in the saddle, stampedes wild horses down a dicey boulder-filled slope. In a later well-executed oil, *The Stampede* (1908), the cowboy is literally part of the stampede where not only is he in danger of being trampled but struck by lightning in a blinding thunderstorm. He desperately fights to control his wild-eyed mount frantically racing along the potholed ground amid the routed night herd. A slip from his horse with a foot still caught in the stirrups, he could be dragged to death, a common accident among cowboys. Remington summed up this nocturnal stampede scene as nature without mercy. Here was the cowboy that Roosevelt, like the artist, held in such high regard.

Remington had help in the cowboy's apotheosis in the public's mind. Wister, along with Roosevelt and Remington, formed a Western triumvirate of sorts. Friends who had their differences but nonetheless supported one another's portrayal of the vanished, mythical West that each nostalgically venerated.

Wister's Western novel *The Virginian* (1902), which he dedicated to Roosevelt, was one of the most widely read works of fiction of its day. That "slim young giant, more beautiful than pictures," as Wister described the protagonist, helped establish the cowboy as an American folk hero. The novel was illustrated fittingly, first by Remington and later by Russell. Roosevelt

acknowledged that Remington not only had the greatest talent of the trio but also the greatest influence.
Writing to Remington in 1895, Roosevelt remarked
that Remington and Wister were doing the best work
among contemporary American artists and authors.

The cowboy inspired Remington, the man, and
Remington, the artist. For him, the cowboy was the
perfect exemplar of manhood. He hoped the Westerner's sturdy traits would become more fashionable in the East. Likewise, Roosevelt and Wister
believed the manly virtues of the cowboy were necessary for the continued success of America. They feared
culture had vitiated out males back East. It is useful
to examine Remington's sculptural representations of
the cowboy in this context, as well as to discuss the
uniqueness of the compositions and the political
undertones of the iconography. With his sculpture,
Remington comes closer to expressing the iconic
because he isolates the figure, unlike his paintings
which use iconic themes. The paintings do not express
the iconic because he does not isolate the figure
enough or make enough of the figure. Furthermore,
the three-dimensionality of the sculpture has a presence that flat paintings do not. Paintings are illusions
of space and depth whereas sculptures create space
and depth.

> *[Cowboys] are smaller and less muscular than the wielders of an ax pick; but they are as hardy and self-reliant as any men who ever breathed—with bronzed, set faces, and keen eyes that look all the world straight in the face without flinching as they flash out from under the broad-brimmed hats. Peril and hardship, and years of long toil broken by weeks of brutal dissipation, draw haggard lines across their eager faces, but never dim their reckless eyes nor break their bearing of defiant self-confidence.*
>
> —Theodore Roosevelt, 1888

Although having no formal training in sculpture, Remington attempted his
first bronze work on the encouragement of a neighbor. The result was the
twenty-four-inch *Broncho Buster* of 1895. With this first sculpture, Remington created the most memorable image of the American cowboy. He broke
the established historical formula of the equestrian statue, an example of
which is the ancient Roman sculpture *Marcus Aurelius* (161–180 CE). Remington's dynamic composition was unique. No one had ever sculpted a three-
dimensional cowboy on a wildly bucking horse. This bronze, however, can
trace in every line of its pedigree to Remington's illustration of a bronco buster
attempting to tame a wild horse in Theodore Roosevelt's 1888 article in *Century Magazine*. From his experience in the Dakota Territory, Roosevelt
described the life of a bronco buster as one who deserved high wages because
he would never grow old in his perilous line of work.

The asymmetrical work was balanced without a central support column.
Exploding with energy, the wild-eyed horse rears on its hind legs in frantic
motion to unseat the cowboy who clutches reins and mane in his left hand
and with extended right hand holds a menacing quirt. The result of the

It was still the Wild West in those days, the Far West, the West of Owen Wister's stories and Frederic Remington's drawings, the West of the Indian and the buffalo-hunter, the soldier and the cow-puncher. That land of the West has gone now, "gone, gone with lost Atlantis," gone to the isle of ghosts and of strange dead memories.

—Theodore Roosevelt, 1893

contest of wills is suspect as the right foot dangles free from the stirrup, while the left foot barely touches the other. The rider's individual skill is pitted against the brutal power of the animal. Remington transformed a cowboy performing a ranch chore of bronco busting into an American icon. The universal theme of struggle is the subject of this equestrian statue. Remington reworked this piece over a ten-year period and with his attention to detail changed arm positions, quirts and reins, and even replaced the original smooth-surfaced leather chaps worn by Southwestern cowboys with the roughly textured woolly chaps of the Montana cowboy. The artist was delighted with his initial sculptural efforts.

For Remington, however, who was obsessively concerned with the imminence of death and predisposed to view life in terms of decline and defeat, bronze would offer an opportunity to stop the onward rush of time. In essence, he was prescient. Immediately following its first casting in 1895, the *Broncho Buster* enjoyed immense popularity at Tiffany's of New York, which subsequently became the first commercial market for Remington's bronzes. Over one hundred casts sold during the artist's lifetime. It became the most popular small bronze of the nineteenth and early twentieth centuries, in part derived from the publicity of the Rough Riders' presentation of this bronze to Roosevelt, who had greatly admired it. The President wrote with great understanding of the cowboy's skill that "Only those who have ridden a bronco the first time it was saddled, or have lived through a railroad accident, can form any conception of the solemnity of such experiences. Few Eastern people appreciate the sky-rocket bounds, grunts, and stiff-legged striking" (Remington, 1889). Today the *Broncho Buster* resides prominently in the Oval Office.

To complement the *Broncho Buster* both thematically and compositionally, Remington designed *The Wicked Pony* (ca. 1898) as a companion piece. Again the cowboy's task of breaking a horse becomes a life-and-death struggle. Although in dire peril of being trampled by threatening hoofs, the thrown cowboy with strong will and determination still grasps the ear of the fiercely kicking horse. A viewer of the bronze asked Remington how the cowhand could possibly have escaped alive, as the horse was not struggling for its freedom, but to kill. Remington answered, "He didn't. He was killed—I was there and saw it" (Samuels and Samuels, 1982).

It is likely Remington could have seen this tragedy while out West. One may also speculate that he also saw the metaphorical death of the American frontier. Moreover, the sculpture could be viewed as an analogue of contemporary events. Remington, as well as many of his contemporaries, perceived America being trampled and crushed by the tremendous influx of immigrants. Whatever its interpretation, this tragic subject proved unpopular with the public. It did not uphold their romanticized view of the brave cowboy with good triumphing over evil.

The Rattlesnake also demonstrates boldness in the combination of composition and technique. In fact, Remington considered this bronze his favorite work. In the 1905 version as the rearing horse recoils from the snake, the rider wearing woolly chaps shifts forward in the same direction as the horse, attempting to control the animal, stay in the saddle, and hold onto his hat simultaneously. A mundane ride on the range becomes another life-and-death battle where the cowboy's abilities and self-reliance are placed in a contest against a dark side of nature.

[Y]our Virginian will be eaten up by time—all paper is pulp now. My oils will all get old wasting . . . my watercolors will fade—but I am to endure in bronze—even rust does not touch. . . . I am going to rattle through all the ages, unless some Anarchist invades the old mansion and knocks it off the shelf.
—Remington to Owen Wister

The cowboy and his horse again confront nature and its power in *The Norther* (1901). Here Remington has depicted the constant struggle and hard life associated with life in the West by emphasizing isolation and suffering. In contrast to the volatile action of the other works, *The Norther* turns inward to itself, standing quietly as if the figures are frozen still by the blizzard. Blasted by the bitterly cold wind, both hunched cowboy and horse close their eyes. The subtle details of the roughly textured winter coat of the horse work together with the tightly wrapped rider whose right hand is tucked under his left for warmth. With this gesture, Remington elicits the bone-chilling cold of the freezing air.

Having met the challenge of surface detail, Remington turned to his most complicated figural group, *Coming Through the Rye* (1902). Based on earlier two-dimensional representations, Remington devoted a year to the modeling and an additional five months to its casting. The four raucous horsemen, brandishing firearms, charge forward straight at the viewer on wildly galloping horses, a favorite compositional motif of the artist. Only five of the sixteen hooves touch the base and serve to support the active sculptural group. Tightly integrated, the four cowboys form a cohesive unit. In 1904 *Coming Through the Rye* was remodeled in large scale for the Louisiana Purchase Exposition in St. Louis, whose theme was "The Winning of the West." Initially received with modest praise, *Coming Through the Rye* increasingly gained notoriety through the years to become another American icon of the life in the West.

To read the image literally, a group of boozing cowhands after many hard-driven days on the range, ride in and shoot up the town for some good ol' wild cowboy fun. The sculpture's formal antecedents are found in Remington's "charge theme" in such illustrations as *Dissolute Cow-Punchers* (1888), *Cowboys Coming to Town for Christmas* (1889), the painting *A Dash for the Timber* (1889), and the tempera *Captain Dodge's Colored Troopers to the Rescue* (ca. 1890). Perhaps the ultimate derivation is the New Testament theme of the Four Horsemen of the Apocalypse—one memorable example is by Albrecht Dürer (1497). Remington was clearly aware of archetypes, shown in his painting *The Last Cavalier* (1895). To carry this analogy farther, one may speculate that this derivation also reflects Remington's cultural and political views. Such an interpretation in this context has been treated in Remington's paintings and we can use these observations to interpret the sculpture.

Although he heroicized the cowboy, Remington also assigned him a role in the politics of the time—a role that to us now appears inglorious. Remington feared and disliked the changing face of America. The cowboy of "Old America," the last pure American hero, was the vanguard of Anglo-Saxon society. Just as the cowboy steadfastly stood against all foes in the past, so he could be a model for Remington's threatened Anglo-Saxon world to meet the future head-on and turn back the waning tides of American society.

Remington was an avid reader of contemporary theories on social evolution, which at the time was a national preoccupation. These theories confirmed his personal philosophy about immigrants and immigration policy. As the Four Apocalyptic Horsemen were unleashed on a sacred mission to conquer and kill so could Remington's cowboys save white America. For Remington, as well as for many other Americans at this time, the perception of an Anglo-Saxon world struggling against the onslaught of immigrants was very real. Public opinion held the immigrants responsible for the social unrest and labor problems of the period. Because of this perception, the immigrants became analogous with the so-called Indian savages. It was not unusual for newspapers to refer to laborers and immigrants as "redskins" and "savages." Even Roosevelt labeled some Caucasians as backward and burdensome, hindering progress. Roosevelt once commented to Remington that he was one person who kept alive his hope in the country. Indeed, modern society was reflected in frontier terms. According to this view, as the cowboys struggled with hostile antagonists such as Indians or nature, so was the Anglo-Saxon world struggling for its survival.

Reiterating Roosevelt's views that the Anglo-Saxon had become soft, Remington turned to the one Anglo-Saxon who was still rugged, courageous, and self-sufficient, the cowboy. In Wister's *Harper's Monthly* series "The Evolution of the Cowboy" (1895), the cowboy is portrayed as knight-errant of Anglo-Saxon lineage. The concept was Remington's and was written with much input from the artist. Remington illustrated this publication emphasizing this fictionalized heritage with the *Last Cavalier*. This publication marked the beginning of the popularization of the mythical cowboy. The critics also applauded Remington's illustrations, preferring them to the prose.

From this examination of Remington's sculpture we can become more objective about our past without diminishing his technical skill and visionary prowess. Western art is more than a documentary transcription of the Western experience. Looking beneath the surface of a work of art reveals a rich, multilayered, and figurative meaning of our history. Roosevelt wrote, "The soldier, the cowboy and rancher, the Indian, the horses and cattle of the plains, will live in [Remington's] pictures and bronzes, I verily believe, for all time" (Roosevelt, 1907). And indeed, it is impossible to think of life of the West without visualizing a Remington bronze or painting. For better or worse, Remington defined the American West and he, himself, became part of the myth of the West.

Perhaps Remington and the cowboy myth had become one and the same, and he realized the immortality of that myth. In his one known self-portrait, Remington chose to depict himself as a cowboy. This is an important statement. The artist had fulfilled his boyhood dreams and that of others of his generation, as well as for many today. How many of his public and friends would like to be that cowboy on horseback? In *Self-Portrait on a Horse* (ca. 1890), Remington portrays himself in full cowboy regalia, mounted on a white horse. He sports a wide, up-turned hat brim, fringed cowhide chaps, and a cartridge belt for the rifle slung across his saddle, rope—all worn by the cowboys in his paintings. The ubiquitous scarf and holstered gun are missing, or possibly hidden by the horse's body. He, too, lacks the sun-worn look that he described of the cowboys he knew. However, he is not a department-store cowboy or dude. He is stripped down to essential work gear.

The artist represents himself as a slender man of action—a man with the bark on, as he liked to refer to his Westerners. Here Remington is that exemplar, a classic icon of manliness for his Eastern cohorts. With a slight smile, he stares out at us with self-satisfaction, perhaps even a challenge. With a sense of ownership, he seems to know something that we don't. Once in a fit of pique, Remington reiterated his lament of modernity: "Cow-boys? There are no cow-boys! Indians! They became extinct thirty years ago! The West is no longer the West of picturesque and stirring events. Romance and adventure have been beaten down in the rush of civilization" (Maxwell, 1907). Yet he knew he had made the cowboy more real than reality.

He possesses authority as he literally towers over the viewer. Larger than life, he blocks our way up the steep hillside into this desolate, sun-seared country, this place of freedom, that only the rugged can inhabit. His portrayal offers a variety of interpretations: a sentry on lookout, a knight on his white horse journeying far and wide, a hired gun?

As protective as he was of his artistic vision, one feels that he is charged with guarding the path to the Wild West of nostalgia where only the select may enter.

When closely looking at the self-portrait, one sees that Remington presents himself rather anonymously. His likeness is a superficial account of a sitter.

My West passed utterly out of existence so long ago as to make it utterly a dream. It put on its hat, took up its blankets and marched off the board; the curtain came down and a new act was in progress.

He appears like he is one of his Western characters in a role. There is little intense self-scrutiny. Hiding who he is, we never really get to see Remington. Like much of his art, Remington never moved from exterior description to interior feeling. He did not penetrate outer surfaces to disclose a more mysterious inner domain of emotions. He designed his work to appeal to the sentimental as opposed to the emotional. As he did with his Western world, the artist gives us a snap-shot of himself: the effect of the instantaneous and fragmentary.

Remington's chameleon-like appearance and per-sonality allowed him to move with ease among different social strata. Refined Eastern society as well as disciplined American soldiers and rough-and-tumble cowboys openly accepted the artist in their company. Remington entertained his friends at elite clubs, such as the Players Club in New York City, as well as conducted his business with the publishers of *Harper's* wearing Western dress and speaking cowboy lingo. Once out West, although sometimes wearing British attire and speaking the language of a Yalie, Remington adopted the demeanor of his companions.

He included himself in illustrations while on assignment with the cavalry in the Southwest. In *Marching in the Desert* (1888), *Method of Sketching at San Carlos* (1889), and *Marching on the Mountains* (ca. 1889), Remington traded in his cowboy hat for a pith helmet along with his ponderous weight for a more muscular form. A cavalry lieutenant, Alvin H. Sydenham, who met Remington in 1890 in Montana recalled his first impressions of "a fat citi-zen dismounting from a tall troop horse . . . The horse was glad to get rid of him." He proceeded to describe his attire, quite different from that affected in the self-portrait: "a brown canvas hunting coat whose generous propor-tions and many swelling pockets extended laterally, with a gentle downward slope to the front and rear, like the protecting expanse of a brown cotton umbrella. And below, in strange contrast, he wore a closely-fitting black rid-ing breeches of Bedford cord, reinforced with dressed kid, and shapely rid-ing boots of the Prussian pattern, set off by a pair of long-shanked English spurs" (Samuels and Samuels, 1982). This was not the cowboy looking out at us in the self-portrait. Regardless of his fashion, Remington shared the caval-rymen's monotonous days and exhausting patrols. He vividly described a day's scouting patrol that covered thirty-five miles: "The heat was awful and the dust rose in clouds—men get sulky, go into a comatose state—the fine alkali dust penetrates everything but the canteens" (Samuels and Samuels, 1982). The artist sweated with the troopers in the heartless desert sun and braved the cold with them in the northern Plains.

Although his outfit brought smiles to the faces of the soldiers, Sydenham found him to be "[a] big, good-natured, overgrown boy—a fellow you could not fail to like the first time you saw him." The soldiers also appreciated his humor. Waking up a cavalry officer early one morning in the Plains, Remington asked for a "cavalryman's breakfast." The officer, unsure as to its meaning, questioned Remington who responded "a drink of whiskey and a cigarette." He had coined a new phrase for the military. Remington's unconventional personality extended to his creations, thematically, technically and stylistically (Samuels and Samuels, 1982).

When Sydenham renewed his acquaintance with Remington a year later at the posh Grand Hotel in New York City, he was astonished with the artist's change in appearance: "His crowning glory was a tall silk hat . . . tan kid gloves, patent leather shoes, and a portly stick with a buckhorn handle combined their effect to enforce the disguise." Sydenham recognized the man beneath his cover, commenting, "for nothing could hide his broad good-natured face and laughing blue eyes . . . As far as I could see he was different only in the surface covering from the weighty party who had descended from the horse at the head of the troop that day on the Tongue river" (Dippie, 2001). Remington would have been pleased with this insightful evaluation. Cavalrymen were his heroes, and he was proud to be accepted by them. Respectful of their sacrifice and bravery, he knew the difference between his chosen career and theirs. Upon election as an honorary member of the U.S. Cavalry Association in 1890, he wrote, "My business in life, as a painter and illustrator is to give other fellows the credit that is due for gallantry—I desire no honors of this kind for myself" (Spelt, 1988). And that he did over and over again, whether in the compelling individual portraits of Lieutenants Edward W. Casey, Francis H. Hardie, and Powhatan H. Clarke or the generic troopers dutifully carrying out their missions as in fateful last stands in *Rounded-Up* (1901), charges at full speed with thundering hooves striking the ground in *The Cavalry Scrap* (1909) or quieter moments of the ordinary camp life in *A Cavalryman's Breakfast on the Plains* (ca. 1892). These soldiers are forever in our memories, especially because John Ford has preserved the images of the paintings in his Western films, most notably in his cavalry trilogy, *Fort Apache* (1948), *She Wore a Yellow Ribbon* (1949), and *Rio Grande* (1950). Remington's beloved cavalrymen live on in these films.

By looking at a chronological series of events that make up Remington's life, we can better understand what shaped the way Remington chose to live and influenced him in his life's choices and the creation of his art.

BIOGRAPHY

Early Life

Born 4 October 1861 in the small town of Canton in upstate New York, the artist was the only child of Seth Pierre Remington, a newspaper owner and editor, and Clara Bascomb Sackrider Remington. From his father, whom he idolized, Remington developed an ever-abiding affection for the outdoors, horses, and the military, which would ultimately propel him westward and to his career. Remington would forever be enthralled with the cavalry. The soldier would remain a steadfast and lovingly depicted stock character of his artistic inventory. Even more so, a horseman whether in a thundering cavalry charge or herding cattle, would be the unifying element of his Western paintings.

Coupled with stories of his father's cavalry action in the Civil War was the contemporary combat of the Battle of the Little Bighorn. Like the rest of the nation in 1876, the fourteen-year-old Remington was riveted by the breaking news, a site he would visit in 1881 on his first trip to the West. A few months after the defeat of the Seventh Cavalry, Remington entered the Highland Military Academy in Worcester, Massachusetts, where he would fill his textbook margins and sketchbooks with soldiers, one of which was a depiction of this battle. This theme of "Last Stands" resurfaced consistently in the mature artist's work, exemplified in the 1890 oil *The Last Stand*.

Entering Yale in 1878, Remington enrolled in the School of Fine Arts, seemingly to purse a career in journalism like his father. Instead he excelled in the masculine pursuit of football, a first-string forward on the Yale team, where he was happier than in the classroom. He also took drawing classes, his first formal artistic studies, under John Henry Niemeyer. Typical of a late nineteenth-century studio curriculum, the function of art was to imitate nature, especially achieving proficiency in the depiction of the human figure. Remington began with the time-honored method of drawing from classical plaster casts. Prominently displayed in Niemeyer's studio was the revered French neoclassical artist Ingres's axiom: Drawing is the Probity of Art. This adage, for better or worse, like the sword of Damocles, held sway over Remington's career. His drawing acumen would establish him as an expert illustrator and eventually damn him in the eyes of some art critics. Nonetheless, as Ingres, one of the most recognized painters in all of art history, legendarily advised a young Edgar Degas (also slated for greatness), "Draw lines, young man, many lines, from memory and from nature; it is the way you will become a good artist," Remington would give similar advice to the aspiring Maynard Dixon practically verbatim. After a year and a half at Yale, Remington abruptly dropped out of college after the death of his father in February 1880.

First Experiences West

In August 1881, Remington journeyed to Montana for a late summer adventure, satisfying his youthful desires to go West. This brief Western excursion of a few months was portentous. Remington inadvertently began his career as an illustrator. With youthful exuberance, he submitted sketches from his travels to *Harper's Weekly*, which they published 25 February 1882 as *Cow-boys of Arizona*, albeit redrawn by a staff artist. The young artist had much to learn, however, not only in creating a successful composition, but also in finding himself and determining his life's course.

Several months later in fall 1882, Remington received a substantial inheritance of $9000 that rescued him from a tedious government clerking position in Albany, New York. Having succumbed to West fever, Remington knew the only cure for himself—following a westward trail. He immediately headed West again in 1883, this time in search of profit and adventure.

An interval of failed business enterprises followed. For about a year Remington tried his hand at sheep ranching in rural Butler County, Kansas, an endeavor that he would later amend in his life's history to cowpuncher. In early 1884, he moved on to Kansas City to invest in a saloon, a risky undertaking because Remington enjoyed imbibing. That spring he traveled to the Southwest and Mexico before returning to New York to marry his beloved Eva Adele Caten on 1 October 1884, after a five-year courtship. The newlyweds immediately departed for Kansas City, but their life together there was brief. Eva had no idea of her husband's business ventures until she arrived. Remington spent his time drawing, painting, riding, boxing, and in the saloon. He also indulged in the rigorous outdoor life that he not only enjoyed but also thought requisite for the male, like his gridiron days at Yale.

By the year's end Eva, feeling alone and isolated and with her husband facing insolvency, returned to New York. Remington remained behind and opted to spend a few weeks in late summer roving and sketching across the Southwest. By the summer's end Remington rejoined Eva in New York. From that time on, Remington contentedly made his home in the East with his esteemed wife, interrupted by occasional trips out West usually on illustrating assignments for a month's time.

Remington's summer of contrition in the Southwest began a series of fortuitous events that would advance his artistic career. In May, Geronimo led an Apache escape from the San Carlos reservation in Arizona. The public, rapt with the resurgence of the Indian Wars, couldn't get its fill of information, whether in the newspapers or dime novels. The very name "Apache" evoked danger and excitement. Some were fearful that the Indians Wars were not over; others were glad they weren't. Geronimo was on his way to becoming a cult figure, thanks to the popular press. Leaning toward a career as an artist, Remington was in the right place at the right time. With an extensive portfolio from his summer wanderings Remington provided the visual complement of scenes of the Apache war, whether he had closely witnessed it or not. He returned to New York with exactly what the magazine publishers wanted. Remington presented the visual drama and the precise detail.

Remington As Illustrator

In the 9 January 1886 issue of *Harper's Weekly*, Remington's illustration *The Apache War: Indian Scouts on Geronimo's Trail* appeared as full-page cover.

Here was the real thing, the unspoiled native genius [Remington] dealing with Mexican ponies, cowboys, cactus, lariats and sombreros. No stage heroes these. . . .

—Poultney Bigelow
(1856–1954)

For the first time his drawing had not been reworked and it carried his name. This illustration had that look of historical truth that would typify his style. A lean cavalryman, the apex in the tightly clustered composition, apprehensively scans the horizon for renegades as friendly loin-clothed Apache Indians run parallel to his sides in groups of two; a lone figure on horseback trails behind. This early composition of a double-axis diagonal, moving from lower left to upper right and from lower right to upper left anticipated Remington's mature pared-down pieces with this recurring geometric framework.

For example, within a year *Harper's Weekly*'s *Pima Indians Convoying a Silver Train in Mexico* presented the same formula. In this drawing, better articulated figures move along a precipitous incline no longer dwarfed by a dominating horizon. The barely clothed Indians have been reduced in number and replaced with fully clad figures in almost identical stances. For the focal point, Remington substituted a mounted Indian on a similar white horse that presses forward at the same gait with head lowered, right front leg striking the ground, the left raised and curving downward. Rather than a lone individual in the vast flat plain bringing up the rear, a mule train edges its way along a steep narrow ledge, which intensifies the jeopardy of the setting. The work also displays another of Remington's preferred compositional conventions: the positioning of three figures with the secondary inclusion of a fourth in the foreground.

Seeing his illustrations in print Remington readily recognized his weak draftsmanship. Thereupon, he enrolled briefly in the Art Students League, from March through May 1886, to improve his artistic skills, a last half-hearted attempt at formal study. Remington gladly abandoned the confines of the Art Students League for boots and saddle as he hastily left in June on a *Harper's Weekly* assignment as a war correspondent and illustrator. He rode along with Company K of the Tenth Cavalry, an African American regiment, in pursuit of Geronimo in the Santa Catalina Mountains north of Tucson. Later, he joined other patrols along the Southwestern frontier, pushing into Mexico. When he returned to New York, he met up with former Yale schoolmate Poultney Bigelow, with whom he had taken Niemeyer's drawing class. Now editor of *Outing* magazine Bigelow was gripped by the rawness of his friend's imagery. He felt as if an electric current had passed through his body from this new visual experience. He saw an unmitigated Western aesthetic in his friend's artistry, and lauded Remington's prowess and spunk.

For this editor, Remington appeared larger than life, the stuff of boyhood yearnings.

This Eastern artist had ridden into the untamed Western country disregarding the danger of marauding Apaches. He exemplified the seemingly distinct

Western traits of his drawn cowboys and soldiers of self-reliance and independence that had shaped American character. Remington took Easterners along for the ride of their childhood dreams and yearnings. Recognizing Remington's market potential, Bigelow immediately signed him on for more. With a commission in hand, Remington was to illustrate a dynamic Apache war series.

He had turned himself into a cowboy, and I had become a slave to my desk.
—Poultney Bigelow

Less than a year later, Remington crossed international borders again, this time to Alberta and Saskatchewan, Canada. With a second *Harper's* commission he sought out new Indian material for the month of April 1887. One result, the composite drawing *In the Lodges of the Blackfeet*, appeared in *Harper's Weekly* that summer. Rather than depicting the Blackfoot in their current throes of acculturation to learn agriculture, the artist preferred to portray them as traditional warriors, an image more appealing to him as well as his publisher and public. His Indians were fighters, not farmers, although there were rare exceptions, as in *The Twilight of the Indian* (1897).

Canada's Western frontier exerted a pull on Remington's sensibilities. The artist recognized an internationalism of frontier spirit that would continue to draw him back for subject matter throughout his career. Moreover, he could project his continuing childhood adoration of his father's military exploits and subsequent devotion to the U.S cavalry onto the North-West Mounted Police who had just put down a Metis confrontation with the government. In *Arrest of a Blackfeet Murderer*, printed in the 18 March 1888 *Harper's Weekly*, Remington easily substituted the dashing Canadians for the U.S. Cavalry.

The year 1888 proved critical to his career. The elite *Century Magazine* published Theodore Roosevelt's six-part series "Ranch Life in the Far West," which Remington illustrated, arguably the most important commission of his career. The magazine then sent him to Texas, Arizona, and New Mexico, which resulted in three publications that he both wrote and illustrated. The artist had now firmly established a place in the public's imagination. More important to Remington, however, he received national recognition as a painter that year. The National Academy of Design, the most respected of American art institutions that sanctioned subjects and styles, accepted *Return of the Blackfoot War Party* (1888) for its annual exhibition. Remington would continue to show at the Academy through 1895, but with festering disappointment. The Academy elected him as an associate member in 1891, his only recognition from this arbiter of taste, with reviews of his paintings becoming less favorable of his technical ability. It was primarily Remington the man they objected to more than his art—his popularity with the public, his great financial success in a variety of artistic undertakings, and his larger-than-life persona. In other words, he was not one of them. He did not fit into their social ilk, nor did he try.

International success quickly followed as *Lull in the Fight*, a gripping last stand subject, earned him a silver medallion at the 1889 Paris Exposition. Filled with confidence, Remington began to create some of his greatest large-scale paintings. *A Dash for the Timber* of 1889 introduced the theme of "the charge" that Remington would develop and to which he would continually return. In this painting Remington unified his learning and experience, about which a *New York Herald* critic stated that he had advanced to one of America's best young artists. It was also the greatest crowd pleaser at the Academy's exhibition.

Subsequently the American Art Galleries in New York hosted an exhibition of twenty of Remington's paintings in April 1890 that for the most part received public acclamation. Some critics, however, were still bloodthirsty. The *New York Times* shrieked: "His colors are so shrill and his temperament is so prone to violent movement that a collection of his pictures gives the impression of a thousand discordant noises, yells of battles, screams of dying horses, and the crudeness of existence between a pitiless sky and a pitiless earth, without the compensation of beautiful colors and noble forms. . . . He remains the illustrator in black and white who, with a magnificent but short-sighted audacity, has taken to color. He is not at home with oils and brushes; his paintings hurt" (*New York Times*, 1890). Remington's national subject matter, his realistic style, and his technical ability did not appeal to all. In the meantime, private sales of paintings were increasing. *Harper's* publications, in particular, put on a publicity campaign for their showcase artist, often praising the man more than his art. They attributed his realistic images to his personal experiences in the West. The result was that he became a celebrity and he delighted in it. These were the years *Harper's* acclaimed him as the soldier-artist. Financially, Remington was riding high, too. He was in the national top 10 percent income bracket.

Remington continued to turn out both illustrations and written material for *Harper's Weekly*, *Harper's Monthly Outing*, and *Century*, among other publications, during the late 1880s and early 1890s. He traveled extensively on assignments including Mexico, Montana, Wyoming, Dakota Territory, the Southwest, Texas, Cuba, and Europe. The trips were arduous as he wrote of his travails to Eva in 1889, "[T]here is not a square inch of my body that is not [mosquito] bitten—and oh oh oh how hot it is here—I have sweat and sweat my clothes full—I can fairly smell myself—I am dirty and look like the devil and feel worse and there is no help for me . . . all this is very discouraging but its an artist life" (Dippie, 2001). But the toil was paying off. No one could compare with Remington as a Western illustrator. In 1893, Remington chose to have his first one-man show and sale at the American Art Association, in lieu of exhibiting at the Academy. This rebellious decision proved financially lucrative for the artist but alienated him from the Academy all the more. His exhibition sales were equal to the entire sales for the Academy.

Remington continued his typically demanding pace of illustrating, painting, and writing. Unfulfilled with illustration and disappointed with lackluster painting sales at this time, he added sculpture to his schedule in January 1895. Before he completed his first sculpture in October, he published his first book, *Pony Tracks*, in July. Well received, one critic maintained the book presented a better understanding of army frontier life than any official documents. Remington's prose in this case proved more real than reality, like his art. Quickly following on the heels of this literary accomplishment was the enthusiastic popular acclaim for the bronze *Broncho Buster*, an original subject for this medium. Few sculptors could achieve this measure of success with a first attempt.

Nine months later Remington completed *The Wounded Bunkie* (1896). Narrating one of his favorite themes of the masculine world of the cavalryman in life and death struggles, the artist translated his "feeling for mud," as he liked to say, into the tensile strength of bronze. The subject itself also literally evokes feeling and strength as a wounded trooper collapses into the arm of his comrade who protectively rides beside him amid the turmoil and noise of war. This heroic image of friendship emotes the virtues of honor, loyalty, and courage. In this complex composition depicting rapid movement, only two legs of the galloping horses, with flaring nostrils, flapping manes, and surging muscles, support the entire group. Remington again employed innovative techniques to emphasize the dramatic.

Remington also found time to complete his book *Drawings* (1897) showcasing sixty-two illustrations. He received superb reviews. Wister's preface in the picture book compellingly expressed the power of Remington's artistic contributions at this time: "I have stood before many paintings of the West but when Remington came with only a pencil, I forgot the rest: It is Homer or the Old Testament again. If Remington did nothing further, already he has achieved: He has made a page of American history his own" (Samuels and Samuels, 1982). For Wister, as well as many others, Remington remained the epic Western historian.

Remington and the Spanish-American War

Corresponding with Wister, Remington wrote of his hope for war with Spain in his typically bombastic crude language deeming it proper to kill Cuba's Spanish oppressors. However, as an advocate of Anglo-Saxon superiority, he believed the Cubans an inferior race and in need of guidance. Yet for all his racist bluster Remington had gained a respect and admiration for the black cavalry he rode with in Arizona.

Shortly thereafter in January 1897, Remington sailed on a secret trip to Cuba on assignment for William Randolph Hearst's yellow press *New York Journal* to illustrate popular correspondent Richard Harding Davis's copy. The artist found himself embroiled in what became one of the legendary anecdotes of the insurrection. Reportedly, Remington cabled Hearst, "Everything is quiet. There is no trouble here. There will be no war." To which

Hearst allegedly replied, "You furnish the pictures. I'll furnish the war." And Remington did.

He returned to New York while Davis remained in Cuba sending dispatches to the newspaper. One story became a lurid sensation. Remington supplied the graphic details. Spanish officials, with the implication they were male, stripped searched a young Cuban woman, Clemencia Arango, sailing under the American flag. As in many of his Western illustrations for accompanying text, Remington used his imagination. The artist depicted a very white curvaceous nude woman encircled by three darkened Spanish men. The shocking drawing, printed five columns wide, attracted much attention, leading some to ponder how it avoided censure because some thought the woman more nude than Remington's Indian depictions. Both Davis and Remington had twisted the actual event. A lone Spanish woman had searched Arango. But the damage was done with the misrepresentation. Many, along with Remington, eagerly anticipated the Spanish-American War. "[T]here is bound to be a lovely scrap around Havana," Remington remarked to Wister, "a big murdering—sure—" (Samuels and Samuels, 1982). Remington finally got his wish to see war up close and personal.

Thrilled for this opportunity to see what he perceived as men at their noblest, he arrived in Cuba 22 June 1898. From the deck of a ship, he watched the Second Division hit the beach. Once on land trying to catch up with the infantry, it became all too apparent this was not the kind of fight he had bargained for. Life was miserable with the poor food, fever, and long, slogging marches on foot in the rain and mud. He became completely disillusioned as his letters revealed: "All the broken spirits, bloody bodies, hopeless, helpless suffering which draws its weary length to the rear, are so much more appalling than anything else in the world that words won't mean anything to one who has not seen it" (Samuels and Samuels, 1982). He could easily have added "images," too. Remington was finished with his long-winded jingoistic saber rattling. The realities of war were inglorious. The bleeding, shattered bodies were not the stuff of his clean whole canvases.

In July 1898, Remington returned home to Endion, his gentleman's estate in New Rochelle, New York. He came back a confused man, trying to understand what he had lived through. Nothing had looked and felt like the reality of his art and imagination. As far as his future painting was concerned, he told a friend, it would only be floral still lifes in the future. Within six months his weight ballooned to 295 pounds and he was drinking heavily. He entered into a frenetic work schedule—painting, illustrating, sculpting, and writing at the same time. The National Institute of Arts recognized Remington as one of the 100 most prominent Americans in literature and the arts. He was unimpressed. At Roosevelt's prodding, he relinquished still life painting to paint *The Charge of the Rough Riders* (1898), which he had observed with binoculars from the safety of a low bank. It became his most celebrated work of the war. Removed from the cry of wounded in his quiet studio, he took artistic license. He painted a traditional valiant portrayal of this charge, explaining one attack was like any other. He could not paint the horror and suffering he had witnessed: "I could not get the white bodies which lay in the moonlight, with the dark spots on them, out of my mind. Most of the dead on modern battlefields are half naked, because of the 'first aid bandage.' They take their shirts off, or their pantaloons, put on the dressing, and die that way" (Samuels and Samuels, 1982). Most likely, the public would not have wanted to see a painting with such horrendous subject matter either. It was not an image of the gallant American dead.

This soldier-artist had had enough of war. "I have had nothing to do with soldiers since the war in Cuba," he related to a journalist years later in 1907, "I only knew the soldier as a part of my West, and the West and the soldier closed together. The uniformed fighting man passed on and off my board a long time since" (Maxwell, 1907). Seemingly, he never felt the disparity between fact and fiction in his work as he profoundly did with the Spanish-American War. By 1899, the artist was back to business with his frontier imagery.

Becoming a Fine Artist

After a four-year absence, Remington submitted the oil *Missing* (ca. 1899) to the Academy. They remained unimpressed. Remington carried over the simple compositional devices of his early paintings and numerous illustrations, but his technique had improved. As the diagonal procession sweeps the eye far back into the high horizon of the composition, Remington adeptly isolated the real subject within the composition of helplessness. He sets the captured solider with hands bound behind his back against the landscape. With this major change in composition, the artist has created a focus, not just a plethora of objects and forms that compete with each other as in his early work. The paralleling Indians ride in more space, light, and air amid the parched sage-brush steppe. As a result, the image becomes more convincing as an historical document—that the artist was there and conveyed truthful information to the viewer.

Missing is successful because it appeals to all of the five senses. The viewer sees, hears, smells, tastes, feels the narrative being presented through its visual language. From the surface reality, the viewer responds to this image without the intervention of the intellect. The painting's pervasive literalness with the detail of a lone cow skull in the foreground, a heavy-handed metaphor, directs the eye to the soldier. No doubt is left to his fate that he unflinchingly accepts, a quality true of all of Remington's military men. Life on the frontier was dangerous and violent, a fact they stoically accepted.

However, this image, and others like it, become a metaphor for some, whether the artist intended it or not. *Missing* takes on implied meanings of duality: savagery versus humanity, wilderness versus civilization. In this clash of cultures, the Indians appear to belong in this remote and barren landscape, the cavalryman an intruder. The Eastern audience would readily identify with the soldier who is part of their heritage. As well this picture supported their mainstream values. It reconciled lamentable acts, making them not only understandable but also acceptable and even heroic.

At the end of the century, Remington found his artistic compass. He wrote to Wister that he had been "trying to paint at the impossible—as Miss Columbia said to Uncle Sam *'That was my war'*—that old cleaning up of the West—that is the war I am going to put the rest of my time at" (Samuels and Samuels, 1907). This time around, however, Indians would play a greater and more emphatic role. In February 1900, he completed his second novel, *The Way of an Indian*. In one of the action-driven illustrations, *He Rushed the Pony Right to the Barricade*, the Indians would triumph. Within a few months Yale awarded him an honorary degree as the "most distinguished pupil" of the Art School, with which he was greatly pleased. But he knew what he wanted most was still out of reach—to be a great American artist. He began taking steps to become a better artist, with the hope of a positive side effect in finding favor with the critics.

Remington became more experimental in the presentation of Western subject matter. He labored with a variety of techniques and styles, although he continued to employ his favorite compositional formulae: the double-axis diagonal, the pyramid and its inversion, and running the action directly at the viewer. Color, however, would be his first undertaking—the technique the critics had most ridiculed. Color was no easy feat for a man who had spent much of his career working in black and white. Writing to Wister in the fall, Remington underscored his need to see color with the eyes of a child. Having concentrated on form in his art, he devoted the next two months to the study of color. This was the man who five years earlier had repudiated painting as wasting his time, saying he couldn't discern a red blanket from a gray overcoat as far as color was concerned.

In October he returned to the Southwest, as he wrote to the famed illustrator Howard Pyle, wishing to improve his color sense. However, upon stepping off the train, he was acutely disenchanted with what he saw. It was the local color, however, that disappointed. He vowed he would never go West again. The region had failed to stay the same as the pictures he had painted. "It is all brick buildings—derby hats and blue overhauls," he fumed (Samuels and Samuels, 1982). Yet, what resulted from this trip was more significant for the artistic goals he had set for himself. He gleefully wrote he now grasped the essence of color and how to render it effectively. Still he maintained the views of a commercial illustrator, observing, "Color is great—it isn't so great as drawing and neither are in it with imagination. Without that a fellow is out of luck" (Dippie, 2001).

The painting *Rounded-Up* (1901) shows his beginning efforts with color. It was traditional in theme and composition: a last stand in an inverted pyramid.

The difference lay in the brighter palette. In the dazzling sunlight, men impassively stay the course in a subdued portrayal of a desperate situation. He had foregone his typical pounding action. The reflective light bounces off the alkaline plains floor more than bullets. Soon Remington would become preoccupied with the properties of light at all hours of the day and night to provide mood rather than a literal transcription of objects. Remington closed out 1901 with what he regarded his first fine art exhibition at the acclaimed Clausen's Gallery on Fifth Avenue. He was moving forward in his working methods.

Shortly thereafter, in 1902, he told a friend that he had found the formula for serious art: "Big art is a process of elimination, cut down and out—do your hardest work outside the picture, and let your audience take away something to think about—to imagine. . . . What you want to do is just create the thought—materialize the spirit of a thing, and the small bronze—or the impressionist's picture—does that; then your audience discovers the thing you held back, and that's skill" (Wildman, 1903). His process was no longer the simple description of nature with which he had worked all of his life as he struggled with light and color.

An exclusive contract with *Collier's Weekly* in 1903 allowed him to focus on painting. With this four-year retainer of $1000 per month, Remington could paint what he wanted while providing twelve color oils per year that the magazine would reproduce monthly. He had the best of both worlds with this contract. His supportive public would have access to his popular work, which mattered immensely to his sense of celebrity. However, as he told Wister, he knew the capricious public had a tendency to forget and needed to be reminded to keep him on their cultural calendar. But the bottom line was he could concentrate on becoming a fine artist. Well-known New York art critic Royal Cortissoz observed a dramatic transformation in his painting that year: "I have seen paintings of his which were hard as nails. But then came a change, beginning with this exhibition of night scenes, where a painter took the place of an illustrator's brittle pen drawings and blaring reds and yellows" (Samuels and Samuels, 1982). The critic continued his ebullient praise for Remington's showing at the Noé Gallery on Fifth Avenue. He wanted to slap the artist on his back for creating painterly works filled with life that no one else could do.

Remington realized his artistic goals in the 1904 painting *Pony Tracks in the Buffalo Trail*, a double-diagonal composition. The subject was oft repeated, beginning with his first published illustrations. This time a frontier scout has joined the lead and a cavalry column brings up the rear. Using a similar arrangement to *Missing*, Remington eliminated the distraction of the skull and scattered sagebrush. Moreover, he loosened his style. Previously his works were tighter, perhaps feeling a need to delineate it all. Now with his mastery over drawing, he is so competent that he does not need to delineate everything. He has mastered his technique and is comfortable with it. At this point he can relax it. Clarity of form and color yielded to broken, bold brushwork; hard contour lines softened.

Nonetheless, Remington remained frustrated with his efforts with color. Writing to a young illustrator, Remington bewailed:

> You know how popular I've been. Every place I go I'm the great Fred Reming-
> ton, but all my life I've planned what I would paint when I had money enough
> and for ten years I've been trying to get color in my things and I still don't get it.
> Why why why can't I get it. The only reason I can find is that I've worked too
> long in black and white. I know fine color when I see it but I just don't get it and
> it's maddening. I'm going to if I only live long enough. (Samuels and Samuels,
> 1982)

Remington always maintained a critical eye with his work. When works did not meet his standards, he would frequently destroy them. He was concerned both with contemporary approval and posterity's.

The critics were beginning to take favorable notice. A reviewer at the *New York Times* compared Remington with European artists, a flattering perception for American artists at this time who needed European art credentials to be accepted by the establishment. Reviewing the 1906 Knoedler exhibition, the journalist wrote with admiration over Remington's softened and harmonized compositions that evoked such celebrated French artists as Corot and Pissarro. In particular, he singled out Remington's shades of night to create tones of mystery that he had found lacking in previous works. The respected American Impressionist Childe Hassam also applauded Remington's paintings, declaring they "are all the best things—Nobody else can do them" (Samuels and Samuels, 1982). These words meant a great deal to Remington, who aspired to join his friend in the ranks of leading American artists.

Nonetheless, Remington remained dissatisfied with his technical improvements. He believed his illustrations, all 2700 of them, had hindered him in his serious artistic objectives. Two months later in February 1907, he burned another set of paintings because they were not up to his new standards. He attempted to eliminate works from his repertoire in which he feared the entrenched art establishment would find too much of the illustrator. Remington remained trapped between the abyss of the commercial art world and that of high art. *Collier's* did not want the nocturnes the critics appreciated. The magazine wanted narrative action at high noon, like the old Remington. He, however, with enhanced technical proficiency, preferred to develop some of his stories with a limited color palette. He emphasized contrast between light and dark rather than contrast among more strong colors, a far cry from the heavy-handed modeling of his first published illustrations. His nocturnes were much more subtle and sensitive than black and white. The coldness of snow and the reflection of the moonlight through tonal color could never be achieved in the black and white illustration.

Fired On (1907) is Remington's mature palette, a sophisticated palette. The New York critics were unanimous in their approval of this painting shown at Knoedler's. They praised his artistic conception, structural composition, and method of expression. In contrast, they came down heavy on the sunlit pictures. It especially hurt when Cortissoz, who had praised Remington's paintings the year before, now saw the hand of the illustrator again. He spared no words lambasting what he saw as crude color technique. The *New York Times* seconded that evaluation. However, Cortissoz, along with the *Times*, tempered their criticisms. In Cortissoz's eyes Remington redeemed himself with the nocturnes, which demonstrated great progress. He added that Remington should be congratulated for his achievement. The critics believed that the night paintings held the greatest promise in Remington's future. They were correct in their assessment.

> *Art is a she-devil of a mistress and, if at times in earlier days she would not stoop to my way of thinking, I have persevered and will so continue.*

The nocturnes at last brought him the critical acclaim he fixatedly sought. His postwar imagery was more reflective; he more often examined tragedy rather than the heroic. The theme of no visible enemy would be consistent in his later art, which crackled with suspense. The tension in his earlier paintings was still there, but shrouded in the darkness of night. This is Remington at his painterly best. Although the nocturnal paintings that replaced the earlier sun-scorched canvases are abstractions of mood and feeling, Remington never forsook narrative content.

The year's end mixed reviews gave rise to an artistic identity crisis. In January 1908, Remington wrote in his diary that he felt he was attempting the impossible because his subject matter required him to be a studio painter not a plein air artist like his academically recognized contemporaries. Yet he saw himself as one with The Ten. Cortissoz, in particular, recognized that Remington had created his own impressionistic style. His understanding of subdued nocturnal color likewise influenced his depiction of the blistering sunlit Southwestern skies. For example, in *Buffalo Runners—Big Horn Basin* (1909), Remington's colors are blended and more tonal rather than chromatic like the French Impressionists. Instead of understanding the impressionist touch or stroke, he mimics it. He does not deal with or clearly grasp the French Impressionist use of color based on the physics of color. In 1908, Remington recorded in his diary that "I have always wanted to be able to paint running horses so you would feel the details and not *see* them" (Samuels and Samuels, 1982). This was a startling statement for an artist who had built so much of his reputation on the accuracy of detail. And indeed, the broken brushed buffalo runners race across the canvas in a double-axis diagonal whipped by the wind in the glaring sun.

He understood this aspect of modernism; he believed true painting was just beginning. He described the new technique he was aspiring to achieve: "Small canvases are best—all plein air color and outlines lost—hard outlines are the bane of old painters" (Samuels and Samuels, 1982). He, too, had joined ranks with the critics in dismissing a previously esteemed painter when he casually commented that Bierstadt did not understand harmony. But some critics disapprovingly maintained Remington's paintings continued to be illustrative. His work was primarily respected for its historical value. A *New York Daily Tribune* critic compared Remington to his predecessor Catlin. He believed Remington's work would serve as pictorial documents of America's past as Catlin's paintings were useful as ethnographical records. This was not the affirmation Remington sought.

He burned more paintings that year as he relentlessly worked with color. By June he found some satisfaction writing in his diary that he completed five paintings that he thought would pass muster. Above all, Remington was pleased with his color discoveries and technique. He happily cited he had learned to use Prussian Blue and Ultramarine properly, and for the first time he created the silver sheen of moonlight. His diligence paid off. At his year's end show at Knoedler's he received good reviews. The *New York Globe* enthusiastically told the public to go see his pictures. The reviewer found his works distinctively American along with glowing praise for his color that was more pure, vibrant and expressive. Remington felt he had triumphed. Proudly, and relieved, he told a friend his exhibition was a huge hit. He pronounced himself no longer an illustrator.

He joyously welcomed the new year as he wrote in his diary New Year's Eve that he had come into his own as a painter, a real artist, at the age of forty-seven. The year 1909 started off right for him. In January, *Craftsman*, a magazine of the arts and crafts movement, extolled Remington as one of America's most outstanding artists; the journal deemed him a revolutionary in bringing about new conditions in American art. Still he had personal doubts as he wrote in his August diary about the upcoming Knoedler's exhibition: "I wonder if this bunch will make artistic New York sit up?" Then *Scribner's Magazine* contacted him about plans for a feature article for 1910 that would examine the whole of his art. This essay would become Remington's memorial. At the year's end Remington would be dead of peritonitis.

He had a few months left of heady living. At the height of his artistic prowess, Remington exulted he not only was happier than ever, but also healthy. The aesthetic pieces were coming together. Railroad financier William T. Evans, a collector of the best of American art, purchased *Fired On* as a gift for the National Gallery, Washington, DC. The Fifth Avenue crowd, as Remington called them, was also buying his work. His December show at Knoedler's opened to large crowds and received rave reviews. Remington was thrilled as he wrote in his diary on 8 December: "[T]he art critics have all 'come down'—I have received splendid notices from all the papers. They ungrudgingly give me high place as a 'mere painter.' I have been on their trail a long while and they never surrendered while they had a leg to stand on. The 'Illustrator' phase has become a back ground" (Samuels and Samuels, 1982). The respect he resolutely sought at last arrived. The *Times*, often his nemesis, affirmed his aesthetic. Other critics followed suit in praise of his style and importance as a historian. One review, however, was ominous: He observed that the shadow of death was close at hand in the faces of Remington's characters, a theme that evidenced genius to him. On 23 December Remington collapsed. Doctors performed an emergency appendectomy on Remington's kitchen table. Peritonitis had set in from a burst appendix. He passed away at 9:30 AM on 26 December.

In his later years Remington tried to separate his art from Remington the man, who made popular copy. "Don't write about me but about my art. It's the art that counts," he implored. "Consider my Art and not myself. I hope the Art is interesting but I assure you I am not. I am utterly commonplace" (Dippie, 2001). Remington was wrong on both accounts. People have continued to write about both the art and the man. He, along with his art, has become part of American legend and lore. He not only created but became part of the Western American myth. He, too, perhaps was prescient as he wrote to a friend a few weeks before his death, "I am the bone in a big art war down here [in NYC] and bones don't have a good time. I stand for the proposition of 'subjects'—painting something worth while as against painting *nothing* well—merely paint" (Spelt and Spelt, 1988). His subject matter—his West—continues to create controversy today.

FURTHER READING

"American Paintings," *New York Times* (10 April 1890), p. 4, in Doreen Bolger Burke, "In the Context of His Artistic Generation," *Frederic Remington: The Masterworks* (New York: Harry N. Abrams, 1988).

Anaconda Standard, 16 Dec. 1901, typescript in the James B. Rankin Papers in Brian W. Dippie, "Cowboys are Gems to Me," *South Dakota History* 32(3) (Fall 2002).

Catlin, George. "The North American Indians: Being Letters and Notes on Their Manners, Customs, and Conditions (1841)" in Brian W. Dippie, "Green Fields and Red Men," *George Catlin and His Indian Gallery* (New York: W.W. Norton, 2002).

"Charles Russell, Cowboy Artist," *Butte Miner* (11 October 1903).

Coffin, William A. "American Illustrations of Today (Third Paper)," *Scribner's Monthly* 11 (March 1892): 348.

"Cowboy Artist, St. Louis' Lion" in Peter H. Hassrick, *Remington, Russell and the Language of Western Art* (Washington, DC: Trust for Museum Exhibitions, 2000).

Dippie, Brian (ed.). *Charles M. Russell, Word Painter: Letters 1887–1926* (Fort Worth, TX: Amon Carter Museum, 1993).

Dippie, Brian W. *The Frederic Remington Art Museum Collection* (Ogdensburg, NY: Frederic Remington Art Museum, 2001).

Dippie, Brian W. "Frederic Remington's Wild West," *American Heritage Magazine* 26(3) (April 1975): 8.

Dippie, Brian W. *Remington & Russell: The Sid Richardson Collection*, rev. ed. (Austin: University of Texas Press, 1994).

"Goings On About Town," *New Yorker* (6 March 1989), p. 14.

Hagerty, Donald J. *Desert Dreams: The Art and Life of Maynard Dixon* (Layton, UT: Gibbs-Smith Publisher, 1998).

Horan, James D. *The Life and Art of Charles Schreyvogel: Painter-Historian of the Indian-Fighting Army of the American West* (New York: Crown Publishers, 1969).

Hough, Emerson. "Wild West Faking," *Collier's* 42(3) (19 December 1908): 18.

Maxwell, Perriton. "Frederick Remington—Most Typical of American Artists," *Pearson's Magazine* 18 (October 1907): 403.

McCracken, Harold. *Frederic Remington: Artist of the Old West* (Philadelphia: J.B. Lippincott, 1947).

McCullough, David. "Remington the Man," in *Frederic Remington: The Masterworks*, p. 30.

"Mr. Schreyvogel Paints the Fact," *New York Herald* (2 May 1903).

Remington, Frederic. "A Few Words from Mr. Remington," *Collier's Weekly* 34 (18 March 1905): 16.

Remington, Frederic. "Cracker Cowboys of Florida," *Harper's New Monthly Magazine* 91 (August 1895): 339.

Remington, Frederic. "Horses of the Plains," *Century Magazine* (January 1889) in *Collected Writings* 20.

Roosevelt, Theodore. "Ranch Life in the Far West," *Century Magazine* 35 (February 1888): 502.

Roosevelt, Theodore. "In Cowboy-Land," *Century Magazine* 46 (June 1893): 276.

Roosevelt, Theodore. Introductory quote in *Pearson's Magazine* 18 (October 1907): 395.

Russell, Charles M. *Good Medicine: The Illustrated Letters of Charles M. Russell* (Garden City, NY: Doubleday, Doran, and Co., 1929).

Russell, John. "Remington's War and Old West," *New York Times* (10 February 1989).

Samuels, Peggy, and Harold Samuels. *Frederic Remington: A Biography* (Garden City, NY: Doubleday & Company, 1982).

Spelt, Allen P., and Marilyn D. Spelt. *Frederic Remington—Selected Letters* (New York: Abbeville Press, 1988).

Wildman, Edwin. "Frederic Remington, the Man," *Outing* 41 (March 1903): 715–716

Wister, Owen. "Introduction to Frederic Remington," *Done in the Open* (New York: P.F. Collier & Son, 1902).

Colt Single Action Army Revolver, 1871. Buffalo Bill Historical Center, Cody, Wyoming; Gift of Brian P. and Ann A. McDonald; 2 February 1999.

Rifles and Revolvers

George M. Stantis

WINCHESTER MODEL 1873

"The gun that won the West." Though there were certainly many other fire-arms that took part in the changing of the American West, few can lay claim to having been as innovative, popular, or long-lived as the Winchester Model 1873 (also referred to as the Model 73). It is the lever-action rifle that most people think of when they bring to mind the rifle of the cowboy, settler, or gunfighter. Determined to improve and expand sales with the development of a center-fire cartridge and a firearm to handle them, the development of the Model 73 was the brainchild of Oliver Winchester. With technical innovation and aggressive salesmanship, by the end of its manufacture in 1923 more than 700,000 Model 1873s had been sold, making it one of the most popular and widely used firearms in American history.

The cartridge used in Winchester's previous model of 1866 (Model 66) was a .44 caliber rim-fire, with a 200-grain lead bullet, a black powder charge of 28 grains, and a muzzle velocity of 1125 feet per second. Development of the new center-fire cartridge allowed for greater powder charges, with com-bustion of the entire powder column assured because the flame of the ignited primer shot forward along the length of the cartridge case. But with increased powder charges, there were also increased internal pressures the Model 66 was not capable of handling. The new round developed for the new Model 1873 would be designated the .44-40, or .44 WCF (Winchester Center Fire). It was composed of a brass case, primer, 40 grains of black powder, a 200-grain lead bullet, and achieved an average muzzle velocity of 1300 feet per second.

With plant superintendent Nelson King and Oliver Winchester's newly hired son-in-law Thomas G. Bennett, a project team was assembled in 1870 to develop both the new cartridge and the rifle to handle it. After three years of intense work the completed design of the Model 1873 and the .44-40 was announced to the public, but production problems stalled mass pro-duction for another year; with only eighteen Model 73s being shipped in its first year of introduction. Many of the newly incorporated innovations were patents held by King and assigned to Winchester. Thus, from the begin-ning of production to the end, in 1923, barrel markings on all 1873s read "KING'S IMPROVEMENT PATENTED MARCH 29, 1866. OCTOBER 16, 1860."

Though many variations and options would be made available, the basic sporting Model 73 was a lever-action, side-loaded, top-ejecting rifle with a twenty-four-inch round barrel, under-barrel tube magazine, American walnut forearm and butt stock, with crescent butt plate. Unlike the earlier Model 66, which had a brass receiver, all parts of the Model 73 were gun-metal, iron, and later steel. Another innovation was a sliding dust cover, which kept debris from entering the internal mechanism at the top of the receiver when the firearm was not in use.

The Model 1873 was an evolutionary design. Its primary appeal was that it allowed the rifleman to fire fifteen cartridges as fast as the lever-action of the new arm could be worked without reloading. In 1875, Winchester began an extensive advertising campaign of its Model 73 in America and Europe, with one result being a most favorable review being written in London's *Field* sporting magazine.

Another advantage was the patenting by Winchester of a reloading tool in 1875 that allowed the owner to reload cases after they had been fired. The new hand-loading tool removed the spent primer, inserted a new primer, seated the bullet, and resized the cartridge to its original factory specifications. This innovation allowed the owner to make his or her own cartridges from components, regardless of how far the individual was from civilization.

I have been using and have thoroughly tested your latest improved rifle. Allow me to say that I have tried and used nearly every kind of a gun made in the United States, and for general hunting, or Indian fighting, I pronounce your improved Winchester the boss.

—William F. "Buffalo Bill" Cody, 1875

Adding to the practical appeal of the Model 73 was Colt's chambering its "frontier" model six-shooter in 1878 with the same .44-40 cartridge as the Winchester. Here was born a combination of rifle and pistol that allowed for the carrying of only one cartridge that was interchangeable between rifle and pistol. It therefore illustrates quite clearly why many early photographs show individuals holding a Model 73 and sporting a Colt revolver slung at their hip. Later, Colt and Winchester 73s were produced in .38-40, .32-20, and the .22 short and long.

Because large government contracts were not immediately forthcoming and seeing that the American domestic market was growing, Oliver Winchester determined to offer the public the Model 73 in various configurations. Winchester was also the first major American firearms manufacturer to offer the public a myriad of factory options.

Standard barrel length for carbines was twenty inches. Special lengths could be ordered from fourteen to nineteen inches, but are considered rare. Carbines with less than the standard length barrel are referred to as "Baby Carbines." It should also be noted that any barrel length could come with a saddle ring.

Rifle barrels came standard with twenty-four-inch round barrels. Octagonal barrels were considered an option, but were found to be popular by a ratio of 6:1 in all calibers. Either round or octagonal barrels could be special ordered in lengths of fourteen to thirty-six inches. Special order short-barreled rifles in either round or octagonal configuration were most often seen at twenty inches. The majority of .22-caliber barrels are found to have octagonal barrels. Heavier than standard weight barrels were also a special, but a not often seen order item. Although part round/part octagonal barrels were offered, they are seldom encountered.

If there is any one feature in which Winchester guns excel all others . . . it is in their remarkable accuracy. This is due to the excellence of Winchester barrels and to the care taken in targeting them. At the plant of the Winchester Repeating Arms Co. there are ranges from 50 feet up to 200 yards. At these ranges every rifle is shot to test its accuracy, the distance varying according to the caliber.

—Winchester Repeating Arms Co.

Muskets were produced with standard thirty-inch tapered round barrels. There are some muskets found with barrels three to four inches shorter than standard. Crowning of the muzzle on muskets and carbines was standard. Rifles did not have crowned muzzles on either their round or octagonal barrels, though some may be found with a semi-crown on the outer edges of the barrel.

Full-length tubular magazines were standard for both carbines and rifles, with the musket having its magazine set back three inches from the muzzle. Standard-length carbine magazines held twelve cartridges. Full-length rifle magazines carried a capacity of fifteen cartridges, and muskets held seventeen cartridges in their magazine. Though seldom publicized in its literature, Winchester recommended that the magazines not be loaded to full capacity to avoid cramping the magazine's internal spring. A magazine with half capacity was available, but extremely rare.

Early carbine front sights were integrated with the front barrel band. Later-model carbines had the blade silver-brazed into the slot on the barrel band, with the blade being of nickel steel or brass. By mid-1880 the post front sight was a two-part post integrated with the barrel. Ivory or copper inserts could also be ordered at an extra charge.

Carbine rear sights had a non-adjustable leaf marked 1, 3, or 5. The adjustable leaf rear sight became standard around 1882. Adjustable leaf carbine sights were fitted and graduated for the cartridge chambered in the gun.

Rifle front sights were initially one piece; with later models having two-piece construction with a silver blade inserted into the base that fit a dovetail milled into the barrel. Rear sights were of one-piece construction on early rifles; with two-piece construction following that incorporated a flat flip-up elevator.

Musket front sights on early models were two-piece, with later models offered in a variety of shapes and configurations. Early model rear sights were nonadjustable for windage. Later, rear sights came standard with windage-adjustable military ladder sights.

Through the course of its long production, Winchester offered a variety of sighting options. Because of this, the upper tangs of rifles were drilled and tapped for tang sights. There were also a number of rear sight options that included a variety of express leaf sights, "peek" or peep sights. Front sights too were available in a number of configurations that included various blade inserts, front blades made of different materials, globe front sights, and the

Beach combination sight. All sights not listed as standard were available at an extra charge.

Winchester bright blue was the standard metal finish. Triggers, hammers, and many of the internal parts were case hardened for durability. Color case hardening of some external parts was a special order item. Another special order item was full white nickel plate applied primarily to the frame, side plates, tang, elevator, dust cover, and butt plate; all other parts then being the standard bright blue.

The Winchester Repeating Arms Co. have [sic] unsurpassed facilities for producing fancy finished guns of all prices and descriptions.
—Winchester Repeating Arms Co.

Standard wood for the Model 73's butt stock and forearm was straight-grained walnut. Selected stocks were first oil finished, sanded smooth, scraped to remove any "whiskers," then a mixture of linseed oil and walnut hull oil was applied to add color and finish. If a high gloss was desired, instead of the standard satin finish, additional coats of oil were hand-applied and rubbed. "Fancy grain" walnut was an additional cost item, and came in either burl grain or crotch walnut. The most popular finish was an extra finish of oil to the walnut to bring out the curl, but was not fancy enough to be deemed deluxe.

Throughout the Model 73's production Winchester offered any feature or extra the customer required and could afford, from gold-plated triggers to the fanciest metal engraving and wood checkering. These options were offered as long as the Model 1873 was in production.

Perhaps the most magical of all Model 1873s is the "One of One Thousand" and "One of One Hundred." Winchester announced in its catalog of 1875 that it would be introducing specially made and finished rifles. These rifles would be tested for accuracy, have set triggers, and extra finished wood and metal as standard. All exposed metal parts such as the receiver, butt plate, hammer, side plates, and for-end caps would be case hardened and colored, while all other external parts would come bright blue. Internal parts would receive special polishing, and be found to have matching assembly numbers. The fancy-grained burl walnut would come checkered. These special rifles were offered from 1875 to 1877.

All One of One Thousand rifles have that inscription engraved on the barrel, close to the front of the receiver. The earliest rifles had "1 of 1000" engraved in numerals, although later models were spelled out. Winchester records indicate that there were 136 of these rifles sold. Barrels marked with the One of One Thousand were later assembled and sold in 1881. An even rarer Model 73 variety was the One of One Hundred; only seven are known to have been manufactured and sold.

Manufacture of the Model 1873's component parts was halted in 1919 near serial number 706,000. Assembly of parts was continued until 1923 when the last Model 73 left the factory with serial number 706,610.

Large Caliber Single-Shot Rifles: The Competition

Winchester claimed that their firearms "won the West," but it was the large-caliber single-shot rifles that put it down for the count. At about the same time that Winchester was introducing its .44-40 cartridge and Model 1873 rifle and variants, companies like Sharps and Remington had shown the world what a large-caliber and black-powder charge could do at 800, 900, and 1000 yards by winning long-range matches in Europe—a feat Winchester at the time could not attempt. The trapdoor, falling and rolling block rifles would become Winchester's greatest competitor for the American frontier and hunting market. Here were firearms that used bullets almost twice the weight of any used safely in a Winchester before the introduction of the Winchester Model 1885 Single Shot, and whose transfer of energy to the target no lever gun of the time could match. These single-shot black-powder cartridge rifles were the big bores of their day. It is interesting to note that the demise of these large-bore rifles coincided with the disappearance of the buffalo herds they were originally designed to harvest. But now, for more than twenty years, there has been a recurring interest in these "buffalo guns," and each is now manufactured by a new generation of craftsmen to the same exacting standards that had brought them to prominence more than 130 years ago.

BUFFALO RIFLES

Though any firearm or rifle was used to hunt buffalo, the rifles most considered "Buffalo Rifles" are those that were used by the professional hunters from 1866 to the early 1880s. These firearms are identified as being single-shot black-powder cartridge rifles with an external hammer and weighing between ten and sixteen pounds. Ranging from forty to fifty calibers, the buffalo hunters fired lead bullets that weighed from 400 to 550 grains (there are 437.5 grains to the ounce). Sharps, Remington, Ballard, and the Trapdoor Springfield are just a few of the models and manufacturers that made rifles suitable for the buffalo ranges. Myth and legend has sprung up concerning their long-range accuracy and killing power. In less than twenty years the professional buffalo hunter with his large-bore rifle decimated the vast herds of bison that once roamed throughout the American West.

Even by today's standards the rifles used by the professional buffalo hunter are accurate and powerful. Their selection of a rifle was dictated by the animal that they were hunting, and by the way in which they hunted the American bison, or buffalo. These are large animals, with males sometimes weighing as much as a ton, and required a heavy bullet that would penetrate deeply. Unlike the Indian and other hunters who chased the buffalo herd from horseback, the professional buffalo hunter preferred taking a "stand" that allowed them to select their targets and to keep the herd within range. For this style of hunting the rifle could be long and heavy to make that killing shot from 200 to more than 600 yards away; whereas those that chased the buffalo from horseback used lighter and shorter-barreled rifles to maneuver it around the head and neck of a running horse.

PROFESSIONAL BUFFALO HUNTING

When the buffalo hunters first came, the buffalo were found in massive herds, and kills were generally made at 200 to 600 yards. As the herds were thinned the buffalo became more wary of the sight and smell of man, which extended the killing range to 700 and even 900 yards.

In the early period of commercial buffalo hunting between 1870 and 1875, the most widely used cartridge was the .44/75 two and a quarter inch and the .50/70 Government. There was also the .50 two and a half inch and the .44 two and five-eighths inch, but these were not used by the majority of hunters. Weights of the rifle in this period ranged from ten and a half to thirteen pounds, with the average being eleven and a half to twelve pounds. Open sights were used, but a greater percentage of hunters fitted special order peep and globe sights. During this period military rifles chambered in .44/70 and .50/70 were often seen. There increased the number of heavy rifles weighing from fourteen to seventeen and a half pounds and chambered for the .44/90 and .50/100 two and a half inch. These rifles had heavy octagonal barrels between thirty and thirty-two inches, many were ordered with set triggers, shotgun butt stock, and were sometimes equipped with telescopic sights.

After 1875 through 1878 there was a growing number of heavier rifles used. There was also a decline in the number of telescopic sights used, with the front globe sight and tang mounted peep rear sight predominating. During this time the .44/90 was the most

There were several methods to kill buffalo, and each hunter adopted his own. One method was to run beside them, shooting them as they ran. Another was to shoot from the rear. The most successful and profitable method of hunting was to leave your horse out of sight after you had determined the direction and course of the wind, and then get as near as possible. If the herd was lying at rest, the hunter would pick out some buffalo that were standing up on watch and shoot the sentinel in the side so that the bullet would not go through, but would lodge in the flesh. A buffalo shot in this manner would begin to mill round and round in a slow walk. The other buffalo sniffing the blood and following would then not be watching the hunter, and he would continue to shoot the outside cow buffalo. In this way the hunter could hold the herd as long as they acted in this way. And just as a trained cowpuncher would hold his herd with his horse and rope, the hunter would use his gun. This was termed mesmerizing the buffalo so that he could hold them on what we termed a stand, which afterwards proved to

(continued)

*be the most successful way
of killing the buffalo.*
    —Details taken from Miles
Gilbert, *Getting a Stand*, Ch. 6
(Union City, TN: Pioneer Press,
1993), pp. 78–79.

used cartridge, with the .45 caliber becoming increasingly popular. Weights of the rifles also increased, with rifles generally weighing thirteen and three-quarter pounds to sixteen and a half pounds. The butt stock was of the shotgun type, and the average barrel length was thirty inches. It was during this latter period that mention of the "Big Fifty" becomes more prevalent in the recollections of some of the old buffalo hunters. This reference is to the .50/100/473 two and a half inch cartridge. That is, a .50 caliber, two and a half inch case, carrying 100 grains of black powder, and firing a 473-grain paper patched or lube-grooved bullet.

Of all the rifles used by the buffalo hunters it is the Sharps Model 1874 that comes most quickly to peoples' minds. The unique profile, with its large side-mounted hammer and distinctive trigger guard that also acted as the falling block lever, is the rifle identified with most of the notable incidents of the buffalo-hunting era. It was with a .50/90 Sharps that Billy Dixon struck one of a group of Indians more than 1500 yards away on the second day of the Adobe Walls Fight (Texas) in 1874.

Actually introduced in 1871, the designation of 1874 came after Sharps began to introduce other models to their line of firearms. Produced for less than ten years, the Model 1874 Sharps has become an American icon and is identified as much with the Old West as is the Colt Single Action revolver or the Winchester Model 1873 lever gun. In fact, it has been contended by some that, "the Sharps made the west safe for Winchester." The reputation of the Sharps far outweighs the actual number made—approximately 6500. Even taking into consideration all the variations, such as the Creedmore, Business Rifle, Long and Mid Range, Military, and Hunter's Rifle, the total production of Model 1874s was between 12,000 and 13,000. The reputation of the Sharps by those that made their living in the hide trade was not only its accuracy, but the fact that the rifle was sturdy and easy to disassemble. A simple pin was pulled from the side of the receiver that allowed the breechblock and extractor to drop out the bottom for inspection, repair, or cleaning. The extractor had an extension that allowed for manual pressure to be applied when removing a stuck case caused by overheating. Due to financial complications, the Sharps Rifle Company closed its doors in 1881 at about the same time the great buffalo herds were on the verge of extinction, and the rifle that killed many of them was potentially responsible for destroying its own market.

One of the most popular buffalo rifles of this era was the Remington Rolling Block; also known as the Remington No. 1. By the time the Sharps Model 1874 was introduced Remington had already manufactured over 600,000 of this model rifle for both the American and foreign military. During the 1870s the Remington Arms Company was working twenty-four hours and producing nearly 1600 rifles for each twenty-four hour period. These military rifles carried 35.2-inch barrels, and offered to the American public chambered for the .43 Spanish, and .43 Egyptian; while the .50/70 Government carried a 35.5-inch barrel. So lucrative were foreign military sales for Remington that the company allowed the American market to take care of itself. It was from the needs of the buffalo hunters and other American hunters that Remington developed their Remington No. 1 Sporting Rifle.

Remington Sporting Rifles were manufactured from 1870 through 1890. It is because of the diverse needs of the American market that the Remington Sporting Rifles are found in a vast array of calibers and stock configurations. One could order a rifle as light as eight and a half pounds to as heavy as fifteen pounds. Barrel length was twenty-six inches, but could be ordered longer for $1.00 per two inches added, up to thirty-four inches. Another more common option was single-set triggers. Remington did not drill and tap the tangs of their rifles for peep sight mounting, as was done with other manufacturers. Sporting Rifles came standard with a blade front sight and buckhorn rear, but offered as an option their "combination open and peep sight" mounted on the barrel just ahead of the receiver.

Operation of the action is done by bringing the hammer to full cock, the block is then brought back by using the thumb tab on the right side, inserting the cartridge, then pushing the thumb tab forward against the breech. Disassembly of the action is accomplished by removing a screw on the left side of the receiver and the securing button and driving out two pins. This will then allow for the removal of the block and trigger. It is the simplicity of the action and the myriad of available options that attracted many of the buffalo hunters.

Marlin Ballard was another rifle that saw use by the professional buffalo hunter. The era of the Marlin Ballard was from 1875 to 1890. The history of the Ballard is complex, having been bought and sold many times. Known primarily for their excellent target rifles, the Marlin Ballard was also made in hunting configurations that did see service out West and on the buffalo ranges.

The Marlin Ballard models most likely used by the hide hunters would have been the Ballard Hunter's Rifle 1-1/2 and 1-3/4, the Ballard Perfection No. 4, Ballard Sporting Rifle No. 4-1/4, and the Ballard Pacific No. 5. Each of these rifles was made from the finest materials then available. They could be ordered with barrels that ranged from twenty-six to thirty-four inches and could be chambered for any caliber, including any number of their proprietary or "everlasting" cartridges. Double-set triggers were also standard on some of these models. Its action is not seen as being as strong as many of its competitors, but it was capable enough to handle the pressures of any of the large cartridges of its day using black powder as its propellant.

As a true falling block action, the Ballard is loaded by simply pulling down on the trigger guard; this then lowered the entire two part block, which also housed the trigger assembly and hammer. Disassembly is done by removing the transverse screw on the right side of the receiver which then allows for the entire block and extractor to be removed.

Perhaps one of the first rifles to be termed a Buffalo rifle would be the Trap-door Springfield. It was developed after the Civil War to save money by recon-structing the large inventory of muzzle-loading Model 1861 Springfields into single-shot cartridge rifles. In September 1865 E.S. Allin was awarded a pat-ent that consisted of milling the breech area of the rifle-musket and attaching a hinged breechblock, or trapdoor. We know it was used as a buffalo rifle because it was the rifle William "Buffalo Bill" Cody used to feed railroad workers building the transcontinental railroad in the late 1860s. It was during this time that Buffalo Bill used his Trapdoor rifle, Leucrecia Borgia, to kill sixty-nine buffalo in one day. It operated by putting the hammer on half-cock, pushing up on the thumb tab to raise the block, loading a cartridge, closing the block, drawing the hammer to full-cock, and firing.

The first cartridges developed for the Trapdoor used a 500-grain .58 caliber bullet propelled by 60 grains of black powder, with a muzzle velocity of 946 feet per second. By 1867 the next cartridge developed for this rifle was the .50/70. It was loaded with a 425-grain bullet and 70 grains of black powder. By 1873 the Army redesigned the Trapdoor and developed a new cartridge to go with it, the famous .45/70. This cartridge is still sold today, but originally it was loaded into a 1.1 inch brass case with 70 grains of black powder and a 500-grain lead bullet.

Trapdoor Springfields came in three basic configurations. There was the infantry rifle with its thirty-five and a half inch barrel, the Cadet Rifle with a twenty-nine and a half inch barrel, and the cavalry carbine with a twenty-two inch barrel. Together there were more than 600,000 Trapdoors manufactured by the Springfield Armory.

Development of the self-contained cartridge and the rifles to fire them evolved in time to meet both political and material need. The rifles used by the professional buffalo hunter were tools that met the criteria for reducing the native people's food supply and by supplying meat and hides to a growing industrial nation. Strangely, it is the rifles that are better remembered than the men that wielded them with such deadly efficiency.

COLT SINGLE ACTION

Perhaps no other American-made handgun is as recognizable as the Colt Sin-gle Action revolver. It is the sidearm seen and used in a dizzying array of mov-ies, television Westerns, books, and magazine articles. Carried by gamblers, cowboys, soldiers, outlaws, farmers, and lawmen, the Colt Single Action car-tridge revolver was the most recognized and popular. It has served as a symbol of an era, and from its acceptance by the U.S. Army in 1873 to its present production, this six-shooter remains an iconic fixture.

The Colt Model P, also known as the Colt Single Action, Peacemaker, or Fron-tier, is one of the most popular and legendary small arms in American history.

Produced for more than 130 years, and still popular, the Colt Single Action was the result of patents held by Charles B. Richards, with his cartridge conversion of open-top Colt revolvers, and William Mason and his improved ejector. Mechanically, no principal changes were made to the internal workings of the revolver from its earlier percussion models, such as the .44-caliber Colt Model 1860 Army and the .36-caliber Colt Model 1851 Navy.

The Workings of the Colt Single Action

The Colt Single Action is a six-shot, solid frame revolver, as compared to the earlier "open-top" Colts, or hinged framed Smith & Wessons. The frame is two parts, the cylinder frame and the grip frame with the trigger guard, which is all assembled with screws. After drawing the hammer back two clicks to rotate the cylinder, loading is done singly into the cylinder through the swing-out loading gate on the right side of the cylinder frame. Empty cases are ejected one at a time through the opened loading gate by pulling forward on the ejector rod, located in the housing under the barrel. The cylinder can be removed by again bringing the hammer back two clicks and removing the base pin by either unscrewing the base pin screw (as in black powder era guns), or pushing the transverse bar to the right, then pulling the base pin forward.

Evolution came with the adoption of the black-powder center fire cartridge and the incorporation of an integrated top strap that bridged the front and back of the revolver frame. This top strap added strength to the frame, and thus allowed the use of more powerful cartridges. Into the frame the barrel was screwed. The back strap and trigger guard were separate components and were attached to each other, and the frame, with screws. But like earlier Colt percussion revolvers there remained the revolving cylinder, hammer, trigger, mainspring or hammer spring, handspring, and a bifurcated spring that operated both the cylinder bolt and trigger.

The original military contract was for 8000 in 1873; by 1891 the U.S. military had purchased more than 37,000. Chambered for the .45-caliber center fire cartridge, early revolvers were issued to selected state militia and various government departments. All specimens are identified by the "U.S." stamped on the left side of the frame, along with the initials of the inspector, and small initial stampings on other parts. These early Colt Single Actions carried seven and a half inch barrels for the cavalry, and were barreled five and a half inches for the artillery. The first unit to be issued the Colt SA (single action) was the Second Cavalry stationed at Camp Douglas, Texas. On 13 April 1874, they received eighty-four. Now officially introduced to the West, the new Colt SA was advertised by the agent for the Colt Company, B. Kitteredge & Company, as the "Peacemaker," a name synonymous with the Colt

SA. But Peacemaker was not the official name. Colt designated their SA as the Model P. The Colt's Patent Fire Arms Manufacturing Company sold their SAA (single-action army) through a number of traveling salesmen. They also had fifteen to twenty "jobbers" acting as wholesalers, whose job was to handle the large-quantity orders for distribution to individual retail stores. Colt also had sales offices in New York and London.

Serious collectors of the Colt SAA separate the manufacturing history of this revolver into three distinct generations.

First generation Colt Single Action's were manufactured continuously from 1873 to 1940, with a total production of 357,859. But it must be taken into consideration that this period was also divided into two subgroups. They are the black powder–era guns and smokeless powder–era guns, and thus into either black powder or smokeless frames. The difference is that the black powder frame has a screw that angles in from the front of the frame which then holds the base pin in position. This differs from the smokeless powder frame in that the base pin is held in place by a transverse spring-loaded pin. Here a warning should be made. Though the smokeless powder frame was adopted in 1892, the Colt factory did not warranty any of their single action revolvers until 1900. Therefore, if the serial number is below 192,000 then it is a black powder–era frame. Revolvers came with seven and a half, five and a half, and four and three-quarter inch barrels, but the factory offered barrels in lengths from two and a half to sixteen inches on special order, and also offered a special shoulder stock that could turn the longer barreled arms into a carbine. During this period Colt offered more than thirty different chamberings for cartridges from the .22 Long Rifle to the British .476 Eley. Most popular was the .45 Colt, with 158,885 sold in this caliber, followed by the .44-40 (71,291), the .38-40 (50,520), the .32-20 (43,264), and the .41 Colt (19,676). It is an interesting note that many of the Colt SA's most popularly sold calibers were also those chambered for the Winchester Model 1873.

Second generation production Colt "Peacemaker" was in response to the influence of television and movie Westerns. Manufactured from 1956 to 1975, the serial number began with 0001, but ended with the suffix SA. Initially offered in .45 Colt, the .38 Special was added later that same year. In 1958, the .44 Special was added, and in 1960, the .357 Magnum also became available. By 1964, the .38 Special was dropped, as was the .44 Special in 1966. Barrel lengths offered were seven and a half, five and a half, and four and three-quarter inches.

Third generation Colt SAs were placed into production after Colt had an opportunity to retool, rebuild, and refit the machinery that had been used in its manufacturing for more than a century. In 1976, Colt reintroduced the Peacemaker, retaining the standard barrel lengths, and offered in a barrel length of seven and a half inches, and chambered in .45 Colt. Soon afterward four and three-quarter and five and a half inch barrels were offered along with the .357 Magnum caliber. By 1978, the .44 Special was offered in all three standard barrel lengths, and by 1982 the .44-40 was offered with only the four and three-quarter and seven and a half inch barrels. Serial numbers in 1976 began at 80,000SA, but when the serial number reached 99,999SA in 1978 Colt began a new serial number range beginning with SA1001, and ending in 1993 with SA99,999. From 1993 to the present serial numbers are found with the prefix of "S" and the suffix "A."

With such a long production run the number of Colt SA options and embellishments are innumerable. As standard, the finish was a case colored frame and hammer, with all other parts being deep blued, and with oil-finished walnut grips; between 1882 and 1896, customer requests led Colt to come out with two-piece, black hard rubber, gutta-percha grips with a single holding screw. But the civilian customer had a vast array of special order options that included nickel, silver, or gold plating; grips could be ordered in plain or fancifully carved exotic materials; or engraving that ran from simple embellishment to full and deep coverage of all its exposed metal parts. So varied and expansive are these specially embellished guns that collectors are still discovering new variations. Colt show guns and presentation pieces that are elaborately engraved and may be inlaid with gold and other precious stones and metals consistently won international recognition and prizes. Many of these embellished Colts were presented to foreign presidents, kings, and sultans; and many more were specially made and presented to notable American businessmen, politicians, and famous personalities.

Of interest are also those models which had either the flat-top or standard top-strap frame as the Model P, but produced with special barrel lengths. These are the Buntline Special, Sheriff's, and Storekeeper's models.

Supposedly dime-novel writer Ned Buntline (Edward Z.C. Judson) had these special twelve-inch barrel, flat-topped Colts made as gifts and presented to notable lawmen Charles Bassett, Neal Brown, Wyatt Earp, Bat Masterson, and Bill Tilghman. And though there is scant evidence to prove that these were actually ordered and delivered, there were customers that indeed special ordered Colt SAs with extended barrels. The Buntline is defined as having barrel lengths from ten to sixteen inches. They were generally ordered with a grooved flat-top frame into which was inserted an adjustable leaf sight. They also came with an extended hammer screw onto which a nickel-plated brass shoulder stock could be mounted. Colt had announced this configuration at the Philadelphia Centennial Exposition, but aside from the first batch, this firearm was never produced in any numbers until the 1960s and 1970s.

At the other end were the Sheriff and Storekeeper models. These are easily identified as having barrels from three to four inches and without having an ejector or rod housing. As a special ordered item they were made in limited numbers through each generation of Colt SAA manufacturing.

Colt used the basic design of its single action throughout its production. A variation from this was the Flat-Top Target models. These are distinguished by having a nonadjustable fixed rear sight mounted on the flat, rather than the more usual radiused top strap, and for having a front sight base into which any variety of sight blades could be inserted and tightened by a screw. Available at first only by special order, these Flat-Top Target models were later listed in both their 1890 and 1892 catalogs. Approximately 917 Flat-Top Target models were made, with the .38 caliber being the most popular.

Western Gunleather

As Americans began migrating West they brought with them their style of carrying pistols and revolvers. Whether one's six-shooter was carried in a California Slim Jim, Mexican Loop, or Buscadero rig, they each evolved in the West in response to their place and times.

Early Eastern hip-belt holsters were generally in the form of a simple sleeve, or cuff. Their simple purpose was to hold the sidearm on the belt, and they were often open-topped and made with thin pliable leathers.

There is some speculation that due to the need to access one's sidearm in a hurry, the rough and tumble mining camps of California led to the development of the California Slim-Jim holster. Popular from the 1850s through the 1870s, the Slim Jim holster was opened-topped and followed the contours of the revolver it was carrying, giving quick access to the grip and trigger. Many existing samples exhibit graceful lines and show the influence of Mexican leather carving and tooling. This contoured design and applied decoration would influence all other Western holster designs to the present day.

Developed in the 1870s, the "Mexican Loop" holster is perhaps the most recognizable of the Western-designed "gun boots," seen most often in photographs of cowboys, lawmen, and outlaws. The Mexican Loop holster allowed for a broader belt loop to accommodate the wider gun belts with their integrated cartridge loops. By the beginning of the twentieth century it had become so popular that the pattern was advertised through the mail-order catalogs of Montgomery Ward and Sears.

The "Buscadero" rig was the invention of the entertainment industry. Its unique suspension and often garishly decorated holster and belt set its wearer apart from the more old-fashioned rigs of lesser characters. The Buscadero dominated Western-themed shorts, films, and TV from the 1930s through the 1970s. It was the rig of most of Hollywood's cowboy heroes and was the precursor to the development of the fast-draw pattern of holster. The fast-draw, like the Buscadero, was worn low on the hip, with the grip near equal to the lowered wrist of its wearer.

The Bisley model was the first major change to the SA design. Colt called it the "Target Revolver model," and it was first introduced and advertised in England through the Holland & Holland catalog in 1895 where the *Illustrated News* called it "Colt's New '95 Model, .455 Caliber Army and Target Revolver in One." The following year the name Bisley was assured by its having performed admirably at the Bisley international shooting matches in England. By 1898 Bisleys were being offered in every variety of the standard Model P, including Flat-Top Target models, and in eighteen calibers. There were 45,326 Bisley models produced until 1912, when the Colt Company ceased its production.

The Colt Single Action is perhaps the most recognized and collected revolver in the world. And though it has undergone some minor improvements in its long history, it has remained virtually unchanged. There are more books, articles, and movies highlighting the Colt SA than any other revolver. Its identifiable status comes from more than a century and a quarter of production, and by its use by some of the American West's most notable personalities.

FURTHER READING

Barnes, Frank C. *Cartridges of the World*, 11th ed. (Iola, WI: Gun Digest Books, 2006).

Boorman, Dean K. *The History of Colt Firearms* (New York: Lyons Press, 2001).

Bowman, Hank Wieand. *Famous Guns From the Winchester Collection* (New York: Fawcett, 1958).

Cochran, Keith. *Colt Cavalry, Artillery, and Militia Revolvers, 1873–1903* (Rapid City, SD: Cochran, 1987).

Cook, John R. *The Border and the Buffalo* (Abilene, TX: State House Press, 1989).

Dutcher, John T. *Ballard: The Great Single Shot Rifle* (Denver, CO: John T. Dutcher, 2002).

Gilbert, Miles. *Getting a Stand* (Union City, TN: Pioneer Press, 1993).

Graham, Ron, John A. Kopec, and C. Kenneth Moore. *A Study of the Colt Single Action Army* (Dallas, TX: Taylor Publishing, 1976).

Grant, James J. *Single Shot Rifles* (Highland Park, NJ: Gun Room Press, 1991).

Haven, Charles T., and Frank A. Belden. *A History of the Colt Revolver* (Iola, WI: Krause, 1999).

Kuhnhausen, Jerry. *The Colt Single Action Revolvers: A Shop Manual*, Vol. 1 and 2 (McCall, ID: Heritage Gun Books, 2001).

Madis, George. *The Winchester Book* (Brownsboro, TX: Art and Reference House, 1985).

Madis, George. *The Winchester Handbook* (Brownsboro, TX: Art and Reference House, 1981).

Mayer, Frank H., and Charles B. Roth. *The Buffalo Harvest* (Union City, TN: Pioneer Press, 1995).

O'Meara, Doc. *Colt Single Action Army Revolver* (Iola, WI: Krause, 1999).

Sellers, Frank. *Sharps Firearms* (North Hollywood, CA: Beinfeld, 1978).

Stone, George W. *The Winchester 1873 Handbook* (East Lyme, CT: Rod's, 1973).

Venturino, Mike. *Shooting Buffalo Rifles of the Old West* (Livingston, MT: MLV Enterprises, 2002).

Venturino, Mike. *Shooting Colt Single Actions, In All Styles, Calibers, & Generations* (Livingston, MT: MLV Enterprises, 1995).

Waite, M.D. "Bud," and B.D. Ernst. *Trapdoor Springfield: The United States Springfield Single Shot Rifle—1865–1893* (Highland Park, NJ: Gun Room Press, 1980).

Wilkerson, Don. *The Post-War Single Action Revolver* (Dallas, TX: Taylor Publishing, 1986).

Williamson, Harold F. *Winchester: The Gun That Won the West* (Washington, DC: Combat Forces Press, 1952).

Wilson, R.L. *Colt, An American Legend: The Official History of Colt Firearms from 1836 to the Present* (New York: Artabras, 1986).

Wilson, R. L. *Winchester, An American Legend: The Official History of Winchester Firearms and Ammunition From 1849 to the Present* (New York: Random House, 1991).

Winchester Repeating Arms Co., New Haven, Ct., 1916. Facsimile Edition, corporate pamphlet. New Jersey: Castle Books, nd.

Statue of Sacagawea and her son, Bismarck, North Dakota. Getty Images.

Sacagawea

Vanessa Gunther

Sacagawea is perhaps one of the most recognizable Indians in American history. Along with Pocahontas, she exemplifies the typical white view of Indian women, amiable to the will of the Anglo-Europeans who seized control of native lands. Because of this, the story of her life often seems to begin and end with the Lewis and Clark Expedition during the years 1805–1806. The assistance she provided to the thirty-two travelers she guided from the Mandan villages in present-day North Dakota to the Pacific and then back again has become emblematic of the conquest of America. In the mind of most Americans this conquest was a fairly neat affair where the Indians either welcomed the arrival of the white man or recognized the futility of fighting against such a foe and assumed a position of subordination. Little could be further from the truth. Although Sacagawea may be an iconic image of the restless nature of nineteenth-century Americans, she has also been an equally iconic image of betrayal to native people much like Malinche, the Nahua woman who assisted Hernán Cortéz in his conquest of the Aztec has become to the indigenous people of Mexico. The story of Sacagawea however, is one of considerably greater fluidity, and speaks of a woman of profound strength and grace whose heart was always with her people.

She was born around the year 1787 in what is now Lemhi County, Idaho, into the Shoshone or Snake Indian tribe. Whether she was given the name Sacagawea at the time of her birth is unknown. There has been considerable debate over whether hers is a truly Shoshone name or a name given to her by the Hidatsa. Her name has been given several meanings, the most common of which is "bird woman," although it must be noted that this is not what the Shoshone would translate her name to mean. To them, Sacagawea means "canoe launcher." Little is known about her life as a child, until she entered early adolescence. She was undoubtedly taught to harvest the native plants of the Northwest and to make moccasins and clothing, because she demonstrated these skills during the months she spent with Lewis and Clark. As an infant she had apparently been promised as a wife to a man within her own tribe, and a bride price had been paid by the prospective groom's family. However, the life that had been planned for Sacagawea by her parents was wrenched from her five years before she encountered Lewis and Clark. In his diary, Meriwether Lewis recounts the event that took her from her people and set her on a course with history. Around the year 1800, Sacagawea and a group of Shoshone were attacked by members of the Minnetares or Hidatsa tribe near Jefferson's River in modern-day Idaho. It is likely the Shoshone were there collecting birch bark and other food items to store for the winter. Although the Shoshone escaped the initial attack, the Hidatsa pursued them and eventually "killed four men, four women, a number of young boys, and made prisoners of all the females and four boys." Sacagawea was among the girls taken. For the next five years she would be a prisoner of the Hidatsa and lived in their village near the Missouri River in modern-day North Dakota. Sometime in 1804 she was either purchased or won in a gambling contest by a French-Canadian fur trapper by the name of Toussaint Charbonneau, who, at the time, was about forty-five years her senior. When Charbonneau was hired by Lewis and Clark to serve as their interpreter during winter 1804–1805, he brought with him his three wives, one of whom was Sacagawea. However, the distinction of being betrothed to Charbonneau apparently was one of convenience for the trapper, and on 8 February 1805, at the insistence of William Clark, Charbonneau married Sacagawea. Three days later, she would give birth to a son, Baptiste.

When the Corps departed the Mandan villages on 7 April 1805, Sacagawea, Baptiste, and Charbonneau accompanied the group. For the next sixteen months, until August 1806, Sacagawea demonstrated her value to the expedition. Six weeks after leaving the Mandan village a squall overturned one of the boats used by the Corps; without the quick action of Sacagawea many of the items carried would have been lost. In addition to this service, she often secured food for the company when game was scarce, served as translator and guide, and provided an unseen aura of protection for the men. As both Lewis and Clark note, her presence was evidence enough to the Indians they came into contact with of the peaceful intent of the group. The relationship between the Corps members and Sacagawea grew into one of genuine affection. When Sacagawea was seriously ill for several weeks in June 1805, Clark tended to her and voiced his concern both for her recovery and of her importance to their mission. Over time, William Clark would assume a greater role in her well-being and later that of her child. On 14 August 1805, Charbonneau was reprimanded over his ill treatment of her, and when the expedition ended in 1806, Clark offered to adopt Sacagawea's child or to provide assistance to the family should they decide to settle in St. Louis.

Perhaps the most poignant reminder of the life that Sacagawea had been torn from came when the Corps met the Shoshone Indians. There negotiations for horses and supplies that were needed to carry the men to the Pacific Ocean were stalled until it was discovered that Sacagawea was the sister of the tribal chief, Cameahwait. Their joyful reunion was marred by the news that virtually all of her family had died, leaving only two brothers and the orphaned son of her eldest sister. Sacagawea, in accordance with Shoshone tradition, adopted the child, who would become known as Bazil. When the expedition left the Shoshone, Sacagawea left Bazil in the care of her brother. She would not see him again for another forty years.

Once the Corps of Discovery had completed its mission to cross the continent and the players returned to their respective lives, the story of Sacagawea's life often ends. However, the relationships developed during the expedition proved difficult to break. William Clark was appointed superintendent of Indian affairs in the Louisiana Territory and pressed his services on Charbonneau, encouraging him to settle with his family in St. Louis and even offering again to adopt Baptiste, Sacagawea's son, of whom he had grown very fond. Charbonneau took advantage of Clark's generosity and in late 1806 he left his family in Clark's care while he trapped furs in the Southwest. It appears that an on-again-off-again relationship ensued over the next five years, with Charbonneau, Sacagawea, and another wife of Charbonneau's alternating residences between the Hidatsa and St. Louis. For many the end of the story of Sacagawea occurs shortly after this time. But the evidence of how much longer Sacagawea lived is contradictory.

In 1811, Charbonneau accepted a job as an interpreter and trapper for Henry M. Brackenridge along the Missouri River. Charbonneau left his younger son Tousant, by his second wife, in the care of William Clark, and then left St. Louis with his Shoshone wife Otter Woman. For the next eighteen months Charbonneau trapped along the Missouri in the vicinity of the Fort Manuel Lisa Trading Post, near modern-day Omaha, Nebraska. Because conditions along the Missouri were frequently unsafe, Charbonneau's wife primarily remained at the fort. At the fort sometime in 1811, his wife gave birth to a child who was named Lisette. Shortly after Lisette's birth it was assumed that Charbonneau had been killed in an Indian attack. A final piece of evidence into the unfolding mystery occurred on 20 December 1812, when John Luttig, a clerk at the fort noted that Charbonneau's wife had died of "putrid fever." It has been assumed that Otter Woman was Sacagawea. Additional proof for this has been a St. Louis Orphans Court record from 11 August 1813 noting the appointment of William Clark as the guardian for both Lisette and Tousant. However, for this to have been the end of Sacagawea's life, it would be necessary for there to be no further mention of her in the historical record. This is not the case. Charbonneau, Sacagawea, Baptiste, and Tousant are mentioned in several additional records. Only Lisette fails to make another appearance.

Scholars note that Baptiste is not mentioned in the court record; the reason for this would be that his mother, Sacagawea, was still alive. According to Missouri law at the time, it was required for both parents to be proven dead for an adoption to take place. Since Charbonneau was known to have three children—Tousant, Lisette, and Baptiste—it would indicate that Charbonneau and one of his other wives had died. Considering William Clark's strong affection for Baptiste, it is inconceivable that he would not have included his name in the adoption order. Additional evidence to suggest that Sacagawea's story continued on well after 1812 can be found; it is, however, not without controversy.

By July 1816 Charbonneau had returned to St. Louis. He again repeated the same itinerant pattern of residence that characterized his life up to this point. In 1820, he again appeared with a new wife, Eagle, from the Hidatsa tribe, but soon obtained employment with another fur trading company that would have necessitated his absence from St. Louis. Charbonneau took both of his wives, Sacagawea and Eagle, with him, but left behind Tousant and Baptiste in the care of William Clark. Clark's records for the year of 1820 note receipts for tuition for both boys. In the early 1820s, while trapping in the Midwest, Charbonneau took a third wife, a member of the Ute tribe. It was this last addition to the family that ended Sacagawea's relationship with Charbonneau. When Charbonneau reportedly beat Sacagawea in front of his new wife, she abandoned him. Here the story of Sacagawea again diverges; William Clark continued to mention Sacagawea in his diary through the 1820s. However in 1830 he made a cryptic note next to her name in one entry, "dead." Whether this was his belief because he was unaware of her whereabouts or whether he had actually seen her body is not recorded. Another story indicates that Sacagawea was very much alive, and after traveling through the Southwest where she met several different tribes, including the Apache and the California Indians, she eventually settled among the Comanche, a tribal group whose language is similar to that of the Shoshone. There she remained for several years, eventually marrying a man and giving birth to five children, although only two survived their childhood. When her Comanche husband was killed sometime in the early 1840s, Sacagawea decided to return to the Shoshone. Taking her daughter Yagawosier with her, she left her son, now a man, behind with the Comanche.

Sometime around 1843, Sacagawea reappeared in the Wind River Valley and was reunited with the people she had been stolen from almost forty years earlier. During that forty year absence the West had beckoned white settlers by the thousands into the lands traditionally held by the Shoshone. Fur traders and adventurers had visited the area and harvested furs almost from the moment Lewis and Clark returned to the United States. They were followed by missionaries and traders. In the year that she reappeared among her people, Jim Bridger established a fort along the Oregon Trail in modern-day Wyoming that served as a way station for the settlers moving into the area and later as a military outpost during the Indian wars that would rock the region from the 1850–1880s. The once open ranges of the West were becoming congested. As a nation reliant on its horses for survival and wealth, the intrusion of settlers into their valleys and plains threatened the survival of the Shoshone people.

When she returned to the Shoshone, Sacagawea was reunited with Baptiste and Bazil. In the years she was absent, Baptiste had completed his education and some accounts have him living in Europe for several years before returning to the Shoshone and serving as a guide and interpreter. However, he eventually took to drinking and as impressive as his early life might have been, his later life was marked by few accomplishments. Bazil, the son Sacagawea adopted from her deceased sister, had risen to a position of prominence in the tribe. Her own son Baptiste regarded her with some indifference; however, her adopted son Bazil and she became quite close. During the 1850s and into the 1860s, Sacagawea was reported to be living near Fort Bridger and annually came into the fort to trade.

As white incursions into the land of the Shoshone continued, the Wind River Shoshone under the leadership of Washakie agreed to a treaty in 1868 that reserved the valley for them. The Fort Laramie treaty, as it was known, was a seminal event in the history of the Shoshone. The native councils that were called to discuss this treaty also drew Sacagawea out from the past.

Several members of the tribe report that she was at the council meetings and even spoke, urging the Shoshone to accept the reservation and to live in peace with the settlers. Here, however, Sacagawea is known as Porivo, or chief, because of her stature within the tribe. She would have been entering her eighties and would have been afforded great respect by members of her tribe because of her age and because of her past dealings with the whites.

In 1871, Sacagawea, Bazil, and his family moved onto the new Wind River Reservation. Because of her previous contact with whites and the respect they afforded her due to her contribution to Lewis and Clark, Sacagawea became indispensable to the Indian agents who were charged with instructing the Shoshone in agriculture. She continued her relationship with Bazil and lived in his home with his family for the rest of her life. There she remained until she died in 1884 at the age of 97.

The story of Sacagawea's life is perhaps the hardest to reconcile between what is truth and what is wishful thinking. Although much of the documentation that supported her living a long and healthy life has been lost, much still remains. For many the controversy surrounds the fact that much of this information has been taken from the oral histories of the Shoshone people. Among the Shoshone, there is no dispute over Sacagawea's long and storied life. For those who believe that Sacagawea died in 1812 of puerile fever there is even less information, and all of it is based on documents written by white men. Historians have noted that Sacagawea's story is one that changes with the needs of the time. Although Lewis and Clark found her services indispensable, the importance of her presence among the members of the Corps of Discovery has also been debated. With the forced opening of the West, she became an icon for generations of Americans who wanted to believe in the myth that the land was easily yielded to them. To the Indians though, many see her as a traitor to her own people because she helped Lewis and Clark, many others see her as a pragmatic woman, one whose knowledge of the Americans prevented untold bloodshed. In all instances she stands as an icon of the West.

FURTHER READING

Ambrose, Stephen E. *Undaunted Courage: Meriwether Lewis, Thomas Jefferson, and the Opening of the American West* (New York: Simon & Schuster, 1996).

Clark, Ella Elizabeth. *Sacagawea of the Lewis and Clark Expedition* (Berkeley: University of California Press, 1979).

Deloria, Philip Joseph. *Indians in Unexpected Places* (Lawrence: University Press of Kansas, 2004).

Howard, Harold P. *Sacagawea* (Norman: University of Oklahoma Press, 1971).

Johnson, Virginia Weisel. *The Unregimented General: A Biography of Nelson A. Miles* (Boston: Houghton Mifflin, 1962).

Wooster, Robert. *Nelson A. Miles and the Twilight of the Frontier Army* (Lincoln: University of Nebraska Press, 1993).

View of Bridal Veil Falls as seen from Wawona Trail, Yosemite Valley, California. Courtesy of Library of Congress.

Yosemite National Park

Kenneth W. McMullen

Of the names that speak to natural beauty in the West, Yosemite Valley probably heads the list. Famous photographers, writers, and artists have publicized Yosemite's grandeur as far back as the mid-1800s. If not completely synonymous with the West, Yosemite has represented an idealized vision of the American West as rugged, untamed, beautiful, and unpopulated. The last descriptor represented a falsehood.

A group of Native Americans populated Yosemite long before other Americans first set foot in the valley. The people, known as the Ahwahneechees (people of Ahwahnee) represented one of the smaller clans of the Central Miwok tribal groups. In Central Miwok Ah-wah-nee meant "place of the gaping mouth," referring to the opening that leads into the valley. It is known that the Ahwahneechees traded with, and sometimes raided, the Paiutes who lived east of the mountains near Mono Lake.

With the advent of the California Gold Rush, whites began infiltrating the area just outside of the valley. When the negative cultural interaction pattern between whites and indigenous peoples took its usual course, it resulted in a serious attempt by the Miwoks to drive the whites from the area around the eastern San Joaquin Valley foothills—the area just outside Yosemite Valley. The native attacks represented their resistance to the whites appropriating anything they wanted—including anything that belonged to the natives.

The officials in Sacramento organized some of the local men and formed the Mariposa Battalion, appointed Major James D. Savage, and made him the commanding officer. Its purpose was to pursue and destroy the Native Americans responsible for the attacks against the miners and settlers along the Merced River. Savage took a personal interest in the mission because he had been the target of some of the attacks, perhaps because he had cohabited with several different native women in the trading post he operated.

Savage's men might have been the first white men to see the valley. Many were taken with its striking appearance. They may have also originated the name of the valley. Dr. Bunnell, a member of the Mariposa Battalion, recorded that one of the men suggested Yosemite for the name of the valley because it meant, "they are killers"—referring to the Ahwahneechees. Another theory holds the name derives from the Central Miwok term for "grizzly bear."

After battles with whites and struggles with the Mono Lake natives, the Ahwahneechees fled the valley in 1853. Later they returned to live in the valley and attempted to survive in their traditional lifestyle while working for the whites that had moved into the area. Some natives found jobs at a sawmill and hotel, located in Yosemite, owned by James Mason Hutchings who at one time partnered with John Muir.

Hutchings helped to promote Yosemite's beauty with his *California Magazine*. Through it publicity artists such as Albert Bierstadt—a member of the Hudson River school—spent two months sketching the valley, and then painted several canvases showcasing the grandeur of the valley.

Although its fame grew, not many came in person due to the difficulty in getting to Yosemite. In the 1850s the trip from San Francisco to the valley took up to seven days. As the number of tourists slowly increased, some individuals filed claims on land within the valley, and a few built hotels. These land claims caused legal problems well into the twentieth century, though they were consistent with federal land policy in the 1800s. The national government wanted to distribute—sell—publicly controlled land to promote economic growth, and in Yosemite's case, help bond California to the rest of the United States by placing settlers on the frontier lands.

In contrast to those who claimed the land, the publicity surrounding the park led many to try to preserve its untrammeled beauty. Frederick Law Olmsted happened to be in California in the mid-1800s, trying to organize and run the Mariposa estate. Yosemite's beauty made an impact on Olmsted to the extent that the creator of New York City's Central Park decided that Yosemite Valley needed to be saved as a public park. Horace Greeley also wrote about the valley after his visit to Yosemite in 1859. In addition, he advocated protecting the giant redwoods just outside of Yosemite.

Working with California's senator John Conness, Olmsted and his group convinced Congress to pass the Yosemite Park Act of 1864, which President Lincoln signed on 30 June 1864. The bill set aside Yosemite Valley and the Mariposa Grove of Giant Redwoods (*Sequoia gigantean*) that Greeley wanted to be saved. The bill also authorized the state of California to oversee the park. The state appointed seven commissioners including Olmsted.

Olmsted assisted the state in formulating guidelines and policies for the maintenance of the park. Although Olmsted returned to the East a few years later, the state eventually invoked all of his recommendations, one of which involved building a road into the park to facilitate tourism.

As with all state programs, the park needed budget allocations and it tended to receive very little money. Sacramento expected, somehow, for the park to be monetarily self-sufficient, even though by 1870 tourism had only reached approximately 2500 per year. Throughout the time the state governed the valley, the park's management commission battled for funding from the state's budget. With the lack of funding, the commission relied on special concessions to private parties to raise the monies necessary for park improvements. This state of affairs left the park administration almost no money to police the boundaries of the park and enforce the rules and regulations. By the late 1880s, development for tourism had led to rundown hotels, taverns, land set aside for raising crops, and vegetable stalls. Thus, the ongoing dichotomy between promoting tourism and protecting the beauty of Yosemite started with the first commission to oversee the park, and continues today. From the view of those who wanted to preserve the land—such as John Muir—the commercialism desecrated holy ground.

The interest in nature that sprang up in the late 1800s retained some of the flavor of the Transcendentalists with the love of the countryside and the belief in the healing power of nature. Earlier writings of authors such as James Fenimore Cooper portrayed the wonderful beauty of the untamed land and spoke of it as being more beautiful than the works of man. The movement had as its impetus a need to return to nature for vacations.

One outgrowth of the urbanization of the late nineteenth century was the feeling that the evils of the growing city need to be offset by wilderness areas and parks so Americans could visit these lands and revitalize themselves. In passing, it needs to be noted that the majority of the people who fought to save Yosemite, and later Hetch Hetchy, consisted of middle-class, educated individuals who had no monetary interest in the various wilderness areas they attempted to save.

The struggle to preserve Yosemite became in some ways a struggle between the East and the West. Many of the proponents for saving natural and wilderness lands lived in the East and saw the pastoral lands in a different light than those people in the West. The Easterners saw the forested lands and meadows as places of refuge and renewal from the crowded, noisome urban environment in which many of them lived. Westerners, as a consequence of their experiences in settling the West, saw the land and all it contained as resources to be used in transforming and civilizing the wilderness.

In 1889, John Muir and Robert Underwood Johnson, publisher of *Century Magazine,* went on an extended camping trip in the Sierra Nevada Mountains. During the trip Muir and Johnson agreed to fight for national control over much of the land surrounding Yosemite Valley to save it from being denuded and destroyed by overgrazing and clear-cutting forestry. Muir was particularly incensed by the mistreatment of the alpine meadows. Their efforts resulted in the Yosemite National Park bill that President Benjamin Harrison signed on 1 October 1890. The act added over two million acres around the valley to the park without changing the status of Yosemite itself. The land added included Hetch Hetchy Valley. The law did not change the status of private holdings that now resided within the park boundaries.

Many residents in the San Joaquin Valley and foothills complained about removing that much land from potential sales. Some wondered if the government knew of valuable resources located in the now protected land and believed that the government did not want anyone else to be able to develop those resources. The bill setting aside the land for Yosemite did not align the boundaries with respect to privately held land. Farmers, herders, and timber interests claimed acres inside the park.

Shortly after he signed the bill expanding the federal holdings around Yosemite, President Harrison signed a directive ordering the U.S. Army to supply troops to garrison and control Yosemite as the army had done in Yellowstone National Park. The U.S. Army, through the efforts of General Philip Sheridan, played a major role in creating and then saving Yellowstone National Park. The army stationed troops within Yellowstone to maintain the park and enforce government regulations. The troops, although part of the War Department, in their duties as park rangers, reported to the Interior Department.

The presidential order caused men of the Fourth Cavalry, Troop I under the command of Captain Abram E. Wood, and Troop K, Captain Joseph H. Dorst commanding, to be stationed—in the spring through autumn months—in Yosemite Valley and the Mariposa Grove of Giant Redwoods, respectively. Captain Wood assumed the position of acting superintendent of Yosemite National Park. The troop's first campsite within Yosemite remains designated A.E. Wood Campsite.

Part of the frustration felt by Captain Wood came because the Interior Department replied very slowly, if at all, to the acting superintendent's repeated requests for guidelines on what his men were to enforce and what penalties Wood could assess for the various crimes encountered during the army's patrols.

A lack of accurate maps also hindered his efforts at containing depredations. Not until 1896 did the army complete its first authoritative map of the Yosemite National Park. During the intervening years, the various patrols kept notes of the terrain to help compile a more authentic composite of the territory the troops guarded. The army administered the park until 1916. The civilian National Park Service personnel replaced the army troopers during a two-year transition.

Due to a lack of thorough planning, the bill establishing the 1890 boundaries of Yosemite laid down the limits along gridlines rather than what was practical, what scenic areas needed to be included, or even with an eye toward allowing for the private holdings.

Because of the continued use of the national park lands by persons who owned holdings within the park—such as grazing or logging—in 1903 Secretary of the Interior Ethan Allen Hitchcock appointed a Yosemite Park Commission to find a solution.

The commission—named for its chairman Hiram M. Chittenden, who had served at one time as a superintendent of Yosemite Park—proposed that Congress remove from the park acreage along the western, southern, and eastern boundaries of Yosemite. This land included many of the private holdings. The legal fights over private land claims in Yosemite Valley continued up to the 1873 ruling by the U.S. Supreme Court in the case *Hutchings v. Low*, which held the government had the right to set the claims aside and regulate the parks to protect the natural beauty.

Worried about the ties between the politicians in the California government and commercial interests such as the Southern Pacific Railroad, Muir and his associates worked to have the state give control of the national park back to Washington, DC. They succeeded, in 1906, in getting the California legislature to pass a bill that relinquished title to Yosemite, and the park reverted back to both federal ownership and control.

Because of construction of a railroad and a road for automobiles leading to the park, visitation increased. To lessen the competitive expansion of facilities, in 1925 the park consolidated the concessionaires into one organization. The park continues to implement the 1980 General Management plan that focuses on integrating the increased tourism with retaining the natural beauty of the valley.

FURTHER READING

Bunnell, Lafayette Houghton. *Discovery of the Yosemite and the Indian War of 1851 Which Led to That Event*, 4th ed. (Los Angeles: G.W. Gerlicher, 1911).

Jones, Holway R. *John Muir and the Sierra Club: The Battle for Yosemite* (San Francisco: Sierra Club, 1963).

Meyerson, Harvey. *Nature's Army: When Soldiers Fought for Yosemite* (Lawrence: University Press of Kansas, 2001).

Miller, Sally M. (ed.). *John Muir: Life and Work* (Albuquerque: University of New Mexico Press, 1993).

Miller, Sally M., and Daryl Morrison (eds.). *John Muir: Family, Friends, and Adventures* (Albuquerque: University of New Mexico Press, 2005).

Wolfe, Linnie Marsh. *Son of the Wilderness: The Life of John Muir* (New York: Alfred A. Knopf, 1945).

See also the National Park Service Web site for Yosemite, www.nps.gov/yose.

Brigham Young. Courtesy of Library of Congress.

Brigham Young

Thomas G. Alexander

Brigham Young's ancestors had emigrated in the seventeenth century from England to New England, where they settled. His father, John Young, a native of Hopkinton, Massachusetts, had fought in the Revolutionary War, and his mother Abigail (Nabby) Howe was born in Shrewsbury, Massachusetts. In November 1800, John and Nabby moved to Whittingham, Vermont, where they purchased fifty acres of land. There Brigham was born on 1 June 1801, the eighth of eleven children.

Believing that the Smyrna district of Sherburne, Chenango County, in central New York offered better land than the rocky Vermont soil, the Young family moved there in 1804. Later the same year, they relocated to near Cold Brook or "Dark Hollow." There they struggled to clear land and find enough to eat to hold body and soul together. In 1813, they moved to Aurelius, Cayuga County, where they had lived only two years when Nabby died. Brigham was then only fourteen years old. John with Brigham and part of the family moved to Tyrone, an area on the Tioga River considered wilderness at the time.

Brigham grew up in a devoutly religious Methodist family. His brothers Phinehas and Joseph served as Methodist ministers. As a youth, Brigham listened to the preaching of circuit riders and attended Methodist camp meetings. Brigham developed a friendship with Hiram McKee, who later joined the ministry and with whom Brigham corresponded long after he had moved to Utah. In 1824, Brigham and his wife Miriam joined the Methodist church, apparently attracted by the emphasis on grace, free will, the witness of the Spirit, and Christian perfectionism, and the rejection of the Calvinist doctrine of election. Local people remembered Young for his "deep piety and faith in God."

In 1817, John married a second wife, Hannah Brown, and about the same time he told Brigham, then seventeen, that he needed to provide for himself. Brigham apprenticed himself in Auburn to John C. Jeffries, from whom he learned carpentry, painting, and glazing. From 1817 through 1822 Brigham helped build a marketplace, the local prison, the theological seminary, and the private home of William Brown, which William H. Seward later occupied.

In 1823 he moved to Bucksville (later called Port Byron) on the Erie Canal. He worked for a number of employers before settling with Charles Parks who manufactured furniture, pails, and buckets. Though a self-styled clumsy speaker, Young helped organize the Bucksville Forensic and Oratorical Society.

On 5 (or 8) October 1824 he married Miriam Angeline Works (1806–1832), a daughter of Asa and Abigail Works. They settled in Aurelius where Brigham continued to work at the pail factory. In late 1827 or early 1828, the young couple moved to Oswego, where they remained only a few months. Late in 1828 they moved to Mendon, where a number of his family had already located. In Mendon he developed a close friendship with Heber C. Kimball, who later served with him in the Latter-Day Saints Church's Quorum of Twelve Apostles and as a counselor in the First Presidency.

Events that took place between 1820 and 1830 changed the Youngs' lives. In 1820, 14-year-old Joseph Smith Jr., born in Vermont but then living in Palmyra, New York, experienced a theophany in which he conversed with God and Jesus Christ. Later in the decade, a resurrected being named Moroni led him to some golden plates, which he recovered, translated, and published as the Book of Mormon. Smith translated the prose into a vernacular reminiscent of the King James Bible. The book contains a religious history of some Israelite people who had emigrated from the Near East and who lived on the American continent until the collapse of their civilization in about 400 AD. The central message of the book is the authenticity of the gospel and the atonement of Jesus Christ, and the central occurrence is the visit of the resurrected Christ to these people on the American continent. Continuing in his spiritual quest, Smith and the associates he attracted to his teachings founded the Church of Christ, later renamed The Church of Jesus Christ of Latter-Day Saints. Members, who are often called Mormons or Latter-Day Saints (often abbreviated LDS), are Christians who believe their religion is the restoration of primitive Christianity, but they are not Protestants.

Smith sent out missionaries to preach the restored gospel, and in April 1830 Samuel H. Smith, Joseph's younger brother, came to Mendon where he gave Brigham's brother, Phinehas, a Book of Mormon. Phinehas read the book and passed it on to the remainder of the family. The book and the teachings of Mormon missionaries converted virtually all of the Young and Kimball families. In April 1832, Brigham, Miriam, and eleven other relatives—all of his immediate family—were baptized into the LDS Church. Like many other nineteenth-century converts, Young began serving as a missionary. He preached in western New York and in Canada.

As neighbors attested, Young had frequently sought religious enlightenment. In Mormonism, Young and his family found answers to troubling questions. The Latter-Day Saints believed in prophetic leadership, continuing revelation, Christ's atonement, universal salvation, and priesthood ordination for all righteous men. Mormons rejected the doctrines of infant baptism and original sin. They also preached a religion that could embrace truth from whatever source, including other religions. This doctrine attracted Brigham perhaps most of all. Brigham also reveled in the expressions of personal piety in the new religion. He and others in the infant church practiced speaking in tongues, the Pentecostal experience mentioned in the Book of Acts.

Early in their marriage, Miriam contracted tuberculosis. To Brigham's intense sorrow, she died from the disease in 1832, shortly after the two were baptized. Her disability left Brigham to care for the household and two daughters, Elizabeth and Vilate, while continuing to work as a carpenter and farm laborer and preaching for the new religion. Vilate Kimball, Heber's wife, helped him care for his daughters.

Members also believed in gathering in covenant communities. During the 1830s, the church established two centers—Kirtland, Ohio, near Cleveland,

and Independence, Jackson County, Missouri, near Kansas City. In fall 1833, Brigham moved to Kirtland where Smith had established the church's headquarters. There Young worked as a builder, and he continued preaching. He helped in construction of the Latter-Day Saints' temple in Kirtland where members participated in the sort of charismatic and Pentecostal experiences Young found enlightening and satisfying. On 18 February 1834 he married Mary Ann Angell (1803–1882), a native of Seneca, Ontario County, New York, who helped rear his two children by Miriam and bore six other children.

Although Joseph lived for most of the 1830s in Kirtland, he had designated Independence as the site of the New Jerusalem, the place for a covenant community and the site for Christ's second coming. He expected members to construct a town; live in an economic system of shared property, goods, and services; and to build temples both for religious and secular purposes. In practice, however, the separation of the two spheres had little meaning throughout most of nineteenth-century Mormonism.

As Mormons poured into Jackson County, they tried to purchase all the property in the area, they preached unusual doctrines, and they seemed to befriend free African Americans. The non-Mormons opposed Mormon settlement, for what reason or combination of reasons is unclear. By 1833, opposition to the Mormons led the old settlers to organize mobs, attack people and burn houses, tar and feather two of the leaders, and kill some of the members. Missouri's political leaders offered little help. Eventually, to escape mob violence, the Mormons fled across the Missouri River to Clay County.

Learning of the mobbing and driving while in Kirtland and believing that Missouri's governor, Daniel Dunklin, would assist in redeeming the Saints' property, Joseph Smith planned a rescue mission. He called on members in the East and Midwest to form a paramilitary unit called Zion's Camp. Members of the unit resolved to travel to Missouri to help recover the property lost to the mobs and to help the members return to their homes in Jackson County. On 5 May 1834, Brigham joined Zion's Camp. The expedition traveled from Kirtland, Ohio, into Missouri arousing curiosity on the way. Missouri's governor disappointed Smith, because when given the opportunity to assist the refugees, he declined to do so. The expedition failed, in part because of a plague of cholera among its members, in part because the governor refused to assist them, and in part because the Missouri mobbers greatly outnumbered them.

On the road to Missouri, however, participants listened to Joseph preach and experienced his charismatic gifts as they traveled from one point to another. Thus participants developed a close relationship with Smith and with each other. It is not surprising that many of the participants emerged as leaders in the fledgling church, some becoming members of the Quorum of Twelve Apostles.

In February 1835 at age thirty-four, Young was called as a member of the original Quorum of Twelve Apostles. Smith assigned the Twelve to preach throughout the world and to preside over outside areas organized into districts called stakes in which large numbers of members lived. At first Young and others in the Twelve preached in Ohio, New York, New England, and Ontario, Canada. His family remained in Kirtland, and Young returned there frequently to work and participate in church activities.

Early in 1837, recognizing the need for a circulating medium, Joseph Smith and a number of the leaders proposed to charter a bank in Kirtland. The Ohio legislature refused to grant them a charter, but they opened the bank anyway. It failed because those outside Kirtland refused to accept its notes, and the ensuing depression of 1837 exacerbated the Mormons' economic plight. Its failure and other problems led a group of men to oppose Smith's leadership and to try to unseat him as church president.

Young rejected the dissenters and supported Smith. Fearful of personal injury, Young left Kirtland for the Mormon settlements in northern Missouri in late December 1837. Smith himself fled to Missouri in early 1838.

After most Mormons had settled in northern Missouri in the area around Far West, conflicts between them and other Missourians quickly developed. These led to the defection of a number of prominent Mormons including Thomas B. Marsh, then president of the Quorum of Twelve, and the killing of Apostle David Patten, senior to Young in the Twelve. The defection and death of these two senior members left Young as president of the quorum. As the battle between the Mormons and Missourians proceeded, Missouri governor Lillburn W. Boggs, who had replaced Daniel Dunklin, issued a proclamation ordering the militia to "exterminate" the Mormons or drive them from the state. In the wake of this order Missouri militiamen arrested and imprisoned Joseph Smith and several of the other leaders. Young, who remained as one of the senior Latter-Day Saints still at large, helped organize the forced exodus of the members from Missouri to Illinois.

The Saints gathered first in Quincy, Illinois, and then, after Smith and his associates escaped from custody, they settled on a bend of the Mississippi in Hancock County at a town called "Commerce." They renamed the town "Nauvoo," said to be a word of Hebrew derivation meaning "beautiful place." Some of the Saints settled west of the river in Iowa, and Young moved his family to Montrose, Iowa, in 1839. Young and others contracted a disease they called fever and ague—probably malaria.

Late in 1839, in a sickened condition, Brigham with most of the Twelve left their families on the Mississippi and accepted a call to proselytize for the church in Great Britain. When they arrived early in 1840, they found Great Britain in upheaval. Rapidly spreading industrialization had attracted men and women from the countryside to the cities, and poverty, filth, and disease seemed the lot of most of the working class. Young and his associates in the Twelve together with other missionaries converted hundreds of people.

Heeding Joseph Smith's teaching to gather with the Saints into covenant communities, most of those who remained faithful emigrated from Great Britain.

Those who traveled during the early 1840s gathered in Nauvoo. Later emigrants joined the Saints in Utah after the exodus.

While in England, Young proposed, and the others agreed, to expand the work in other ways. They published a British edition of the Book of Mormon and a hymnal. They also began the publication of the *Latter-day Saints Millennial Star*, appointing Parley P. Pratt, one of the senior members of the Twelve, as editor.

Young and most of the Twelve returned to Nauvoo in April 1841. After their return, Joseph Smith enlarged the responsibilities of the Twelve by laying the major business of the church on their shoulders. The membership of the church ratified this decision in a conference held in August 1841. Thereafter, the Twelve assumed responsibility for calling missionaries, assigning them to their fields of labor, and otherwise directing the proselytizing efforts of the church. Young and the other apostles took responsibility for other matters including the publication of the *Nauvoo Neighbor*, a local newspaper, and the *Times and Seasons*, a religious periodical.

Young, members of the Twelve, and others continued to preach Mormonism, and they took care of their own affairs. Young, Heber C. Kimball, Apostle Wilford Woodruff, and others built brick homes in a town that had previously been filled with log cabins. A number of these homes, including Brigham's, have remained and have been restored. Young also joined the Masons as did many of the men in Nauvoo, and he participated as an actor in local dramatic presentations.

During the Nauvoo period, Smith also announced a number of new doctrines. These included temple ordinances called "endowments," which presented a series of dramas explaining how to achieve salvation. In the temple services, members entered into religious covenants in which they pledged an additional degree of righteousness and commitment. Temple ordinances included also vicarious baptism and endowments on behalf of the dead who had not heard the gospel while they were alive and marriage for time and all eternity for the living and the dead. Smith also preached that the existence of each human being reached backward co-eternally with God, that after death the righteous could return to Heaven to live as resurrected beings with God and Christ, and that the faithful could become Gods and Goddesses themselves.

Young and other select members received the earliest endowments in rooms above Smith's red brick store, but under Smith's teaching they came to realize that they must construct a temple to perform the ordinances. Young and others in the Twelve assisted in collecting funds for the temple, and, after construction began, they assisted in building the new edifice.

Smith had already begun the practice of plural marriage himself as early as 1835. In Nauvoo, however, he married a number of other women. As Smith married additional women, including some with living husbands, the practice became an open secret in Nauvoo. In 1843 he began revealing the principle to a select group, including Young and other members of the Twelve. Young and others resisted the practice at first because it contradicted their moral codes, but most eventually accepted it because they believed Smith was a prophet authorized to reveal God's will to them.

Anti-Mormon activity had begun to rear its ugly head in Illinois as it had in Ohio and Missouri, and the Mormons tended to vote as a block for candidates friendly to them. Disturbed by the failure of the federal government to help them as the Missouri government assisted in driving them from their homes, Smith sought to find out the views on the Mormons of prominent presidential candidates as the 1844 presidential election approached. To do so, he sent letters to a number of them. He received replies from some of them, but none was satisfactory. As a result, in spring 1844, Smith announced his candidacy for the presidency of the United States. He sent representatives, including Young, on missions to stump for his candidacy throughout the Northeast, Midwest, and upper South.

In the meantime, anti-Mormon rhetoric had turned to violence in Hancock County as it had in Ohio and Missouri. Mobs attacked outlying settlements, burning homes and outbuildings and forcing many of those outside Nauvoo to flee to the city for refuge. Anti-Mormons followed the lead of Thomas Sharp, editor of the *Warsaw Signal*, who urged community violence against the Mormons. Sharp and other anti-Mormons preached that the local citizens should either kill the Mormons or drive them from the state.

While Young and the others were away preaching, internal opposition surfaced as well. A group of dissidents including one of Smith's counselors in the First Presidency published a newspaper—the *Nauvoo Expositor*—in which they denounced Smith and excoriated the practice of polygamy. Outraged by the personal attacks, the city council, with Smith's approval, declared the newspaper a public nuisance and had the city police force destroy the press.

In response to this action, county authorities swore out complaints against Joseph Smith and his brother Hyrum. Though they at first considered escape, the Smith brothers eventually surrendered to the authorities and were taken to the county seat at Carthage where a judge ordered them jailed.

Illinois governor Thomas Ford had promised to protect Joseph and Hyrum Smith, but on 27 June 1844, a mob made up principally of Illinois militiamen stormed the jail. They murdered Joseph and Hyrum and severely wounded Apostle John Taylor, who was visiting them. In a letter to William W. Phelps following the murders, Ford said that though he deplored the murders he joined with the majority in believing that it was a good thing the Smiths were dead.

News traveled slowly in 1844, but when members of the Twelve and Smith's remaining counselor Sidney Rigdon, who were all in the Eastern states, learned of the murders, they returned to Nauvoo. In a special conference in Nauvoo on 8 August 1844, the majority of the members spurned Rigdon and voted to accept Young and the Twelve as a collective presidency. Some dissidents, including Rigdon and James J. Strang, organized competing churches, and a number of those who remained in the Midwest, including Joseph's wife Emma Hale Smith and his immediate family, later founded the Reorganized Church of Jesus Christ of Latter Day Saints with Joseph's eldest son, Joseph Smith III, as president.

Joseph Smith's death did not end the anti-Mormon violence or the pressure to force the Mormons to flee from Illinois. Young and the other leaders in Nauvoo continued to construct the temple and to give baptisms and endowments in the partly completed structure. At the same time they began to plan for a westward movement. They read accounts of the West from mountain men and travelers, and they studied the reports of John C. Frémont's expeditions, especially of the exploration of the Bear River country and the Wasatch Front, both in present-day Utah. They also read Lansford Hastings's emigrant's guide that proposed a route into the Great Basin as a part of the trail to California.

Continued anti-Mormon violence led most of the Saints to abandon Nauvoo. Young directed the exodus. Beginning on 4 February, the Mormons struggled through the muddy trails of an Iowa spring, making several settlements along the way. In early 1846, the Mexican-American War broke out, and President James K. Polk authorized the recruitment of a battalion of 500 Mormons to assist in opening a route to California. The Mormon Battalion journeyed to California by way of Santa Fe, southern New Mexico, and the Gila River in present-day Arizona. The pay for this battalion helped finance the exodus to the Salt Lake Valley while taking a large number of emigrants West as well.

At the same time, Samuel Brannan, leader of the Saints in New York, chartered passage on a ship, the *Brooklyn*, to take Eastern Saints to California. They rounded South America, touched in Hawaii, and sailed to San Francisco, then called Yerba Buena. They also established a settlement called "New Hope," and Brannan traveled eastward to try unsuccessfully to convince Young to bring the Saints to California.

Instead of pushing on west in 1846, Young and the other leaders decided to winter on the Missouri. They established settlements along the Missouri stretching outward from Council Bluffs, then called Kanesville, on the Iowa side and Florence, then named Winter Quarters, on the Nebraska side. In April 1847, Young led the first group of pioneers westward from Winter Quarters to the Salt Lake Valley.

The route west became a journey in which the participants transported themselves not only from the Midwest to the Far West, but also from conventional time to sacred time. In a sense, it recapitulated the exodus of the Children of Israel from Egypt to the promised land, except in this case, Young played the role both of Moses and Joshua.

On the way, they met with explorers who had visited the region previously. These included Father Pierre De Smet, Jim Bridger, and Miles Goodyear, who had established a settlement at the confluence of the Weber and Ogden Rivers at the site of the later city of Ogden, Utah.

Two of Young's colleagues, Apostles Orson Pratt and Erastus Snow, arrived in the valley on 22 July, and the bulk of the original party entered on 23 July. This group began plowing, damming City Creek for irrigation water, and planting crops.

Young had been afflicted with what they called "mountain fever," a disease that later authorities have labeled "Colorado tick fever." As a result, he did not enter the valley until Saturday, 24 July.

The ecology of the valley of the Great Salt Lake elicited divergent responses from the emigrants. Wilford Woodruff thought it a beautiful sight—a fit dwelling for the Latter-Day Saints. Harriet Young, wife of Brigham's brother Lorenzo, however, said that she would gladly travel another thousand miles rather than settle where no self-respecting white man could make a living. Incapacitated and laying in the back of Wilford Woodruff's carriage, Young asked Woodruff to turn around the carriage. According to later observers, he lifted himself to view the valley and told those present that this was the place for the Saints to build their kingdom.

On Sunday, 25 July, members of the party conducted religious services, and for the next couple of days they made a circuit of the valley. Returning to the site where the first group had begun to plow and plant on 23 July, the explorers determined it offered the best place for their initial settlement. On 28 July, Young designated the site for the temple.

Young and his associates laid out the city on a variation of a plan that Smith had devised for Jackson County, Missouri's city of Zion. Blocks were to be ten acres in size and lots were to be large enough to hold gardens and domestic animals like cows and chickens. Young said that he wanted the streets built wide enough so teamsters could turn around wagons with ox teams without having to back them up. Larger farms were located in fields south of the city. At first, because of Young's general policy, no one paid for their town lots or farms. Each occupant paid a $1.50 surveying fee.

Several additional parties entered the city during the summer and early fall. By the end of the year perhaps 2000 people had immigrated to the Salt Lake Valley.

In August 1847, Young and many of the pioneer party returned to Council Bluffs to bring their families and escort others to their new Zion. In a conference held in December 1847, the members at Council Bluffs sustained him as church president and prophet, seer, and revelator. Young returned to Utah in 1848 and remained there the rest of his life, except for a short excursion to Mormon settlements in Oregon Territory.

In presiding over the church, Young recognized no division between the secular and sacred. He directed the establishment of nearly 400 settlements in Utah, Idaho, Wyoming, Arizona, Nevada, Washington, and California. To preside over ecclesiastical and secular work in the settlements Young called bishops with two counselors to lead each congregation, which the Mormons called "wards." Young organized the wards in each county into units called stakes, presided over by a stake president, two counselors, and a twelve-man stake high council. People in the settlements carried out normal tasks such as apportioning land, building homes, planting farms, and constructing irrigation works.

In the larger settlements, Young divided the communities into multiple wards. He organized Salt Lake City, for instance, into nineteen wards. He eventually established a twentieth ward after the development of the Avenues area in the northeastern portion of the city.

Young sent out exploring parties to determine the best sites for agricultural communities and the location of needed minerals and lumber. In general, the people established the first settlements along the eastern edge of the Great Basin on the west side of the Wasatch Mountains, which bisect Utah in a north-south line from Cache Valley on the north to Nephi in Juab County on the south. From Nephi south, high plateaus continue the north-south–trending high country line. Present-day Interstate Highway 15 follows the general line of the Wasatch Mountains and plateaus. Over the next decade settlements first moved north to Davis County, Ogden, and Brigham City and south to Utah Valley and to Sanpete Valley east of the I-15 corridor.

Young used various methods to select settlers for these ventures. In some cases, he or one of his associates read names from the pulpit at conferences. In others, he called someone to lead the settlement and authorized them to select others to go with them. In a number of places, he simply allowed the people to choose to go on their own volition.

Young also envisioned a line of settlements stretching from Salt Lake City to the southern California coast at San Diego. Some of these were designed to supply the Saints with needed commodities. He sent an iron mission to Parowan and Cedar City in southern Utah in an attempt to supply iron for manufactured goods. A lead mission went to Las Vegas Springs near present-day Las Vegas, Nevada, to supply lead. Farming and ranching communities were established in San Bernardino in California and at Carson Valley in what is now western Nevada. Following the discovery of gold at Sutter's Fort in present-day Sacramento, Young even dispatched missionaries to pan for the yellow metal.

In spite of the proximity to Salt Lake City, because of information from Lansford Hastings and Jim Bridger, Young erroneously believed that freezing cold during the summer made settlement in Cache Valley in northern Utah unwise. As a result, the first settlements there did not take place until several settlers from Tooele petitioned to move to Cache Valley in 1856, long after settlements in southern Utah, western Nevada, and southern California.

Young, himself, occupied the property east of Temple Square. He first constructed a row of log cabins on what is now First Avenue, near the current site of the private cemetery in which he and some of his family members were buried. During the 1850s he constructed two adobe houses, the Beehive House and Lion House, on what was then called "Brigham Street"—now South Temple. He housed some of his families in these two houses. Between the two dwellings, he built a one-story building that served as his office. Behind these structures, Young developed a compound that included a gristmill, facilities for livestock, granaries, other outbuildings, a store, and a schoolhouse. In addition, Young owned a farm in the southern Salt Lake City and a number of other farms, ranches, and mills. He grazed cattle on public land in Cache Valley. A deed of trust, written in 1855, transferring his property to the LDS Church listed the total worth at $200,000. Like other deeds of trust written during the 1850s, this was never executed.

Because Native Americans already lived in Utah, the expanding Mormon settlements quickly conflicted with the hunting, fishing, farming, and gathering settlements of these peoples. Salt Lake Valley stood between lands occupied by the Shoshone to the north, Goshute to the west, and Ute to the south. Conflicts occurred almost immediately with the Shoshone to the north and the Ute to the south. The bloodiest of these conflicts undoubtedly occurred in Utah Valley. In fact, after receiving reports from local Mormon leaders, Young authorized what amounted to a war of extermination against the Utes of Utah Valley. He rescinded his order, however, when cooler heads let him know that the settlers had caused most of the problems that led to the conflicts.

What amounted to a virtual full-scale war occurred with the Goshute during the early 1860s. Also during the early 1860s, the U.S. Army under Patrick Edward Connor carried on a series of campaigns that nearly eradicated the Shoshone from Utah. The Mormon militia participated in most of the conflicts with the Utes, including the Walker War of 1853–1854 and the Black Hawk War of 1865–1872. These conflicts and federal policy led to the removal of most of these tribes to reservations. The major exceptions were the Paiutes, who remained in southern Utah but who were eventually settled on reservations in that region, and the Navajo, who remained in southeastern Utah.

Young also presided over the economic development of the territory. He supervised the establishment of a telegraph line, cooperated in building the transcontinental railroad, directed the construction of local railroads, and founded cooperative ventures. Anxious both to mitigate the impact of rowdy railroad construction teams on the community and to accumulate funds for local development, Young contracted to grade roadbeds for the Union and Central Pacific Railroads in Utah territory. His associates recruited workers to construct the railroad grade from various communities in northern Utah. Unfortunately, the railroads declined to pay the full agreed-upon amounts, and in some cases he had to accept ties, tracks, and equipment in payment. These were used to help construct the Utah Central Railroad from Salt Lake City to Ogden, the junction point of the Union and Central Pacific. The church leaders also donated land for the Central (later Southern) Pacific marshaling yards in Ogden to locate the yards in a Mormon community and bypass Corinne, which had been founded by non-Mormons as a competitor to the Mormon communities.

Young also projected railroads south from Salt Lake City and north from Ogden. The Mormons completed the Utah Southern Railroad to Chicken Creek in Juab County before selling it to the Union Pacific, who completed it to Milford and Frisco in Southern Utah in the nineteenth century and eventually to San Pedro, California, in the twentieth century. The Mormons completed the Utah Northern to Franklin in southern Idaho before selling a controlling interest to the Union Pacific interests who completed it to Dillon, Montana.

Young espoused an economic philosophy of mercantilism rather than agrarianism or laissez-faire capitalism. He wanted to promote the self-sufficiency of Utah's intermountain kingdom. As a result, he had the Saints undertake several activities aimed at promoting self-sufficiency. The agricultural settlements generally succeeded as did some of the mining ventures, such as coal mining at various places and salt mining on Great Salt Lake. Some of the manufacturing ventures failed miserably. John Taylor brought equipment for sugar manufacture from France, but the Saints lacked the technological skill to make it function properly. The group of Welsh, Scots, and English who settled Cedar City succeeded in making a few iron implements, but in general that effort failed as well, and Young released those who wished to leave from their responsibility to the mission. During the 1860s, Young attempted to promote the local growth of cotton and the manufacture of cotton textiles. These ventures succeeded only partially.

On the other hand, some of the manufacturing ventures succeeded. These included the Consolidated Wagon and Machine which produced various implements into the early twentieth century. A number of wool mills, including a mill at Provo, also succeeded during the nineteenth century.

During the 1850s, Young also sent out missionaries to spread the gospel to Native Americans. These missions went, among other places, to Fort Lemhi in what is now Idaho; Fort Bridger in what is now Wyoming; and Moab Harmony, Pinto, and Santa Clara in Utah. With the exception of the three in southwestern Utah, most of the missions failed to achieve their goals and were abandoned, in the cases of Fort Lemhi and Moab after attacks by the local Indians.

Young also worked with his two counselors and the Quorum of the Twelve Apostles in organizing the church in the intermountain area and in spreading the gospel abroad. Missionaries proselytized in Asia, South America, Oceana, the United States, and Western and Southern Europe. Unlike the current situation in which members of the Quorum of Twelve Apostles generally live in the Wasatch Front area and take assignments to supervise missionary and church work in various parts of the world on a temporary basis, Young assigned Apostles to settle in various areas and visit Salt Lake City infrequently for council meetings. Orson Hyde, for instance, established settlements in Wyoming

and in Carson Valley, Nevada, before settling in Sanpete County. After pros-
elytizing in various parts of Europe including Northern Italy, Lorenzo Snow
supervised the cooperative settlement in Brigham City. Charles C. Rich and
Amasa Lyman superintended the settlement at San Bernardino, California.
Afterward, Rich supervised the settlement in the Bear Lake region of northern
Utah and southern Idaho. After Lyman returned from San Bernardino, Young
assigned him to supervise settlements in and near Fillmore in central Utah.
Young sent Erastus Snow to St. George to supervise the cotton mission. He
sent Franklin D. Richards to Ogden to supervise the Weber County settlements. Marriner W. Merrill went to Cache Valley to oversee the settlements in
northern Utah.

Young also concerned himself with the educational welfare of the Saints.
He instructed each bishop to organize an elementary—then called common—
school in their ward. Ordinarily the school children met in the ward meeting-
house, though in some cases separate school buildings were constructed. Local
people financed the schools from taxes, contributions, and tuition.

Young also promoted various types of recreational activity. Various wards
and groups regularly held dances, theater presentations, and concerts that
were open to both Mormons and non-Mormons. Young and most of the
church leaders eschewed what were called round dances—waltzes, polkas,
and other dances in which partners came in close contact. They favored
instead square dances, schottishes, and reels. It was said that Young, himself,
danced well. Choirs sprang up in various wards, and Young promoted the
development of the Mormon Tabernacle Choir which emerged in later years
as a world-renowned organization.

Perhaps the most important recreational activity was the theater. Young
encouraged the development of theater groups in wards throughout the
church. He helped organize the Deseret Dramatic Association in 1850. Most
important, he threw his wholehearted support into the building of the Salt
Lake Theater. The theater, which was completed in 1862, held an audience of
7500. Young and other church leaders subscribed to boxes at the theater. The
theater boasted its own resident company, and it gave employment to a number
of skilled artists who painted scenery for its various productions. In addition,
the theater hosted traveling companies and became noted as the most important
venue between the bend of the Missouri and the Pacific Coast. Young himself
believed that the theater could be a great educator and enjoyed, in addition to
romantic comedies, Shakespearean dramas. During Young's lifetime, the theater mounted multiple performances of *Hamlet*, *Macbeth*, *Richard III*, *Romeo
and Juliet*, *Othello*, and *Merchant of Venice*.

As leader of the Latter-Day Saints people, Young also ventured into politics.
After the Mormons arrived in Utah, they organized the provisional State of
Deseret. They drew the boundaries of the state to include all of the Great
Basin, Arizona to the Gila River, and a portion of Southern California stretching
to the Pacific Coast at San Diego. The people elected Young governor of the

provisional state. Utahns then petitioned Congress to grant them either state-hood or territorial status. Consulting with Pennsylvania aristocrat Thomas L. Kane, they concluded that territorial status would burden them with unfriendly outside appointees; they favored statehood.

President Zachary Taylor declined to do anything for the Utahns, but after his death and the succession of Vice President Millard Fillmore to the presidency, Congress organized Utah Territory as part of the Compromise of 1850. Fillmore appointed Young as territorial governor and superintendent of Indian affairs, and he split the appointive positions between Mormons and non-Mormons—or Gentiles as they were generally called in the nineteenth century.

Young continued to serve as governor until 1857, and Kane's prediction proved prophetic. Conflicts with federal judges and other Mormon haters led to tense relations with the federal government during much of Young's tenure. Utahns elected Mormons as territorial delegates and as members of the territorial legislature, but many of the presidential appointees—including the majority of territorial secretaries and territorial district and Supreme Court judges—were Gentiles. Frightened by their contact with Utahns, two of the judges and the territorial secretary had fled during the early 1850s.

In 1856 and early 1857, Young had followed the lead of his counselor, Jedediah M. Grant, in promoting a "Reformation" among the Mormon people. The leaders urged the members to renew their commitment to Mormonism by presenting themselves for rebaptism.

They devised a catechism with a series of questions to be asked the members to determine their level of faithfulness. Of the nineteen questions, none asked about the members' beliefs. Rather, all inquired into actions. The catechism asked whether members had committed murder, theft, or adultery, spoken against principles in the scriptures, lied about others, paid their tithing, taught the gospel to their families, bathed frequently, paid their debts, worked six days a week, worshiped on Sunday, taken God's name in vain, or drunken alcohol to excess.

Young also preached some of his most controversial doctrines, some of which the subsequent church leadership has repudiated. These included the notion that Christ's death and resurrection did not cover some of the most serious sins and that to achieve salvation those who had committed murder would have to present themselves to have their own blood shed. In a second doctrine, also repudiated, Young had argued that God, the Father, and Adam were the same person.

In 1854 following the 1853 massacre of John W. Gunnison and his party on the Sevier River, Maj. Edward W. Steptoe led an investigating party to Utah. After investigating the massacre, Steptoe concluded, rightly, that Young and the Mormon leadership had played no part in the massacre, which had been perpetrated by Pahvant Utes in retaliation for the murder of several of their people by a passing emigrant train. Three of the Pahvants were later convicted of manslaughter, a verdict that upset the presiding judge, John F. Kinney. Kinney had wanted a verdict of first-degree murder.

Following this trial, conditions in Utah deteriorated. Kinney, territorial surveyor general, David H. Burr, and Judge William W. Drummond all sent letters to Washington condemning the Mormons in general and Brigham Young in particular. Drummond's letters, in particular, carried a number of lies including charges that Young had masterminded the Gunnison massacre, the murder of federal judge Leonidas Shaver, and the massacre of former territorial delegate Almon W. Babbitt and members of his party.

Instead of conducting an investigation of these charges President James Buchanan ordered Young's removal as governor, the appointment of Alfred Cumming of Georgia as his replacement, and the dispatch of an army supposed to have been 2500 men (though in actuality much smaller) to escort the new governor. He also replaced all of the Mormon appointees with Gentiles, many of whom were antagonistic to the Mormon majority. Following these removals, no Mormons were appointed to federal positions until after 1890. Fearful of the possibility of army-initiated massacres reminiscent of the treatment they had received in Missouri and Illinois, the Mormons under Young's orders and under the command of Daniel H. Wells prepared to repel the expedition.

In preparation for the defense of Utah, Young sent Apostle George A. Smith to the settlements south of Salt Lake City. Smith told the people to prepare for a possible siege, to muster the territorial militia, and to avoid selling supplies to emigrants. Unfortunately, the first emigrant train to pass through Utah following Smith's southern journey ran afoul of zealots from Cedar City and points south. Led by Jack Baker and Alexander Fancher, the party, whose journey originated in Arkansas, consisted of perhaps 150 men, women, and children and 500 to 800 cattle.

After some conflicts over the unwillingness of the settlers to sell goods to them, members of the emigrant party ran into difficulty in Cedar City. They declined to pay what they considered an exorbitant price for milling some wheat, and they reportedly harassed Barbara Morris, wife of a counselor in the bishopric and mother of a member of the stake presidency. Wanting to chastise the party, stake president Isaac Haight sent some militiamen after them and ordered John D. Lee, then serving as Indian farmer in New Harmony to gather Paiutes to assist in attacking the emigrants. He also called a meeting of the stake high council, and when the high council balked at his proposal to chastise the party, they agreed to send James Haslam to Salt Lake City to ask Brigham Young for his counsel on the matter.

In the meantime, while Haslam rode to Salt Lake City, the militiamen and their Paiute allies attacked the emigrants, who were then camped at Mountain Meadows. The militia killed some of the party, and the Indians suffered some casualties on Monday, 7 September, but they continued sporadic attacks during the week as Haslam continued toward Utah's capital city.

Haslam arrived on Thursday, 10 September 1857, and when Young heard about the proposal, he figuratively hit the ceiling. He sent Haslam south with a letter telling Isaac Haight to let the party pass unmolested. Haslam did not reach Cedar City until Sunday, 13 September.

In the meantime, Haight had sent more militiamen to Mountain Meadows with an order to massacre the party, except children under eight. Under a ruse that drew the emigrants from their hastily built fort of wagons, the militiamen murdered the men, women, and most of the children in cold blood. They saved only seventeen of the small children. Just what role the Paiutes played in the massacre is not clear, but the militiamen did most of the killing.

Some writers have asserted that Young, himself, ordered the massacre. There is no direct evidence that he did so, and the circumstantial evidence also leads to the conclusion that beyond the fact that he had sent Smith south to warn about the coming army and to instruct the people to prepare for possible conflict or siege, there is no evidence of his complicity. Mormon—or Brigham—haters, however, have continued to insist on his complicity substituting rhetoric or seriously flawed logic for evidence.

In 1858, after disputes over the Utah war had been settled, federal officials investigated the massacre, and they had the story fairly well worked out by 1859. Young, himself, also had associates conduct investigations. In 1859, he offered to go south himself to maintain order while the federal judges conducted trials of the accused. Young had the support in these efforts of Governor Cumming and U.S. Attorney Alexander Wilson. Some other federal officials, especially Chief Justice Delana R. Eckels and U.S. Marshal Peter Dotson, spurned Young's help. In 1859, however, Young had Apostles Smith and Amasa Lyman remove the perpetrators from their ecclesiastical positions. After a further investigation conducted by Apostle Erastus Snow and Bishop Lorenzo Roundy, in 1870 the Quorum of the Twelve excommunicated John D. Lee and Isaac Haight for complicity in the massacre. Young reinstated Haight in 1874, apparently because his supporters erroneously convinced the president that the stake president's only sin was his inability to control Lee.

Lee was the only person convicted of the crime. Tried successfully in 1876, Lee was executed at Mountain Meadows in 1877. None of the other perpetrators was tried, in part because of lack of evidence, in part because some of them received immunity by turning state's evidence, and in part because some of them, including Haight, were never captured.

In retrospect, the Mountain Meadows Massacre remains as a blot on Utah's history, and for some on Young's reputation. It is impossible to prove a counterfactual proposition, but some things seem evident. Most probably, without the hysteria generated by the advancing army and fear of a possible repeat of the mobbings and murders of Missouri and Illinois, the massacre would never have taken place.

In the meantime, the good offices of friends of the Mormons and of federal officials settled the conflict. Thomas L. Kane, who had developed sympathy for the Mormons, secured the support of President Buchanan to travel to Utah to try to negotiate a settlement. Arriving in Salt Lake City on 25 February, Kane met with Young and other church leaders. After securing approval of Young for his course of action, Kane traveled under Mormon escort to Fort Bridger, called Camp Scott by the army, where the army and federal appointees had camped for the winter. He met with Governor Cumming, who agreed to come with him to Salt Lake City.

Instead of a state of rebellion, Cumming found the Mormon community prepared to acknowledge him as governor but so afraid of abuse by the army that they had abandoned the city and fled south. Cumming and Kane began a journey south to investigate the Mountain Meadows Massacre, but word of the incapacity of Kane's father led them to return to Camp Scott. Cumming told the army commander Col. Albert Sydney Johnston that the Mormons had everywhere acknowledged him as governor, but that they feared the army.

An official delegation led by Lazarus Powell and Ben McCulloch came to Utah with a proclamation of amnesty issued by President Buchanan. Young and the Mormons accept the amnesty, Cumming took office, and the federal officials took their places. The army marched through a deserted Salt Lake City and on to Cedar Valley where they established Camp Floyd, named for Secretary of War John Floyd. Afterward the Mormons returned to their homes in Salt Lake City.

During the late 1860s, Young became particularly concerned about the disruption that the coming of the railroad would cause. He and other Latter-Day Saints favored the introduction of the railroad because it would make the gathering of the members easier and more economical. Nevertheless he understood that it would also introduce more of a rowdy element into the Mormon community.

In part to combat the influence of the railroad, in part to promote communitarian economic development, and in part to promote increased spirituality, Young initiated a number of programs during the 1860s. He re-inaugurated the School of the Prophets, a program in adult spiritual and secular education first inaugurated by Joseph Smith in Kirtland. Entrance to the school was by ticket issued by Young and by bishops, and the organization spread throughout the territory. To promote thrift and spirituality among young women, Young inaugurated the retrenchment association, which eventually grew into the Young Women's Mutual Improvement Association. This organization promoted a number of educational, cultural, and recreational activities for young women.

During the 1850s, a number of wards had successfully inaugurated relief societies. These were organizations of mature women who sought to alleviate poverty among whites and Indians and to assist in the temporal and spiritual welfare of women and families. During the 1860s, Young promoted the development of a church-wide organization. To do so, he enlisted the skills of Eliza R. Snow, one of his plural wives and the acknowledged leader of women in the church. The organization continued the sort of compassionate service promoted by the ward organizations during the 1850s and promoted Pentecostal experiences, blessings, and healings among women. During the late 1860s and afterward, the Relief Society promoted woman suffrage that Utah inaugurated with church approval in 1870.

The *Deseret News* editorialized in favor of cooperative merchandizing on the Brigham City model citing British cooperatives as models. As the railroad neared Utah and the potential importation of cheap goods seemed to threaten the kingdom, Young and the church leadership stepped up their efforts to organize cooperative businesses under religious leadership. In December 1868, a group of merchants made a preliminary organization, and in May 1869 the first of the enterprises belonging to Zions Cooperative Mercantile Institution (ZCMI) opened. Most of the early stockholders were merchants who traded their merchandise for an equivalent value of ZCMI stock. Spreading from this first organization, most of the towns organized similar cooperatives. The larger towns like Ogden and Provo organized more than one, and in Salt Lake City most of the wards organized individual co-ops.

In addition, enterprising women organized and operated a number of cooperative stores. Eliza R. Snow organized the Women's Cooperative Store and Exchange in Salt Lake City in 1876, and women organized similar stores in Ogden, Brigham City, Provo, Parowan, and St. George.

With few exceptions, the men and women organized as producer cooperatives rather than as consumer cooperatives on the British Rochdale plan. Though ZCMI and the local CMIs tended to mitigate price gouging by merchants in a position to take advantage of shortages or monopolies, the profits from the businesses went to the stockholders rather than to the consumers.

Nevertheless, Young and the other church leaders tended to view the CMIs as halfway measures—stepping stones to the Law of Consecration and Stewardship. Young and other church leaders like Apostle George Q. Cannon feared the increasing integration of Zion's economy with that of Gentiles outside the community, and they wanted to promote economic equality among the membership.

The coming of the Civil War in 1861 created a number of particularly severe difficulties for the Mormon community. Workers completed the construction of the transcontinental telegraph in 1861, and Young sent what is said to have been the first message from Salt Lake City. Reflecting on the secession of the Southern states, he said that Utah had not seceded but remained steadfast by the Union.

Shortly after the outbreak of the war, the federal government requisitioned two units of the Nauvoo Legion for short-term service in guarding the transcontinental mail route in Idaho and Wyoming. Young, himself, encouraged the militiamen to participate in the venture.

These were the only requisitions made of Utahns by the federal government during the war. In fact, the Mormons suffered from the occupation by units of

California Volunteers under the command of Col. (later Brevet Brig. Gen.) Patrick Edward Connor. Decidedly anti-Mormon, Connor established his headquarters on the bench overlooking Salt Lake City at a station he named Fort Douglas after Illinois senator Stephen A. Douglas. Connor carried on most of his campaigns against the Shoshone, but he and his adjutant, Maj. Charles H. Hempstead, established an anti-Mormon newspaper, the *Union Vedette*, through which they attacked Young and the Mormon community. They also established a provost office in downtown Salt Lake City ostensibly to prevent the rejection of greenbacks, a paper currency issued by the federal government during the war. It served to harass the Mormons.

Connor also undertook the task of trying to promote the growth of Utah's Gentile community. He did so by granting liberal leaves to his soldiers to allow them to engage in mining, and he and his wife undertook a number of mining ventures themselves. After the war, Connor remained in Utah, founding the town of Stockton south of Tooele in eastern Utah.

In the 1870s Young supervised the organization of communitarian United Orders. In general, members of the church founded four types of orders. These included manufacturing and marketing cooperatives like the one at Brigham City in northern Utah, which had actually been organized by Lorenzo Snow much earlier; United Orders in which each person deeded their property and contributed their labor to the order and received income according to their needs like the one at St. George in far southwestern Utah, which Young organized in 1874; and a cooperative system in which the order owned all the means of production and distribution collectively and the people worked within the system like the one at Orderville in southern Utah. In the cities of the Wasatch Front, many of the wards organized a fourth type of United Order in which they operated cooperative business ventures making goods such as shoes or clothing. In general with the exception of the Brigham City and Orderville orders, most of the orders failed within a year, generally because of the inability of the members to agree on an equitable distribution of contributions and rewards.

He also promoted spiritual welfare. He and others preached and ministered to the members. Meetinghouses were constructed in the various settlements. To provide for sacred ordinances, Young began the construction of temples in Salt Lake City, St. George, Manti, and Logan, Utah, and an endowment house in Salt Lake City. The endowment house in Salt Lake City opened in 1855 and the St. George Temple in 1877, eight months before his death. The other temples were not completed until after his death.

He continued the practice of plural marriage, which Joseph Smith had instituted in Nauvoo. Young married at least twenty-three women besides Works and Angell. By fourteen of them he fathered forty-nine children.

Perhaps Young's most serious difficulty during the 1870s resulted from the activities of Utah Territorial Chief Justice James B. McKean. McKean set as his task the defeat of the Mormon community and the prosecution of Young and the church leadership for crimes he believed they had committed. To indict and convict Mormon leaders and others, McKean ordered U.S. Marshal Matthewson T. Patrick to pick grand and petit jurors off the street rather than selecting them from lists made from the tax rolls as required by territorial law. With a packed jury, the U.S. attorney secured indictments against Young and other leaders, including George Q. Cannon, Daniel H. Wells, and dissident Henry W. Lawrence for lewd and lascivious cohabitation under territorial law. Significantly, he did not prosecute them under the Morrill Anti-Bigamy Act that Congress had passed in 1862 and was directly aimed at the Mormon practice of polygamy. He granted Young bail while announcing from the bench that the case, though called *The People v. Brigham Young*, was really "Federal Authority versus Polygamic Theocracy." On the testimony of confessed murderer and now-lapsed Mormon William A. Hickman, the U.S. attorney also secured indictments for the murder of Richard Yates during the Utah War against Young, Wells, and Hosea Stout.

In addition Young faced McKean over the divorce petition of one of his plural wives, Ann Eliza Webb Dee Young. Ann Eliza petitioned McKean's court for divorce. Young replied that he was legally married to Mary Ann Angell, that Ann Eliza was not divorced from James Dee at the time of the alleged marriage, and that the sealing was a plural or celestial marriage and not legal under the Morrill Act.

Instead of just dropping the matter, McKean placed the burden of proof on Brigham and ordered him to pay Ann Eliza $500 per month alimony pending the outcome of the litigation. Young refused to do so and McKean fined him $25 and ordered him to the penitentiary for one day for contempt of court. Significantly, Charles Hempstead, Patrick Edward Connor, and numerous other Gentiles came to Young's defense in the matter. Eventually, however, the U.S. Attorney General ordered the case thrown out of court on the grounds that Brigham and Ann Eliza could never have legally married.

In the meantime another case that undermined McKean's plans and his illegal method of empanelling jurors reached the U.S. Supreme Court. Shortly before McKean's appointment, Paul Englebrecht, who owned a saloon in Salt Lake City refused to post a bond for the sale of liquor as in the city ordinance. Jeter Clinton, an alderman and justice of the peace for the city, ordered the city police to destroy Englebrecht's liquor supply. Engelbrecht sued the city for $59,000 to recover the value of the liquor. A jury empanelled by the U.S. Marshal from Gentiles found on the street convicted Clinton and ordered him to pay Englebrecht. Clinton appealed the decision to the Supreme Court, which ruled that Utah's courts must follow territorial law in empanelling juries.

The decision in the Englebrecht case threw out Clinton's fine, but it also nullified the indictments McKean had secured with packed juries. As a result, the federal officials had to throw out the indictments against Young and his associates.

In 1874 Congress passed the Poland Act that changed the method of empan-elling juries. Henceforth both the probate court judges and the clerk of the U.S. district courts were involved in selecting jurors. This meant that the U.S. marshal could still not simply select unfriendly Gentiles from the streets and secure trumped-up indictments. As a result, the indictments against Young and others were never renewed and Young lived a free man until his death.

Before 1840, most Mormon converts had come from New England, New York, the Midwest, eastern Canada, and the upper South. By 1850 that pat-tern had changed, and the majority came from the British Isles, Scandinavia, and elsewhere in Western Europe. In a significant statistical study, Dean L. May concluded that by the 1860s, the great bulk of Utah's adult population consisted of "recent European immigrants to the Mormon Zion."

Why should the Mormons have felt the need to immigrate to the United States? When people converted to the restored gospel, they accepted more than the obligation to live moral lives, cultivate personal piety, and attend church. They also believed they must flee Babylon and "gather" with the Saints in Zion. The doctrine of the gathering had roots both in the desire to build towns in a new Zion and in the belief that the Saints must seek refuge in covenant communities to prepare for Christ's second coming. As premillen-nialists, following a period of tribulation promised in the Book of Revelations Mormons expected Christ to return to the earth to rule for a thousand years. Unlike conventional premillennialists, however, the Latter-Day Saints believed that if they gathered with God's covenant people in towns they could avoid the tribulation that would precede Christ's second advent. Moreover, they could build a kingdom that they could turn over to Christ and that would spread throughout the earth as promised in Daniel Chapter 2.

Thus, for religious and social reasons, until forced by U.S. land laws after 1868 to change their patterns of settlement, the Mormons colonized by towns. Following the pattern of most American cities, they generally platted these towns in a grid system oriented to the compass's cardinal points. Although patterns varied, they usually reserved some space in the town center for civic and religious buildings. In a pattern quite unlike most rural areas of the United States, but similar to those of New England and the Spanish Southwest, they divided the land outside the towns into farms and pastures. Like the Spanish, they also developed irrigation systems. After 1868, these patterns changed considerably in part because the preemption and homestead laws required farmers to reside on the land they claimed. Since the Mormons had already laid out most of the core settlements by that time, they tended to homestead in dispersed sites more frequently in Idaho and Canada than in Utah.

In spite of Utah's relative poverty and the efforts of the church leadership to promote equality, Utah was not an egalitarian society. Studies by economists Clayne L. Pope, James R. Kearl, Larry T. Wimmer, and L. Dwight Israelsen have shown that although the nineteenth century Mormons managed to build a community with relatively greater economic equality than the rest of the United States, wealth and poverty dwelt side by side. Family connections and native ability tended to promote prosperity while foreign birth tended to lead to greater poverty.

Nevertheless, despite the predominant emphasis on action rather than belief, in Sunday sermons and conference addresses, Young and other Mormon leaders discoursed on the gospel and on the way to redemption and salvation. Although a few sermons discussed speculative doctrines such as the belief that Adam was God and the need for murderers to shed their own blood as a part of the atonement, the overwhelming majority focused on conventional topics such as Christ's atonement; the necessity for faith, repentance, and baptism; and practical subjects like charity for others, establishing settlements, and building the kingdom.

Most focused on the mission of Christ as son of God, a member of the Godhead, and redeemer, and on the restoration of Christ's gospel through Joseph Smith. They considered the first principles of the gospel: faith in the Lord Jesus Christ, repentance of sins, baptism by immersion, and the laying on of hands for the gift of the Holy Ghost. They discussed the fall of Adam, the atonement and redemption through Jesus Christ, and the resurrection of the body. They essayed on the apostasy of Christ's primitive church and its restoration and the restoration of the priesthood through the prophet, Joseph Smith. They emphasized the need for latter-day prophets and for continuous revelation. Some discussed the scriptures, including the Bible, the Book of Mormon, and revelations to Joseph Smith. They discussed Christ's second coming and his millennial reign. They talked about spiritual gifts such as healing, visions, and visitation of angels. They discussed the Godhead, and though they differed in details, they all rejected traditional Trinitarian doctrine and considered God and Christ as separate beings. Some discussed eternal marriage, and Richards argued for plural marriage and for the communitarian United Order. Some of them discussed aspects of the ten commandments.

In comprehending the teachings and practices of Young and Mormon leaders, it is important to understand the relationship of the Latter-Day Saints and the American Indians. We should understand that it is often extremely difficult to make sense out of the association, in part because of ad hoc statements and in part because of the diverse rhetoric and actions that appeared in different contexts. The Book of Mormon places the Indians (called Lamanites in the book) in the House of Israel, and thus Latter-Day Saints perceive them as part of God's chosen people. At the same time, it records that after immigrating to America, the Indians had rejected the Abrahamic covenant and had chosen a life of barbarism. Still, the book promised their conversion to the gospel of Jesus Christ, their redemption through Christ's atonement, and their central role in the establishment of Zion.

Convinced by the Book of Mormon and drawing on meager resources, under Young's leadership Mormons spent enormous financial and human capital in supporting missions to various tribes in Utah, Idaho, Wyoming, Nevada, Arizona, and New Mexico. In virtually every case except short-term relationships such as those cultivated by Jacob Hamblin and his associates with the Paiutes in southwestern Utah and the Hopi in northern Arizona and by Louis Robison, Isaac Bullock, and William Hickman and their associates with the Shoshone in southwestern Wyoming, the missionaries failed to establish good relations with the Indians and the missions failed within a few years.

In most cases Mormons initiated the contact with the best of intentions. At base, although the Mormons considered the Indians equal before God and infinitely perfectible, they viewed their cultures as degraded. Like most nineteenth century friends of the Indians, they held a progressive view of history and they expected that the Native Americans would adopt Euro-American culture. They expected the missionaries to help facilitate this acculturation by close contact and teaching. Thus, although the Mormons respected the Indians, they also viewed them from the perspective of colonialists.

Still, because of the belief in Indian perfectibility, the Mormon view of the Indians differed from that of the average Westerner. Indeed Mormon views were closer to those of the Jesuits since Brigham Young expected the missionaries to learn the Indians' languages and to participate with them in cultural and social activities as part of their proselytizing activities. The Mormons invited the Indians to associate with them and encouraged them to send their children to local schools. The Mormons also ingratiated themselves with the Paiutes by suppressing the slave trade. They also established a system of adoption and indentured servitude and offering formal education to the Indian children.

In practice, however, the expansion of Mormon settlements led to the confiscation of Indian lands, the disruption of Indian culture, and the economic decline of the Indian people. With the exception of some like the Paiutes near Santa Clara who had previously engaged in irrigated agriculture and who labored with the Mormons in constructing irrigation works, the Indians rejected the Mormons' efforts to transform them into agrarians. Within a short time, even the Paiutes found themselves dispossessed of their lands and resources. With the disruption of their economic and cultural life, the Indians turned to begging or stealing at worst, or, at best, they became day-laborers in the Mormon towns or on farms.

Near the end of his life, Young's health began to fail. He died 29 August 1877 in Salt Lake City from an abdominal disease then called cholera morbus.

His principal accomplishments include extensive and successful proselytizing activity, maintaining the integrity of the LDS Church after Joseph Smith's death, supervising the settlement of a large region of the American West, and promoting Christianity, economic development, and spirituality among the people.

FURTHER READING

Arrington, Leonard J. *Brigham Young: American Moses* (New York: Knopf, 1985).

Arrington, Leonard J., Feramorz Fox, and Dean May. *Building the City of God: Community and Cooperation Among the Mormons*, 2nd ed. (Urbana: University of Illinois Press, 1992).

Black, Susan Easton, and Larry C. Porter (eds.). *Lion of the Lord: Essays on the Life & Service of Brigham Young* (Salt Lake City, UT: Deseret Book, 1995).

Cornwall, Rebecca, and Richard F. Palmer. "The Religious and Family Background of Brigham Young," *BYU Studies* 18 (Spring 1978): 286–310.

Palmer, Richard F., and Karl D. Butler. *Brigham Young: The New York Years* (Provo, UT: Brigham Young University Press, 1982).